Inventing Acadia Artists and Tourists at Mount Desert

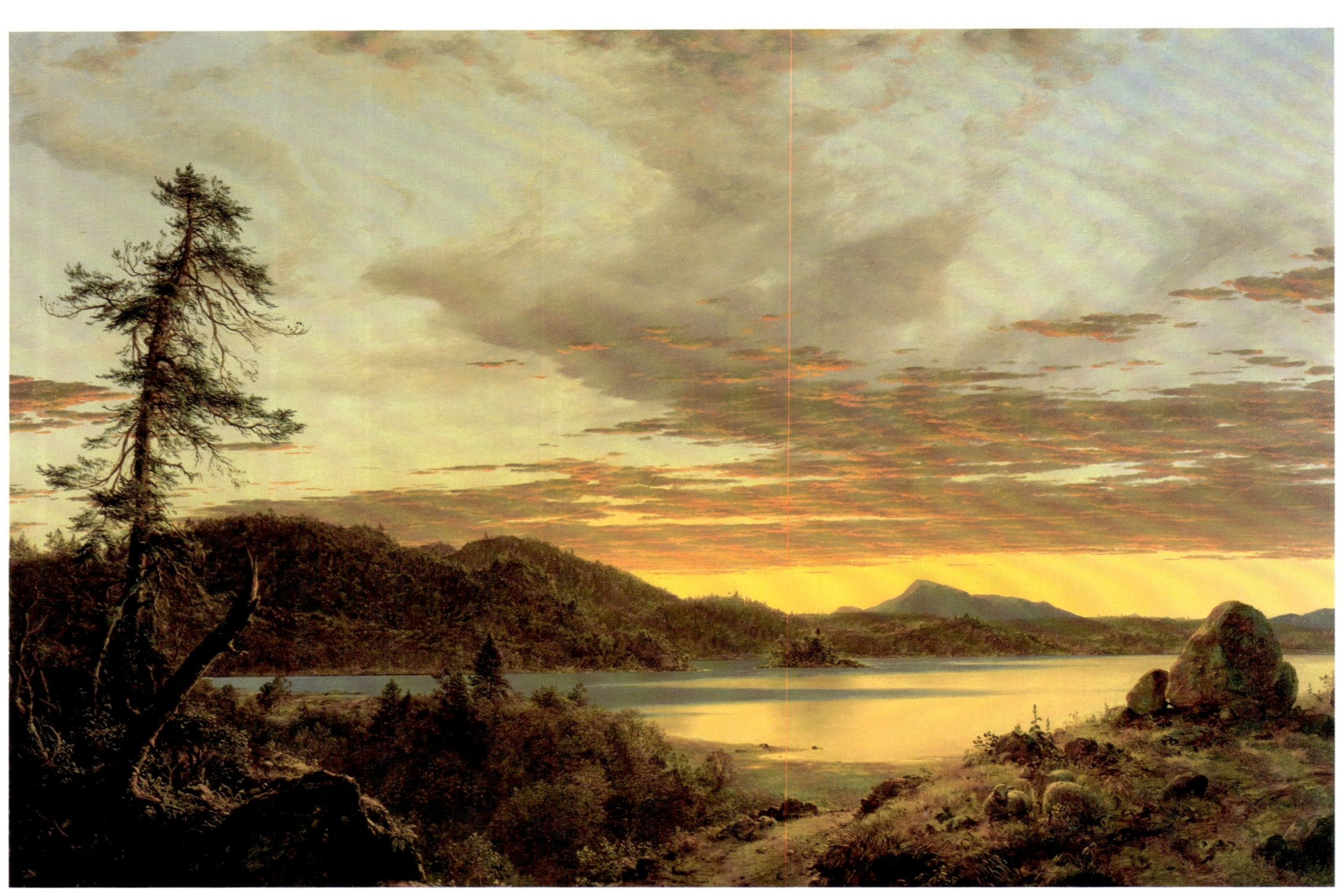

Inventing Acadia

Artists and Tourists at Mount Desert

PAMELA J. BELANGER

With Contributions and Essay by J. GRAY SWEENEY

Foreword by JOHN WILMERDING

The Farnsworth Art Museum

Distributed by University Press of New England

For John Wilmerding and Merl M. Moore, Jr.

Generous Spirits of American Art

Published in conjunction with the exhibition
Inventing Acadia: Artists and Tourists at Mount Desert
organized and curated by Pamela J. Belanger at
The Farnsworth Art Museum.

The Farnsworth Art Museum, Rockland, Maine
13 June–24 October 1999

Edited by Dawn Hall
Designed by Malcolm Grear Designers, Providence, Rhode Island
Separations by Elite Color Group, Providence, Rhode Island
Printed by Meridian Printing, East Greenwich, Rhode Island
Bound by The Riverside Group, Rochester, New York

Library of Congress Catalogue Card No. 99-71192
ISBN 0-918749-09-3 (paper)

FRONT COVER: Sanford Robinson Gifford, *The Artist Sketching
at Mount Desert, Maine*, 1864–1865, oil on canvas, 11 x 19".
Collection of Jo Ann and Julian Ganz, Jr. (fig. 67)

FRONTISPIECE: Frederic Edwin Church, *Sunset*, 1856, oil on canvas,
24 x 36". Munson-Williams-Proctor Institute Museum of Art, Utica,
New York, Proctor Collection, PC.50. (fig. 48)

CONTENTS

PREFACE

For half a century the Farnsworth Art Museum has been dedicated to American art and especially art related to Maine. From Thomas Doughty, Thomas Cole, Frederic Edwin Church, Fitz Hugh Lane, and Sanford Robinson Gifford to Winslow Homer, Marsden Hartley, John Marin, N. C. Wyeth, Louise Nevelson and, today, Andrew and Jamie Wyeth, Neil Welliver, Alex Katz, William Wegman, and Richard Estes, artists have been captivated by a natural environment that is both exquisitely subtle and sharply contrasting. Nowhere is this more apparent than on Mount Desert where an American Acadia was invented and where the heart of Maine art, a blend of romantic aspirations for a new Eden, and a clear-eyed, Yankee insistence on truth, was first envisioned. *Inventing Acadia: Artists and Tourists at Mount Desert*, the exhibition and accompanying publication celebrates this legacy to the nation.

The Farnsworth Art Museum is located in Rockland, Maine, a sea-side community of fewer than eight thousand people. It lies at the gateway to Penobscot Bay and the Gulf of Maine and on the mainline to Mount Desert. On a clear day, from the heights of the nearby Camden hills, Cadillac Mountain is visible, along with spectacular profiles of the Maine archipelago and Acadia National Park. Once a community of fishermen and shipwrights and a trans-shipping center for lime, ice, granite, and lumber, Rockland is now becoming an art center boasting dozens of commercial art galleries and numerous studios tucked into the upper floors of the Main Street business district. What began during the early years of the nineteenth century on Mount Desert, with adventuring artists providing the impetus for tourism, has now evolved into the state's second largest industry. Today, the Museum attracts visitors from all over the world and every state in the nation.

Inventing Acadia: Artists and Tourists at Mount Desert could never have been possible without the dedication and perseverance of Pamela J. Belanger, Farnsworth Curator of Nineteenth-Century American Art, who initiated this project and directed every aspect of its development to its realization. Her study of the art historical intersection of tourism and artists on Mount Desert is a splendid contribution to the region and the nation's awareness of this magnificent place.

Special thanks to John Wilmerding, Christopher Binyon Sarofim '86 Professor of American Art at Princeton University, whose knowledge of the artist's Mount Desert is unsurpassed. J. Gray Sweeney, Professor of Art History at Arizona State University, generously contributed to the publication, and we appreciate his expertise.

We are also extremely grateful to the Henry Luce Foundation, the David Rockefeller Fund, and the Wyeth Endowment for American Art, for generous financial support. These grants have enabled the Farnsworth to culminate its Fiftieth Anniversary Celebration with a sharply focused exhibition that looks to the past and speaks to the present about a "regional" subject with national relevance. *Inventing Acadia: Artists and Tourists at Mount Desert* emerges from the very center of our institutional identity and we believe it is a model for what small, regional museums can achieve with a sure sense of place.

Christopher B. Crosman
Director

INTRODUCTION AND ACKNOWLEDGMENTS

The cultural and social historians Raymond Williams and Eric Hobsbawm first proposed the idea that nineteenth-century Europeans "invented" traditions, developed cultural symbols, and produced images to support the establishment of national identities. David Lowenthal, the cultural geographer, demonstrated that the identity of a nation is not simply the product of geology, climate, or the intrinsic physical conditions of a place, but its formation is a complex process in which images and language about the environment are transformed to serve social, economic, and political needs. In the United States the discovery and transformation of Mount Desert by landscape painters into a tourist destination and a national symbol of New England wilderness is a prime example of the invention of culture and place. The result is known today as Acadia National Park.

The approach taken in this study is an examination of the particular and specific ways images functioned in this production of geographical place, which seeks to understand how works of art that served this purpose were themselves part of a market culture of commodities whose existence was necessary to the development of Mount Desert. The field of cultural production in New York in the 1850s and 1860s laid the foundation for Acadia National Park, hundreds of miles distant and half a century later, based on the idea that scenery was valuable. Today as the twentieth century ends there is a renewed emphasis on investigating the ways deep historical and cultural processes operate, and on illuminating the complex connections of visual art to larger social and ideological changes. A critical examination of the first group of artists to explore and paint Mount Desert and the reception of these images at that time are the principal focus of the inquiry. These works of art are keys to understanding the invention of Acadia National Park by the turn of the nineteenth century. The pre-Civil War processes of cultural invention played out around Mount Desert were preliminary to larger and more complex constructions of national identi-

ty that resulted in the emergence of national myths of an "Old New England," in which scenic destinations like Mount Desert, Nahant, or Newport became vital components in assertions of regional identity.

The analysis of the work of a number of historians of American art who are engaging in rewriting critical her/histories of the visual culture of this period has been essential in offering this interpretation. This new work has been stimulated by recent methodological and theoretical discourses that prompt reconceptualization of traditional assumptions about visual culture and its function in society. By situating paintings, drawings, prints, and photographs of Mount Desert within deep historical and social contexts it becomes possible to observe patterns of meaning and to focus more sharply on the operations and transformations of aesthetic conventions of representation and symbolism. An examination of paintings from the perspective of their production as luxury goods for elite audiences in New York allows another perspective to surface. Finally, J. Gray Sweeney offers an essay on the production of landscape images and the various ways their meanings were produced, inflected, and assimilated. His essay is helpful for understanding how visual culture was fundamental to cultural identification of special geographical places in the East and West that became National Parks. These places were "shrines" of scenery. Tourists came there to worship, recreate, and consume the visual experience of the landscape, both as actual place, and as cultural artifact in paintings and other imagery. At the same time the artists who represented the Island, in particular Frederic Edwin Church, gained renown for doing so, and by linking their names to the place they came to occupy dominant positions in the urban market for landscape paintings.

Among the intellectual and academic debts incurred in preparing this study are the contributions of many colleagues in the discipline who have supported this inquiry. The late David C. Huntington first investigated the cultural importance of Frederic Edwin Church's work, and his inter-disciplinary, often text based, approach to American visual culture has been a ground for this study. More recently, theoretical writings of the French sociologist and historian Pierre Bourdieu have stimulated a rethinking of the economic and social implications of artist's visual inscription of Mount Desert as scenery and as national symbol. Struggles for position and distinction among individual painters, their rivalries for status and patronage, was characteristic of the achievements of New York artists and was an essential part of the larger historical process through which the Island was promoted as a scenic destination. The wide field of cultural production that emerged with artists who painted Mount Desert is an important example of the early production of belief in the mission of the fine arts to educate, inspire, and motivate audiences in the United States to buy art and travel. The social conditions in which this happened were marked by the rapid transformation of art as part of a commodity culture that would force a redefinition of the modern artist's identity by the end of the nineteenth century.

This attempt at defining the complex relationships among art producers, collectors, dealers, critics, publishers, tourist interests, and the consumers of culture that resulted in the establishment of an identity for Mount Desert has benefited from recent studies and several helpful readings of the manuscript. The analysis of American Studies historians Stephen Nissenbaum and Dona Brown in rethinking issues of regional history and its construction are essential to reformulating the field of visual cultural as it merged interests with tourism across the Northeast. The National Museum of American Art's study *Picturing Old New England: Image and Memory* arrived too late to be assimilated for this text, although the studies share interpretive objectives and methodologies. John F. Sears and Dean MacCannell's investigations of the history and theory of tourism (the largest industry on the globe today) have been fundamental in clarifying the Mount Desert artists' participation in this aspect of the field of cultural production. James C. Moore read the entire manuscript and offered clarifications and appropriate cautions. Cole scholar Alan Wallach's investigation of the powers of panoramic perception, and his analysis of the role of cultural and social elites in the production of American visual culture has been indispensable. William H. Truettner also provided thoughtful advice about the project's concept and text. Merl M. Moore, Jr. generously shared from his immense archives important documentation. His vital contribution is recognized on the dedication page. Moore's sleuthing in newspapers of the period enables a more complete critical reassessment of the reception of paintings of the Island. Church scholar Gerald L. Carr shared important archival documentation about Cole's and Church's paintings, and offered a very helpful reading of the manuscript. Church scholar and curator Franklin Kelly provided helpful advice and assisted with lenders. Eleanor Jones Harvey's recent study *The Painted Sketch* has been helpful by sharpening the focus on issues of technique and the production of personal style during the period. Her early reading of essays is appreciated. Joni M. Kinsey's study of Thomas Moran's paintings of the western national parks and the critical reception of Moran's work has been very helpful. Nancy Anderson's studies of Albert Bierstadt and Thomas Moran are valuable additions to the literature on American art, and Dr. Anderson has been especially helpful in clarifying issues related to these artists. Eric A. R. Ronnberg provided helpful advice about Fitz Hugh Lane's nautical pictures. Ila Weiss provided important information about Sanford R. Gifford's work at Mount Desert. Most importantly, John Wilmerding has been tireless in assisting with the loan of works and his pioneering study, *The Artist's Mount Desert,* first opened the door to this rich trove of American art and culture.

Many individuals provided assistance and it is a pleasure to offer my thanks: Paul Haertel, Brooke Childrey, Acadia National Park; Mary Alice Mackay, Albany Institute of History and Art; Sandra Markham, McKinney Library; Alexander Acevedo, Hillary Bangash, Alexander Gallery; Edwin Atlee Garrett, III, Deborah Dyer, Bar Harbor Historical Society; James Berry, Frederick D. Hill, Bruce Webber, Berry-Hill Galleries; Janice Chadbourne, Katherine Dibble, Val Evans, Boston Public Library; Barbara Dayer Gallati, The Brooklyn Museum; Carl Little, College of the Atlantic; Dianne H. Pilgrim, Marilyn Symmes, Gail S. Davidson, Susan Vicinelli, Cordelia Rose, Steve Langehough, Cooper-Hewitt, National Design Museum, Smithsonian Institution; Maurice Parrish, Ellen Sharp, The Detroit Institute of the Arts; Richard Estes; James Cuno, Fogg Art Museum, Harvard University Art Museums; Muriel Sandford, Special Collections Department, Raymond H. Folger Library, University of Maine; Diane Gutscher, Sean Monohan, Hawthorne-Longfellow Library, Bowdoin College; Ned Rifkin, Lacey Jordan, High Museum of Art; Stuart Feld, Eric Baumgartner, M. P. Naud, Hirschl & Adler Galleries, Inc.; Laura Vookles, The Hudson River Museum; Komar and Melamid; Dr. Susan Bandes, Kresge Art Museum, Michigan State University; Latham Lipfort, Maine Maritime Museum; Gary Nichols, Maine State Library, Augusta; William McCue; Jaylene Roths, Mount Desert Historical Society; Dr. Paul D. Schweizer, Debra Ryan, Munson-Williams-Proctor Institute; Daniel Rosenfield, Museum of Art of the Pennsylvania Academy of the Fine Arts; Malcolm Rogers, Theodore E. Stebbins, Jr., Erica E. Hirshler, Museum of Fine Arts, Boston; Annette Blaugrund, National Academy of Design; Mary Sue Sweeney Price, Audrey Koenig, Margaret Molnar, The Newark Museum; Lawrence J. Wheeler, North Carolina Museum of Art; Robert Pyle, Northeast Harbor

Historical Society; James Ryan, Karen Zukowski, Dorren Martin, Robin Eckerle, Anne Ricard Cassidy, Olana State Historic Site, New York State Office of Parks, Recreation and Historic Preservation; Dr. Harold L. Osher, Yolanda I. Theunissen, Osher Map Library, University of Southern Maine; James H. Fyke, Wesley M. Paine, Susan Shockley, The Parthenon; John Arrison, Librarian/Archivist, Penobscot Marine Museum; Charles E. Pierce, Jr., Robert Parks, Christine Nelson, Marilyn Palmeri, The Pierpont Morgan Library; Allen Rosenbaum, Barbara Ross, Maureen McCormick, Karen Richter, The Art Museum, Princeton University; Michele Hiltzik, Rockefeller Archive Center; Hope Alswang, Brian Alexander, Sharon Green, Shelburne Museum; Bill Vose, Nancy Jarzombek, Lynnette Bazzinotti, and Jennifer Kaminsky, Vose Galleries; Deedee Wigmore, D. Wigmore Fine Art, Inc.

I would like to add special thanks to all the lenders to the exhibition: Acadia National Park; McKinney Library, Albany Institute of History and Art; Alexander Gallery, New York; Mr. and Mrs. Douglas Barr; Boston Public Library; Cooper-Hewitt, National Design Museum, Smithsonian Institution, New York; The Detroit Institute of Arts; Michael J. Ettner; Fogg Art Museum, Harvard University Art Museums, Cambridge, Massachusetts; Raymond H. Folger Library, University of Maine; Jo Ann and Julian Ganz, Jr.; Bob Gottlieb; Hawthorne-Longfellow Library, Bowdoin College; High Museum of Art, Atlanta, Georgia; The Hudson River Museum of Westchester, Yonkers, New York; Barbara Tyson Iselin; Mrs. Gustav D. Klimann; Kresge Art Museum, Michigan State University, East Lansing; Maine State Library, Augusta; Museum of Fine Arts, Boston; The Newark Museum; North Carolina Museum of Art, Raleigh; Olana State Historic Site, New York State Office of Parks, Recreation and Historic Preservation; Osher Map Library, University of Southern Maine; The Parthenon, Nashville, Tennessee; Museum of Art of the Pennsylvania Academy of the Fine Arts, Philadelphia; The Pierpont Morgan Library, New York; The Art Museum, Princeton University; Raymond Strout; D. Wigmore Fine Art, Inc., New York; and several from private collections.

The Henry Luce Foundation awarded a generous grant to The Farnsworth Art Museum to support our Fiftieth Anniversary Permanent Collection Celebration. *Inventing Acadia: Artists and Tourists at Mount Desert* is part of this celebration and highlights important paintings from our permanent collection. I am very grateful to Ellen Holtzman for her encouragement. The David Rockefeller Fund and the Wyeth Endowment for American Art both supported *Inventing Acadia* with generous grants. The Margaret E. Burnham Charitable Trust, *Down East Magazine*, and Bonnie Lunt Management (in Memory of Dennis D. Troxell), also supported the exhibition and the book.

I would like to acknowledge editor Dawn Hall who has smoothed and strengthened the publication in many ways. Also, sincere thanks to Malcolm Grear Designers who within a very tight deadline produced a beautiful book. At The Farnsworth Art Museum I would like to thank Director Christopher B. Crosman for his unfailing commitment to the art of Maine. Also, thanks to Helen Fisher who was an invaluable assistant and to other staff members for their interest and enthusiasm for the project.

Special thanks to Professor J. Gray Sweeney who has supported me during the course of this project. Beginning with my thesis on the subject at Arizona State University in 1990 and continuing with recent contributions that enriched this study, Dr. Sweeney has been very generous with his time and expertise.

My deepest thanks go to my parents, Roy and Omerine Belanger, whose calm spirit and constant encouragement sustained me throughout the various stages of this study— Also, my four sisters, Lela, Debra, Trina, and especially Judy Belanger, who has always been my best friend. My deepest gratitude to Craig Brown, who supported me in this endeavor in every way, from the earlier production of this study through to its completion.

To all these individuals and institutions my sincerest thanks. Without their collaboration, *Inventing Acadia: Artists and Tourists at Mount Desert* could never have been realized.

Pamela J. Belanger
Curator of Nineteenth-Century American Art

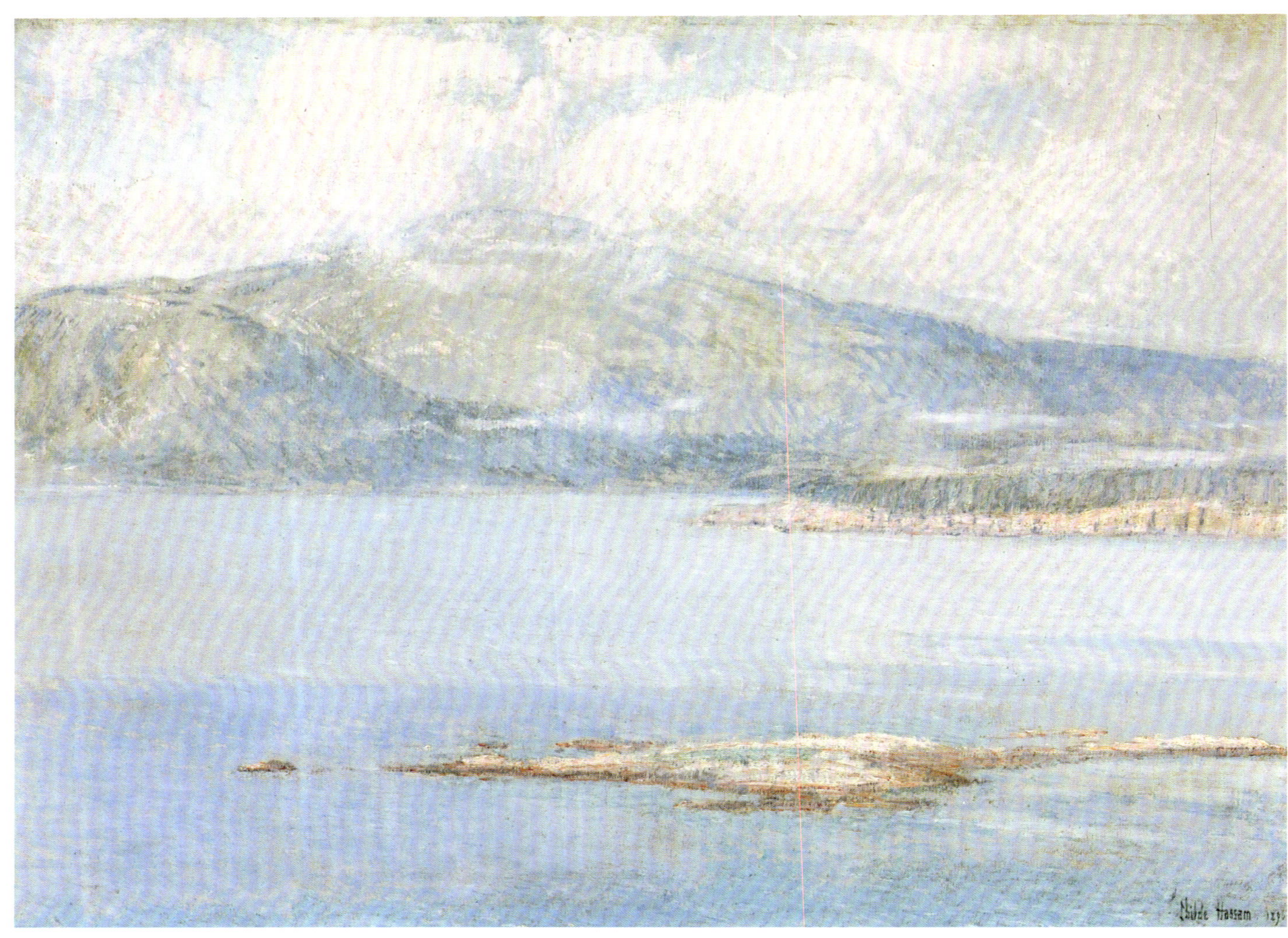

FIG. 1   Childe Hassam, *Looking over Frenchman's Bay at Green Mountain*, 1896, oil on canvas,
26⁷⁄₁₆ x 36⅛". Courtesy of the Pennsylvania Academy of the Fine Arts, Philadelphia.
Gift of Orton P. Jackson in memory of Emily Penrose Jackson.

Drawn to Maine

The idea of an exhibition devoted to the principal artists of Mount Desert has circulated as an especially appealing project for some time. Now, the Farnsworth Art Museum has seized the initiative and brought it to a glorious resolution. The museum has assembled many of the most interesting and beautiful images of Maine's Island jewel. Coastal Maine has attracted artists since Hudson River School painters Thomas Cole, Frederic Edwin Church, Sanford R. Gifford, and Fitz Hugh Lane first painted its magnificent geography, some sixty square miles in extent. Their work is the focus of this exhibition, which places Mount Desert in its rich historical, cultural, and social contexts.

The gathering of pictures included in the exhibition has many special attractions. Foremost among these is its inclusion of noted masterpieces by major American landscape painters. Particular favorites are Fitz Hugh Lane's *Entrance of Somes Sound from Southwest Harbor* of 1852 (see fig. 58), Frederic Church's *Sunset* of 1856 (see fig. 48), and Sanford Gifford's radiant masterpiece of luminous light, *The Artist Sketching at Mount Desert* of 1864–1865 (see fig. 67). These singular pictures are complemented by strong concentrations of these artists' other works, and by the works of Thomas Cole, Thomas Doughty, and Alvan Fisher. In addition, there are present here for the first time surprises, ranging from Thomas Cole's oil sketch of Sand Beach, to Robert Swain Gifford's *Island of Mount Desert from the Mainland* (fig. 2), to George H. Smillie's *A Memory of the Coast of Maine* (fig. 3), to a recent example of water panoramas by Island resident Richard Estes.

American geography has always captured the national imagination and ideas of nature have helped to shape national identity. One of the geographical and geological anvils on which the visual culture of the nation was forged is Mount Desert Island on the Maine coast. Peculiar to its topography are the confluence of sheer cliffs rising dramatically to form sculptured mountains in an island-dotted sea. Because its mountain summits run directly into the sea, forming a unique geological junction of the east coast of the North American continent with the Atlantic Ocean, there is an additional visual drama to the Island's massive silhouette against the horizon. From the sea almost all the intersecting lines of land and water appear clean and sharp, a visual characteristic that continues to appeal to American artists who have recorded and engaged the Island for almost two centuries. Evergreen forests, springing from its unique pink granite, cover the Island today. In the summer, its favored time, the clear, brilliant northern light makes Mount Desert especially attractive to visual artists.

By virtue of its location Mount Desert seems—and is—isolated. Extending south some twenty miles into the Gulf of Maine, the Island lies approximately two-thirds of the way along the Maine shore from New Hampshire to the Canadian border. Nearly three hundred miles from Boston, it is reached even today by a long overland trip from New England's largest cities. The most common early approach was by water. And from the water, the Island's majestic topography achieves its maximum visual drama. Samuel de Champlain, in the seventeenth century, learned that coastal travel to Mount Desert was endangered by sudden fogs, strong seas, extreme tides, and many treacherous, and for a time unmarked, ledges. Coming upon a place of such bold beauty after a long journey and often arduous effort only heightened visitors' feelings of reaching a New World island of Cythera or the longed-for Norumbega.

The most indelible contrast for the visitor today is that between past and present; almost every experience of the moment is enhanced by the awareness of the area's geological and historical past. Only a few places in the continental United States, especially in the East, exist where the surface of the earth so directly reveals the weathering, destructive face of time. The striking sloped hills were produced in

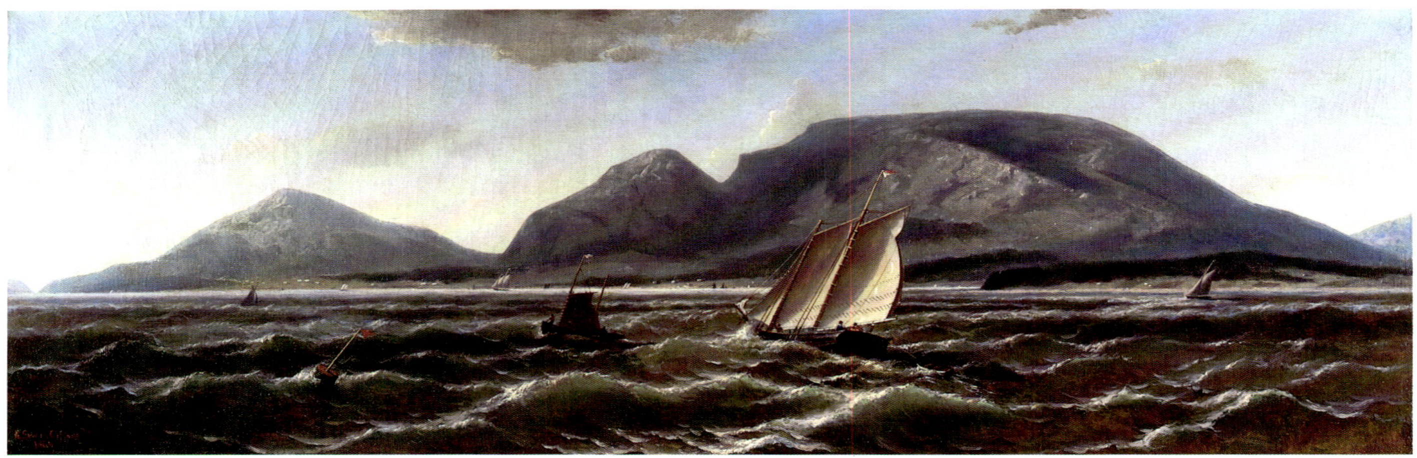

prehistory's elemental polarities: fire and ice, volcano and glacier. According to geologists, most of what is now New England was covered by the sea around 450 million years ago. Since then opposing forces of water and stone have engaged each other to shape this awesome landscape. Epochs of settling of the earth's crust featured alternating periods of lifting and sinking land masses. Underneath the sea, ash and sediment stratified; then as pressures arose from within the earth, land formations protruded above sea level and in turn were subject to further patterns of erosion. One sequence of volcanic eruptions produced the Cranberry Islands off the southern coast of Mount Desert, but they were covered again by the sea during a settling of the crust. Today, we can readily see two basic types of rocks around the Island: the rounded popplestones, formed by constant erosion from the movements of the sea, and the cubic blocks of rock walls, created by ages of layered deposits.

Toward the end of this process, about sixty million years ago, the combination of volcanic eruption and resistance of erosion by the strongest granite produced a nearly continuous mountain range along this part of the coast. Its crest was almost even, and the ridge extended in an approximately straight line from east to west. During another period of uplift in the earth's crust, what is now Mount Desert and the offshore islands were all joined to the mainland. Further upheaval resulted in the promontories and Island formations we recognize today. The so-called Mount Desert mountain range was then subjected to a final great phase of geological actions, that of the Ice Age beginning a million years ago.

Scientists state that at least four major continental glaciers spread southward from the polar ice cap. The glacier that most recently covered New England began about a hundred thousand years ago and reached its maximum extent some eighteen thousand years ago, before beginning its rapid retreat during the age of man. As it encountered the hard granite of the Mount Desert range, which extended across its path at right angles, the ice pack gradually mounted the ridges, grinding them down, which accounts for the gently curving slopes of the Island's north side today. Once reaching the summit, the glacier, whose thickness reached more than two thousand feet, pressed down on the resisting rock beneath, gouging deep canyons running from north to south through the range. When the glacier finally retreated, it left behind some dozen separate peaks of varying heights. Several of the valleys between them became deep freshwater lakes within the Island, while the central one, scoured deeper and longer than the rest, was flooded by the sea. This cut is Somes Sound, a mariner's delight, a dramatic passage reaching up the middle of Mount Desert as a coastal fjord. On the Island's southern slopes the glacier abruptly broke off granite blocks and deposited random pieces of stony debris, prominent today in the sharp cliffs and massive seawalls of the present ocean coastline.

The modern land formation that resulted after the cooling of the fire and melting of the ice comprised about 108 square miles; the Island is roughly an irregular circle, twelve miles across and fourteen miles long. Perhaps the most appropriate description of its dramatic outline comes from its earliest inhabitants, Native Americans, who called Mount Desert "Great Crab Island" in an allusion to its rounded shape. American artists from the early nineteenth century to the present have responded to these powerful primal geographical formations produced by the shaping hand of time and accident.

Shown for the first time in this exhibition are some of American art's greatest images of a place whose hold on the imagination has proven unshakable for more than a century. In

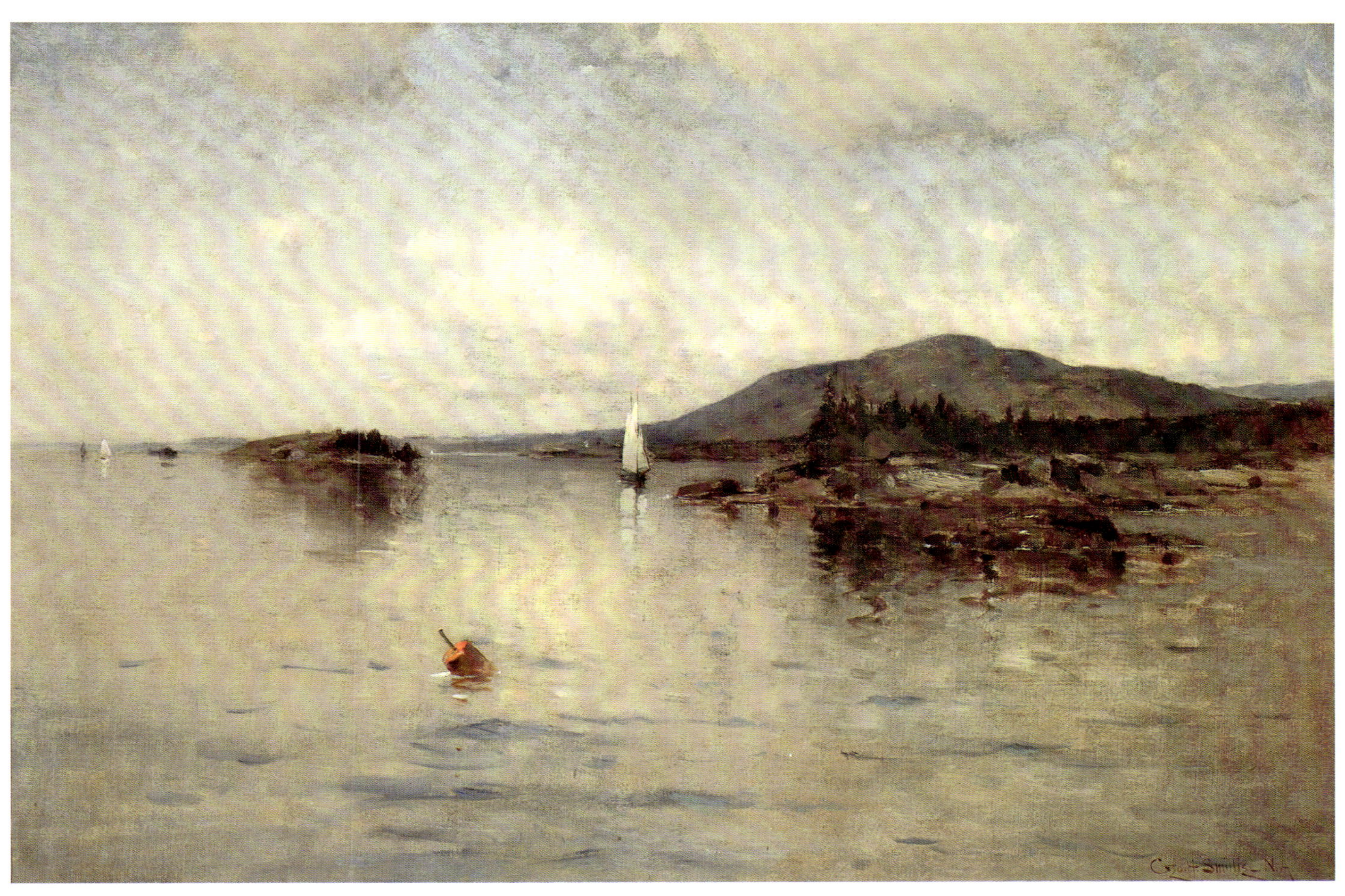

FIG. 3   George H. Smillie, *A Memory of the Coast of Maine*, c.1895, oil on canvas, 20 x 30".
Private Collection.

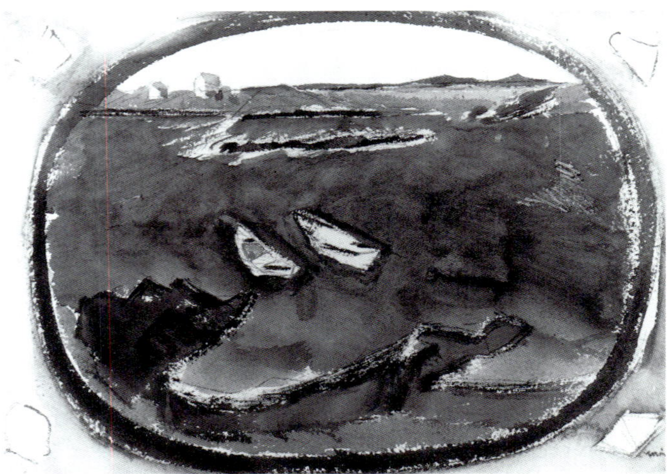

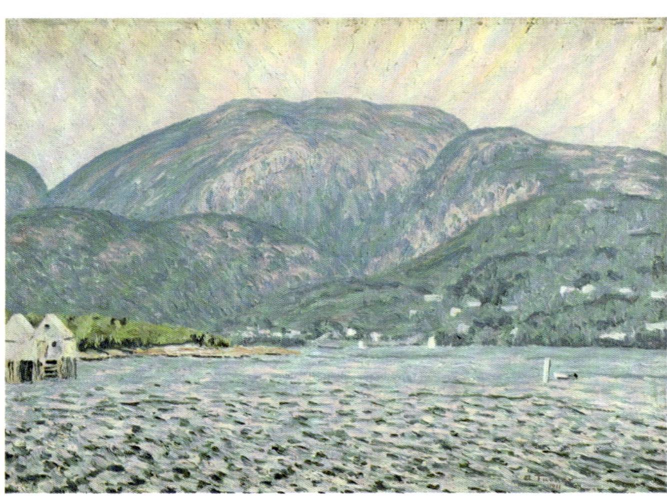

FIG. 4a   Allen Tucker, *Green Mountain, Mount Desert*, 1911,
oil on canvas, 25¼ x 34¼". High Museum of Art, Atlanta,
Georgia. Gift of the Allen Tucker Memorial, 60.16.

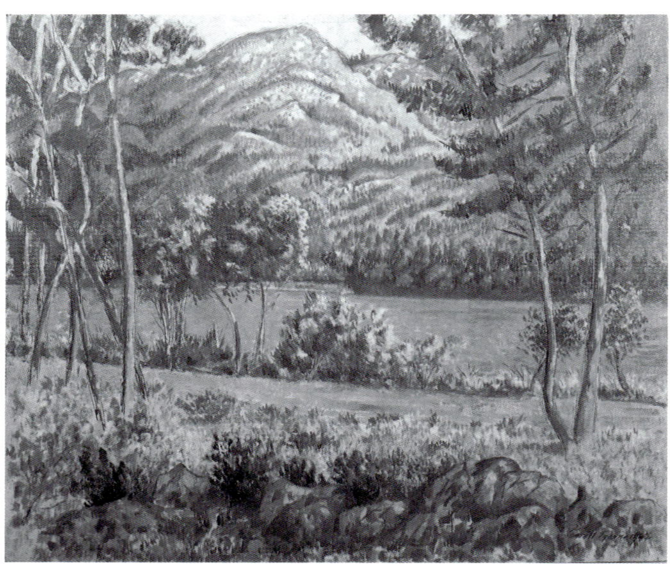

FIG. 4b   Carroll Tyson, *Bubble Pond, Cadillac Mountain*, 1947,
oil on canvas, 25 x 30". Collection of Barbara Tyson Iselin.

addition to the great figures of the Hudson River School and
of Luminism, the exhibition includes a provocative picture by
Childe Hassam, *Looking Over Frenchman's Bay at Green
Mountain* (fig. 1), that is a virtual American Impressionist's
reprise of Cole's first great painting of Island scenery from
1845. Twentieth-century artists often painted the Island, and
this exhibition includes examples that suggest a continuity
of interest in the place since the Hudson River School
painters first were captivated by its light. Allen Tucker's
Green Mountain, Mount Desert and Carroll Tyson's *Bubble
Pond, Cadillac Mountain* represented the Island's most
famous mountain in a favored style of Impressionism during
the early twentieth century (figs. 4a, 4b). Their work, along
with the work of many others, continued the promotion of
Island scenery begun a century earlier. John Marin expressed
the energy of Mount Desert's famous seascapes in *Looking
Toward Mount Desert, Maine* (fig. 5). More recently Richard
Estes has painted *A View of Somes Sound* in which he turns
from his familiar street scenes of reflected windows in lower
Manhattan to an equally meticulous panoramic representation of the Island's great natural fjord (fig. 6). Conceptual artist
Bob Gottlieb's *Bog Walk through Great Meadow* explores the
rich ecological diversity of Mount Desert that is underfoot
(fig. 7). These artists, from the nineteenth century to the present, have marveled at the Island in awe, curiosity, or love.

Inventing Acadia: Artists and Tourists at Mount Desert
offers new studies of the social and cultural significance of
the first artists who painted Mount Desert in the middle
decades of the last century. As this exhibition demonstrates,
Mount Desert is a geographical and cultural place of enduring importance to the national imagination.

John Wilmerding
*Christopher Binyon Sarofim '86 Professor of American Art
Princeton University*

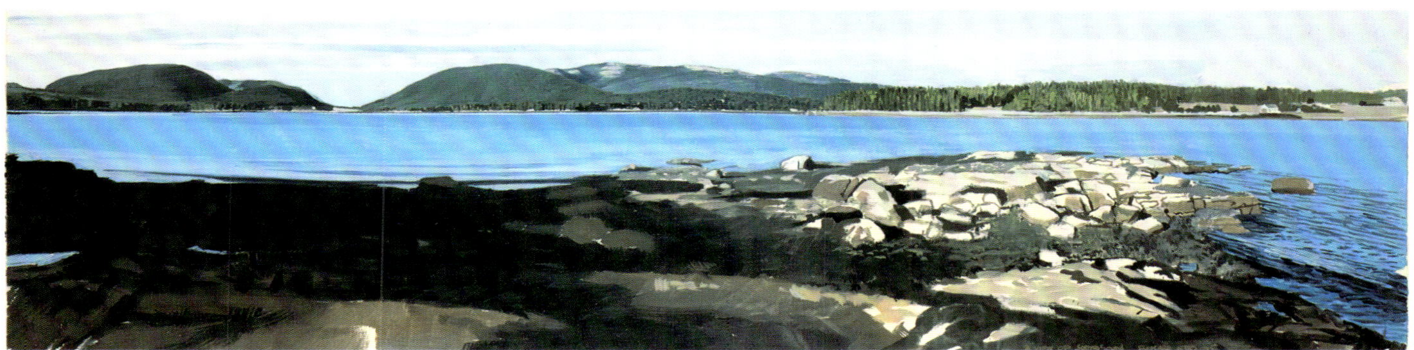

FIG. 6   Richard Estes, *A View of Somes Sound*, 1995, oil on board, 9 x 30⅜". Private Collection.

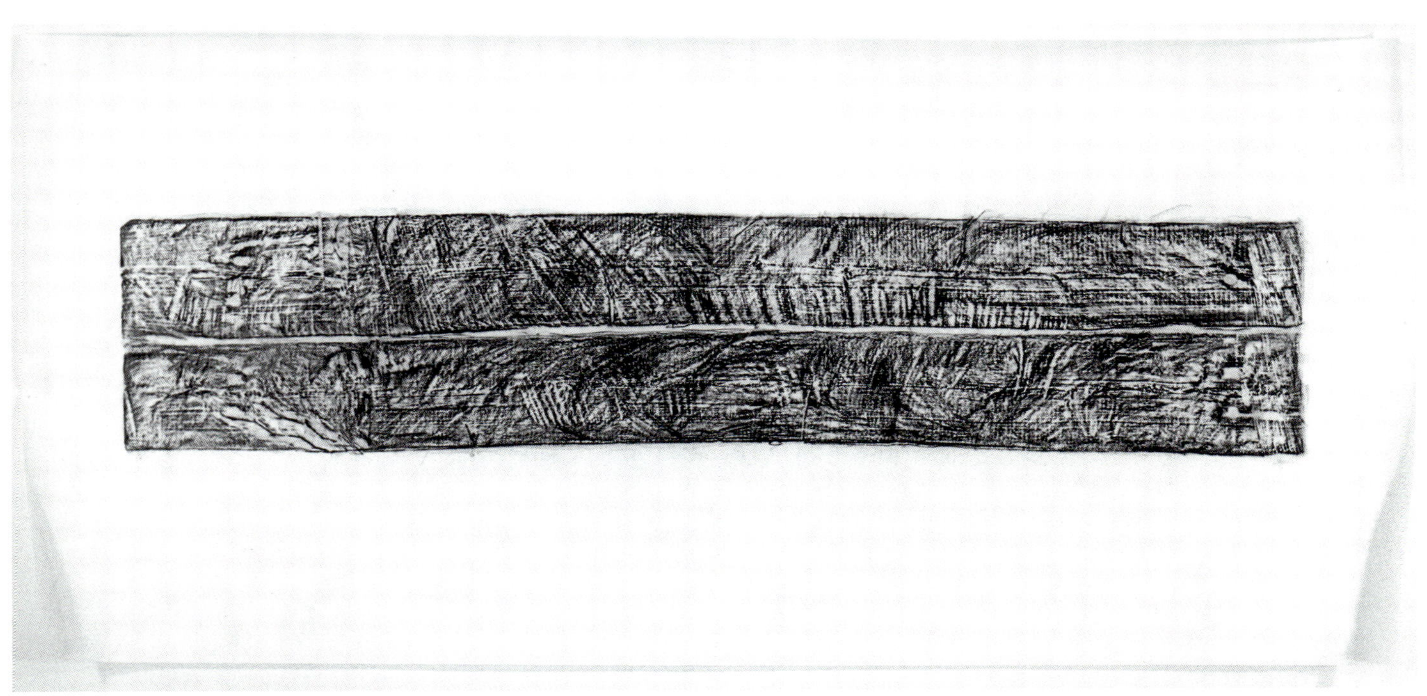

FIG. 7   Bob Gottlieb, *Bog Walk through Great Meadow, No. 12,* 1999, mixed media, 38 x 88".
         On Loan from the Artist.

Inventing Acadia Artists and Tourists at Mount Desert

PAMELA J. BELANGER

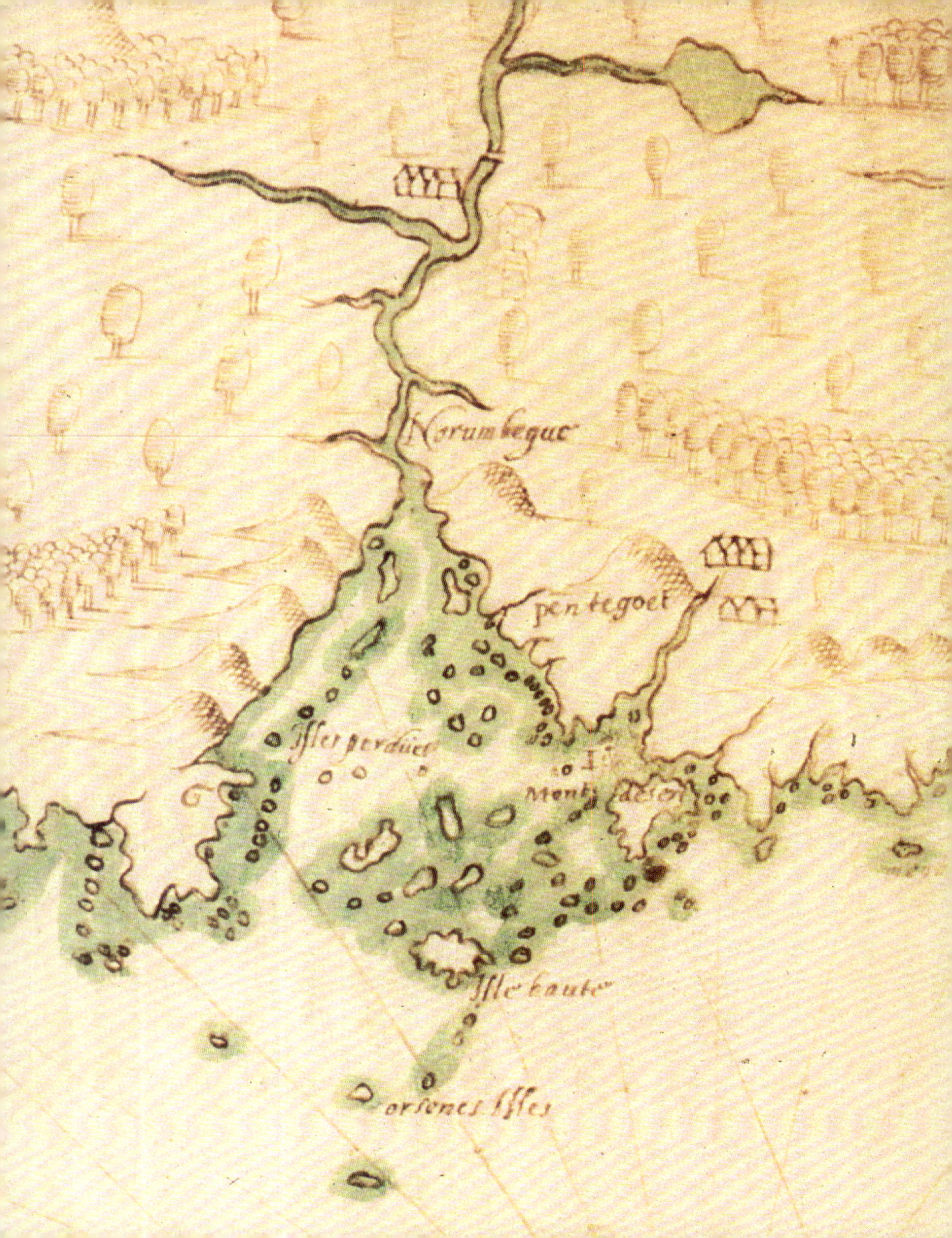

Norumbegue
pentegoet
Isles perdues
Monts deser
Isle haute
orsenes Isles

CHAPTER 1

Mount Desert: Island Wilderness "Down East" [1]

Mount Desert Island owes its nineteenth-century distinction to the painters from New York who discovered this historic area in the early decades of the 1800s. In less than half a century the Island, first regarded as merely a rocky, barren, and largely inhospitable wilderness, far distant from emerging metropolitan centers along the Eastern seaboard, became a scenic destination for thousands of Americans, especially the nation's wealthy elite. To protect the beauty of this remote region from over-development visiting tycoons acquired land that eventually became the 35,000-acre Acadia National Park, the first national park east of the Mississippi River. The cultural work of landscape painters of the Hudson River School initiated the transformation of Mount Desert, around the Civil War, into a travel destination. Today over three million visitors tour the Island park annually.

This remarkable process of cultural transformation must be placed against the background of the Island's spectacular geology, rich natural history, and sporadic, largely unsuccessful European efforts at early settlement. The physical characteristics of the Island that fascinate artists and visitors today resulted from epic geological processes millions of years in duration. Glaciation and eruptions produced the coarse-grained, rose-hued granite that attracted the nineteenth-century landscape painters. The smoothing erosion of glacial advances and retreats dramatically softened the rugged topographic character of the Island, leading to mountains that look in places as if they have been sculpted by some unseen gigantic hand, their surfaces smoothed, rubbed almost to the finish of antique sculpture. An episode of glaciation produced what is today Somes Sound, the only true fjord on the New England Coast. With its dramatic narrow entrance, this aspect of the Island's distant profile excited nineteenth-century visitors as they approached by sea. They were reminded of the Palisades of the Hudson River and the Delaware Water Gap. Coastal erosion produced impressive headlands: Great Head, Schooner Head, and Otter Cliffs surround the only beach in the region, Sand Beach, with its rose-pink color beloved by artists.

The geological uniqueness of Mount Desert excited wonder among early visitors, including the famed naturalist and Harvard professor, Louis Agassiz, who visited the Island to study the effects of glaciation on the geology of Maine. His signature on the Agamont House Hotel Register dated September 6, 1864, is found along with the signatures of many early artists who visited over the years, including Frederic E. Church (1826–1900). Church's paintings of the Island were responsible in large part for its fame as one of the nation's great scenic places.[2] Agassiz's book *Geological Sketches* of 1866 speculated about the awesome size of the mountains and the epic history of glaciation that produced the Island's sublime scenery.

Mount Desert . . . must have been a miniature Spitzbergen, and colossal icebergs floated off from Somes Sound into the Atlantic Ocean, . . . We are justified in supposing that the icefields, when they poured from the north over New England to the sea, had a thickness of at least five or six thousand feet.[3]

Mount Desert's Native American history began around 7,000 years ago. Various groups of people inhabited parts of the Island, particularly the Abenaki Indians who lived there long before the arrival of white settlers.[4] During the warm summer months Native residents lived near the tidal flats of Mount Desert where ocean fish could easily be found in abundance and where farming was productive. The Abenaki referred to their summer home as Pemetic (sloping land). By the 1760s, New Englanders began to claim and settle Mount Desert; the Abenaki gradually abandoned their summer sites, and were pushed westward.[5] After the American Revolution the Abenaki population dwindled to less than one thousand. Today, the Abenaki live in two communities in Quebec, on seven reservations in New Brunswick, and on three reser-

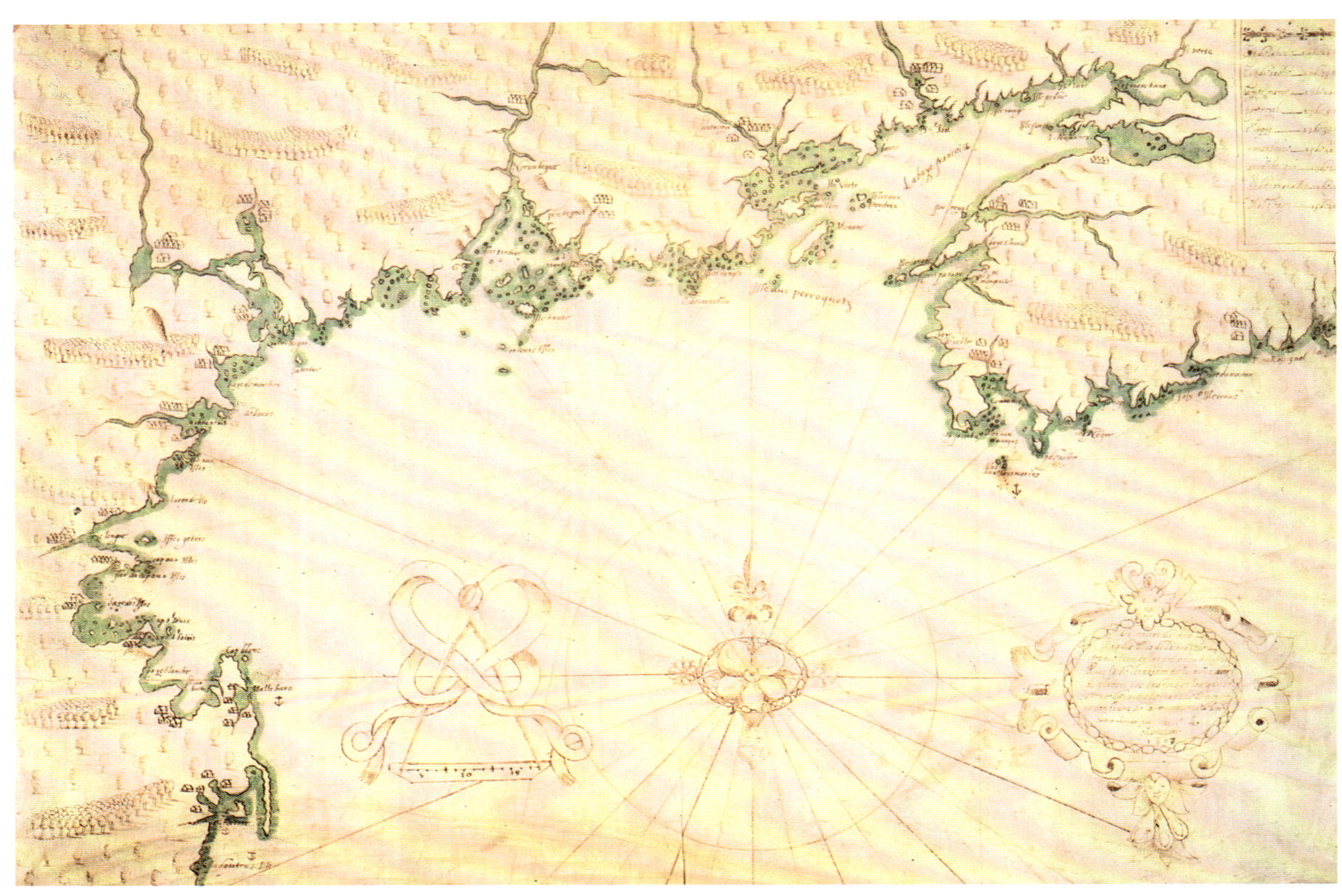

FIG. 8   Samuel de Champlain, *Descripsion Des Costs & Isles De La Nouvelle France,*
Faict et Observes par Le Sr. de Champlain, 1607, ink on vellum, 14¼ x 21½".
Courtesy of the Library of Congress. (detail p. 18)

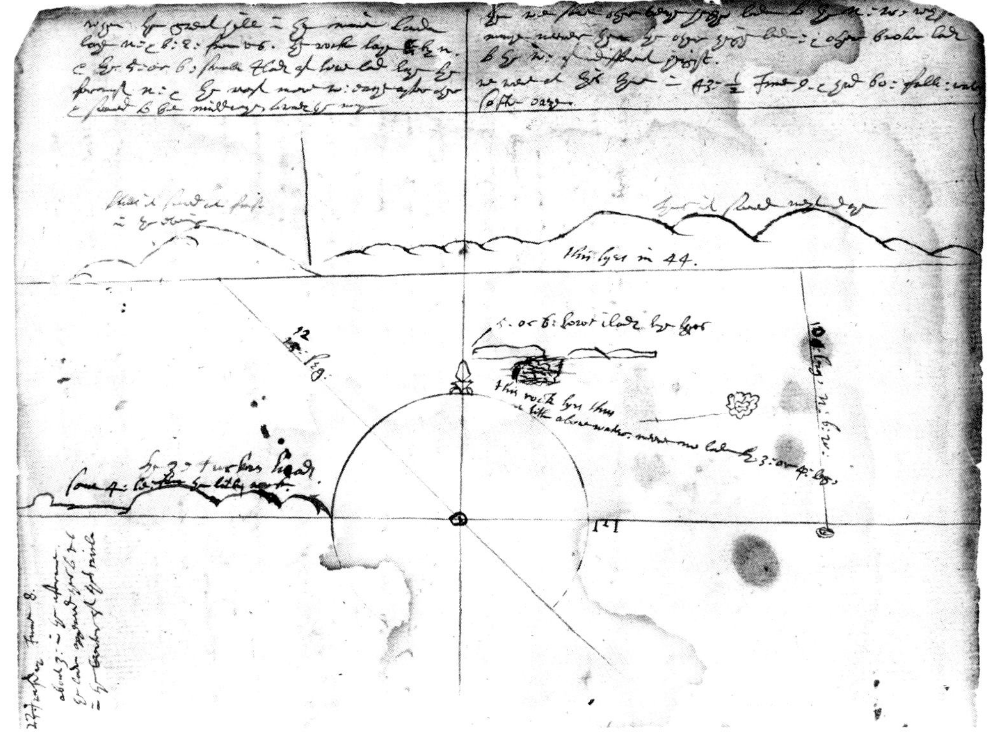

vations in northern Maine; their population has recovered to almost twelve thousand.

While the Abenaki Indians and previous Native Americans were the first seasonal inhabitants of Mount Desert, the first European to see Mount Desert was the Portuguese explorer, Estéban Gomés (1478–1530). Sent by the Spanish in 1525 to search for the fabled Northwest passage to the Pacific Ocean, Gomés sailed into Somes Sound. He found the area disappointing, but named the sound the Rio de Montañas (River of Mountains). He was unaware that he had "discovered" Mount Desert Island. It was not until eighty years later that the French navigator Samuel de Champlain (1567–1635) charted the Island while on expedition for his countryman Pierre du Gua, sieur de Monts. De Monts had a royal land grant to claim "La Cadie," also called L'Acadie, or Acadia, which is French for the Indian name meaning "The Place." This region comprised the whole of the French claim in North America.[6]

Champlain, Winthrop, and Cadillac

Champlain journeyed westward along the Maine coast to explore Acadia and search for "Norumbega," a mythical walled city of riches rumored to be on the Penobscot River.[7] He explored the coastline, entering Frenchman Bay and landing at Otter Creek on 6 September 1604. In 1607, Champlain produced a map of the region, *Descripsion Des Costs & Isles De La Nouvelle France, Faict et Observes par Le Sr. de Champlain* (fig. 8), confirming his discovery of Mount Desert Island. Champlain described the Island as "very high, and cleft into seven or eight mountains, all in a line. The summits of most of them are bare of trees, nothing but rock. I named it l'isle des Monts-deserts" (Isle of Bare

The name survives.[9] As for the riches of Norumbega, Champlain was disappointed, for there were no cities of gold on this rocky inhospitable coast. When Acadia National Park was established, however, one of the Island's mountains was renamed after the fabled city.

Over the next century and a half the Colonial French in New France and the Colonial British in Massachusetts staked rival claims to the region. During this time Mount Desert served as an important landmark for ships heading west to the colonies. In good weather, Cadillac Mountain can be sighted from sixty miles out at sea, and the distinctive profiles of the Island's mountains were often the first sight of land for mariners coming from Europe. In fact, the first known illustrations of Mount Desert were rendered at sea by Governor John Winthrop aboard the *Lady Arbella,* which carried members of the Massachusetts Bay Company in June 1630 (fig. 9). In his *Journal,* Winthrop sketched profiles of the distinctive rounded mountain forms of the Island. He wrote, "We stood N: N: W: with a stiff gale, & about 3: in the afternoon had sight of lande to the N. W.: about 15 leagues which . . . proved Mount Mansell."[10] Mount Mansell was the short-lived English name for the Island that Champlain had named Mount Desert. Winthrop's sketch map with legends illustrates the *Arbella's* course from the sighting of the Island on 8 June to 10 June. The maritime historian Samuel Eliot Morison first deciphered the image, noting that "it seems certain that the center of the circle represents the point whence Mount Desert was sighted on June 8."[11] By 1706, the rugged contours of Mount Desert were a standard navigational landmark, recorded in all printings of the indispensable sailor's navigational guide, *The English Pilot.*[12] From 1770 to 1773, Samuel Holland and his team of six surveyors, thirty-five assistants, and four local guides surveyed more than 3,000 miles of New England coastline, estuaries, and islands. Land features were mapped only as they would be seen by sailors: hills, towns, and areas under cultivaton. All of Holland's work was engraved and published by Joseph F. W. Des Barres, in the monumental *Atlantic Neptune,* printed in London between 1774 and 1780. His "Coast of Maine: Mount Desert Island, Frenchman's Bay, Long Island," July 1776 (fig. 10) is one of over 250 large-scale maps by Holland.

The first European attempts at settlement on Mount Desert failed. Through the missionary Father Pierre Biard, Antoinette de Pons, the Marquis de Guercheville of France, tried to establish a Jesuit mission colony in 1613 in order to convert and teach Indians. Father Biard established his ill-fated mission near Fernald Point, Mount Desert, and named the site Saint Sauveur. The settlement survived only one month–an English attack led by Samuel Argall destroyed the mission.[13]

Another effort to settle Mount Desert in 1688 failed even before it was established. Antoine Laumet, the ambitious self-appointed "Sieur de Cadillac," immigrated to New France hoping to establish a feudal estate, having received a royal land grant that comprised one hundred thousand acres of land along the Maine coast, including all of Mount Desert. His grand scheme, however, dissolved when plans for easier opportunities became more attractive.[14] The French wanted to take control of the Island for reasons other than just settlement. For several years the deep bays on the eastern coast of Mount Desert concealed French warships. These well-sheltered bays allowed lurking French warships to strike at English settlements and disrupt colonial English shipping. As a result, the most prominent of these strategic waterways became known as Frenchman Bay.

Mount Desert and the Colonial Era

With the end of the French and Indian Wars in 1760, the British made their first attempt to colonize Mount Desert. In 1771, the Governor of Massachusetts, Francis Bernard, finally succeeded in securing a royal land grant for the Island.[15] Because it was necessary to survey and inhabit the Island in order to maintain the grant the Governor used a grant of free land to persuade Abraham Somes and James Richardson of Gloucester to settle along what would later be named Somes Sound. Thus, Somesville was the first permanent European town on Mount Desert. Meanwhile, on the eastern side of the Island John Hamor of Kennebunkport, Maine, established a small community at Hull's Cove.[16] Governor Bernard enticed other families to build homes along the eastern shore, including William Lynam's family at Schooner Head. With the start of the American Revolution in 1775, Bernard was forced to abandon his efforts at further settlement and returned to England, but the small community of Somesville survived. After the war,

Sir John Bernard, the governor's son, and Marie Theresa de Gregoire, granddaughter of Cadillac, both laid claim to Mount Desert and each was awarded half of the Island. However, neither moved there and they eventually sold off most of their holdings.[17]

With fertile agricultural land in short supply along the coastal regions of New England, the urge to go "Down East" emerged strongly in the years after 1760. Down East pioneers established the first significant settlement at Mount Desert. Surprisingly, the term "pioneer," usually reserved for travelers heading west, also refers to those who ventured east along the rock-bound Maine coast and the farthest reaches east of the mainland. Like the western pioneer, the Down East pioneers left their homes in search of free land, timbered areas, harbors and waters filled with fresh and salt water fish, and wild areas with game and fast-moving streams that could provide power for lumber and flour mills.

By 1820, farming and lumbering began to rival fishing and shipbuilding as major occupations in this remote area. Through very hard labor, by 1850, these farmers, fishermen, sailors, and shipbuilders had created an economy closely linked to the sea.[18] Little did they realize that their remote region would become a "picturesque" place whose scenery would attract artists and tourists from all over the Northeast. As a result of the work of these artists and tourism interests, within four decades Mount Desert was transformed into a mecca for the well-to-do, revolutionizing the local economy. The development of this new economic order relied on the emergence of a new and uniquely American attitude toward wilderness landscapes, an attitude that encouraged the Island's use as "landscape scenery."

The romantic aura of Mount Desert's early history that developed around the time of the Civil War was frequently associated with early European adventurers, missionaries, and their ill-fated efforts to claim and settle the Island. Tourist and summer-colony interests transformed the Island's history with Victorian sentimentality or overlaid narratives appropriating the Island's early history as one of rich national traditions. This invention of Island history began with the work of the explorer-artists who discovered the Island for their New York and Northeastern audiences, and continued with its eventual transformation by tourist interests that profited local citizens. The residents transported and housed tourists and provided local information and lore. Local prosperity was also related to the expansion of steamboat and railway companies, and the arrival of land speculators and real estate developers. Moreover, when the park was renamed Acadia National Park in 1929, the commonplace or vernacular names originally given to the lakes, headlands, and mountains of Mount Desert were replaced with the more impressive-sounding "historical" names of colorful early explorers and settlers; a few were largely fictitious.[19]

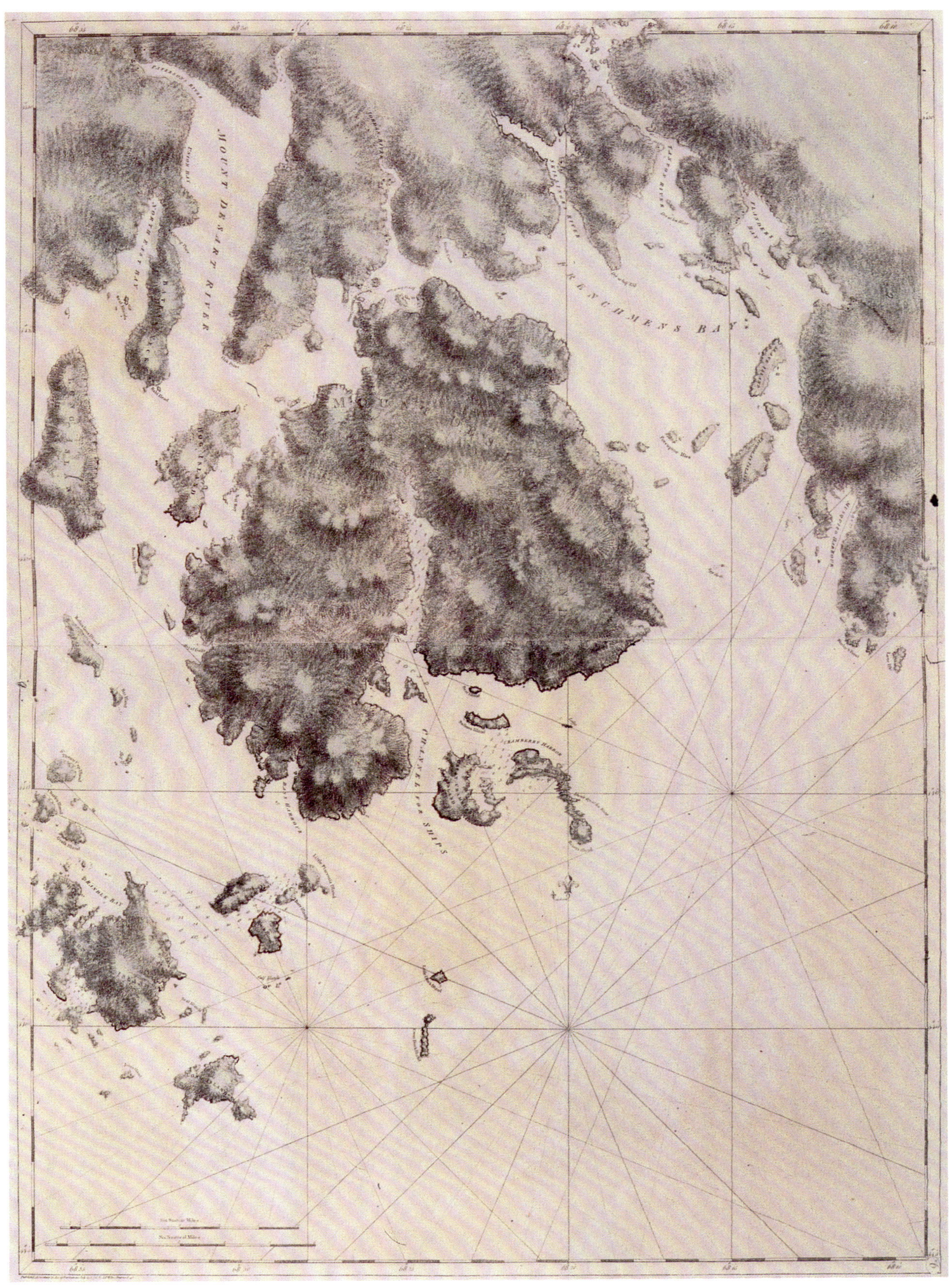

FIG. 10   Samuel Holland, "Coast of Maine: Mount Desert Island, Frenchman's Bay, Long Island,"
July 1776, engraved and published in Joseph F. W. Des Barres, *Atlantic Neptune*, London:
1780, n.p. Courtesy of the Osher Map Library, University of Southern Maine.

The Wilds of America

Long before they settled in the New World, Puritans and other early New England colonists learned to view the wilderness as a sinister and hostile place, and believed that conquering it was a moral duty.[20] For them the linguistic origins of the word "desert," with its Biblical associations of wilderness, made the naming of Mount Desert seem entirely appropriate. Enterprising New England settlers interpreted God's charge in the book of Genesis to "subdue" the earth as meaning the New World wilderness they had come to exploit.[21] Threatened by the vast trackless wilderness of America the first colonists revived old Judeo-Christian associations about nature, and established types of landscapes as either pastoral or as wilderness.[22] One version of the "promise" of the New World held forth a mythical view that led settlers to expect an Eden-like landscape. But soon after arriving settlers found the American wilderness was not paradise after all. Converting the wilderness into their vision of the garden required hard toil and struggle. The nineteenth-century French social commentator, Alexis de Tocqueville, noted the self-proclaimed mission of Americans:

> *In Europe people talk a great deal of the wilds of America, but the Americans themselves never think about them; they are insensible to the wonders of inanimate nature and they may be said not to perceive the mighty forests that surround them till they fall beneath the hatchet. Their eyes are fixed upon another sight, . . . the march across these wilds, draining swamps, turning the course of rivers, peopling solitudes, and subduing nature.*[23]

Tocqueville recognized that Americans generally looked past the beauty of wilderness to the vast potential it held in becoming a cultivated and civilized landscape of farms, towns, and cities. Prophetically, he believed that the wilderness would have to be subdued, or mostly destroyed, before Americans could begin to appreciate it.[24] Tocqueville might not have been surprised by the emergence later in the century of the social phenomenon of scenic tourism. These tourists were new urban dwellers with the leisure and funds to vacation in search of precisely those scenes of wilderness purity that their grandfathers might have worked to erase.

Although American victory in the Revolutionary War had established political independence from Britain, national identity could only be achieved by building a prosperous economy, a sound government, and particularly by establishing a strong cultural identity.[25] During the early nineteenth century the concept of wilderness was increasingly transformed to apply to special scenic places that became prized as the nation's greatest cultural assets.[26] A belief in the socially redeeming and "softening" influences of natural divinity on society became an idea allied to the desire to create an emerging national identity. The American landscape, with its extensive western wilderness was now touted as superior to the civilized, but over-developed Old World.[27]

God's Holy Book

Although their specific Protestant theologies varied, the educated elites in the Northeast held a common-sense perception that the natural world was permeated with divine purpose and manifestations of "transcendent truth." Thus, the landscape itself could become a master symbol imbued with religious meaning. Representations of nature enabled individuals to better grasp how God's holy work was manifest in the landscape. Henry Ward Beecher's *Star Papers* of 1855 expressed a typical Antebellum conception of the natural environment as the direct manifestation of God's handiwork:

> *The soul seeks and sees God through nature, and nature changes its voice, speaking no longer of mere material grandeur and beauty, but declares through all its parts the glory of God. . . . All the aspects of the earth ministered sublime conceptions of God. Mountains were his highway. The clear, open sky, declared his glory. The light was his raiment of joy; the darkness of storms his terrible apparel of judgment. Flowers and sparrows taught his providence and care.*[28]

For many nineteenth-century Americans, however, the wilderness still represented land to be conquered and exploited, and they eagerly embraced the "official" mandate of progress.[29] During the 1860s, however, the concept of the wilderness as a symbol of national pride expanded and became an important issue for the conservation movement that sought to protect vast unspoiled landscapes. Many artists and writers of the Antebellum period recognized the contradiction between the national ambition for expansion and the perception of God in nature, and as a result advocated the preservation of nature against the excesses of civilization. Reflecting this sentiment, a critic for *The Literary World* in 1847 advised American landscape painters to expose the destruction of America's wilderness as "their mission." Paraphrasing Thomas Cole's *Essay on American Scenery* the writer thought that:

> *The axe of civilization is busy with our old forests, and artisan ingenuity is fast sweeping away the relics of our national infancy. What were once the wild and picturesque haunts of the Red Man, and where the wild deer roamed in freedom, are becoming the abodes of commerce and the seats of manufactures. . . . "The aged hemlocks, through whose branches have whistled the winds of a hundred winters," are losing their identity, and made to figure in the shape of deal boards and rafters for unsightly structures on bare commons, ornamented with a few peaked poplars, pointing like fingerposts to the sky. Yankee enterprise has little sympathy*

with the picturesque, and it behooves our artists to rescue from its grasp the little that is left before it is for ever too late. This is their mission.[30]

Landscape painters responded to such pleas in two ways: with images that subtly exposed the contradiction associated with the rapid destruction of the American wilderness, and that also presented landscapes as symbols of national pride in a rapidly disappearing natural history. Occasionally their pictures suggested an emerging scientific awareness of the need to preserve the wilderness for future generations. Mostly, however, they saw in the wilderness landscape a new opportunity to link their fortunes with the emerging industry of tourism and railroads.

Scenic Pilgrims

The earliest tourists of the 1820s and 1830s actually stimulated the emergence of American landscape painting, an industry that "played a powerful role in America's invention of itself as a culture."[31] As Americans developed the idea of wilderness into a symbol of national identity it followed that tourists would come to visit the locations that represented this national greatness. Landscape painters from New York City and other northeastern metropolitan centers sought out wilderness views and through their pictures served an essential cultural purpose, directing an emerging leisure class toward places with grand scenery. A belief that city life required corrective sojourns to the powerfully consoling and redemptive wilderness, for the maintenance of spiritual and physical health, supported this tourist ideology. Both artists' representations of nature, vicariously enjoyed by spectators at exhibitions in cities like New York, and actual searches for scenery by tourists provided momentary escape from the ugliness and commercialism of city life.[32] The production and consumption of paintings of major tourist attractions such as the Catskill Mountains and Niagara Falls further bolstered this notion. Thomas Cole insisted that Americans should learn to appreciate the wilderness not only for physical health's sake but for spiritual health, since the wilderness held the "power to mend our hearts."[33] Travel was believed to revive and renew the spirit. By the 1860s, escape to the wilds had become so popular that the artists' chronicler, Henry T. Tuckerman, wrote that "our times might not inaptly be designated as the age of travelling."[34]

The tourist, in fact, was often referred to as a "pilgrim." With promises of spiritual renewal, "worshiping" nature required a pilgrimage to a "sacred" site, a place where one could read moral lessons in the great book of nature. The writer Willis Gaylord Clark recalled a landscape view after making his "pilgrimage":

Good Reader!—expect me not to describe the indescribable. I feel now, while memory is busy in my brain,

in the silence of my library, calling up that vision to my mind, much as I did when I leaned upon my staff before that omnipotent picture, and looked abroad upon its God-written magnitude.[35]

A Summer Cruise

In 1864, the Washington correspondent for the *New York Tribune*, Robert Carter, wrote, in *A Summer Cruise on the Coast of New England,* about his 1858 voyage to Mount Desert on the sailing yacht *Helen*. He was accompanied on a scenic "pilgrimage" by an artist and a professor. As the vessel approached Mount Desert from Eggemoggin Reach, "bounded on every side by superb views," the peaks of Mount Desert came gradually into view, "at first misty and blue, then green and wooded."[36] Carter observed, "The approach to Mount Desert by sea is magnificent. The Island is a mass of mountains crowded together, and seemingly rising from the water. As you draw near, they resolve themselves into thirteen distinct peaks. . . . It is difficult to conceive of any finer combination of land and water than this view." Only tropical islands could excel it, "on the coast of America it has no rival, except, perhaps, at the Bay of Rio Janeiro."[37]

Carter's party spent two days "exploring the recess of Otter Creek, whose wild mountain passes equal in grandeur the Notch of the White Hills [sic]." They explored "the other bold rocky promontories rising for hundreds of feet directly from the sea, which makes the island so fascinating for the landscape and marine painter."[38] Carter started to recount the storied early history of the Island under French and English explorers, but quickly turned to its present condition. "Of late years, Mount Desert Island has become a favorite resort for artists and summer loungers," Carter observed. "But it needs the hand of cultivated taste for the full development of his matchless natural beauties." In a passage that foretold the "improvements" in the Island's landscape by wealthy summer residents, particularly John D. Rockefeller, Jr., Carter called for "Half a century of judicious clearing of the trees . . . surrounding these savage mountains with lovely glades and charming, yet stately groves, converting the swamps into rich meadows, [to] create picturesque and proper contrast of light and shade." The result would be a park-like place where, "rural grace and wild and stern grandeur would make this island, with its mighty cliffs and somber ravines and multitudinous ocean beaches, a place of pilgrimage from the ends of the earth, to all lovers of the beautiful and sublime in nature." It was impossible, Carter thought "to conceive of any finer field for the exercise of the highest genius of the landscape gardener."[39]

As a recent scholarly study has shown, many nineteenth-century tourists conceived that "their journey was a metaphor for their passage through life to heaven and their destination a porthole into eternity."[40] By the early years of the twentieth century Carter's call for the improving hand of the landscape architect resulted in Rockefeller's improvements and the movement to establish the Island as a protected national park. The invention of Acadia National Park by landscape painters and tourists demonstrates how visual art helped to produce a place whose scenic importance is second only to western parks such as Yosemite, Yellowstone, and the Grand Canyon.

NOTES

1. Charles Franklin Parker, *Come Unto Me: Pictorials from the National Parks of the United States* (New York: Rinehart and Co., Inc., 1949), 53.

2. *Agamont House Register,* 6 September 1864, "Proff. Louis Agassiz & wife Cambridge Mass," Bar Harbor Historical Society, Bar Harbor. Other names listed on the Agamont House hotel register were: J. F. Kensett on 5 July 1855, Charles Tracy on 15 August 1855, Samuel W. Griggs on 20 and 21 August 1858, S. R. Gifford on 23 July 1862, and F. E. Church in 1855, 1856, and 1860.

3. Louis Agassiz, *Geological Sketches* (reprint, Boston: Houghton, Mifflin, and Co., 1896; reprint, Reprint Services Corporation, Jan. 1985), 151–2.

4. Samuel Eliot Morison, *The Story of Mount Desert Island, Maine* (Boston: Little, Brown, and Co., 1960), 3–4.

5. The permanent villages of the Penobscot and Passamaquoddy tribes of the Abenaki were situated along the Penobscot River near Orono and at the headwaters of the Machias and Narraguagus Rivers. While the French were able to maintain peaceful relations with the Abenaki, the English fought three separate wars with them in the late seventeenth century. For more information on the Abenaki at Mount Desert see George E. Street, *Mount Desert, a History,* Samuel A. Eliot, ed., 2nd rev. ed. (Boston: Houghton, Mifflin , and Co., 1926), 62–70; Morison, *The Story of Mount Desert Island, Maine,* 3–6; and Sargent F. Collier, *Mount Desert Island and Acadia National Park: An Informal History,* revised and edited by G. W. Helfrich (Camden, Maine: Down East Books, 1978), 4–6. For Abenaki relations with European colonists see Kenneth M. Morrison, *The Embattled Northeast: The Elusive Ideal of Alliance in Abenaki-Euramerican Relations* (Berkeley: University of California Press, 1984); and J. A. Maurault, *Histoire des Abenakis, Depuis 1605 Jusqu'a Nos Jours* (Quebec: Sorel, 1866; facsimile reprint, New York: Johnson Reprint Corp., 1969). For various Indian tribes in New England see Alden T. Vaughan, *New England Frontier: Puritans and Indians, 1620–1675* (Boston: Little, Brown, and Co., 1965), 27–63.

6. See Vaughan, *New England Frontier.* The French claim included all territory between the Saint Lawrence River and the Atlantic Ocean to Philadelphia with an indefinite western boundary. Another theory about the name Acadia suggests the Italian navigator, Giovanni da Verrazzano. He sailed on behalf of Francis I of France and landed near Cape Fear, North Carolina, in March, 1524, far from Mount Desert. But, because he commanded a certain influence in the region and seems to have originated the term Arcadia, the beauty of the area reminded him of descriptions of idealized Arcadian landscapes of ancient Greece, the region's name of Acadia may be derivative of Verrazzano's "Arcadia."

7. What, if anything, the Indians may have said about Norumbega is not known, but they were an amiable people, fond of telling tales. It has been suggested that this tale may be the product of David Ingram, who had traveled up the Maine coast and upon returning to England paid for his tavern bills by telling fantastic stories.

8. Morison, 9. Historians agree that in Champlain's writing the word desert simply describes a secluded, unexplored area, lacking habitation rather than vegetation.

9. However, the pronunciation of *Desert* in English has remained controversial. There are two opinions on the matter; Desert as in "Sahara" and Desert as in "Ice Cream and Cake," with the accent moving from the first to the second syllable. For a full explanation of the controversy see Morison, 9.

10. See James Kendall Hosmer, ed., *Winthrop's Journal, "History of New England," 1630–1649* (New York: C. Scribner's Sons, 1908)**.**

11. Samuel Eliot Morison, "The Course of the Arbella from Cape Sable to Salem," *Colonial Society of Massachusetts Publication* 28 (1930): 289–93.

12. Morison, *The Story of Mount Desert Island, Maine,* 17. Morison adds that the 1729 edition of the signal guide noted Schooner Head, the prominent headland on the eastern shore of Mount Desert.

13. After crossing the Bay of Fundy from Nova Scotia, Father Biard and the crew of the Jonas encountered a tremendous fog. Strong winds rose but the ship was able to find calm waters in Frenchman Bay. Shortly after, the company rowed to shore, gave thanks and named the area Saint Sauveur. A few Abenaki appeared and asked for help for their chief, Asticou, who was sick and wanted baptism. Father Biard understood Algonkian from the Indians in Nova Scotia, and acceded to Asticou's request. The chief's accommodating ways persuaded Father Biard to settle closer to the summer residence of the Abenaki at Fernald's Point, on Somes Sound. The name Saint Sauveur was transferred to the Point. See Morison, 11–15.

14. Among his activities he founded the thriving frontier outpost of Detroit, where the Cadillac name and coat of arms was later used to promote automobiles. Although he failed to establish his estate in Mount Desert, the tallest mountain on the island was given his name in 1917.

15. 150 years prior the Vice Admiral of the English Navy, Sir Thomas Mansell, had purchased the Island from England for 110 pounds. He named it Mount Mansell, but after failing to settle the Island the claim was revoked.

16. He settled in 1768 with his wife Mary Rodick. Daniel Rodick, Mary's brother, soon joined the Hamors at Hull's Cove. Several families from Cape Cod settled near Hull's Cove in the early 1770s. Most of the settlers in a specific area on the Island came from the same general vicinity. For example, those who settled along Somes Sound were from Gloucester, Massachusetts. For a listing of the settlers along the eastern shore see Street, *Mount Desert, a History,* 150–70.

17. Maine belonged to Massachusetts at the time, and the General Court was influenced by the fact that Bernard Jr. had been a Yankee sympathizer, and was awarded the western half of the Island in 1785. However, after mortgaging his claim, like his father, he went back to England. Marie de Gregoire based her right on Cadillac's claim of 1688, even though it had been rescinded at the Treaty of Utrecht in 1713. Massachusetts was again sympathetic toward France for its support in the Revolution, and Marie de Gregoire was given title to the eastern half of Mount Desert. She moved to Hull's Cove with her family but they were unsuccessful at farming and by 1806 had sold off their land and home.

18. For Mount Desert history see Street, *Mount Desert, a History;* Morison, *The Story of Mount Desert Island, Maine;* and Collier, *Mount Desert Island and Acadia National Park.*

19. Further influences of romantic notions have found expression in individuals who have dug for hidden treasure, novels written about the Island's past, names given to physical attributes which secure its historic past, and the many charming speculations by amateur historians. Listed here are some of the stories written about Mount Desert: Mrs. Burton Harrison, *Golden-Rod: An Idyll of Mount Desert* (New York: Harper and Brothers, 1880); Augustus Allen Hayes, *The Jesuit's*

Ring: A Romance of Mount Desert (New York: Charles Scribner's Sons, 1887); Alsop Leffingwell, *The Mystery of Bar Harbor: A Melo-Dramatic Romance of France and Mt. Desert* (New York: G. W. Dillingham, 1887); Mrs. Burton Harrison, *Bar Harbor Days* (New York: Harper and Brothers, 1887); and Mrs. Burton Harrison, *A Virginia Cousin and Bar Harbor Tales* (Boston, Lamson and Wolffe, 1895).

20. See Perry Miller, *Errand into the Wilderness,* 2nd ed. (Cambridge: Belknap Press of Harvard University Press, 1990), 1–15. For early American concepts of wilderness see Peter N. Carroll, *Puritanism and the Wilderness: 1629–1700, The Intellectual Significance of the New England Frontier* (New York: Columbia University Press, 1969); Leo Marx, *The Machine in the Garden: Technology and the Pastoral Ideal in America* (New York: Oxford University Press, 1967); and Sacvan Bercovitch, *The Puritan Origins of the American Self* (New Haven: Yale University Press, 1975, 1986).

21. Carroll, *Puritanism and the Wilderness,* 3.

22. See Carroll, "The Good Land," and "Sad Stormes and Wearisom Dayes," in *Puritanism and the Wilderness,* 7–44; Roderick F. Nash, *Wilderness and the American Mind,* 3rd ed. (New Haven: Yale University Press, 1982, 1986), 8–22; and Merle Curti, "Traditional Ideas in New Situations," and "Puritan Views and Visions," in *Human Nature in American Thought: A History* (Madison: University of Wisconsin Press, 1980), 3–69.

23. Alexis de Tocqueville, *Journey to America,* George Lawrence, trans., J. P. Mayer, ed. (New Haven: Yale University Press, 1960), 335.

24. See Tocqueville, "A Fortnight in the Wilds," in *Journey to America,* 328–76.

25. Lillian B. Miller, *Patrons and Patriotism: The Encouragement of the Fine Arts in the United States, 1790–1860* (Chicago: University of Chicago Press, 1966), 8–23.

26. See Nash, *Wilderness and the American Mind,* 67–83; Ralph N. Miller, "American Nationalism as a Theory of Nature," *William and Mary Quarterly* 12 (January 1955): 74–95; and Perry Miller, *Errand into the Wilderness,* 210.

27. See James Collins Moore, "The Storm and the Harvest: The Image of Nature in Mid-Nineteenth Century American Landscape Painting" (Ph.D. diss., Indiana University, 1974), 29. For a discussion on the American idea of the moral influence of nature and wilderness see Neil Harris, *The Artist in American Society: The Formative Years, 1790–1860* (New York: George Braziller, 1966), 170–216. See also Henry D. Thoreau, *The Maine Woods,* Joseph J. Moldenhauer, ed. (Princeton, N.J.: Princeton University Press, 1972).

28. Henry Ward Beecher, *Star Papers; or, Experiences of Art and Nature* (New York: J. C. Derby, 1855), 307, 312. For a treatment and interpretation of historical and religious content in nineteenth-century landscape painting see Moore, "The Storm and the Harvest." The founder of American Studies, Perry Miller summarized the idea; "Nature is not man's but God's," ibid., 206. Many of the most popular literary heroes of the period, like James Fenimore Cooper's Leatherstocking, symbolized the ambiguous response Americans felt as they watched in dread and at the same time in fascination the rampant devastations of the wilderness as the nation pursued civilization. For more on the anxiety of some Americans over the loss of wilderness see Perry Miller, ibid., 211–6. See also Albert K. Weinberg, *Manifest Destiny: A Study of Nationalist Expansionism in American History* (Baltimore: Johns Hopkins Press, 1935; reprint, Chicago: Quadrangle Books, 1963).

29. J. Gray Sweeney, "The Artist-Explorers of the American West, 1860–1880" (Ph.D. diss., Indiana University, 1975), 49.

30. "The Fine Arts: Exhibition at the National Academy," *The Literary World* (15 May 1847): 348, quoted in Perry Miller, *Nature's Nation* (Cambridge: Belknap Press of Harvard University Press, 1967), 197; and Perry Miller, *Errand into the Wilderness,* 205–6.

31. John F. Sears, *Sacred Places: American Tourist Attractions in the Nineteenth Century* (New York: Oxford University Press. 1989), 4. See also Dona Brown, *Inventing New England: Regional Tourism in the Nineteenth Century* (Washington, D.C.: Smithsonian Institution Press, 1995). Large scale tourism began in America when a stronger national identity and economy after the War of 1812, the growth of cities, and improved transportation provided, especially for the middle and upper classes, the need and the means to travel. The revolution in transportation began with the Erie Canal in 1825, and the construction of railroads in 1830. Improvements in transportation also hastened development of urban areas, and helped to create a middle class with the time and money to travel.

32. For another view of tourism and travel in nineteenth-century America see also Peter J. Schmitt, *Back to Nature: The Arcadian Myth in Urban America* (New York: Oxford University Press, 1969); and Edward Halsey Foster, *The Civilized Wilderness: Backgrounds to American Romantic Literature, 1817–1860* (New York: The Free Press, 1975).

33. Thomas Cole, "Essay on American Scenery," *The American Monthly Magazine* 7 (January 1836): 1.

34. Henry T. Tuckerman, *The Optimist* (New York: G. P. Putman and Son, 1850), 31, quoted in Edward Halsey Foster, *The Civilized Wilderness,* 9. See also Edward Halsey Foster, "The Greatest Travelling Nation in the World," *The Civilized Wilderness,* 3–25.

35. Willis Gaylord Clark, "Ollapodiana. Number Twenty," *The Knickerbocker* 10 (August 1837): 171–2, reprinted in Lewis Gaylord Clark, ed., *The Literary Remains of the Late Willis Gaylord Clark* (New York: Burgess, Stringer, and Co., 1847).

36. Robert G. Carter, *A Summer Cruise on the Coast of New England* (Boston: Cupples and Hurd Publishers, 1888), 251.

37. Carter, *A Summer Cruise,* 252.

38. Carter, 257.

39. Ibid., 259.

40. Sears, *Sacred Places,* 6.

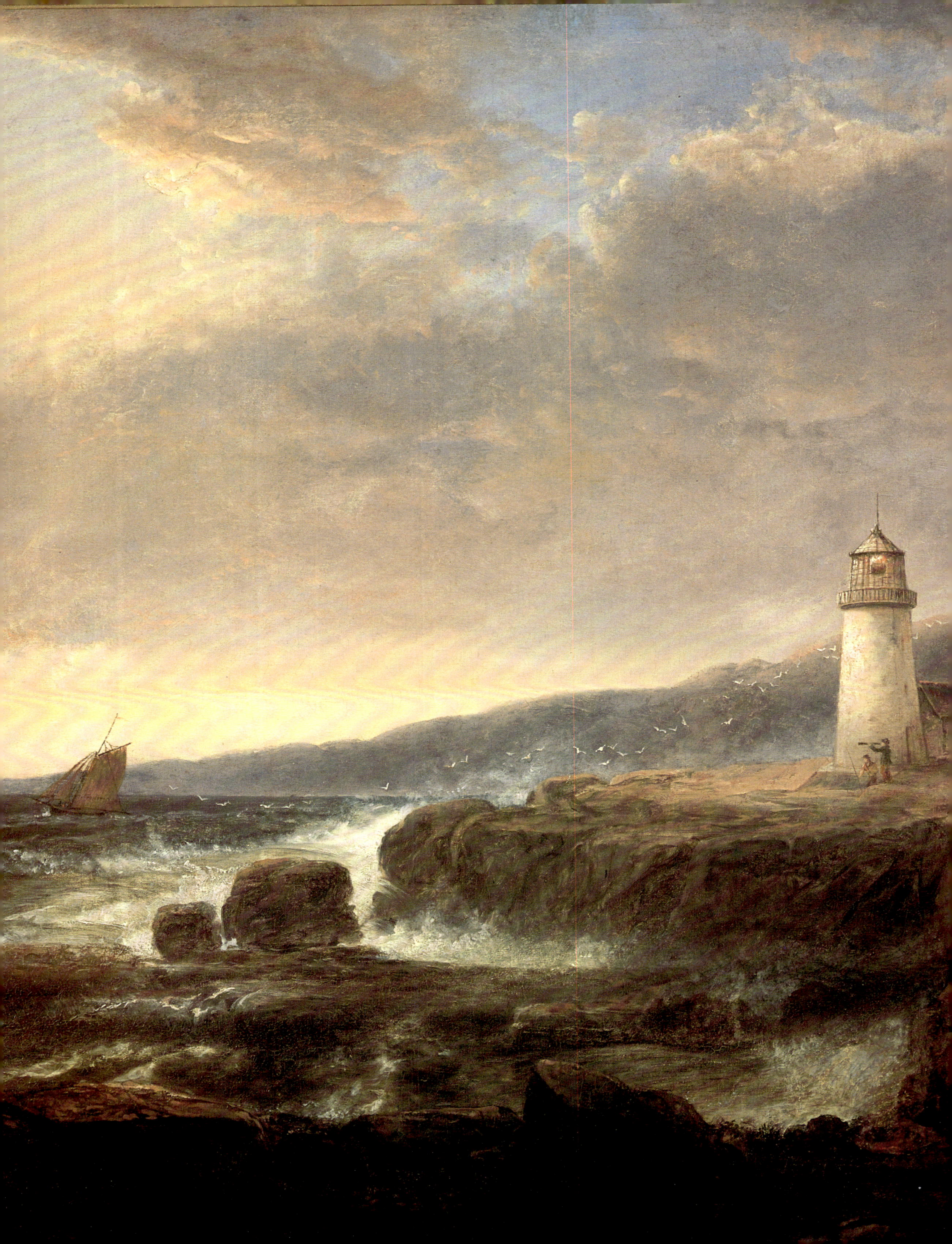

CHAPTER 2

The Grandest Coast Scenery: Thomas Cole and the Discovery of Mount Desert Island [1]

Thomas Cole and Thomas Doughty, artists associated with the Hudson River School, first painted the Island's scenery for northeastern audiences in New York, Boston, and Philadelphia. The paintings of these exploring-artists established a few favorite sites, beginning the process of mediating "appropriate" responses of visitors. Simultaneously, the appreciation of wilderness scenery created a market for landscape art, and the artists' paintings developed an audience for Mount Desert. The early exploring-artists were often motivated by a concern for wilderness preservation and a belief that nature offered assurances of both personal and national transcendence. For individuals thus disposed, Mount Desert soon became a focus of northeastern discourses about national identity.

Access to the Island, until the 1830s, was still difficult, achieved primarily by slow and uncertain passage in coastal sailing vessels that embarked from one of the nearby fishing ports. The maritime approaches presented many difficulties; calm seas could be followed by violent storms, and rock ledges offshore and prevalent fogs were serious navigational hazards. Although Thomas Doughty's 1836 painting *Desert Rock Lighthouse, Maine,* provided a glimpse of the Island, Mount Desert remained a remote, little noticed place until 1844, the year that marked the visit of Thomas Cole. His formidable reputation and the exhibition of his Mount Desert landscapes in New York the following year generated an excitement among New Yorkers and Northeasterners for the Island's northern wilderness scenery.

In the decade preceding the Civil War, Mount Desert came to be regarded as one of the nation's great scenic wonders. Cole had first "discovered" Mount Desert and then in the 1850s his successful student Frederic Edwin Church furthered the Island's growing reputation. Church dedicated a substantial part of his professional career to painting the Island. In the 1860s other artists followed Cole's and Church's example. Numerous paintings of the Island were exhibited in New York at the National Academy of Design and elsewhere in New York, in Boston, Philadelphia, and other cities.

Thomas Doughty: Artist-Explorer of Maine

The first artist to depict Mount Desert was Thomas Doughty (1793–1856), although there is sparse documentation about his expedition to the Island. He may have visited as early as 1828 when he toured the area with the Boston painters Chester Harding and Alvan Fisher. Doughty may have visited and painted Camden, Maine in 1833, but none of the images he produced can be precisely identified. By 1835 Doughty must have been back in Maine, because the next year he exhibited his first version of a lighthouse subject, *Desert Rock Lighthouse, Maine* (fig. 11) at the Boston Athenaeum.[2] Two years later, the picture was also exhibited in London at the British Institution.[3] The following year, while the painting was still in London, an engraving titled "Desert Rock Light House" was produced by W. Radclyffe. These images remain the primary visual evidence that Doughty actually visited the waters around Mount Desert sometime before 1836. Other sketches he was said to have produced of the Island are unlocated.

Doughty's interest in Maine's scenery may have been unconsciously stimulated by the careers of his brothers, one a naval draftsman and another a mariner. Because of their interests his fascination with lighthouses was understandable. The painting of 1836 prominently represented the recently erected lighthouse, a large stone tower with an attached keeper's house. The three figures gathered around its base offer reassurance that lightkeepers, who also served in coastal rescue missions, were on duty. Under a dramatic, cloud-filled sky a good sea runs, represented in the conventional manner of the Dutch marine masters. A single-masted coastal schooner sails by smartly, passing well-off the menacing rocks. The Radclyffe engraving after Doughty's picture

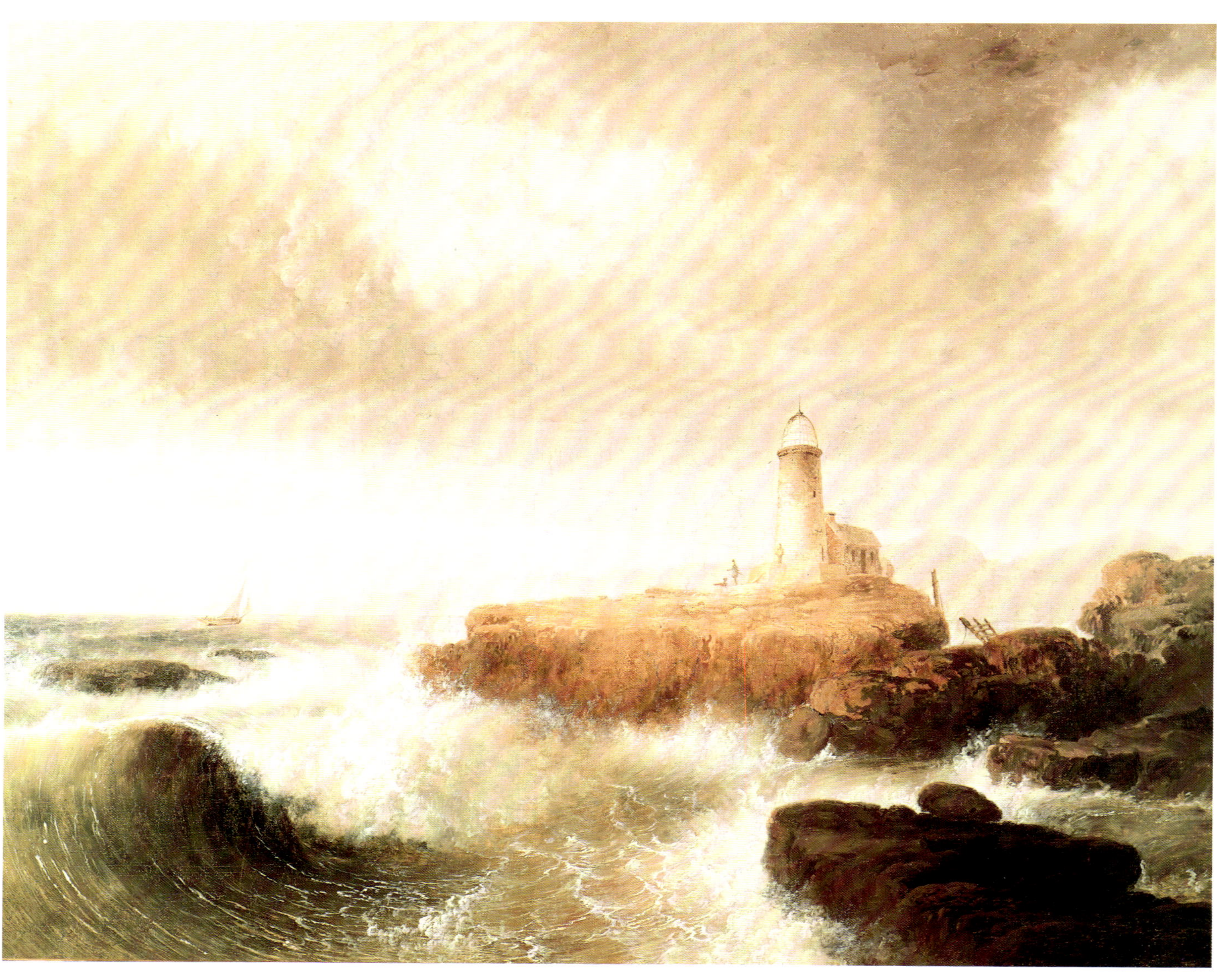

FIG. 11 Thomas Doughty, *Desert Rock Lighthouse, Maine,* 1836, oil on canvas, 26½ x 34". Collection of Mrs. Gustav D. Klimann.

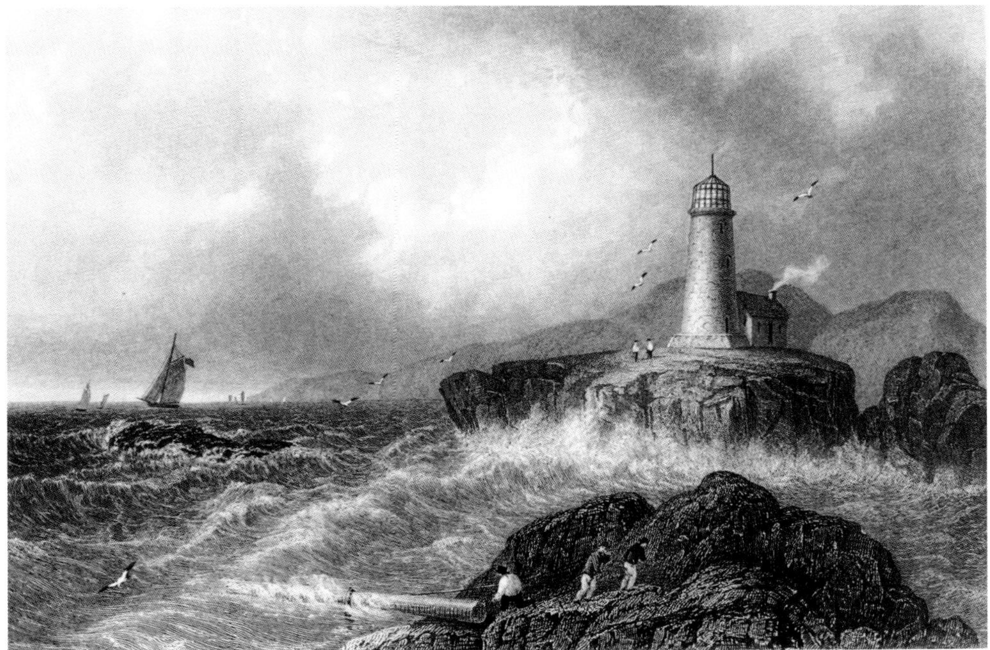

was published in Nathaniel Parker Willis's 1840 travel book *American Scenery* (fig. 12). In the accompanying essay Willis wrote "There *is* beautiful scenery in Maine, and Mr. Doughty made a tour in search of it, and filled a portfolio with sketches which might belong to any Tempe for the summer look."[4]

Not Tempe

But Doughty's image represented a northern rockbound coast with waves crashing at the base of a stout lighthouse, not a sunny antique Vale of Tempe. So, not surprisingly, Willis, the consummate early promoter of American scenery, implied criticism when he stated that Doughty's "forte lies in scenery of a softer and inland character."[5] However, most of Willis's narrative about the Island consisted of a long commentary on a nearly fatal shipwreck on the point where Desert Rock Lighthouse was built, and the heroic rescue of its crew by the people on board a passing vessel. When the engraver produced his image he added salvagers in the foreground removing a wrecked ship's spar from the water.

The frequency of wrecks around the ledge-filled waters in the channels approaching Mount Desert led to appeals for the Federal Government to construct navigational aids such as permanently staffed light stations. The construction of these lighthouses provided a major Federal subsidy for commercial interests developing coastal Maine. These massive stone structures were enormously expensive to build and required impressive feats of engineering, especially in locations where, as at Desert Rock, materials had to be brought to desolate, wave-washed sites by sailing vessels. Doughty's dramatic image in Willis's popular book first revealed to the national public the recently protected approaches to Mount Desert. A photograph from the 1880s shows the structures on the ledge (fig. 13).

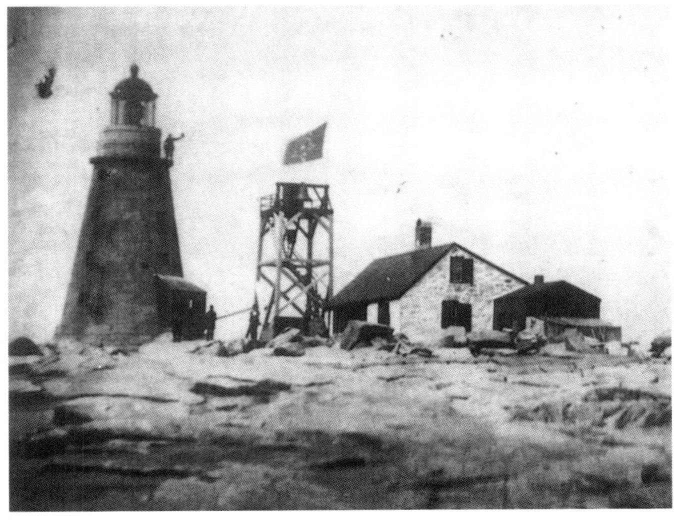

Desert Rock Lighthouse

Doughty painted his second version of the subject, *Desert Rock Lighthouse* (fig. 14), in 1847 while living in Paris. Like many artists, Doughty often repeated successful images. When he had first visited the Island it was still largely inhabited by fishermen, lumbermen, and a few hard-scrabble farmers. The Island's prospects as a scenic attraction were problematic, and reaching its remote northern location was difficult. But in 1845, after Cole's paintings of the Island had introduced the coastal landscapes of Mount Desert to the New York public, and his companion Henry Cheever Pratt exhibited pictures of the Island in Boston, a competitive spirit may have stimulated Doughty to revise and repro-

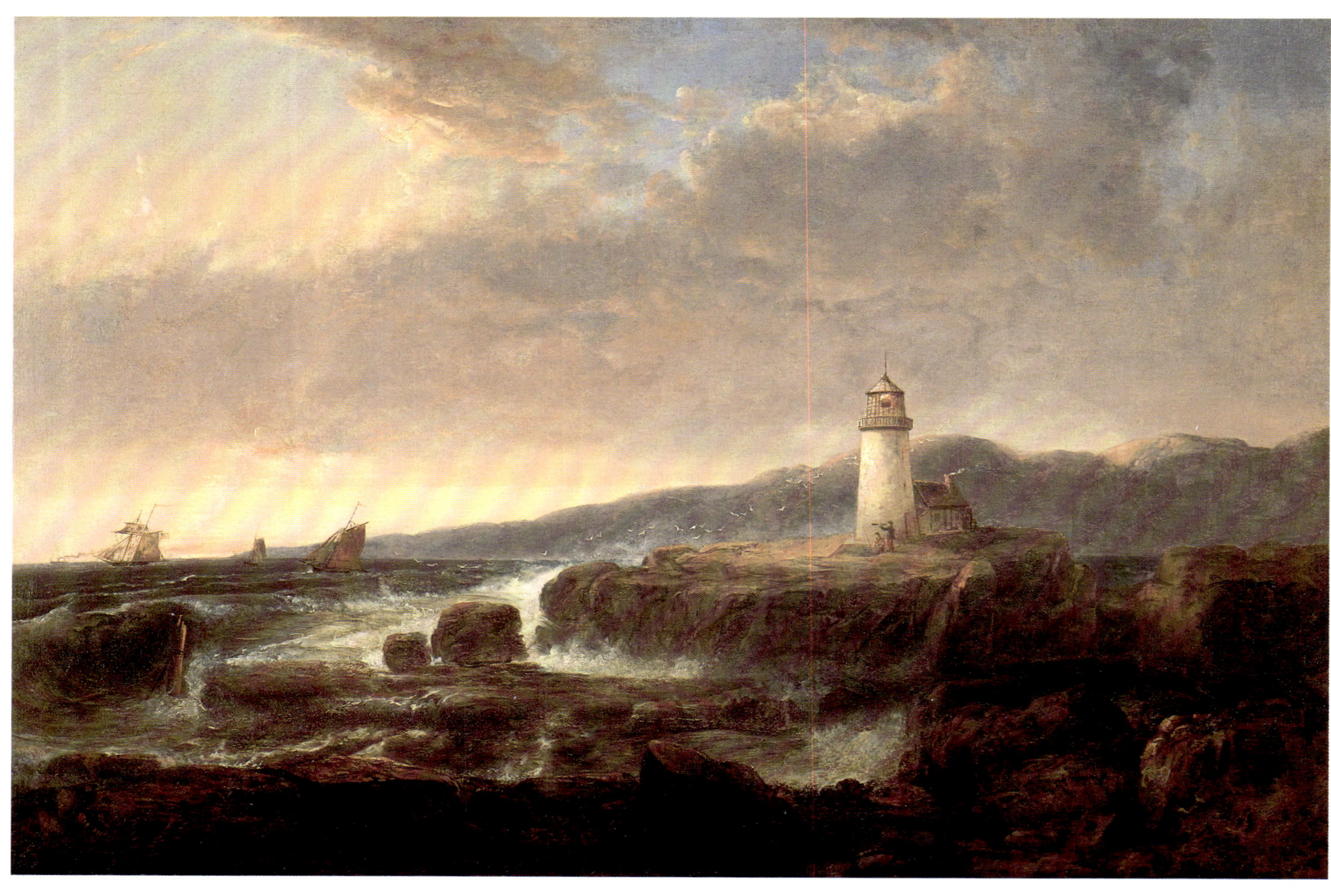

FIG. 14   Thomas Doughty, *Desert Rock Lighthouse,* 1847, oil on canvas, 27 x 41". Collection
of the Newark Museum, New Jersey, Gift of Mrs. Jennie E. Mead, 1939. (detail p. 28)

duce his earlier picture.[6] Because of his contentious personality Doughty often felt unfairly served, and, after all, he *had* painted the lighthouse nine years before Cole visited the Island. Why Doughty did not exhibit his second version, *Mount Desert Lighthouse,* in New York is unknown.[7]

Effective promotion of the Island's scenery to tourist interests required that maritime access appear safe. For Doughty the issue of visual composition was how to accomplish this while balancing conventional aesthetic and representational concerns with other interests. In both pictures, to achieve these conflicting objectives, Doughty conflated distance and manipulated space. Doughty's 1847 painting cannot be a specific view from Desert Rock looking toward Mount Desert.[8] Desert Rock stands as a lonely ledge in open ocean over twenty miles to the South of Mount Desert.[9] Even on a clear day, Mount Desert can hardly be seen from Desert Rock. Doughty's vantage point on the distant landscape recalls a mariner's perspective, from the open sea approaching Frenchman Bay from the South with the mountainous profile of the Island in the distance. In composing his picture, Doughty transported the heroic history and actual lighthouse associated with distant Desert Rock to a similar ledge much closer to the Island. In the process he created a less threatening seascape and a more saleable picture.

He may also have been subtly pleading, visually, for the construction of yet another lighthouse, one that would stand on Egg Rock, a dangerous ledge at the entrance to Frenchman Bay. Lighting this ledge was necessary for access to the well-sheltered harbor village of Eden. Egg Rock Light was finally built in 1875. Doughty's images of Desert Rock Lighthouse actually represent a view from Egg Rock, and when the light was finally lit, the village of Eden was quickly transformed by an influx of tourists on steamboats coming past this lighthouse into Bar Harbor.

The 1847 painting *Desert Rock Lighthouse* differs in other ways from the 1836 picture. The later image visually offers an enhanced sense of security in a remote maritime wilderness. Doughty depicted the lighthouse and ships with uncharacteristic clarity of detail. A sighting of the lighthouse from the sea was often the first time early visitors became aware they were approaching their destination. In the painting, four passing vessels suggest ease of navigation. Two coastal schooners and a two-masted, fully canvassed brig pass, and on the horizon the plume of smoke of a distant steamer symbolizes the new ease of mechanized transportation that would soon reach Mount Desert from the South. The dominating white shaft of the lighthouse tower, topped by a brilliant light, stands assertively before the comfortable keeper's house with smoke coming from the chimney. Two relaxed figures, including a man looking through a telescope at the distant vessels and a woman seated at the base of the lighthouse behind him, suggest that with the faithful attendance of vigilant lighthouse keepers, ships entering the waters of Mount Desert faced little danger.

Doughty was obsessed with public acceptance and the quick sale of work, both of which increasingly eluded him during the last years of his career. Doughty's irascible personality and difficult, competitive attitude toward other artists, particularly Cole, often provoked hostility, and unfavorable reviews by critics, whom Doughty believed unfairly bolstered the careers of "certain" artists at his expense. In a revealing letter to *The Home Journal* in 1851, Doughty wrote that although artists should always paint "pictures of equal merit," he insisted that to earn a living he was required to paint "a *very* great number," and that "the majority of them have been mere 'pot boilers,' or hastily painted pictures." He reasoned that because he was "prostrated by a severe illness . . . I did not labour *very hard* to produce good pictures."[10] A few months earlier the same year, *The Home Journal* noted that Doughty was "still laboring under an attack of inflammatory rheumatism." Around that time Doughty apparently completed still another version of the Island scene. The article further explained that even though he was ill his "picture of 'Desert Rock' is nearly completed."[11] Although Doughty may have been the first artist to visit Mount Desert, his career benefited little from it. His later life was plagued with poor health, sparse critical acceptance, and finally, abject poverty.[12]

Alvan Fisher at Mount Desert

Alvan Fisher may have visited Mount Desert with Doughty around 1835, because he bought some real estate on speculation in Ellsworth at the north entrance to Mount Desert and both artists were known to have been in Maine.[13] Like Doughty he too was interested in lighthouses, but he also knew that softer, gentler scenes, not stormy seas, had a better chance of attracting patrons. Capitalizing on the surge of interest in the Island, and stimulated by Cole's and more recently by Church's success with landscapes of the Island, Fisher's sketch *Bear Island Light and N.E. Harbor,* completed 6 August 1848 (Private Collection), was probably used by the artist to complete several canvases of the important light station on Bear Island, including *Bear Island* (fig. 15). Built in 1839, after Doughty's visit, this light marked the entrance to Northeast Harbor, which was emerging as a major shipping, fishing, and lumber port. Fisher's painting shows the lighthouse at the center of the picture, perched atop the suggestive shape of Bear Island. In the foreground, two figures have landed their small rowboat and come ashore to take in the view. In the distance several schooners move confidently over the sunny bay, one lowering its sails as it approaches a landing at the base of Bear Island. At left, grazing cattle and sheep provide evidence of the proximity of civilization.

Fisher painted a number of images of Mount Desert based on sketches he made during a tour of the area in 1847 and

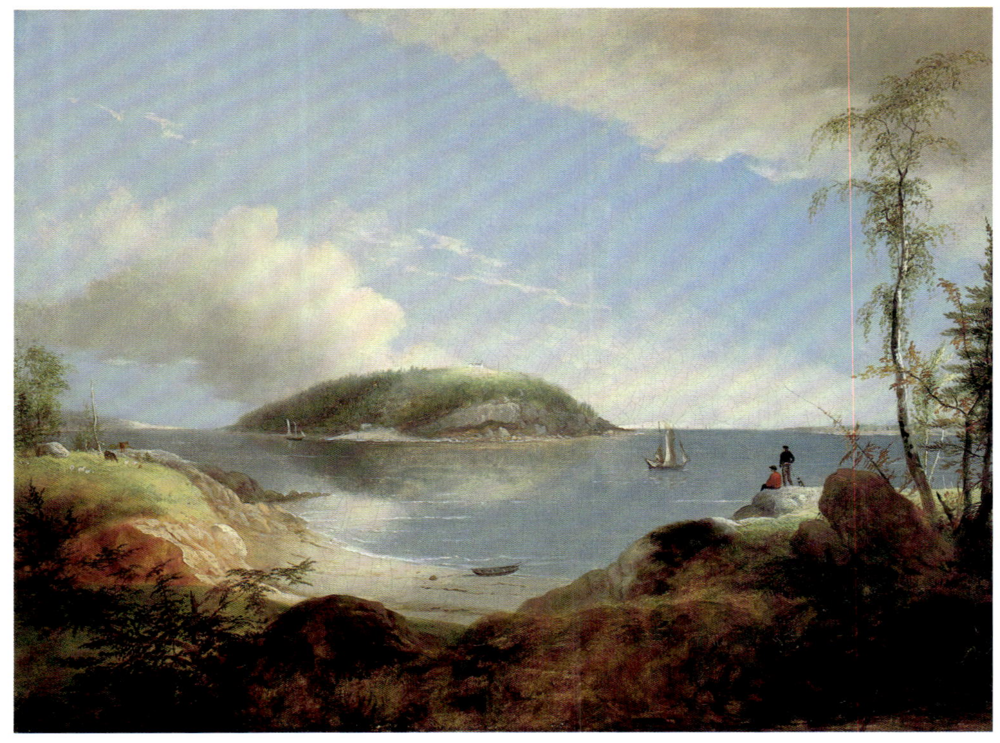

FIG. 15   Alvan Fisher, *Bear Island,* 1851, oil on canvas, 18 x 24". Collections of the Shelburne Museum, Shelburne, Vermont.

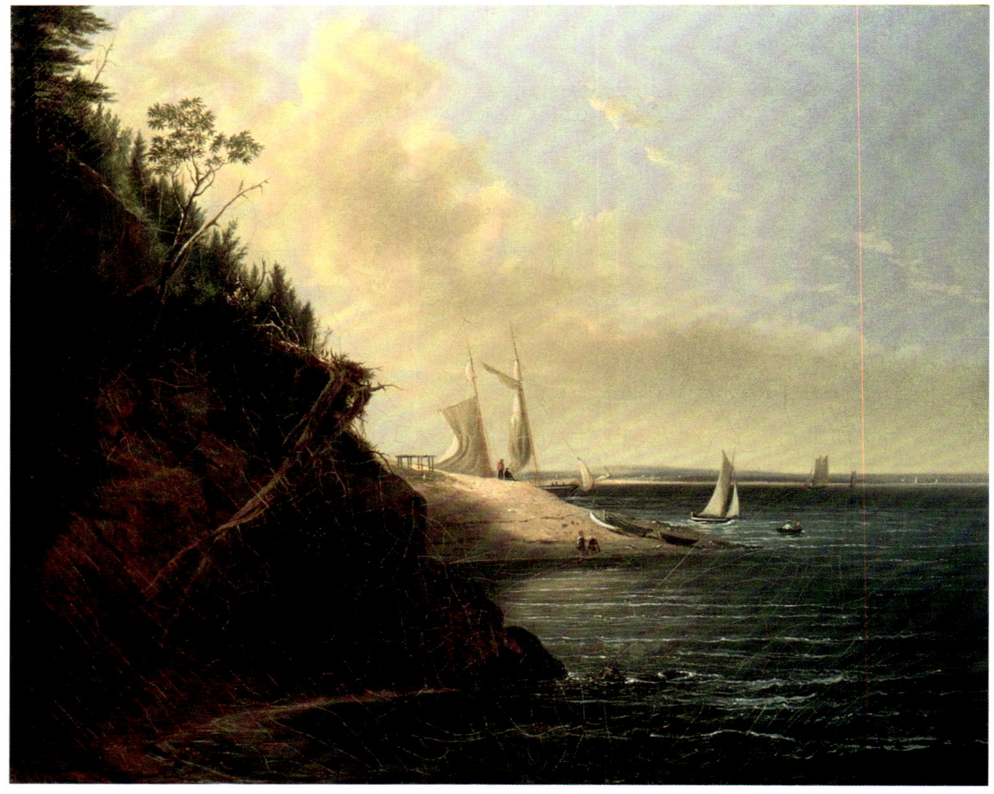

FIG. 16   Alvan Fisher, *Sutton Island, Mount Desert,* c. 1848, oil on canvas, 22 x 27". The Farnsworth Art Museum, Museum Purchase, Roswell Dwight Hitchcock Fund, 1960.

1848. *Sutton Island, Mount Desert,* c. 1848, (fig. 16) is a picturesque view that shows a boat landing, and a two-masted schooner and several other vessels out on the bay. In 1849, in a letter to a friend, Fisher wrote about Mount Desert and Bear Island, hoping to introduce the friend to "the romantic Landscape views, and fishing in your vicinity. Any attentions to Mr. and Mrs. W. which may go to bear out my recommendation of Bear Island will confer a favour on your Obt. Serv't?"[14] The letter suggests that Fisher painted a picture of Bear Island in order to display the romantic attractions of its scenery and its fishing. *Sutton Island, Mount Desert,* remained in the artist's family before it entered the Collection of the Farnsworth Art Museum.

As Spirited as Possible

Thomas Cole probably first became aware of the scenic potential of the Island through the publication of Doughty's 1840 engraving "Desert Rock Light House" in Willis's *American Scenery,* and from the exhibition of the 1836 canvas in Boston. Perhaps he also heard about Doughty's putative early visits to Maine from his good friend in Boston, Henry Cheever Pratt (1803–1880). Such information would have fed Cole's competitive nature. By the mid-1840s Cole needed to find new scenery to stimulate his market for landscapes in New York, and he decided to visit the Island. Indisputably the most influential artist to visit Mount Desert, Cole arrived on 3 September 1844, accompanied by Pratt. The date is considered pivotal to the history of Mount Desert.[15] Cole wrote his wife Maria, "I intend to be as spirited as possible, and to get as many fine sketches as I can."

Cole began his trip by stopping briefly in New York; he then went to Hartford with his new student Frederic Edwin Church, where he spent the day "very pleasantly." Perhaps to Church's disappointment, the youthful artist did not join Cole and Pratt on their long and somewhat difficult journey to Mount Desert.[16] Instead, as Cole informed his wife in his letter of August 22 (fig. 17), "Mr. Church will be with you, [in Catskill] in a few days."[17] Church's later fascination with Mount Desert scenery resulted in as many as eight trips to the Island, from which resulted numerous drawings, oil sketches, and major canvases. Church's sustained interest in the place must have started when Cole told of his exciting visit to the Island upon his return to Catskill. Church, who then lived with Cole and worked with him daily, had ample opportunities to see the master's drawings and oil sketches that resulted from the trip.

From Hartford, Cole then traveled to Boston, and on by railroad to Dresden Mills, Maine, where he met Pratt. Longtime friends, Cole and Pratt first sketched together on a trip to New Hampshire in 1828. The artists' adventure began in Dresden Mills. Cole's August 30 letter to Maria (fig. 18) from "Island of Mount Desert" explains that "we left Mr. Pratt's

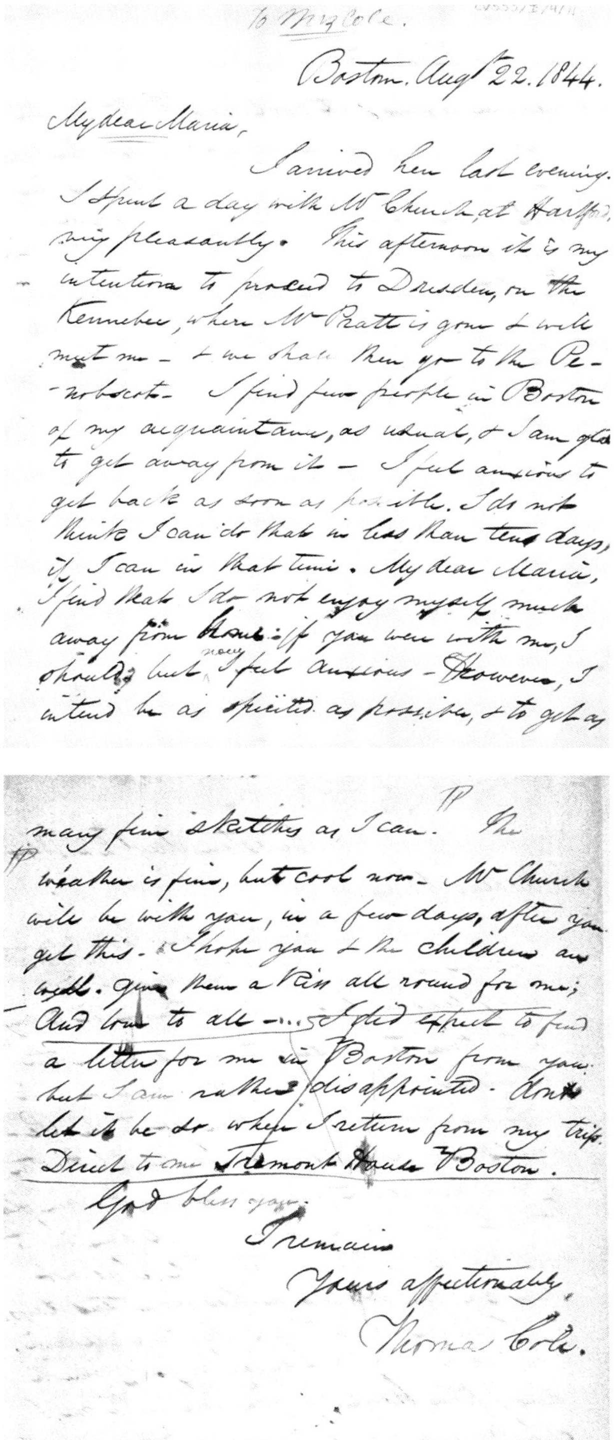

FIG. 17   Thomas Cole, Boston, to Maria Cole, Catskill, 22 August 1844. Thomas Cole Collection, McKinney Library, Albany Institute of History and Art.

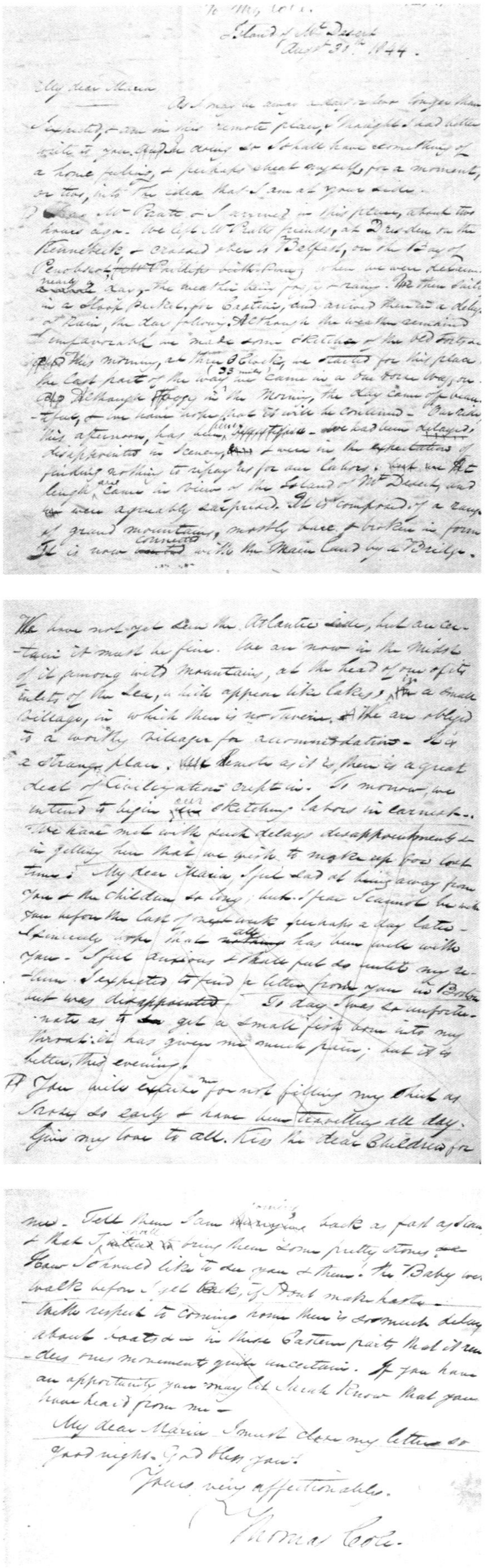

friends, at Dresden on the Kennebeck - crossed over to Belfast, on the Bay of Penobscot." After a day's delay because of fog and rain, they "sailed in a sloop packet for Castine, and arrived there in a deluge of rain the day following." Cole added that "although the weather remained unfavorable we made some sketches of the old fort here."[18] In the early morning of August 30, they continued their journey by wagon from Castine to Bucksport, on to Ellsworth, then turned south toward Mount Desert. Cole nearly despaired about a successful sketching trip, writing, "we had been delayed, disappointed in scenery, and were in the expectations of finding nothing to repay us for our labors." As they approached the Island, however, Cole's hopes began to rise. He wrote, "at length we came in view of the Island of Mt. Desert, and were agreeably surprised. It is composed of a range of grand mountains, mostly bare and broken in form." Here, Cole paused to sketch the panoramic *View of Mt. Desert from Trenton on the Main Land*, 1844 (fig. 19). The appurtenances of civilization were already evident: a barn nestles in the valley and a schooner sails on the bay. Always quick to note improvements, Cole observed that the Island "is now connected to the main land by a Bridge." Yet this dramatic view was prelude, for even from the start of his trip Cole anticipated the scenery on the eastern side of the Island. "We have not yet seen the Atlantic side, but are certain it must be fine," he wrote to his wife.[19]

Among Wild Mountains

Traveling south past the village of Somesville, Cole continued his dramatic description: "We are now in the midst of it, among wild mountains, at the head of one of its inlets of the sea, which appears like lakes, is a small village." Within this wilderness, he noted, "remote as it is, there is a great deal of civilization. Tomorrow, we intend to begin our sketching labors in earnest." On August 29, Cole found himself in a pure wilderness. Adopting the persona of an explorer, he wrote as if he were visiting the far West or some distant, exotic place. "We are now at a village in which there is no tavern, in the heart of Mount Desert Island. One might imagine himself in the center of a continent with a lake or two in view."[20] Cole would have been especially pleased with the aspects of a "small village" and "civilization" even in this "remote" area among "wild mountains." Cole had linked tourism, nearly-wild scenery, and sites of early history ever since he painted Catskill Falls, in 1826.[21] Almost two decades later he used this linking technique—he had used it with pictures of the Catskills, the White Mountains, the Adirondacks, and Niagara Falls—to depict Mount Desert. The Island's potential as a tourist attraction, and its mix of rugged wilderness and emerging civilization, suited Cole's interests perfectly.

After a few days sketching around Somesville, Cole and Pratt traveled across to the eastern coast of Mount Desert. In a letter to Maria, Cole described their carriage ride over

FIG. 18   Thomas Cole, Mount Desert, to Maria Cole, Catskill, 30 August 1844. Thomas Cole Collection, McKinney Library, Albany Institute of History and Art.

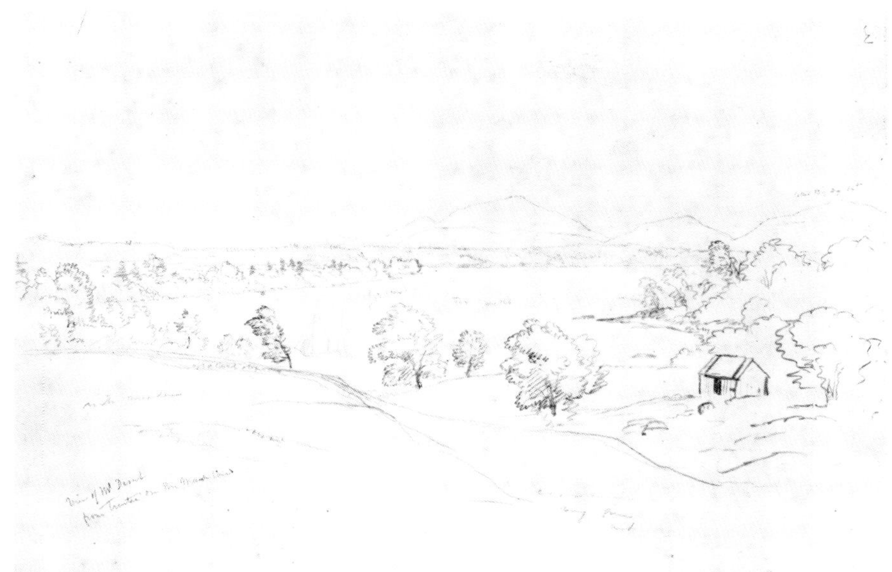

FIG. 19 Thomas Cole, *View of Mt. Desert from Trenton on the Main Land,* 1844, pencil on paper, 11½ x 16¾". Cole Sketchbook, folio 14 v, The Art Museum, Princeton University, Gift of Frank Jewett Mather, Jr. Photo: Clem Fiori.

the Island to the Lynam homestead at Schooner Head where he and Pratt were to be guests. The Lynam's were early settlers and avid promoters of the Island, and their house or homestead (fig. 20) where most of the early artists stayed was a short distance from Sand Beach and Sand Beach Head, or, as it was later named, Great Head. Cole continued, "the ride here to Lynam's was delightful, affording fine views of Frenchmans' Bay on the left, and the lofty peaks of Mount Desert on the right." Cole was fascinated with the new science of geology and was impressed to see "mountains [that] rise precipitously—vast bare walls of rock in some places of basaltic appearance." The road was exceedingly bad, stony, and overhung with beech and spruce, and, for miles, without inhabitants. The party lost the road at one point and "came to a romantic place near a mountain gorge, with a deserted house and a piece of meadow. One might have easily fancied himself in the forest of the Alleghenies, but for the dull roar of the ocean breaking on the stillness."[22]

A Very Grand Scene

On the eastern side of the Island, Mount Desert's only extensive sandy beach particularly excited Cole and Pratt. It is one of the few places where access to the water's edge can be gained without imperiling life, and one of the few places where a pulling boat could be easily landed. Cole's excited letter to Maria continued:

Sand Beach is the grandest coast scenery we have yet found. Sand Beach Head, the eastern extremity of Mount Desert Island, is a tremendous overhanging precipice, rising from the ocean, with the surf dashing against it in a frightful manner.[23]

Cole's enthusiasm for the beach was evident in a small oil sketch he produced of the scene, entitled *Sandy Beach, Mount Desert Island, Maine,* 1844 (fig. 21). The coarse, distinctively pink-colored granitic sand on Sand Beach made it an especially attractive subject. The expanse of sandy beach, situated spectacularly between rocky headlands, lay a short walk away

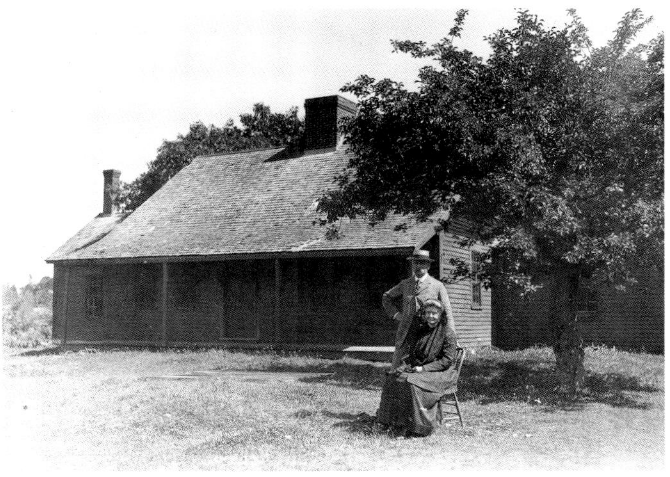

FIG. 20 *George B. Dorr and Mrs. J. P. Morgan (Frances Tracy), in front of the Lynam House,* c. 1920. Courtesy of Raymond Strout.

from the Lynam House where the party lodged. Sand Beach and nearby Great Head afforded spectacular distant views of Schoodic Point and its offshore islands. Today Sand Beach is among the most visited sites at Acadia National Park.

Cole's oil sketch, with its jewel-like precision, represented a corner of the sandy beach at low tide with eroded rocks exposed along the base of cliffs. The saturated, brilliant crisp light of the northern sky reflects from a luminous, calm sea. In the distance sailing vessels are glimpsed and in the sky the moon's faint orb is subtly etched, establishing sentiments of beauty and repose, far removed from the stormy scenes of the Island Cole would later produce back in his New York studio. Cole captured the visual drama of the scene in a letter to Maria: "The ocean with vessels sprinkling its bosom— is magnificent."[24] On the margin of a pencil sketch made on Sand Beach looking inland, Cole noted "This is a very grand scene. The craggy mountain, the dark pond of dark brown water—The golden sea sand of the beach and the light green with its surf altogether with woods of varied color—make a magnificent effect such as is seldom seen created in the sun."[25]

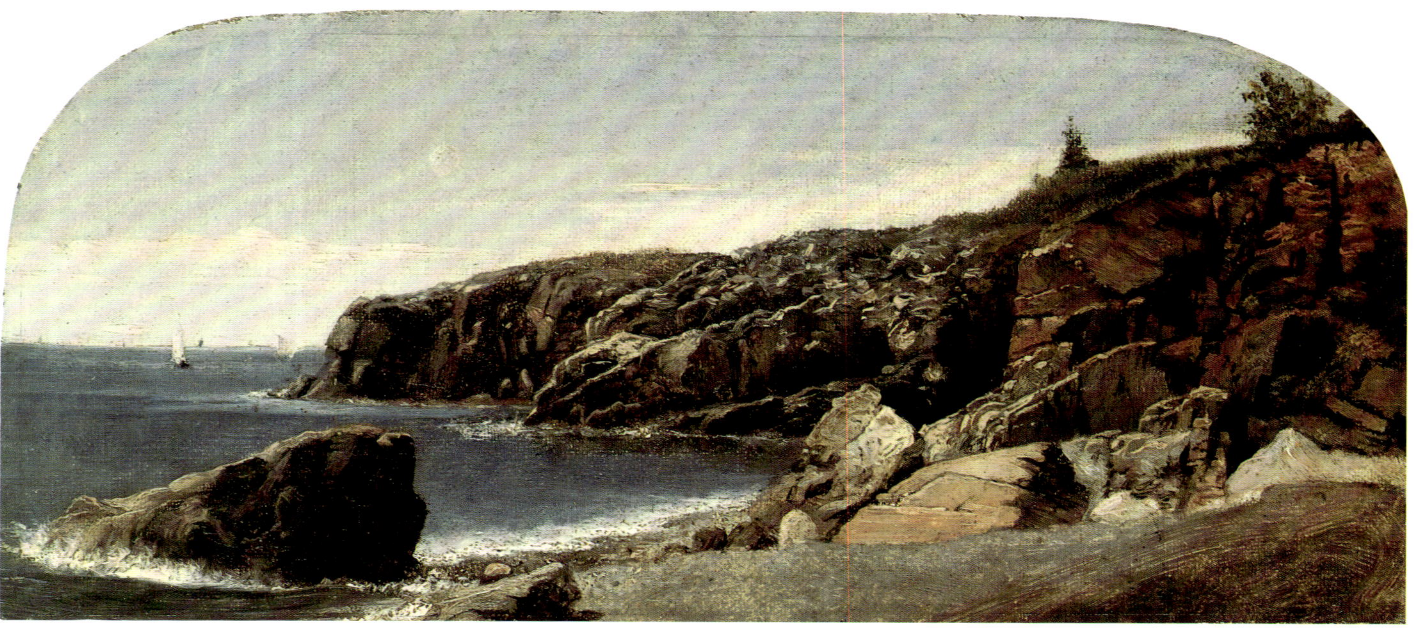

FIG. 21   Thomas Cole, *Sandy Beach, Mount Desert Island, Maine*, 1844, oil on canvas, 5¼ x 11½". Private Collection.

Church must have seen Cole's sketch in Catskill when he returned from Mount Desert in September because Church painted an almost identical view during his first visit there in 1850 (see fig. 31). Neither artist exhibited their sketches of the beach scene, although judging from the unusually high degree of finish in Cole's sketch, he may have intended to produce a larger version. Perhaps he was preempted from doing so by Pratt, who subsequently painted two pictures of Mount Desert that are now unlocated (see Appendix).[26] One of Pratt's pictures was titled *View of Sand Beach at Mt. Desert, Maine, Taken from Nature, 1844*, which was exhibited at the Boston Athenaeum the following year.[27] The fact that Pratt's picture was described in its title as "from nature" suggests that Pratt and Cole may have worked side by side at Sand Beach *en plein air*, and Cole's oil study or oil sketch survives as a memento of this artistic fraternity.

Frenchman's Bay

Frenchman's Bay, Mount Desert Island, Maine, 1845, (fig. 22), a small but potent image finished in the studio, dramatically represents towering red granite cliffs, foaming waves, and a stormy, blustery sky.[28] Cole described the scene: "The whole coast along here is iron bound—threatening crags, and dark caverns in which the sea thunders."[29] The tension between the elements of nature and the pummeled cliff is heightened by Cole's calculated exaggeration of the headland near Sand Beach called Great Head.[30] Always concerned about representing man's place in the natural world, Cole's solitary figure and distant vessel affirm human scale and presence amidst the sublime power of the sea. The viewer empathizes with the person who peers excitedly over the cliff at the roaring white-topped waves. In the distance a small ship heels sharply, spray breaking on its bow as it sails dangerously close to the rocky shore, its pennants streaming out in the wind. The gesturing, excited figure is a prospective tourist type, invited visually by Cole to visit Mount Desert to experience, in the safety of an art gallery, an exhilarating encounter with Maine's remote maritime wilderness.

Cole's *View Across Frenchman's Bay From Mt. Desert Island, After a Squall* (fig. 23), painted the same year as *Frenchman's Bay* and produced especially for public exhibition, gave New Yorker's their first opportunity to view a large-scale image of the wilderness scenery of Mount Desert. Cole completed the painting in his New York studio, basing it on one of sixteen views he sketched on his visit to the Island the previous year. The sketch was inscribed *Islands in Frenchman's Bay from Mt. Desert* (fig. 24).[31] In a letter to his wife on 3 March 1845 from New York, Cole wrote, "I arrived here safely with the pictures . . . [and] have commenced sketching on the canvass for the Sea View."[32] Cole had tourism on his mind as he completed his large picture of Island scenery; he was also finishing a view of the Catskill Mountain House Hotel, entitled *A View of the Two Lakes and Mountain House, Catskill Mountain, Morning* (Brooklyn Museum). Cole exhibited his sea view at an 1845 exhibition at the National Academy of Design along with the Catskill hotel painting, and one of his large religious pictures. *View Across Frenchman's Bay* remained unsold until the late summer of 1847, perhaps because of unfavorable reviews, when it was purchased by William W. Scarborough of Cincinnati.[33]

Cole expressed his enthusiasm for the eastern side of the Island in a letter to his wife, which includes a passage that is a virtual description of *View Across Frenchman's Bay*. Cole wrote, "the view of Frenchman's Bay and islands is truly fine. Some of the islands, called porcupines, are lofty, and belted with crags which glitter in the setting sun." Cole continued with a narration of the distant view beyond the Porcupine Islands: "Beyond and across the bay is a range of mountains

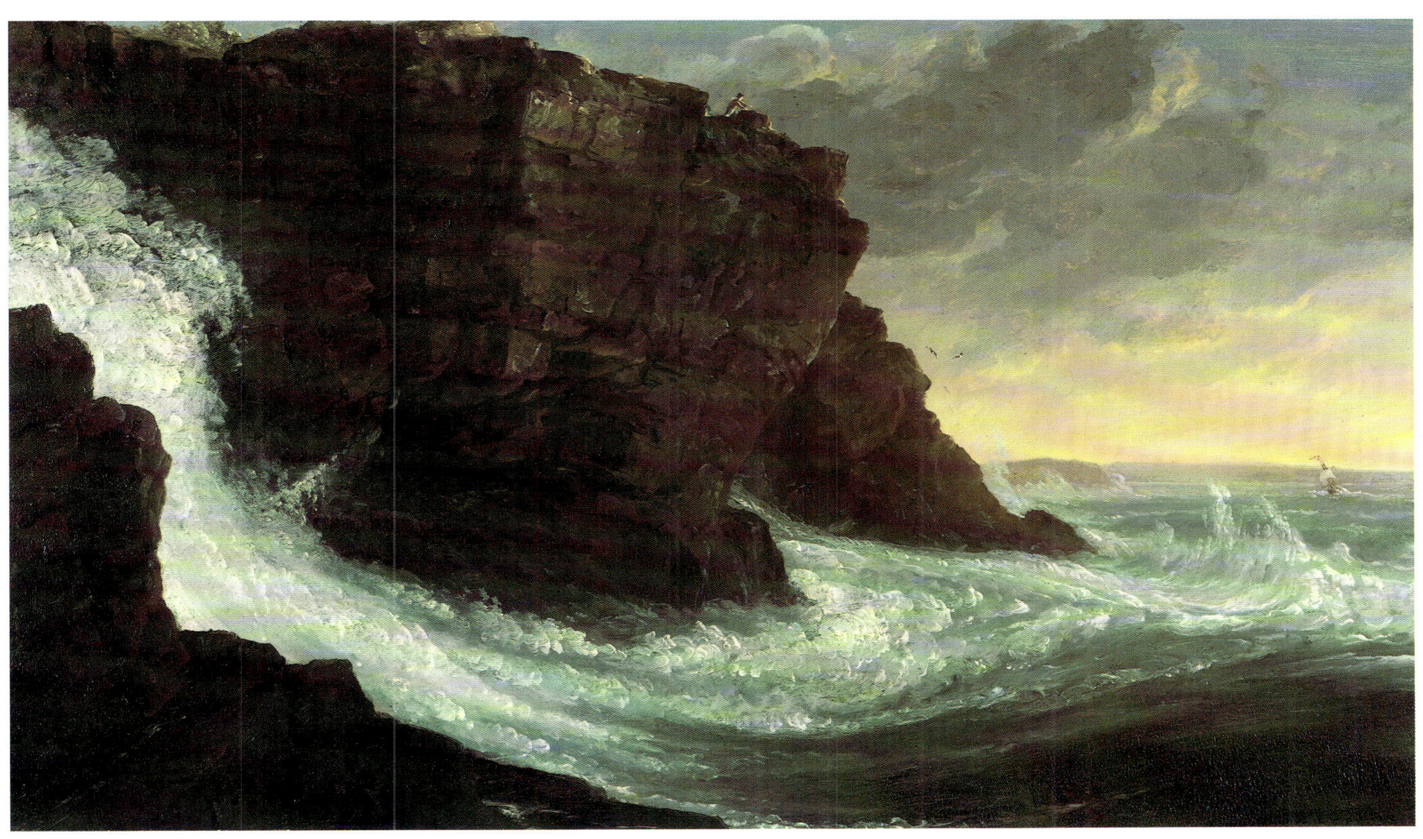

FIG. 22 Thomas Cole, *Frenchman's Bay, Mount Desert Island, Maine,* 1845, oil on wood panel, 14 x 23". Collection of the Albany Institute of History and Art.

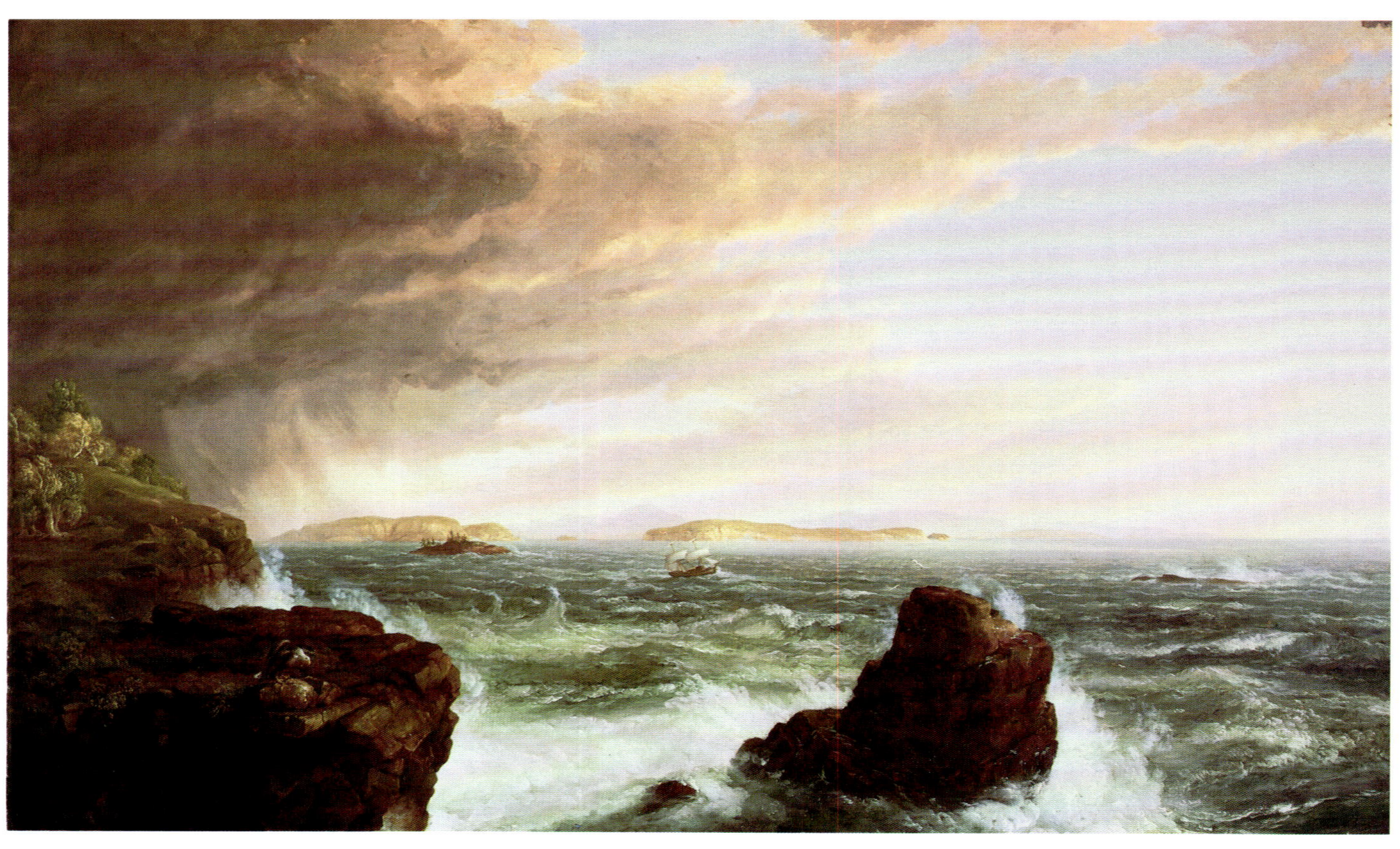

FIG. 23   Thomas Cole, *View Across Frenchman's Bay From Mt. Desert Island, After a Squall,* 1845, oil on canvas, 38¼ x 62½". Cincinnati Art Museum, Gift of Miss Alice Scarborough.

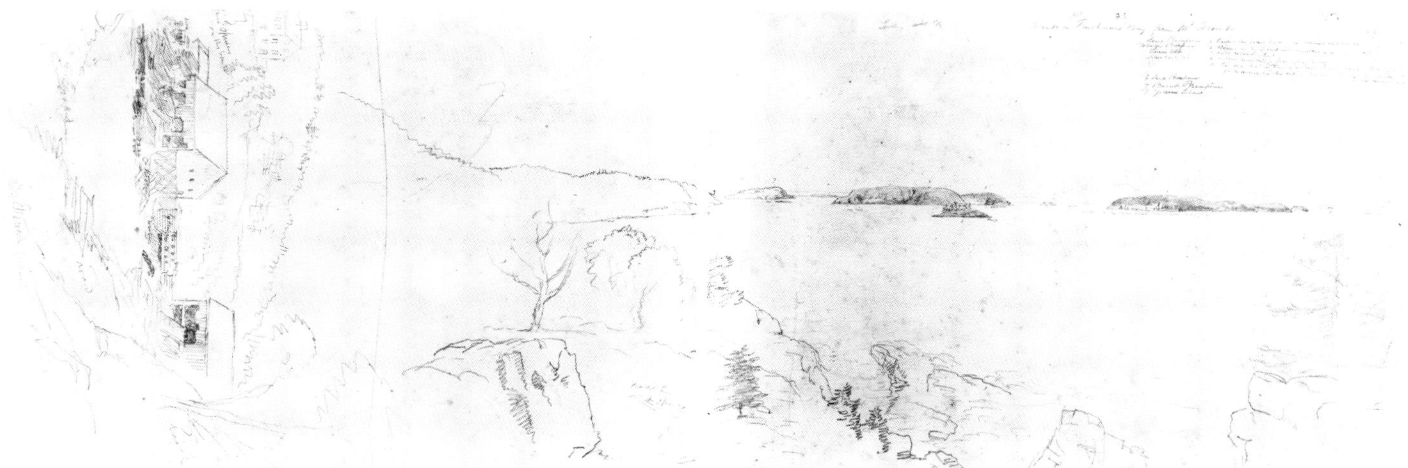

FIG. 24   Thomas Cole, *Islands in Frenchman's Bay from Mt. Desert,* 1844, pencil on paper, 11½ x 16¾". Cole Sketchbook, folio 13v and 14, The Art Museum, Princeton University, Gift of Frank Jewett Mather, Jr. Photo: Clem Fiori.

of beautiful aerial hues."[34] As he completed the picture the following spring, Cole included all the geographical details he mentioned in the letters. Using an expansive horizontal format, the artist relied on a broad sky in the composition to emphasize strong horizontal, even panoramic qualities. The pencil sketch that formed the basis of the painting was made from a vantage point at the top of Great Head or Schooner Head. The view is directly north from these high headlands. He manipulated the foreground to achieve the effect of seeing the bay as if from a high overlook, and he translated the background islands and distant mountains directly to canvas from the pencil sketch. From left to right they are readily recognized and labeled in Cole's pencil sketch as Bald Porcupine, The Thrumpcap, Burnt Porcupine, Rum Key, Schoodic Mountain, Long Porcupine, The Hop, Black and Tunk Mountains, and Stave Island.[35]

Cole made one major change in actual topography by inserting within the frame of his composition the rocky ledge known as Egg Rock, which is actually farther south. The vessel at the center of the composition heads directly toward this dangerous ledge that sits dead athwart the entrance to Frenchman Bay. The artist represented a two-masted square-rigged coastal brig in an unusually detailed manner. The vessel is well-reefed for a gale, with a staysail, a fore topsail, a main topsail, and spanker. Four red-shirted figures are discernible on the vessel. They appear to be struggling to sail her in the strong winds that roughen the sea. She flies masthead pennants, or wind flies, and from their position and the angle of the sails it is clear that she is sailing very close to the wind, perhaps attempting to hold a course and navigate past the danger of Egg Rock and on out to the safety of open water. Emphasizing a portentous moment, the deep orange color in the clouds opens to a luminous sunrise sky.

A Tale Rationally Told

Cole knew about various types of vessels; he had sailed aboard coastal ships to reach Mount Desert, and he had taken large passenger packets to Europe. The brig, already

an old-fashioned type of sailing ship, passed out of service in the American merchant marine in the late 1840s. Brigs were replaced by newer schooner-rigged ships that could sail closer to the wind and required fewer crew members; these soon came to dominate coastal trade. Brigs navigated the waters around Mount Desert from the mid-eighteenth century until the 1850s, at which time the availability of good taut manufactured cotton made the larger and heaver sails of the schooners more affordable. Primarily a ship of an earlier era, the coastal brig is Cole's nostalgic allusion to the storied history of Frenchman Bay, site of colonial naval conflict, and more recently of pioneers heading "Down East" to claim and settle the Maine coast. In Cole's art, objects often held multiple levels of symbolic meaning. The artist had often used boats as metaphors for the "life voyage"; the best known of these boat metaphors is the small shallop in his allegorical series *The Voyage of Life. The Consummation of Empire,* the central panel in Cole's series *The Course of Empire,* is filled with minutely detailed boats. Plausibly, the passing brig also suggested ideas of "passing history," "passing life," to the artist and his audience.[36]

Cole's New York public may have been pleased to discover the splendors of Mount Desert in Cole's large and dramatic picture, and a few critics praised the painting, but most reviews were negative. A harsh critic for *The Broadway Journal* found much to fault. He began by praising the beauty of New York harbor, and complained that instead of painting such local glories, "our artists" such as Cole have "gone down to Frenchman's Bay, four or five hundred miles off toward the North Pole, and has come back and painted a pea-green sea with ledges of red rock."[37] Noting that it was unusual for Cole to paint marines, the critic thought the water well drawn but strangely colored, and "the rocks are of a kind that no geologist would find a name for; the whole coast of Maine is lined with rocks nearly black in color and tinged with a greenish hue, as all marine rocks are. These in Mr. Cole's picture are red." The critic was unaware that the peculiar granitic rock formations on Mount Desert are in fact an unusual pinkish color. "An artist should be something of a geologist to paint rocky scenes correctly," the critic complained. He also thought that the "picture is a good deal too large. So wide a surface for so meager a subject must be filled up chiefly with common places."[38] The *New York Herald* critic was even harsher, calling it "a glorious sky, but the ocean appears like a vast cabbage garden."[39] However, a reviewer for *The Anglo American* was impressed by the originality of Cole's sea-piece. "A storm with rain going off, at the left, surf dashing boldly on the rocks, the sea has become gradually smoother [on the right]. The Picture tells its tale clearly, and rationally, and it is one of the gems of the exhibition."[40] *The New York Daily Tribune* was the most complimentary, giving the picture two notices. The reviewer thought the picture "exhibits his [Cole] peculiar excellence. The mist driving inland from the sea—the vexed waters, and the spray shooting up from every rock, and the deep green of the waters are all true to nature, and seem like a remembrance to one who has witnessed such scenes." Two days later the paper's reviewer remarked on Cole's picture again: "Cole has thrown together some fine and startling effects in this sea-piece. He is a Bold Man."[41]

A Bold Man

The artist's visual construction of complex local, regional, and nationalistic associations in his historical narrative emerges today as the most important element in *View Across Frenchman's Bay*. Cole's complete elimination of the human figure in the foreground of the picture may have made the aforementioned critic uncomfortable with the "meager subject." He was also uneasy with Cole's new interest in the specifics of geological science, mistaking Cole's interest in specific geological types of rock as concern with "common places." Cole's interest in geology and geologic history would have been stimulated by the unusual color of the Island's coast and mountains and its fascinating variety of geological formations.

Another issue concerned the artist: providing a position from which the spectator could gaze upon the scene. The expansive width of the canvas Cole selected provided an opportunity to develop the new wide horizontal or panoramic convention that was gaining favor. This style of composition was perceived as an alternative to the conventional framing devices inherited from the European landscape tradition.[42] By suspending the spectator over the rough water, as if on the edge of an unseen rock ledge, like those at the left, Cole heightened the visual drama of the passing squall. The prospect is shared with no other human presence. On a rocky ledge at left a fierce eagle feeds on its catch. Its precise function is unclear, but its specificity may suggest Cole's interest in "another new branch of the natural sciences in the United States, ornithology."[43] The eagle, which may also symbolize national pride, was at that time a bird still commonly seen in the region. In several drawings from his 1850 expedition to the Island Church also showed eagles or other large birds. He noted in 1850 that "farther down the bay towards the sea, is a great resort of eagles, hawks, sea pigeons, gulls, snipe, ducks, etc."[44]

In *View Across Frenchman's Bay,* Cole attempted to exhibit a scientifically accurate recording of geological forms while preserving his conventional use of sky and rock for associative, narrative, and expressive purposes. Cole's collector's case of mineral specimens and other geological curiosities (at the Bronck House Museum, Coxsackie, New York), and his friendship with Benjamin Silliman, the leading American geologist of the period, exemplify his interest in the new science of the earth's history. In a sketch of *Monument Rock Near Sand Beach* (Detroit Institute of Arts) Cole inscribed "a multitude of granite boulders," indicating his new more specific interest in the types of rock formations. The large rock at right center of the painting, isolated from the coast, demonstrates Cole's interest in the geology of Mount Desert. But the formation may also be another of Cole's manipulations of geographical and geological fact, since it resembles the large offshore rock called "Old Soaker" that is just to the south, and is difficult to see from this vantage point.

While Cole used a new panoramic composition and represented his up-to-date knowledge of geology, he also fell back on iconographic conventions he had relied upon since the beginning of his career. He enthusiastically personified his landscapes with anthropomorphic emblems, and as he completed his composition of Frenchman Bay in his New York studio, Cole overlaid profiles on the pinkish granitic rocks to symbolize the vitalistic power of nature in which he also believed. The most noticeable face in the rocks is strongly profiled in the ledge at the left. The shape is one that Cole employed often, and its sea-sprayed gaze looks out impassively toward the ocean and passing ship. Its presence offered reassurances that every rock, cloud, tree, or wave could speak of both the local and the specific as well as a universal belief in the transcendent power of nature.[45]

An American Scene

Cole's representations of Mount Desert scenery also included several inland views. In a 31 August 1844 letter to Maria, Cole explained that on his carriage ride to Lynam's house he "came to a romantic place near a mountain gorge, with a deserted house and a piece of meadow."[46] He produced a drawing and later back in his New York studio a small oil painting of *House, Mt. Desert, Maine* (fig. 25 & fig. 26). The painting was exhibited at the American Art-Union in 1845 and purchased by the politician Nathaniel Silsbee, of Salem, Massachusetts.[47] The probable site of Cole's painting may be the Great Meadow, near the Sieur De Monts Spring. The distinctive bald peak of Champlain Mountain defines the location of the painting. *Picturesque America* described similar scenery found on the way to Schooner Head. Its commentary might be a description of the location of the deserted farm house.

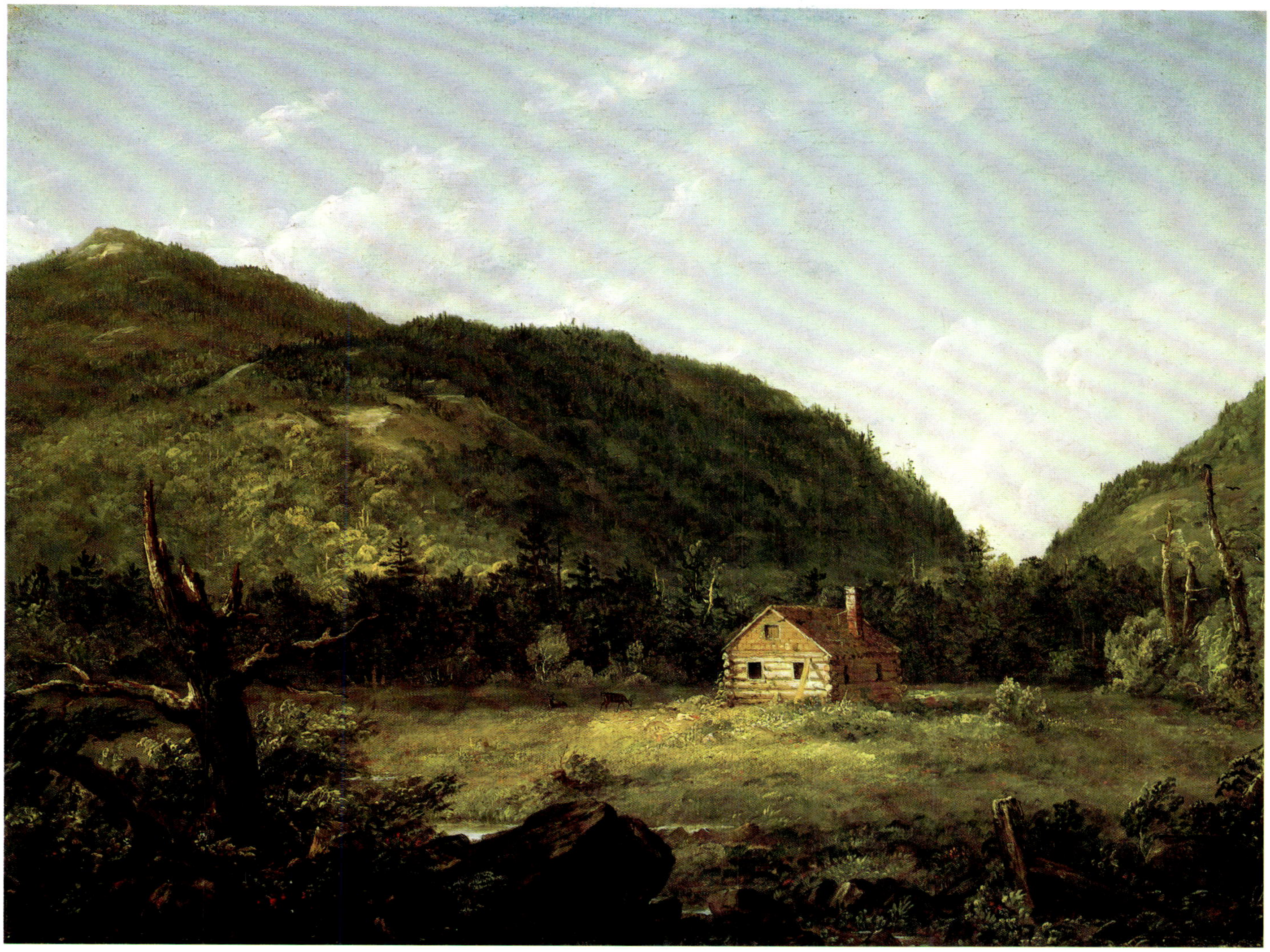

> *The drive derives great interest from the wild and narrow notch between Green and Newport Mountain, through which the road lies for a mile or two. The sides of the mountains are high, precipitous, and savagely rugged. The lower base of each is covered with a thick and tangled forest-growth; half-way up, a few gnarled and fantastic growths struggle for place amid the scarred and frowning rocks, while the upper heights show only the bare, seamed, and riven escarpments.*[48]

Bryant continued to compare the notch at Mount Desert to the Notch of the White Mountains that had become "famous" just a few years earlier. He wrote of Mount Desert's Notch: "It is a wild picture, inferior, no doubt, to the famous Notch of the White Mountains, but possessing, notwithstanding, very strong and impressive features."[49]

In *House, Mt. Desert, Maine,* nature has rapidly undermined man's handiwork settling the wilderness. The foreground is filled with details that demonstrate nature's reclamation of the Down East frontier cabin and its cleared land.

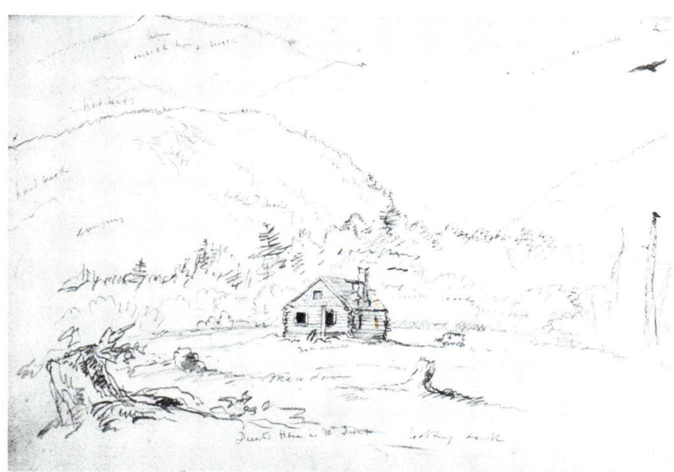

FIG. 26   Thomas Cole, *House in Mount Desert/Rocks,* 1844, pencil with gouache on paper, 9¾ x 14". Lent by the Detroit Institute of Arts Founder's Society Purchase, William H. Murphy Fund, DIA 39.282.

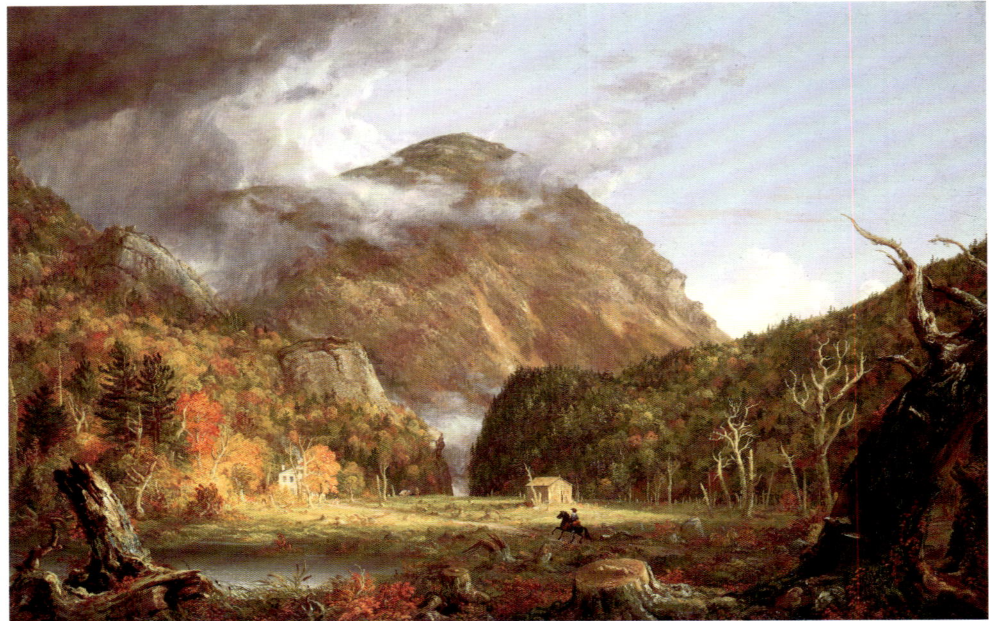

At the left, a single stump, symbol of man's work, is surrounded by new growth. The right reveals only the remains of a fence. The blasted tree in the foreground, which is not in the sketch, functions as a potent emblem of natural antiquity. Its form suggests human associations, complete with the semblance of a face and gesticulating branches. This expressive presence provides a surrogate inanimate actor from whose perspective the viewer may experience the scene; it directs the viewer's attention by gesturing toward the deserted cabin. The cleared land, once used to grow food, becomes transformed into a sylvan meadow—now inhabited by two deer, prime symbols of the wilderness—not quite transformed into an arcadian state.

Cole completed his critically successful picture, *A View of the Mountain Pass Called the Notch of the White Mountains (Crawford Notch)* (fig. 27), five years before *House, Mt. Desert, Maine*. It set an important precedent for Cole's conceptualization of Mount Desert's failed attempts at early settlement. *A View of the Mountain Pass* was acclaimed by *Knickerbocker* as "truly an American Picture," and similar sentiments are expressed in *House, Mt. Desert, Maine*.[50] The White Mountain image depicts a marginally successful attempt to settle the land, marked by freshly cut tree stumps. The stump, most visible in Cole's drawing, is an important symbol and a "focus for very strong associations. In many cases, to the American, the tree which was no longer there was as important as trees that remained. The stump became the tangible indicator of man's workings on the land."[51]

Although Mount Desert proved to be useless for agricultural purposes, it would soon be recognized for its scenic, geological, and geographic uniqueness. Cole opened the way for tourists and subsequently for civilization to come to Mount Desert. He was followed by Church, whose numerous dramatic canvases greatly increased the visibility and appeal of the Island during the 1860s.

NOTES

1. "Mount Desert," *Harper's New Monthly Magazine* 45, no. 267 (August 1872): 324.

2. Robert F. Perkins, Jr., and William J. Gavin III, comps., eds., *The Boston Athenaeum Art Exhibition Index, 1827–1874* (Boston: Library of the Boston Athenaeum, 1980; Cambridge: distributed by MIT Press, 1980), 50.

3. Algernon Graves, *The British Institution, 1806–1867* (first published 1875; reprint, Bath, U.K.: 1969).

4. Nathaniel Parker Willis, *American Scenery*, vol. 2, (London: George Virtue, 1840; reprint, Barre: Mass., Imprint Society, 1971), 36.

5. Willis, *American Scenery* 37, quoted in Frank H. Goodyear, Jr., *Thomas Doughty, 1793–1856: An American Pioneer in Landscape Painting* (Philadelphia: Pennsylvania Academy of the Fine Arts, 1973), 48.

6. In 1939 The Newark Museum received the painting as a gift from Mrs. Jennie E. Mead, of Caldwell, New Jersey.

7. The lost painting *View of Mount Desert, Maine,* exhibited at the Albany Gallery of Fine Arts in 1848, is problematic. It is possible that Doughty could have exhibited his 1846 version of the *Desert Rock Lighthouse* under a new title. See James L. Yarnall and William H. Gerdts, *The National Museum of American Art's Index to American Art Exhibition Catalogues: From the Beginning Through the 1876 Centennial Year* (Boston: G. K. Hall and Co., 1986), 1078.

8. Ron Beard of the University of Maine's Cooperative Extension Service believes that the painting depicts the Mount Desert Island profile from across Frenchman Bay at a point on Schoodic Peninsula.

9. John Wilmerding, *American Marine Painting* (Richmond: Virginia Museum of Fine Arts, 1976; Newport News, Va.: The Mariners' Museum, 1976), 14.

10. "Art and Artists," *The Home Journal* (21 June 1851): 3.

11. Ibid.

12. Goodyear, *Thomas Doughty,* 11–20.

13. Fred B. Adelson, "Alvan Fisher in Maine: His Early Coastal Scenes," *The American Art Journal* 18, no. 3 (1986): 64–65.

14. Quoted in Adelson, 69.

15. By long-standing convention Mount Desert historians customarily assign this date as the moment when Bar Harbor was founded. Richard Walden Hale, Jr., *The Story of Bar Harbor* (New York: Ives Washburn Inc., 1949), 126; see also G. W. Helfrich and Gladys O'Neil,

eds., *Lost Bar Harbor* (Camden, Maine: Down East Books, 1982), 3.

16. Since Church was only eighteen years old, his parents quite possibly forbade him to join Cole on the difficult trip to the wilderness region of coastal Maine.

17. Thomas Cole, Boston, to Maria Cole, Catskill, 22 August 1844, Thomas Cole Papers, McKinney Library, Albany Institute of History and Art.

18. Thomas Cole, Mount Desert, to Maria Cole, Catskill, 30 August 1844, Thomas Cole Papers, McKinney Library, Albany Institute of History and Art.

19. Ibid.

20. Ibid.

21. See Kenneth Myers, *The Catskills: Painters, Writers, and Tourists in the Mountains 1820–1895* (Yonkers, N.Y.: Hudson River Museum of Westchester, 1987); and Alan Wallach, "Making a Picture of the View from Mount Holyoke," *Bulletin of the Detroit Institute of Arts* 66, no. 1 (1990): 35–45.

22. Louis Legrand Noble, *The Life and Works of Thomas Cole,* Elliot S. Vesell, ed. (1853; reprint, Cambridge: Belknap Press of Harvard University Press, 1964), 270.

23. Noble, *The Life and Works of Thomas Cole,* 270.

24. Ibid.

25. John Wilmerding, *The Artist's Mount Desert* (Princeton: Princeton University Press, 1994), 38. Cole's sketch remained with his family until the late 1970s.

26. Alice Doan Hodgson, "Henry Cheever Pratt (1803–1880)," *The Magazine Antiques* 102, no. 5 (November 1972): 846.

27. Perkins and Gavin, *The Boston Athenaeum Art Exhibition Index,* 113.

28. The painting is in the collection of the Albany Institute of History and Art. In November 1964, the painting was purchased from Kennedy Gallery, who obtained the painting from the Cole House and Edith Cole Hill (Silberstein), the great-granddaughter of the artist.

29. Noble, 270.

30. Although the headland in the painting is cited by Wilmerding to be Otter Cliffs, it is thought that the headland more closely depicts Great Head. Moreover, Cole himself alludes to "Sand Beach Head, the eastern extremity of Mount Desert Island," which would be a reference to Great Head since the headland is the easternmost point of the Island. The engraved illustration for *Picturesque America* was titled *Great Head* and appears to resemble Cole's painting, thus suggesting the contemporary understanding of the site as Great Head.

31. An illustration of the sketch for the painting is in Louis Hawes, "A Sketchbook by Thomas Cole," *Record of the Art Museum Princeton University* 15, no. 1 (1956): 15.

32. Noble, 272.

33. The painting is currently in the Cincinnati Art Museum. In 1925 the museum received the painting as a gift from Alice Scarborough. We wish to thank Stephanie Eha at the Cincinnati Art Museum for curatorial information on the painting. For details of Scarborough's collection see Joseph E. Holliday, "Collector's Choice of the Gilded Age," *The Cincinnati Historical Society Bulletin* 28, no. 4 (Winter 1970): 294–315.

34. Noble, 270.

35. John Wilmerding states in "Thomas Cole in Maine," *Record of the Art Museum Princeton University* 49, no. 1 (1990): 19, that the view is a "panorama of 180 degrees, at once looking north to the islands and southeast to the open end of the bay and Schoodic Point."

36. The "storm-tossed boat" in the distance would have evoked associations of a ship in distress, a figure long used to "dramatize man's struggle against fate or against nature, or to point up the need for salvation." Such ships could be used to "spell out a moral or religious message concerning the fate of man." See Lorenz Eitner, "The Window and the Storm-Tossed Boat: An Essay in the Iconography of Romanticism," *The Art Bulletin* 37, no. 4 (December 1955); also J. Gray Sweeney, "A 'Very Peculiar' Picture: Martin J. Heade's *Thunderstorm over Narragansett Bay,*" *Archives of American Art Journal* 28, no. 4 (1988): 8. See David Miller, "The Iconology of Wrecked or Stranded Boats in Mid to Late Nineteenth-Century American Culture," in David Miller, ed., *American Iconology: New Approaches to Nineteenth-Century Art and Literature* (New Haven: Yale University Press, 1993), 186–208.

37. Cited in Ellwood C. Parry, *The Art of Thomas Cole: Ambition and Imagination* (Newark: University of Delaware Press, 1989), 308, n. 115. Parry notes that this harsh review was probably written by Henry C. Watson, rather than Edgar Allan Poe, the other editor of the newly established *Broadway Journal.* "Twentieth Annual Exhibition of the Academy of National Design [sic]," *The Broadway Journal* (3 May 1845): 275.

38. "Twentieth Annual Exhibition": 276.

39. "National Academy of Design," *New York Herald*, 28 April 1845. Thanks to Gerald L. Carr for bringing this humorous review to my attention.

40. "Painting," *The Anglo American,* 26 April 1845. Thanks to Gerald L. Carr for bringing this citation to my attention.

41. "National Academy of Design," *The New York Daily Tribune,* 24 April 1845: "National Academy of Design," *The New York Daily Tribune,* 26 April 1845.

42. Rebecca Bedell, "Thomas Cole and Fashionable Science. Art and Science in America: Issues in Representation," *Huntington Library Quarterly* 59, nos. 2, 3 (1998): 349–78.

43. Parry, *The Art of Thomas Cole*, 304.

44. Frederic E. Church, "Mountain Views and Coast Scenery, by a Landscape Painter," *Bulletin of the American Art-Union* (November 1850): 130.

45. For a discussion of anthropomorphism and "emblematic personification" in Hudson River School painting see J. Gray Sweeney, "The Nude of Landscape Painting: Emblematic Personification in the Art of the Hudson River School," *Smithsonian Studies in American Art* (Fall 1989): 42–65.

46. Noble, 270.

47. Mary Bartlett Cowdrey, *American Academy of Fine Arts and American Art-Union Exhibition Record, 1816–1852* (New York: New-York Historical Society, 1953), 81. Currently in the collection of the Fogg Art Museum, the painting was a bequest made by Edward Charles Pickering to Harvard in 1919.

48. William Cullen Bryant, ed., *Picturesque America: or, the Land We Live In* (New York: D. Appleton and Company, 1872), 11.

49. Ibid.

50. "The Fine Arts: National Academy of Design," *The Knickerbocker* 16 (July 1840): 81, quoted in William H. Gerdts, "American Landscape Painting: Critical Judgments, 1730–1845," *The American Art Journal* 17, no. 1 (Winter 1985): 56.

51. James Collins Moore, "The Storm and the Harvest: The Image of Nature in Mid-Nineteenth Century American Landscape Painting" (Ph.D. diss., Indiana University, 1974), 122. See also Nicolai Cikovsky, Jr., "The Ravages of the Axe: The Meaning of the Tree Stump in Nineteenth-Century American Art," *The Art Bulletin* 61 (December 1979): 611–26.

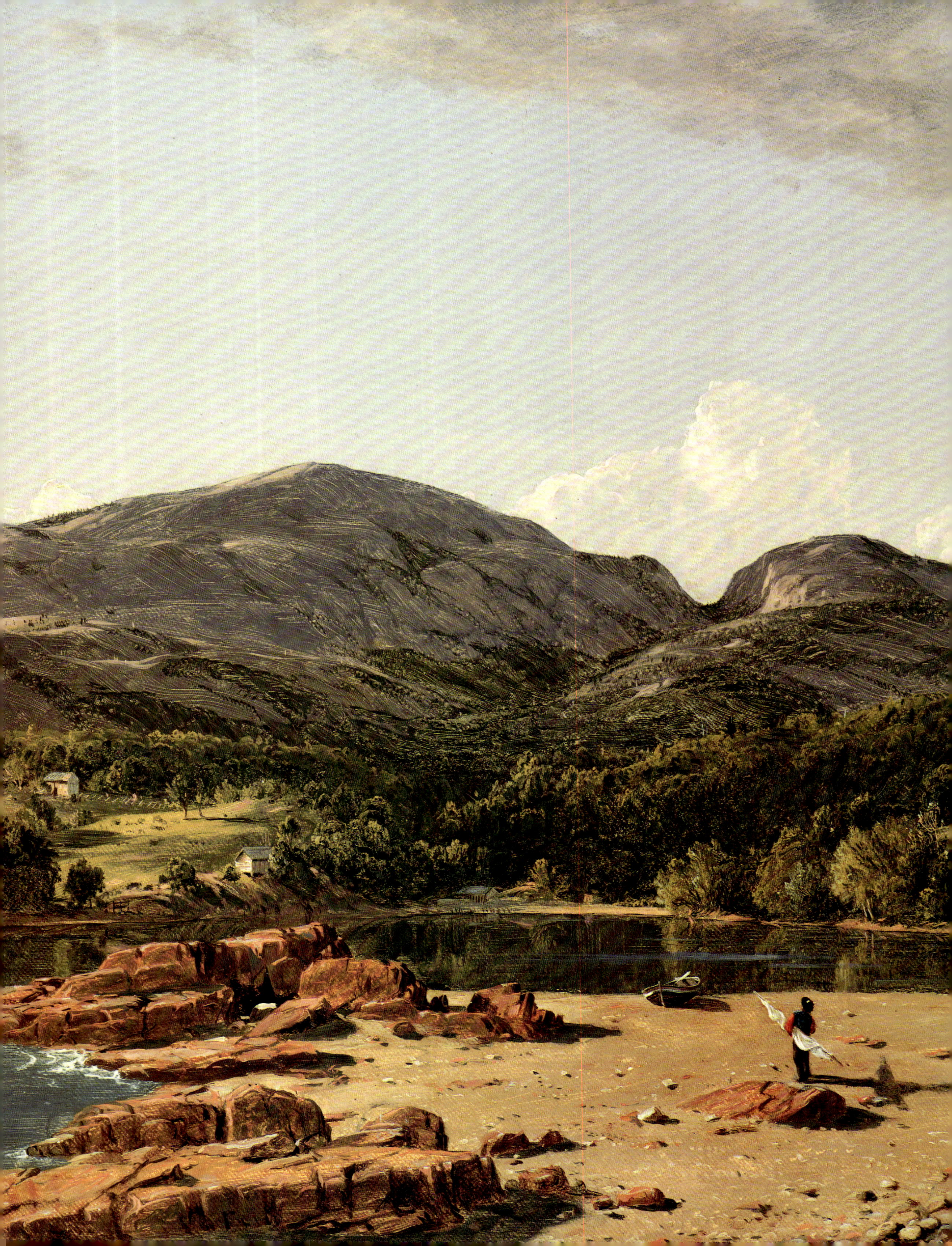

CHAPTER 3

"That Which We Do Not See, or Seeing, Do Not Perceive" [1]

Frederic Edwin Church and Mount Desert

Thomas Cole introduced the impressive coastal scenery of Mount Desert to New Yorkers, and potential tourists, in 1845, but during the 1850s and 1860s it was Frederic Edwin Church, his talented student, who promoted the Island's visual attractions. With their impressive critical success in the Northeast, Church's paintings generated enthusiasm among metropolitan audiences for the increasingly accessible wilderness. Mount Desert combined the preferred cultural and environmental symbols of American national identity, and Church represented it as a mountainous wilderness whose bold sculptured coast appeared to be the work of a divine creator.

A "Genius" Visits

The early settlers at Mount Desert had little to fear from the slow but steady increase of tourists who visited after seeing the paintings of Doughty, Cole, Fisher, and others. Despite government-sponsored improvements in navigation, Mount Desert remained distant and comparatively inaccessible. This remoteness began to change when the youthful Frederic Church first visited in 1850. Only twenty-four years old, he was already considered by his admirers to be "endued with rare genius." Maine's Mount Desert and nearby Mount Katahdin became central themes for the painter who was arguably on his way to becoming America's most renowned landscape artist. In Church's paintings over the next decade Mount Desert became a symbol of the northeastern landscape, the bedrock of the nation. Other landscape painters soon followed his example of touring and painting Island scenery.[2] Commercial development was precisely what Church and other promoters of American scenery sought to stimulate, along with a variety of complex cultural and artistic agendas that made the place attractive to educated, elite visitors. After the Civil War, just two years after Church's last great painting of the Island was exhibited in New York, Clara Barnes Martin, a contributor to *The Nation* published

a travel guide, *Mount Desert on the Coast of Maine*. In it she described the scenery of Mount Desert as a perfect blend of several of the best summer resorts: "It is to find in one [place] the Isles of Shoals and Wachusett; or Nahant and Monadnock; Newport and the Catskills."[3]

In July 1850, six years after seeing Cole's sketches of Mount Desert, Church made his first trip to the Island.[4] Following the visit, Church wrote a series of letters published as "Mountain Views and Coast Scenery, by a Landscape Painter" for the *Bulletin of the American Art-Union*. The article was unsigned, but it can only be by Church. In it he vividly described his tour of the Island.[5] It is the first and one of the most important statements by the artist about his objectives and intentions. Over the next decade Church visited Mount Desert on his way to Grand Manan Island in 1851 and 1852. In 1854, and particularly during his extended visit to the Island in 1855, he made many sketches in pencil and oil that resulted in several major paintings. He visited again in 1860 with his new bride, and again for the last time in 1862. For Church, the quintessential New Englander, going "Down East" to Mount Desert was an adventure like going West would be for other artists of an explorative age.

Dismal Accommodations and Fleas in Abundance

Reaching the Island in 1850 required numerous modes of transportation and many transfers—train, steamboat, and finally fishing schooner. After sketching in the White Mountains, Church traveled by train from New Hampshire to Portland, Maine, where he embarked on the steamboat *Governor* for an overnight journey. Sea-swells made sleeping on board difficult, but by morning the party reached Castine. Church and his traveling companions, who remain undocumented but who may have included Regis F. Gignoux and Richard W. Hubbard (see Appendix), "came to Seal Cove, on the southeastern coast of the island."[6] There they explored the "dilapidated palisades, the sole relics of the fort erected here by the French under Baron Castine." After a hasty dinner, they boarded the schooner *Charles*, and headed for Mount Desert. Proceeding only twelve miles in four hours the ship, which was "only a fishing schooner, bound for the [Grand] Banks, and thence for California with a load of mackerel," anchored, and the party went ashore to find "dismal accommodations . . . and fleas in abundance for room-mates."[7]

After their long journey, and excited about the Island from Cole's accounts six years earlier, Church, Hubbard, and Gignoux anticipated the rewards of wilderness scenery for sketching. Church exclaimed to his companions: "we have not come thus far to be disappointed, I assure you." The Island's natural scenery, Church declared, was comparable to the Isle of Wight, which he had never actually seen, but "picturesque cottages and noble mansions . . . are never a feature of American landscape, save by accident." Had Church returned half a century later he would have seen "accidents" proliferating with a vengeance.[8]

An Immense Range of Mountains

Church pronounced himself "exceedingly delighted with the scenery, and with the people too." The local inhabitants of Mount Desert were "all Irishmen nearly," although "polite, respectful, and kind-hearted." "But what do you think of going to church in a boat?" the earnest Calvinist Church asked his *Art-Bulletin* readers. At meeting-time, he noted a picturesque scene when numerous sailboats and rowboats put off from Mount Desert and the Cranberry Islands and made for Southwest Harbor, "where there is a very decent house of worship, and attended by a congregation as respectable and devout as you will see in any New England village."[9]

The artist's commitment to the development of tourist culture appears emphatically in key passages from his 1850 letter published in the *Bulletin of the American Art-Union*. "It is a pity, he wrote, "that there is no better provision for the enjoyment of 'creature comforts' here than there are." His other comments read almost like an invitation to tourists and entrepreneurs to come to the Island to enjoy "trout fishing, (one of us, with a friend who has just arrived, took a hundred this afternoon,) and deep-sea fishing, and deer and partridges, and an occasional 'bar' on the mountains, and riding and sailing, an air which cannot be surpassed for purity, sea and mountain both, and charms of scenery, composed likewise of both." In an inducement to developers to provide the conveniences befitting a summer destination, Church declared that "it is surprising that some shrewd Bostonian has not erected some sort of hotel here."[10] To be sure, Church was primarily interested in developing a market for his landscape paintings, but he understood that in doing this his art could also stimulate tourism.

Church was immediately interested in finding high vantage points—commanding panoramic views—for his sketch-

ing. One of the first excursions included climbing to the top of Cadillac Mountain (then known as Green Mountain) to survey "the whole of the seaward part of the island at our feet." In a long passage Church shared his excited response to the view from the summit:

There is an immense range of mountains running through the island, one some two thousand feet high, of admirably varied outline—in some places covered with forest, and broken with rocks and precipices overhanging gems of lakes, and in others showing nothing but bare rock from summit almost to base. From the highest peak . . . we could see Mount Desert rock, twenty-five miles off in the ocean; and the mountain on which we stood is sixty miles at sea. From our elevation, we had the whole of the seaward part of the island at our feet. On an adjacent [Bear] island, a fine stone light-house, with outer building, enlivened by their white color, the dense green foliage in which they were buried, while far out in the offing, the soft, hazy blue floor of the ocean was studded with nearly a hundred white sails of fishing smacks.[11]

A Wide and Commanding Prospect

After ascending the summit of Cadillac Mountain, Church painted a small but intense oil sketch, *Eagle Lake Viewed from Cadillac Mountain, Mount Desert* (fig. 28). Although not dated, the work may have resulted from his first trip, or maybe from a trip later in the 1850s. The visual drama of brilliant sunlight reflecting from the surface of the lake makes this one of Church's most compelling panoramic views of the Island and of the vastness of Maine's forested wilderness.[12] In the far distance is the peak of Mount Katahdin, which would be the object of Church's first visit the next year, and of a pilgrimage with Theodore Winthrop in 1855. All told, Church seemed to be exceedingly delighted with the scenery, as Cole had been before him. It had only been two years since Cole's death and his exhilaration at the summit may have resulted from his long-held desire to visit places Cole had told him about. Perhaps he also recalled his memorial painting *To the Memory of Cole* (see fig. 34) that he had painted in 1848.

In the oil sketch he produced from the experience at the summit Church included a Cole-like tree, shaped as a cross, in the left foreground. The sun setting on the distant horizon forms a luminous cross of light, a compositional device introduced by Cole that Church developed over the next decade. The sun's position at the exact center of the composition, and the broad band of horizontal light intersecting with vertical reflections from the lake below, stretching to the horizon, formed this cross of light. Five years later Church returned to the summit and espied Eagle Lake at sunset. This time he was accompanied by the wealthy New Yorker Charles Tracy, whose party Church had joined at Mount Desert for a summer excursion. Tracy's description of the sunset captures an effect similar to that which Church

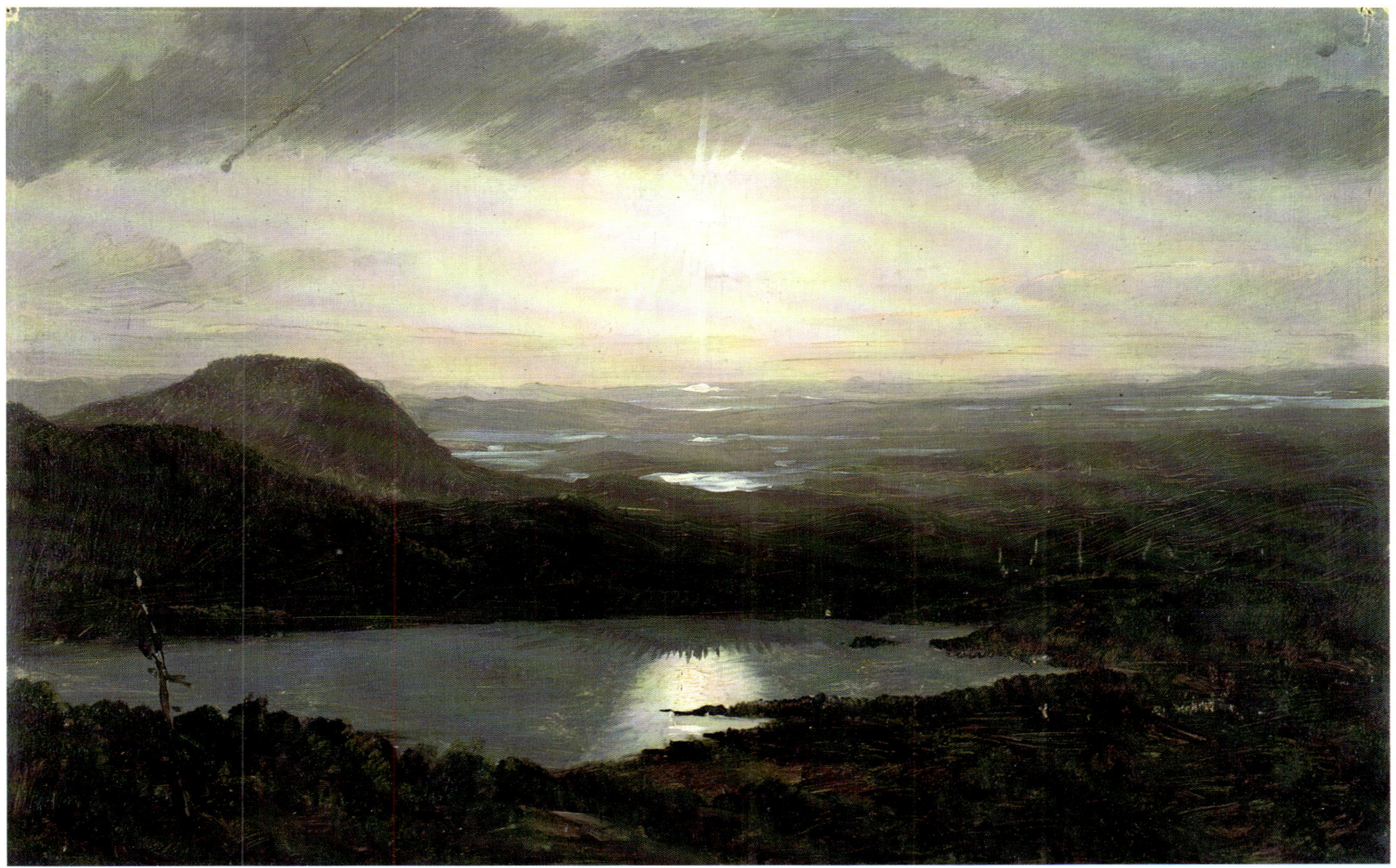

painted in his plein-air oil sketch. "We soon gained a height from which the sunset itself was visible, and then again we had one of the most superb displays of tinted clouds, and bars of light, over a distant horizon. The whole prospect was wide and commanding."[13]

Following Cole's Footsteps

After his excursion to the summit of Cadillac Mountain, Church made his way to the stormy coast on the eastern side of the Island with its rocky cliffs and grand headlands. His letter reveals his excited anticipation of experiencing the scenery firsthand. "There are precipitous rocks that come down abruptly to the water, some four hundred feet high." Barely able to contain his delight upon his arrival Church wrote "you face the East there; and, in stormy weather, the surf dashing against the rocks must be grand. We shall go there soon, and make a permanent settlement [at Lynam's cabin]."[14] At this point Church was essentially retracing Cole's steps. After a brief stay at Seal Cove and sketching in the vicinity, Church and his companions moved to the eastern side of Mount Desert, to Lynam's cabin at Schooner Head, where Cole had stayed six years before. Church's purpose was to see "the surf dash against the rocks," and for "visiting these Porcupine islands that lie just off Bar Harbor," the same scenery Cole had found so compelling.[15] More

than a decade later, in the middle of the Civil War, Church would return to the subject in his *Coast Scene: Mount Desert* (see fig. 52).

Rough Surf

Evidently Church considered the trip a great success, because upon his return to New York he set about transforming his drawings and oil studies into exhibition-scale paintings. During the next year Church exhibited five pictures of Mount Desert scenery at the National Academy, the American Art-Union, and the Pennsylvania Academy of the Fine Arts. The well-received and critically successful paintings bolstered the young artist's reputation and brought the attractions of Mount Desert to a New York audience. A reviewer for *The Home Journal,* surveying the National Academy of Design exhibition, commented that several "meritorious pictures, painted whilst on a professional tour on the coast of Maine, bear witness to the freedom of his pencil and the graceful drawing of the water." The critic also acknowledged that Church's "first essays on the coast of Maine are the best *draughts* a young artist can take, who is thirsting for eminence in a yet unexplored field."[16]

A small oil sketch that Church completed in 1850 during his visit, *Rough Surf, Mount Desert Island, Maine* (fig. 29), may be one of the first pictures of the Island he exhibited in

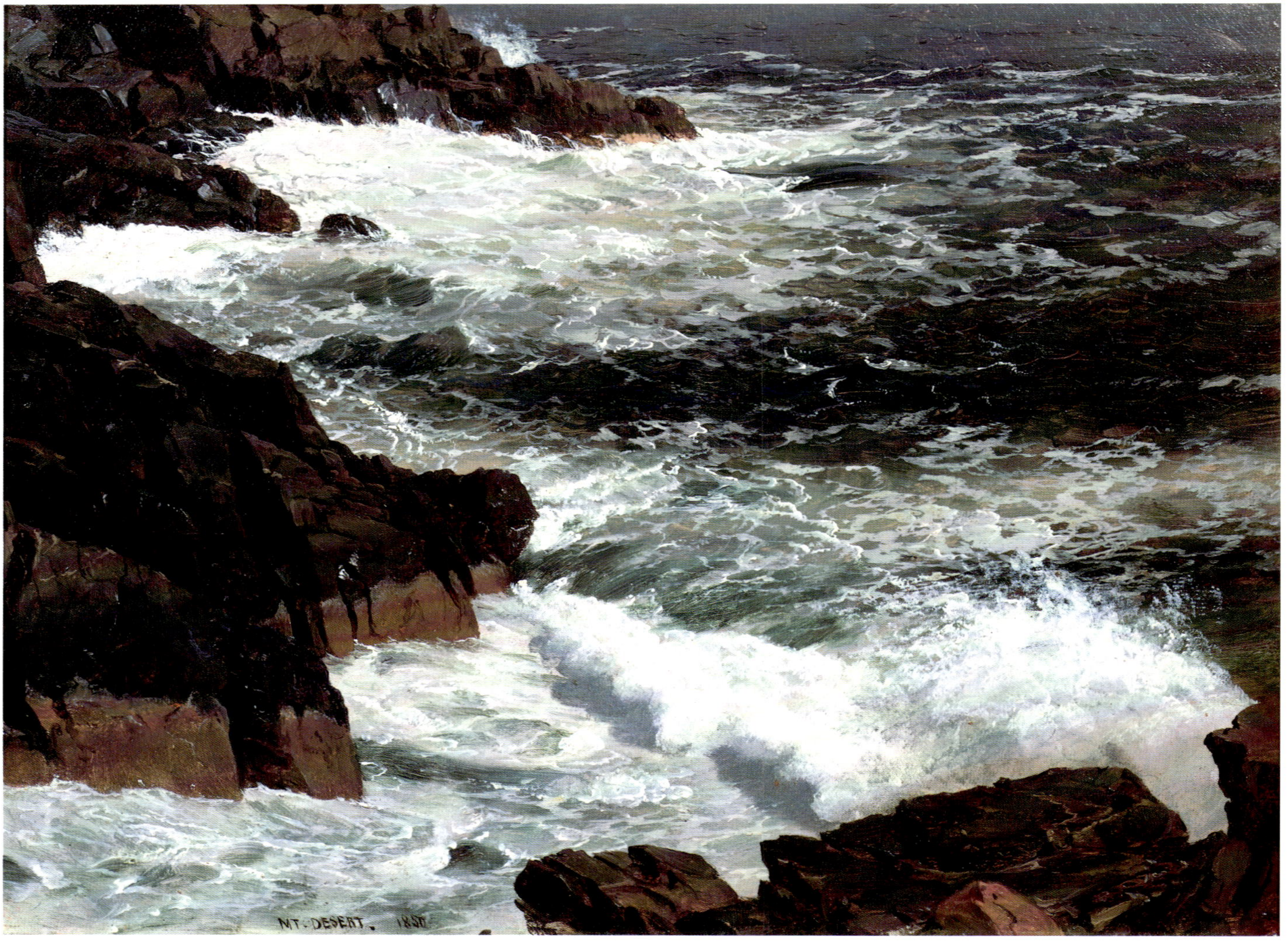

FIG. 29   Frederic E. Church, *Rough Surf, Mount Desert Island, Maine*, 1850, oil on paper mounted on wood, 12 ½ x 16 ¼". Private Collection, Courtesy of Berry-Hill Galleries.

New York in 1851 at the American Art-Union. Its dramatic composition reflects Church's earliest response to representing "surf dashing against the rocks" on the Island's rock-bound eastern shore.[17] The catalogue description of a companion work read: "The water extends in the foreground, while through the fog, in the distance, vessels are indistinctly seen."[18] A series of 12 x 16" oil-on-paper and academy board sketches were painted as Church recorded his impressions of the rocks and sea, and some of these were retouched later in the studio.[19] Church began *Rough Surf* in oil, working out-of-doors on paper which he then mounted on board, adding finishing touches to the foaming whitecaps and rocks later. The unusual angle of the composition is evidence of its plein-air conception and execution (for the most part); the broad sure strokes define the rocky shoreline in contrast to the surging forms of water.

It was a scene that would have undeniable importance for Church, both in terms of his later fascination with moving sea water at Mount Desert and in his representations of Niagara Falls later in the decade.[20] In retrospect, it is clear that

Church's early pictures of Mount Desert merited such favorable review because in them he demonstrated his remarkable technical mastery and his special talent for capitalizing on fashionable American sentiments for certain types of wilderness pictures.[21]

Sand Beach

Church must have been particularly eager to visit Sand Beach, which Cole and Pratt had first sketched in plein-air in 1844. Church made several pencil drawings in the vicinity, including one that depicted a distant view, *Sand Beach & the Beehive from Great Head, Mount Desert Island* (fig. 30). At the beach Church produced his own plein-air oil sketch of the identical scene Cole had painted, *Coast at Mount Desert Island (Sand Beach)* (fig. 31). It displays the refined technique for sketching in oil that Church had perfected since his study with Cole. Church's image shares a visual immediacy and spontaneity with Cole's oil sketch, *Sandy Beach, Mount Desert Island* (see fig. 21). It depicts the same eroded pink rocks and the golden rose-colored sand of the beach at low

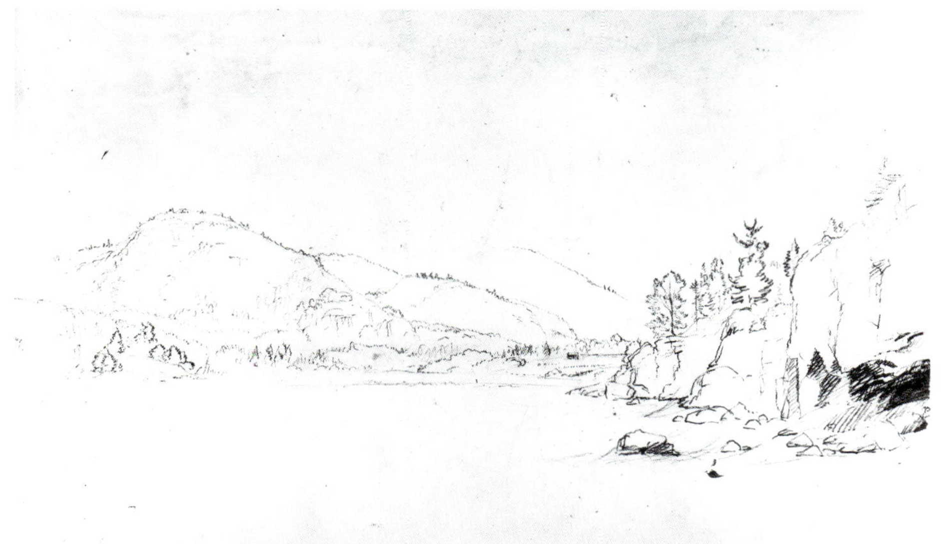

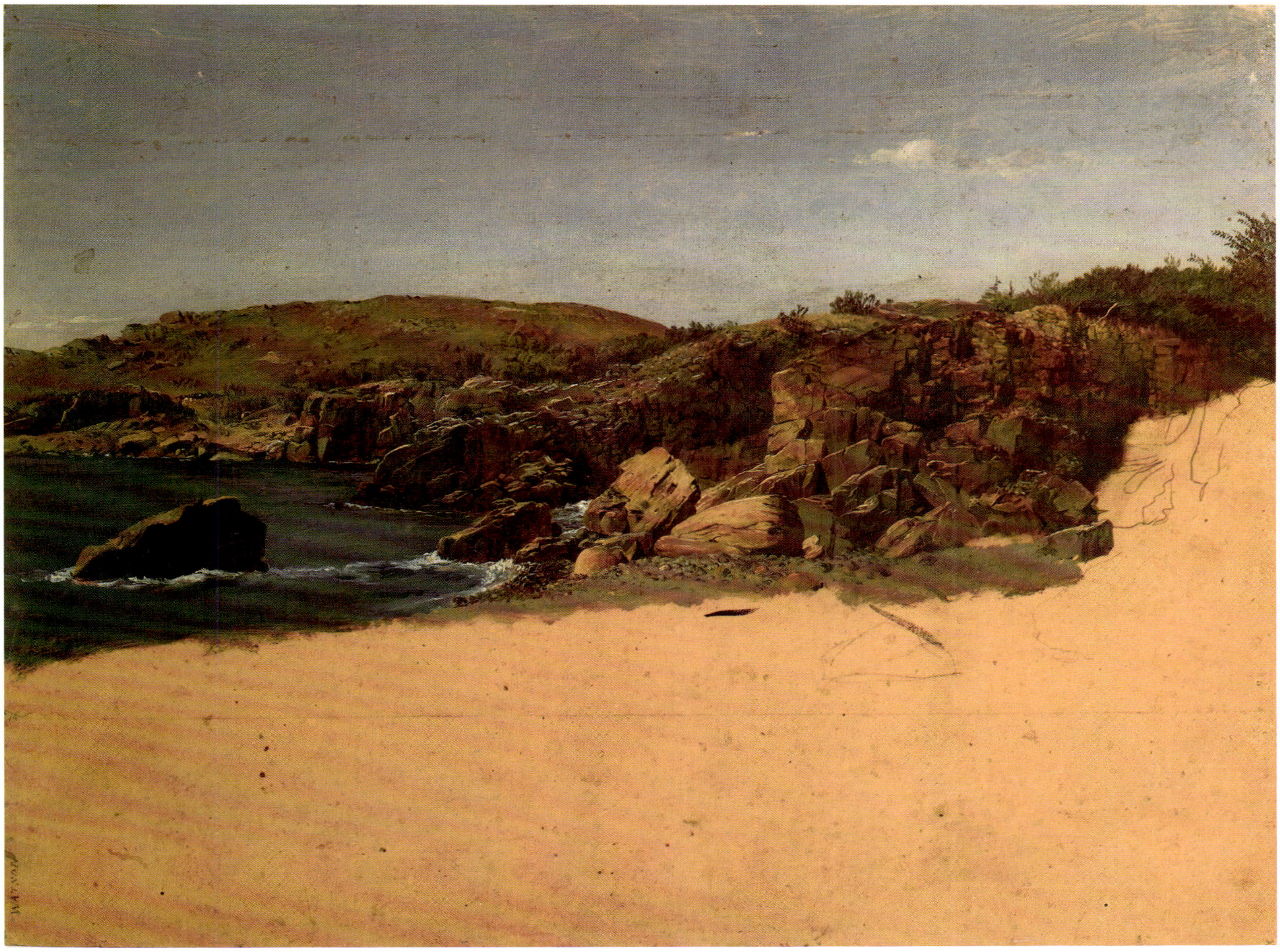

FIG. 31 Frederic E. Church, *Coast at Mount Desert Island (Sand Beach)*, c.1850, oil, graphite, over red ground on board, 12¹⁄₁₆ x 16". Cooper-Hewitt, National Design Museum, Smithsonian Institution/Art Resource, NY, Gift of Louis P. Church, 1917-4-645.

FIG. 32 Frederic E. Church, *Coastline Rocks, Mount Desert Island*, 1850, graphite on coarse light-brown paper, 11¹³⁄₁₆ x 14⅝". Olana State Historic Site, New York State Office of Parks, Recreation and Historic Preservation, OL.1977.57.

tide, but from a tighter perspective. Church's sketch is more geologically rigorous and faithful to the actual scene than Cole's picture. Unlike Cole, Church did not twist the coastline to represent the distant headland, which cannot actually be seen from this position on the beach. He avoided obvious anthropomorphic emblems, relying on close observation of the visual facts of the location in a subtle and more scientifically correct concept of nature as a vitalistic presence. Yet Church was intensely aware of this convention, and in a drawing of the Island's rocky coastline Church wrote "face" on one rocky profile which he darkened to exaggerate its dramatic personification (fig. 32).[22] In paintings produced in his studio for exhibition and sale Church often added his own original, imaginative personifications to enrich meaning and direct the spectator's gaze within the image. Cole's romantic and emotional *Sandy Beach, Mount Desert Island*, despite its small size, seems constructed for dramatic, expressive purposes, as if it could actually have been a sketch for a large painting to be executed later in the studio. True to his extensive practice of emblematic personification Cole shaped the headland to resemble a human face, in this case, literally and symbolically a "great head." In the left foreground, he etched the wave lapping at a minute face. Church's sketch avoided personification, concentrating instead on the observable facts, the "truth to nature" of the scene.

Otter Creek, Mount Desert

Otter Creek, Mount Desert (fig. 33) is a prime example of Church's ability to fuse a rugged maritime seascape—complete with sublime mountain views of Mount Desert and a touristic foreground—with provocative symbolism. On the surface its bright, cheerful, crisply painted scene represents an immanently safe, settled, and accessible place. The

appealing combination of beach scene, settlement, and an inviting valley framed by rugged but smooth mountains of unusual shape made the subject an attractive one for Church. Martin's early travel guide of Mount Desert described the scenery beyond the headlands of Otter Cliff, characterizing what Church would have seen from Cadillac Mountain. "On the other side of this headland lies Otter Creek Cove, repeating Somes' Sound on a tiny scale."[23]

For his view Church chose a position at the northeast bank of Otter Cove that encompassed a portion of the settlement and afforded a fine perspective for a view of Cadillac Mountain. His stay at the Lynam cabin was especially convenient to the little community of Otter Creek, included in the middleground of the painting, for "there is a sort of bridle path from the Otter Creek to Newport Beach [Sand Beach near Lynam's] that might be taken."[24] The pebbled beach in the foreground, filled with the characteristic red rocks of the area, is shown at low tide when the beach is wide and exposed. This setting furnishes a stage for the unusual figure, as well as an expansive perspective for a view of the distant mountain. A young boy carries a rolled-up sail and walks toward his beached boat. The figure walks erectly, his face turned away from the spectator toward the north-northwest across Otter Creek, to the small buildings of the town of that name, and beyond them to the majestic form of Cadillac Mountain. He gazes upward, perhaps to check weather conditions for his voyage, and as he does so he directs the viewer's attention to the swelling mountain forms, which Church thought would become in time a tourist attraction.

Recognizing Church's strong interest in promoting tourist culture, the stance of the figure in *Otter Creek* may suggest a leisurely summer visitor. Like Church himself, this forerunner of the later crowds of Mount Desert tourists is shown

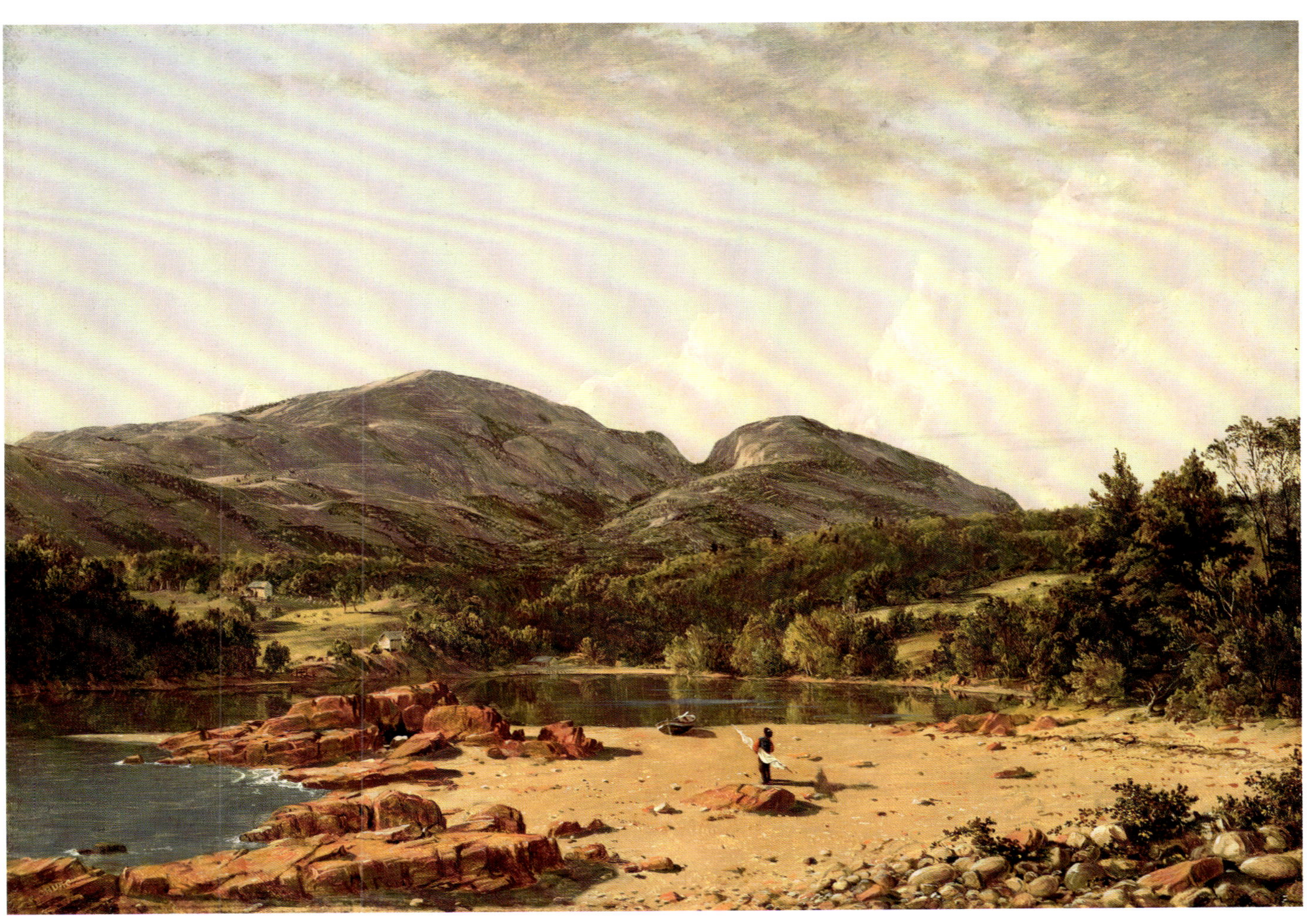

FIG. 33   Frederic E. Church, *Otter Creek, Mount Desert*, c.1850, oil on canvas, 16¾ x 24".
Museum of Fine Arts, Boston, Seth K. Sweetser Fund, Tompkins Collection, Henry H.
and Zoe Oliver Sherman Fund, and Gift of Mrs. R. Amory Thorndike. (detail p. 46)

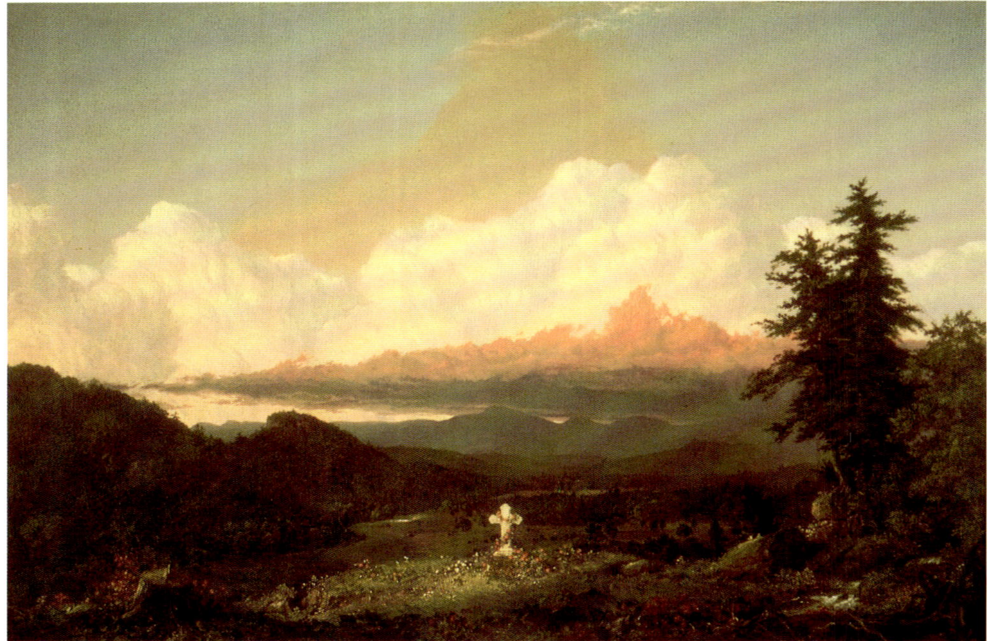

near his small sailing boat after an afternoon of recreation, rock hunting, or hiking. The account of a visiting Quaker family in July 1866 is suggestive: they had reached Otter Creek in a small boat, and after landing the group hiked in the direction to which Church's figure points in *Otter Creek*. As the "rain commenced in earnest, and the gentlemen donned their yellow 'oilers' and the ladies put on india rubber overcoats and oil-cloth caps . . . [they] marched gaily off in the rain . . . [taking] the old path under the Mountain."[25] Thus, tourists already knew the place and even the particular path to use. In fact, tourists would soon be attempting to reach the summit of Cadillac Mountain to take in the spectacular views that Cole and Church had first engaged.

Local Lore

Otter Creek emerged over the next decade as one of several settlements competing for the attention and business of Island visitors. Robert Carter noted in the record of his 1858 trip to Mount Desert that he "spent two days exploring the recesses of Otter Creek, whose wild mountain-passes equal in grandeur the Notch of the White Hills."[26] In *Otter Creek, Mount Desert* Church, however, chose to focus on the pastoral and potentially touristic aspects of Otter Creek rather than on its wildness. Church's interest in tourism was shared by Clara Martin and others who were trying to promote the place. Observing that the rural community of Otter Creek was on the brink of rapid development from tourism, Martin asserted that the "the day cannot be far distant when the little hamlet at Otter Creek will be the successful rival of Bar Harbor." In her promotion she added, "the views from it, whether of the sea, the long slopes of Green Mountain, or the beautifully rounded spurs of Newport, far surpass anything at Bar Harbor." She contended that "it is much nearer the attractive spots at Schooner Head and Great Head, and

a road up the southeast side of Green Mountain would be far more interesting than the present one."[27]

In 1854, just three years after Church painted his view of *Otter Creek,* religious associations were attributed to Cadillac Mountain. Professor Alexander Dallas Bache, superintendent of the United States Coast Survey, determined that Cadillac Mountain with its great height would be an ideal location for a survey station. Bache decided that since the mountain's shape suggested a burial mound and was situated near the town of Eden (Bar Harbor) that a fitting name would be "Adam's Grave." The name was used in Martin's guide, which noted the term and its source.[28] The idea that a mountain could suggest Adam's grave would have been appealing to Church, who often relied upon such local historical symbolism as part of his production of visual narratives.

Adam's Grave and American Symbolism

Church's works were complex. As Cole's student he had absorbed the belief that a work of art could contain multiple levels of meaning. At one level, Church's picture could appeal to prospective tourists, where at another it could produce nationalistic associations and suggestions of transcendence. In an easily overlooked passage, Church subtly inscribed a powerful religious symbol. The shadow of the rolled-up sail and young sailor forms a cruciform image on the beach. Were this not the work of Church such forms might be considered unremarkable. But Church followed Cole in developing cruciform symbolism for his concept of a national landscape, and his memorial painting commemorating the death of his teacher, *To the Memory of Cole* (fig. 34), included several crosses. Cole had a long interest in cruciform symbolism, and in 1850 the issue was still on Church's mind because of Cole's recent death and unfinished last series *The Cross and the World,* which remained unsold despite the efforts of Church and others to find a buyer for it. In Church's 1848 memorial to Cole, the key symbol is a large white funerary cross, prominently positioned at the center of the picture, and the original image may have included a cross formed of clouds which was subsequently removed by the artist from the top of the picture.

The symbolism suggested by the shadow of a cross in the foreground of *Otter Creek* was combined with other symbolic associations that Church had absorbed into his personal style under the influence of Cole's mentoring. The most important of these is Church's subtle manipulation of the profile of Cadillac and Dorr Mountains. Church compressed the actual forms of the mountains, manipulating them in such a way that they form a grand human profile. The face in the mountain gazes upward, and the curious tourist glances toward it. The mountain's visage is positioned so that its chin is to the right, while the cleft between the mountains forms a mouth, and the remainder of the face and the forehead extends to the left. The notion of seeing faces in mountain profiles was a part of tourist culture. For example, visitors along the Hudson River near Catskill were advised to look for profiles in the distant Catskill Mountains where the face of sleeping Rip Van Winkle might be glimpsed. Farther down the Hudson, Anthony's Nose was a renowned landmark. Travel literature of the period is filled with references to faces, figures, battlements, castles, and sculptures.

The fact that Cadillac Mountain was called Adam's Grave may have suggested the appropriateness of such a startling personification of the mountain, and this was reinforced by ample precedent in Cole's work. By 1850, Church had demonstrated complete command of the conventions of emblematic personification, painting faces in the rocks in his *Hooker and Company* (Wadsworth Atheneum) as early as 1846. In *Otter Creek* Church ingeniously transformed a rugged seacoast visited until recently only by fishermen and local inhabitants into a beckoning scene that could attract the tourist or the elite lover of fine arts able to discern Church's subtle conceit.[29]

The picture was the first view of Mount Desert scenery to be seen by the Philadelphia public.[30] Little is known of its early history except that the painting was purchased by James LeFevre of Philadelphia and exhibited at the Pennsylvania Academy of the Fine Arts in 1851 under the longer descriptive title, *Otter Creek and Mount Desert Island, Coast of Maine (Inland View)*, and again in 1862. LeFevre purchased another Church painting, *Twilight, A Scene at Mount Desert Island* (unlocated), which was exhibited along with *Otter Creek* both in 1851 and 1862.[31]

An Old Boat in Fog

In a small and deceptively simple painting, Church found that even fogs at Mount Desert could be used to represent the romantic associations of the place. In his July 1850 let-

ter to the *Art-Union,* he acknowledged that "the only drawback to the enjoyment of the beauties of the island is an occasional fog." Church added that "we have just got into the edge of one, which however, has not prevented our transferring to canvas an old hull of a boat, and some rocks, this morning."[32] The fog and the hull of an old boat would be put to great use in *Abandoned Skiff,* then known as *The Old Boat* (fig. 35), which Church exhibited at the National Academy of Design in 1851.[33]

The spectator is positioned near the old and weathered hull of an abandoned skiff in the foreground. Not far from shore are two couples in a small pleasure craft. George William Curtis described the picture in a review that appeared in the *New-York Daily Tribune*. He made mention that "'An Old Boat,' is also a singular success. It is a very small picture, representing an old boat high upon the shore, and the fog stealing in over the sea." He also observed the particular attention Church paid to seacoast fogs, praising the "moist, white opacity of the mist [that] is remarkably well rendered. We do not recall any finer sketch of that peculiar effect."[34] Church's remarkable technical ability in capturing the ephemeral sentiments of nature gained him fame at the outset of his career. The critic of *The Home Journal* also found Church's modest picture compelling: "this 'Old Boat' is a sea-side pastoral. We are always attracted by it, unpretending as it is." The same reviewer further exclaimed, "our pleasure was greatly enhanced by hearing two well-known *connoisseurs* talking in a delightful strain on its merits."[35]

The theme of the small rowboat abandoned by its owner and left to rot evoked multiple levels of association to Church and educated members of his audience. At one level it was a well-worn metaphor for the human condition, the convention of representing vessels as symbols of life's journey.[36] Church, like most of his audience, knew Cole's allegorical series *The Voyage of Life*. In the last painting of the series, *Old Age*, the traveler's boat is wrecked.[37] Cole used fogs and vapors in *Old Age* to symbolize the veil of darkness that shrouds the material world near the end of life. The "merits" of Church's painting remarked on by *The Home Journal* may have alluded to these associations of the cycle of life. The foreground boat and shore are painted with a detail and clarity that contrasts with the indistinct foggy background. The minutely painted daisies around the boat, and the many precise details of the boat's aging condition—rotted spots on the hull, peeling paint chips, stained and weathered marks—all contribute to sharply define the aura of the decaying hull and the new growth emerging around it. A large gray stone embedded in the earth at the right suggests an eroded profile, complete with a large forehead, eye socket, nose and mouth—a silent natural witness to the old boat.[38]

The visual possibilities that Church had found in the Island fogs would be echoed often by later writers in their

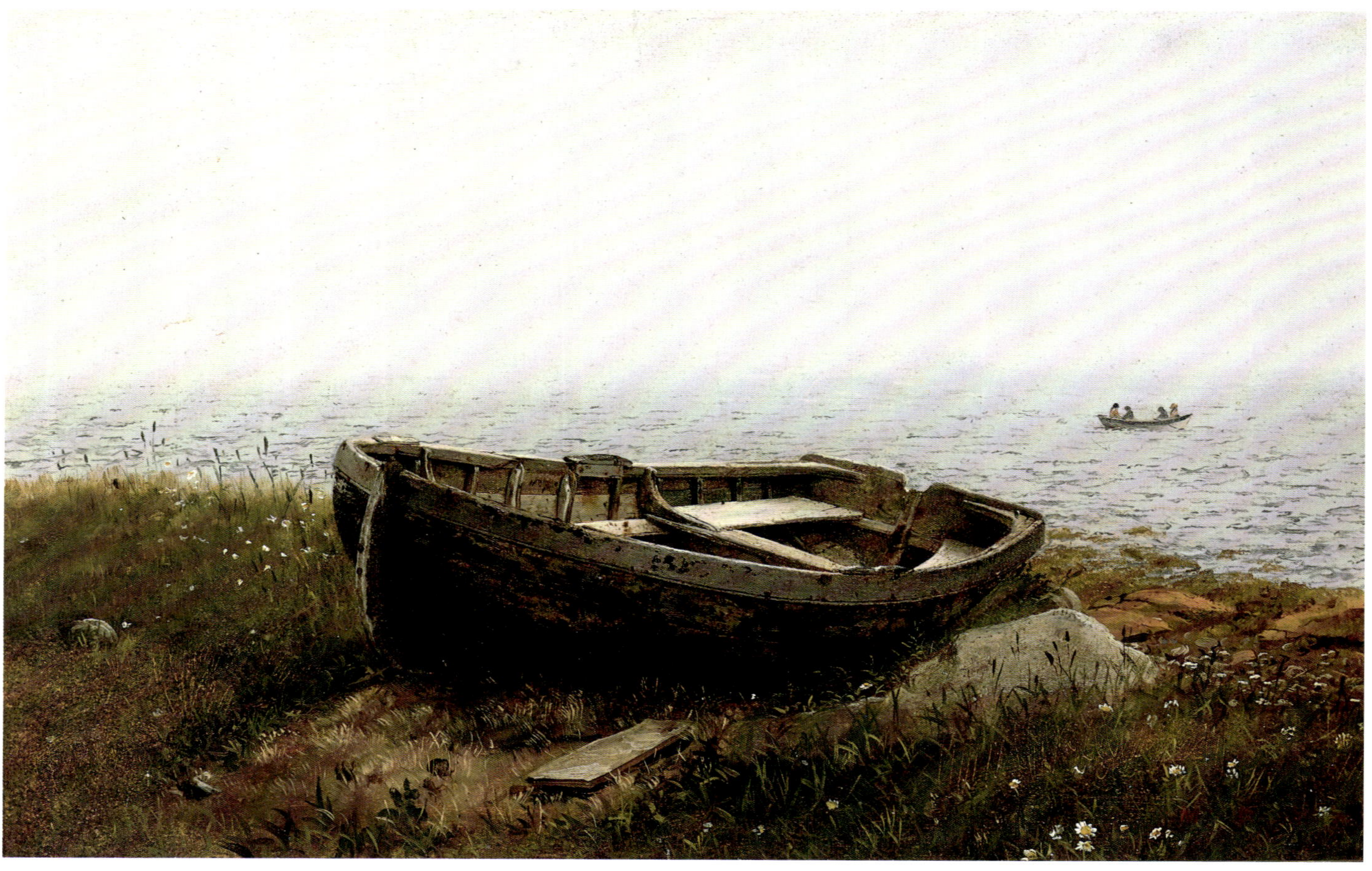

descriptions of Mount Desert. *Picturesque America's* essay resonated with Church's comments on the inconveniences of the Mount Desert fogs which "in July and August especially interfere with the pleasure of the tourist." However, the author believed as Church did that the "impenetrable banks far out at sea, with occasional incursions upon the shore are full of interest." Enlisting the vocabulary of a painter, he wrote "it is a rare pleasure to sit on the rocky headlands, on a day that the fog and sun contend for supremacy, and watch the pictures that the fog makes and unmakes." He carefully analyzed that "the pictures thus formed vary like a succession of dissolving views, and often produce the most striking and unique effects." In a passage beautifully describing one of the mysterious views created by fogs, he wrote "sometimes there is the marvelous exhibition of a mirage, when fleets appear sailing through the air."[39] Martin's guide book also stressed the picturesque effect of Island fogs, remarking that "it lies off at sea by day, drifts in at night or shifts with the tide, now arches the valleys from peak to peak, now caps the mountains, now folds them in softest fleeces, then rolls off in films of gossamer."[40] The appreciation for fogs at Mount Desert was symptomatic of the influence that landscape paintings had on creating the tourist taste for romantic associations in the landscape, although to mariners at sea the fog remained what it had always been—a grave danger. Perhaps an *Abandoned Skiff* is Church's meditation on the transitoriness of life, and

as such provides an interesting contrast to other images that might be read primarily as invitations to tourists.

Newport Mountain, Mount Desert Island

In 1851 Church produced *Newport Mountain, Mount Desert Island* (fig. 36), depicting the dramatic beauty of the pinkish-rock seacoast and the suggestive mountainous forms of the Island. The painting represents the mountain seen from the vantage point of a slippery rock outcrop at the very edge of Frenchman Bay and is based on a sketch completed 12 September 1850 titled *New Port Mountain, Mt. Desert Island* (Olana State Historic Site), from which the modern title of the picture is derived.[41] The point of view demonstrates Church's agreement with Cole's opinion that the eastern side of Mount Desert possessed the best views. Church himself had taken excursions by water across Frenchman Bay to Gouldsboro on Stave Island, east of Mount Desert, and to Sorrento on the mainland, north of Mount Desert. He was interested in the view of the mountains that comprise the Island from that vantage point, as Cole had been.[42] Like Cole, Church chose a less distant view for *Newport Mountain*, and a position on the exact edge of sea and rocky shore. Yet, on closer examination this coastal scene was subtly transformed in the painting to enhance its visual appeal.

Church manipulated the foreground, lowering the horizon and increasing the vertical proportion. He also shifted to a

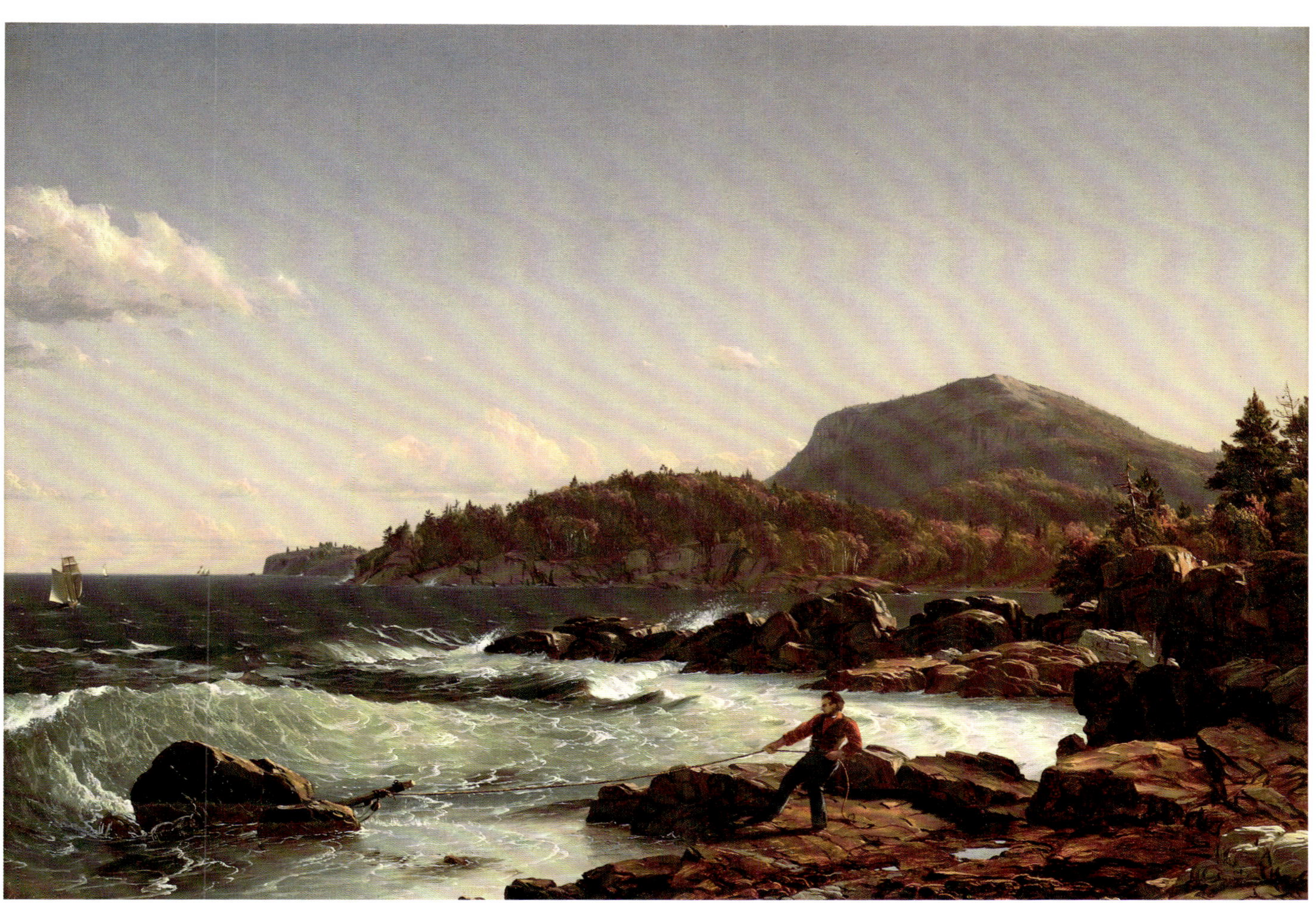

FIG. 36   Frederic E. Church, *Newport Mountain, Mount Desert Island*, 1851,
oil on canvas, 21¼ x 31¼". Private Collection.

higher vantage point, adding distance to the scene and vividly capturing the effects of waves as they encountered the rocky shore. Church roughly sketched the foreground rocks in his plein-air drawing, but in the completed painting these rocks were highly finished and brightly colored. Church added boulders and trees to the right foreground of the finished painting. The middleground and background were evidently taken without much change from the field drawing, including a visual description of Church's notation for a "pebbly beach."

In his letter to the *American Art-Union* Church compared the dramatic differences between his location at the Lynam cabin, directly beneath Newport Mountain, to the community of Bar Harbor to the north. Church noted that Bar Harbor "is quite a settlement compared with the total isolation of Lynam's, where the mountain shuts out the sun by four or five o'clock on the landward side, and the ocean beats against the rocks on the other."[43] Visually developing these sentiments, Church positioned himself with his back to Bar Harbor and facing south. He selected the only foothold just south of Bar Harbor to view Schooner Head in the distance at the left, while providing for a view of Newport Mountain at the right. A writer in *Picturesque America* later argued that the best place for a dramatic view of the Island mountains, including Newport Mountain, was *from* the water, as Church himself had discovered, noting that "Newport rises apparently from the very water's edge in one abrupt cliff a thousand feet in height. It is a dissolving view that for an hour or more presents a superb succession of scenic effects."[44] Church has positioned his figure precisely at the end of Sols Old Cliff Trail, just north of where Bear Brook empties into Frenchman Bay, a view that was opposite the perspective Cole had represented in *View Across Frenchman's Bay*.

In the foreground a picturesque local resident—a salvager—contrasts with the leisurely tourist or sailor in *Otter Creek*. The salvager works, he does not gaze. Perhaps with his red shirt and manly figure he is one of the "respectful" local Irish mariners who had settled the Island. The figure strains to recover a ship's spar from the rocky shallows that is still fitted with its valuable turning block and lines, suggesting that wreckage from a recent storm at sea is worth claiming. At left, a well-canvased brig bears off the distant headland on a leeward tack. Farther off, the sails of other ships are seen, reminding viewers that the waters around the Island were heavily trafficked with vessels.

Grim Ramparts: Bare, Hard, Unyielding

Early Mount Desert guides praise Newport Mountain's rugged features that Church found so compelling. *Harper's* article remarked that "on your road to and from Schooner Head and Great Head you pass by Newport Mountain, which also guards the entrance to Bar Harbor on the side of the

sea."[45] In the same article, Newport Mountain's position against the sea was acclaimed as "the greatest of all Nature's grand displays—the mountains rising out of the sea. . . . [Their] summits bare, hard, and unyielding."[46] Furthermore, Martin wrote that "like all the eastern faces of the mountains, its [Newport Mountain] cliffs are steep and rugged. They rise in 'grim rampart and solid bastion' against the fury of the eastern gales."[47] Church has effectively depicted in the middleground of *Newport Mountain* the "total isolation of Lynam's." The sun has not set, only a few tree tops are touched with light. This is particularly evident in the rocky shore where "the ocean beats against the rocks" despite the warm, late afternoon colors reflected on the rocks, foliage, and sunset sky.[48]

Church's concerns for the promotion of Mount Desert would have allowed the introduction of emblematic associations to help establish the beauty of this place. Rocks at the right, expressively contrived by Church, suggest human profiles. Some of these visages reprise visual conventions for representing such emblematic profiles found in the rocky cliff at the left in Cole's *View Across Frenchman's Bay* (see fig. 23). Gazing toward the local seaman and the vessels at sea, the stony profiles become silent yet vitalistic presences, and the divine work of the great creator is evident even in a remote seaside wilderness. The protective associations of these personifications of nature are reinforced by the rosy hue in this passage of the painting, which demonstrates Church's commitment to geological specificity. In fact, in Church's mind, as in Cole's, there was no contradiction in demonstrating knowledge of the most updated scientific theories of geology and merging it with the iconology of personification. To the modern viewer, unfamiliar with these obscured codes of meaning, perhaps the most surprising personification is Church's manipulation of the left side of Newport Mountain where he subtly inscribed a great profile gazing heavenward.

An 1851 article in *The Home Journal* endorsed the salubrious effects derived from the visual reproductions of wilderness: "To persons dwelling amidst the dust, and noise, and hot revelers of a city, landscape paintings produce the effect of a visit."[49] For those who could not travel easily and those who found it tedious or frightening, these pictures allowed them to be "arm chair" travelers, and functioned in a manner similar to popular travel books. Wild and compelling pictures of the Island with just a hint of accomodation served to entice tourists to experience Mount Desert firsthand.

Red Skies at Sunrise: Day Markers for Sailors

Church's *Beacon, off Mount Desert Island* (fig. 37), is deceptively simple. It depicts at first glance, little more than a stone mariner's beacon in open ocean, beyond that a broad expanse of "empty" sea and a radiant cloud-filled sky. Yet like

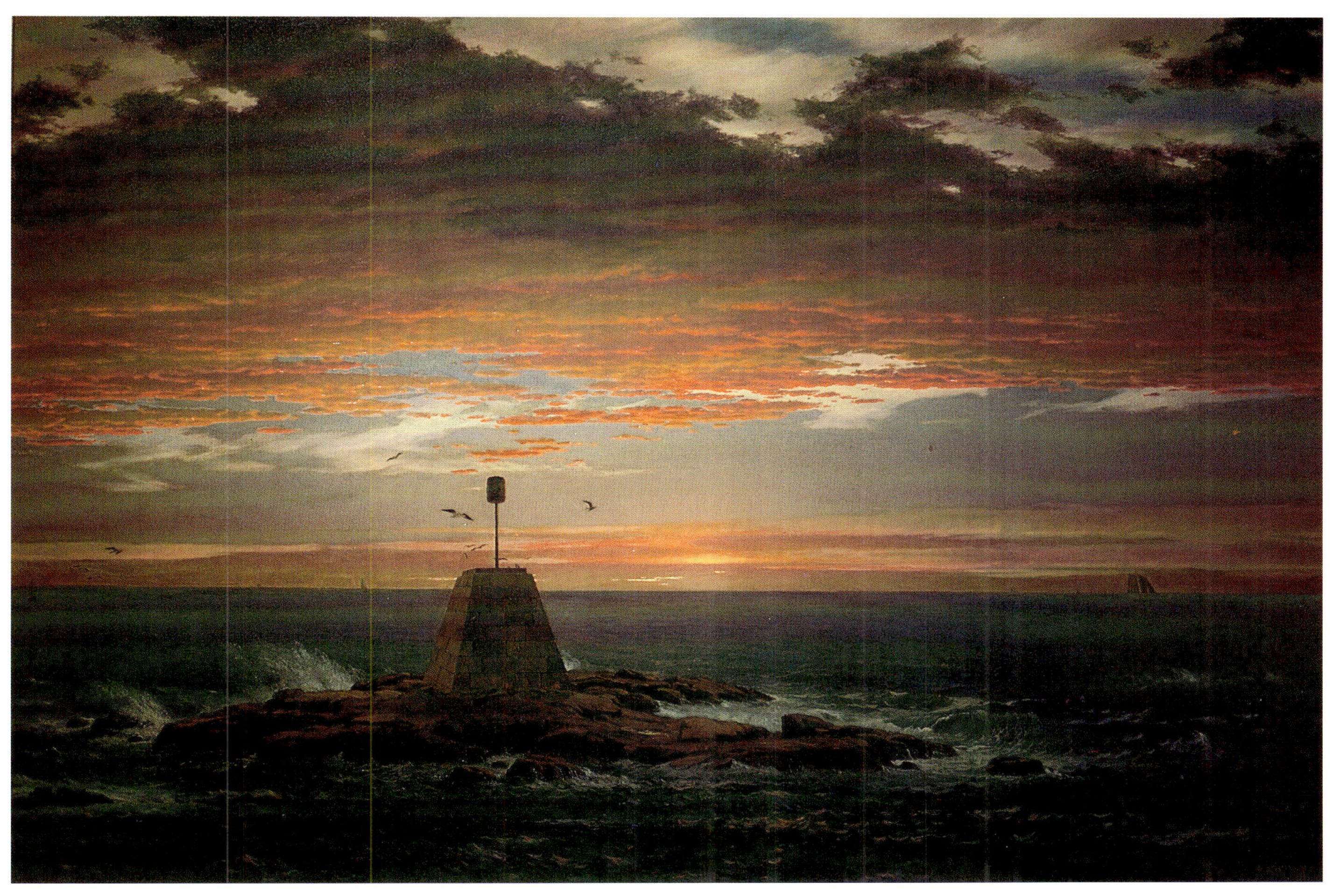

FIG. 37 Frederic E. Church, *Beacon, off Mount Desert Island*, 1851,
oil on canvas, 31 x 46". Private Collection.

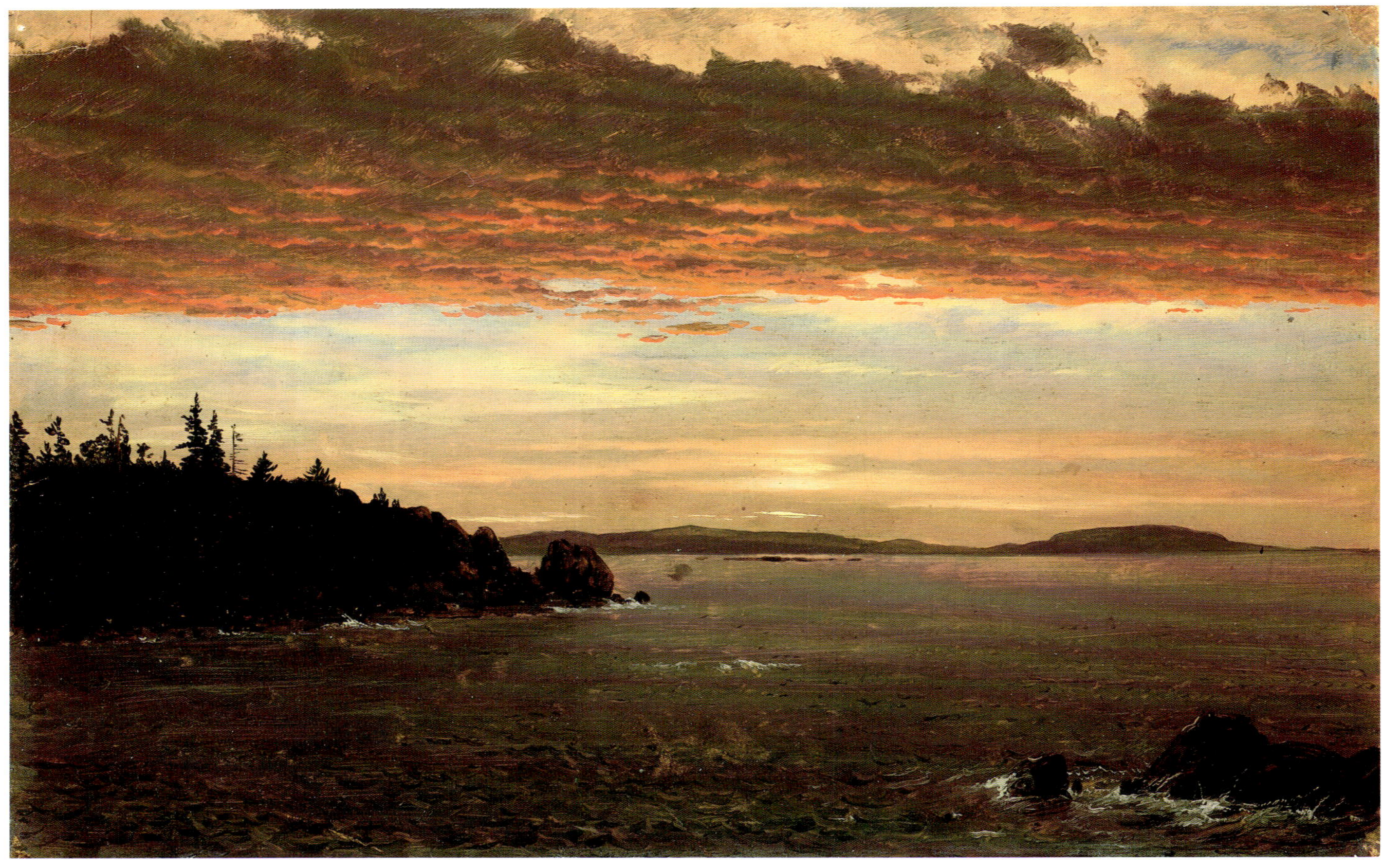

FIG. 38   Frederic E. Church, *Schoodic Peninsula from Mount Desert, Sunrise*, 1850–1855,
oil on board, 8⅞ x 14". Cooper-Hewitt, National Design Museum, Smithsonian
Institution/Art Resource, NY, Gift of Louis P. Church, 1917-4-332.

other large pictures intended by the artist for public exhibition and eventual sale the image contains multiple layers of
meaning. It presents literal, symbolic, and typological associations promoting elite attitudes about the cultural and historic value of the Maine seacoast as a symbol of America's
national identity and a visual meditation on Protestant ideas
of personal salvation. Some of these associations had already
emerged in Church's work and he extended and elaborated
upon them in *Beacon*.

The dramatic sunrise sky of *Beacon* is based on an 1850
oil sketch, *Schoodic Peninsula from Mount Desert, Sunrise*
(fig. 38). The oil sketch is brilliantly illuminated with red
and pink clouds layered in horizontal bands, and a distant
sky saturated with golden radiance. Church retained the horizontal bands of clouds from his sketch almost exactly in composing *Beacon,* but he imported another subject from a different part of the Island, placing the mariner's beacon on
East Bunkers Ledge, just off the coast at Ingraham Point
near Seal Harbor, in the foreground near the center of the
composition. The view represents the area of Western Point
looking east across Frenchman Bay, past Egg Rock to Birch
Harbor Mountain, Buck Cove Mountain, and Schoodic Head
on Schoodic Peninsula.

A detailed delineation of the day marker, seen in a pencil
drawing entitled *Study of Sailing Ships and Coastal Scenery*

(fig. 39), is probably from Church's 1850 trip. It indicates
that the artist took a boat out to the site to make a close-up
field sketch. Rather than show the beacon in relationship to
the shore, Church selected a vantage point looking directly
out to sea. Mariners would have seen a similar view heading out into the broad expanse of the Atlantic Ocean between
Little Cranberry and Baker Island on the right and Schoodic
Peninsula on the left. He also represented the beacon at high
tide when most of the dangerous ledge is submerged.

Long before Church saw the beacon for himself, he saw
Cole's 1844 sketches of Mount Desert. In them he could have
observed the beacon in the corner of a drawing of *Penobscot
Bay* (fig. 40). Church would have seen the beacon from the
water as he traveled through Eastern Way on his first trip
to Mount Desert aboard the schooner *Charles*. The area was
heavily trafficked, in fact, the 1854 *Coast Pilot* stated that
on occasion more than four hundred sailing vessels had been
sighted near this point at Southwest Harbor, attesting to the
need for a permanent marker.[50] As Doughty and Fisher recognized earlier, the public was interested in the placement
of lighthouses and markers, and patrons of art also found
them to be desirable subjects for paintings. In 1838 the government had responded with a special Act of Congress that
enabled the placement of three navigational markers on rock
shelves at the approaches to Northeast and Bass Harbors.

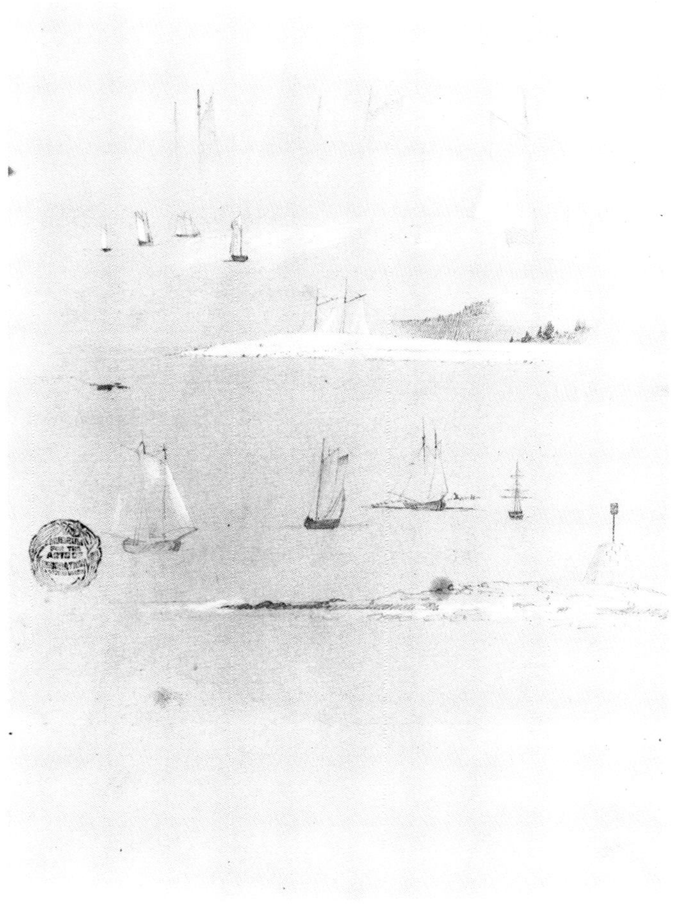

FIG. 39   Frederic E. Church, *Study of Sailing Ships and Coastal Scenery*, c. 1850, pencil on paper, 9⅞ x 7 1/16″. Cooper-Hewitt, National Design Museum, Smithsonian Institution/Art Resource, NY, Gift of Louis P. Church, 1917-4-271A.

As part of this effort, this region's first day marker built of masonry was constructed on East Bunkers Ledge in 1839–1840, to guide vessels into the fine harbors at the end of Somes Sound.[51] The beacon is situated between Rhodes Cliff on Mount Desert and Little Cranberry Island just south of Seal Harbor, changed today only by a coat of reflective white paint, and the removal of the pole and barrel depicted in Church's picture.

Rare and Gorgeous Color: *Beacon, off Mount Desert Island*

Church's *Beacon, off Mount Desert Island* attracted considerable attention during its exhibition in the spring of 1851 at the National Academy of Design.[52] It was the most visually challenging and complex painting to result from Church's 1850 visit to Mount Desert. In the same exhibition Church also showed his painting *The Deluge*. The two images looked very different but were related conceptually through typological concepts of history. *The Deluge* was Church's largest effort at historical painting, and it was to be his last of exhibition scale. *The Bulletin of the American Art-Union* noted that *The Deluge* "showed the terrible power of the elements of Water with originality and success." But it added: "There will be three or four striking views from his easel, made up from sketches taken by him, last summer, at Mount Desert Island, and on the coast of Maine." One of these was *Beacon,* which critics generally liked as much as they disliked *The Deluge*. The pictures were often compared, with critics agreeing that *Beacon* is "a strong and truthful picture, with more imagination in its reality than the effort at the

FIG. 40   Thomas Cole, *Penobscot Bay*, 1844, pencil on paper, 11⅜ x 16 15/16″. Cole Sketchbook, 7v, The Art Museum, Princeton University, Gift of Frank Jewett Mather, Jr. Photo Clem Fiori.

Deluge by the same artist." Another critic alluded to the brilliant use of color in *Beacon* that owed a considerable debt to the famous English landscape painter J.M.W. Turner. He thought the view of the "Beacon 'From Mount Desert Island' by Church, seizes upon those glowing metallic bars, rare and gorgeous in color, which lie along the summer sunset, with a depth of view which carries the eye far to seaward."[53] A critic for *The International Magazine* thought that "all greatness has its own manner . . . and a very happy and brilliant career seems open to him. The works of none of the younger artists have attracted more attention." He went on to assert that the fame and position of [Joseph M.W.] Turner would be the reward of "a devoted student and artistic delineator of the peculiarities of atmospheric phenomena. We exhort Mr. Church to entire boldness in his attempts."[54]

Effect and Sentiment, Sunrise or Sunset

Effects of light were thought to express the vital, spiritual qualities of a picture. Thus the times of day and their "effects" or "sentiments" had special significance at mid-century. They not only suggested the various qualities of light, shade, and atmosphere, but subtly expressed the vital quality of a picture—its "spirit."[55] Time of day and the specific attributes of sunrise or sunset were subjects of frequent discussion. Although the perspective established in *Beacon* cannot easily be mistaken for anything but an easterly view, "We are not to forget, however, that the *time* represented in this picture is a matter of doubt among the spectators." Curtis believed that the time of day was sunset, and acknowledged there were "partisans both of sunset and of sunrise." "One side asserts that the light in the middle distance of the sky is too white and cool for the evening," he wrote, "and the other that the water is too dark for morning; but both agree that it is that character of atmospheric phenomena in which morning and evening effects resemble each other." The ambiguity could "be resolved only by the closest observation and knowledge of these precise effects, and meanwhile the uninitiated may adopt as they please, the morning or evening theory." Curtis finally admitted that "for our own part the suggestion and sentiment of the picture seem to indicate evening, although such a feeling might, perhaps, be traced to special association."[56] By later in the year another critic commented, "Mr. Church has given, in addition to other works, his famous *Beacon, off Mount Desert*, in which is one of those marvelous sunset effects, for which he is so celebrated."[57] Yet what did the effects and the sentiment of *Beacon* actually *mean* to Church's audience?

Church's history painting *The Deluge* is considered by many art historians today as a pendant or companion painting to *Beacon*.[58] If *Beacon* is luminous, and a picture of light-filled repose, critics complained that *The Deluge* was "weakened by the feebleness of [its] accessories. There is a crumpling effect of the rocks, more like the dilapidation of a stack of chimneys than the vast Neptunian movements of the early world." "Had Church seen the deluge," a critic observed, "he would no doubt have painted it to far better advantage."[59] Viewers may not have realized that the rocks in Church's Old Testament scene had recently been sketched in Maine. Church's champion Curtis had the most devastating criticism. He thought the "fatal defect" of the work was its unmitigated horror. . . . The eye reels about this canvas disrobed and dismayed."[60] Harsh criticism of *The Deluge* was evidence of a growing preference for Church's naturalistic landscapes as opposed to historical or allegorical work.

The two paintings were closely associated in Church's imagination. Both drew upon his experiences at Mount Desert the previous summer, yet they depicted opposing aspects—the sublime hopeless raging disaster of the historical Biblical flood contrasted with a luminous and calm American landscape of spiritual promise and potential peril. The typological links between the two images may have been evident to the most discerning viewers, and particularly those accustomed to typological sermons so commonly preached from pulpits all over New England. Calvinists such as Church believed that the Old Testament Past, in this case the marine disaster called the deluge, washed away the sins of the Old World so that mankind could be reborn into a New World of Christian faith. Church's beacon in this concept of history would symbolize the emergence of this New World, namely America.[61]

Church had imparted complex typological meaning to his pictures before and would do so again. He had also depicted ambiguous times of day, as in his 1848 memorial picture to Cole, but in *Beacon* he achieved a new level of iconographic inventiveness. Lacking at first glance a traditional subject, the painting establishes a primary meaning through association of the beacon as an emblem of safety, or even salvation, because of its grounding on rock. These symbolic elements combined with the luminous sunrise sky were the "sentiments" that Curtis and others praised. He observed that the "sentiment of this picture (and the sentiment of pictures is the sole ground upon which the esoteric critic may speak with authority) is finely sustained throughout." Curtis noticed, "The sails of a few vessels stretching out to sea, and the surf combing over the rocky ledge upon which stands the Beacon, forming the central point of the foreground of the picture, are full of broad and genuine feeling. . . . There is great repose in the picture."[62] The pyramidal, geometrically formed beacon functions as the principal visual protagonist rather than the distant ship. Seen in this way the stone beacon can be read as "a passive hero."[63]

Rocks, Emblems, Metaphor

Beacons, like ships, were understood as metaphors of the human condition.[64] A day marker directs vessels to safe channels and harbors, a beacon offers assurances of safe passage, and at an emblematic and symbolic level, it could offer guidance to salvation, both personal and national. Long established religious associations of the "rock of ages" are obvious—it was a powerful verbal and visual metaphor of safety from shipwreck or the perils of the life voyage. The frontispiece from *Religious Emblems*, published in 1851, the same year as Church painted and exhibited *Beacon*, depicts a lone rock in a storm-tossed sea. An evocative passage accompanying the frontispiece reads: "in my distress I called upon the Lord . . . he drew me out of many waters."[65] Accompanied by a long poem entitled "Salvation" the visual device in *Religious Emblems* is accompanied by an illustration of a single rock ledge surmounted by a large, luminous, beacon-like cross with two suppliant figures. They are surrounded in a tumultuous sea by a sinking ship and a woman in the water about to drown (fig. 41). The poem explicated the associations of the Rock of Ages.

> So when mankind were wreck'd on Eden's shore,
> Loud was the tempest, . . . /
> Shall man be saved, or lost? / . . .
> The Rock of Ages lifts its lofty head;
> With glad surprise, more clear his moral sight,
> He sees besides, a cross of heavenly light;
> The Rock he clambers to the cross he clings,
> And saved from danger, of Salvation sings.[66]

The poem suggested that "the vessel . . . may represent the safe and happy condition of our first parents." The text also explains that the "drowning mariners denote the deplorable state of mankind since the fall." Finally, the hoped-for salvation is represented by the "rock," it is a type of "Christ, the Rock of Ages, . . . who, by his cross, giveth life to a dying world."[67] In this case, the rock of Christ's faith is reborn in the New World after having been washed away in the deluge of the Old World, rematerialized at sunrise for those with "eyes to see and minds to understand" on the coast of Maine's Mount Desert.

Interpreted in the context of concerns about national identity, Church's painting contains associations of both safety and danger. The only signs of life in the picture are the ships in the distance and the sea birds hovering close to the beacon. Metaphorically they could be read by Church's contemporaries as emblems of divine presence, reinforcing Protestant symbolism of personal transcendence and salvation.[68] Contemporary comments reveal that Church's audience consisted of receptive and sympathetic observers attuned to an array of subtly encoded messages. The picture is "deservedly one of the most popular in the Gallery; for it is broadly conceived, and its feeling and association command a universal sympathy." Further, the same reviewer recognized "there is great repose in the picture. As the spectator looks, he muses; and

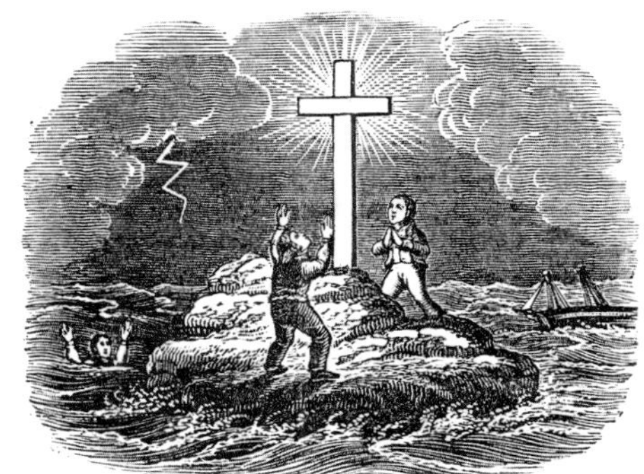

SALVATION.

Lo! where amid appalling dangers dread,
The rock undaunted lifts its welcome head;
Tho ship of commerce gayly sail'd along,
All hands were merry with their evening song;
When lo! they scud before a sudden blast,
The sails are shiver'd, broken is the mast;
The ship is wreck'd, the storm rolls wildly round,
The sinking sailors have no footing found.
In drowning plight, stunn'd by the wave's rude shock,
The lightning kindly points them to the rock;
The Rock they grasp, and raise themselves on high,
In conscious safety bid the storm pass by.
    So when mankind were wreck'd on Eden's shore,
Loud was the tempest, loud the thunder's roar,
Earth, sea, and skies affrigl ted were, and toss'd,
Tumultuous all. Shall man be saved, or lost?
In that wild ocean of despair and dread,
The Rock of Ages lifts his lofty head;
The sinner, sinking, stunn'd by Sinai's shock,
By Sinai's lightning, now beholds the Rock;

FIG. 41   Rev. William Holmes and John W. Barber, *Religious Emblems: Being a Series of Emblematic Engravings, with Written Explanations*, Cincinnati, Ohio: John H. Johnson, 1851, "Salvation," 25.

the sea and the shore and their eternal mystery and sadness gather in his mind."[69] The day marker is seen against the band of light above the horizon. Given Church's predilection for redefining the cruciform symbolism of his mentor Cole, these forms might be read as evoking associations of salvation in a dangerous world.

Gorgeous *sky-scapes*

The sky in Church's *Beacon* supports such a transcendental interpretation. Curtis wrote "'Beacon, off Mt. Desert Island,' is another of the artist's gorgeous *sky-scapes*, if he will tolerate so doubtful a term." He added that "these are the poetic strokes, with which the subdued brilliance of the ranks of high clouds is in admirable harmony."[70] Church and Cole had long considered the sunset and sunrise sky as a principal manifestation of divinity. Cole wrote emotionally of sunrise skies a year after Church left his studio.

> Rise! For the sun has breathed upon the sky
> And the cold ether . . . melts like dusk metal in
> the forge's flame . . .
> Be still! For in this sacred solemn deep
> Of silence all things mute do pray.[71]

A critic for the *American Art-Union* alluded to such celestial repose, recognizing that Church had "chosen the pure ether

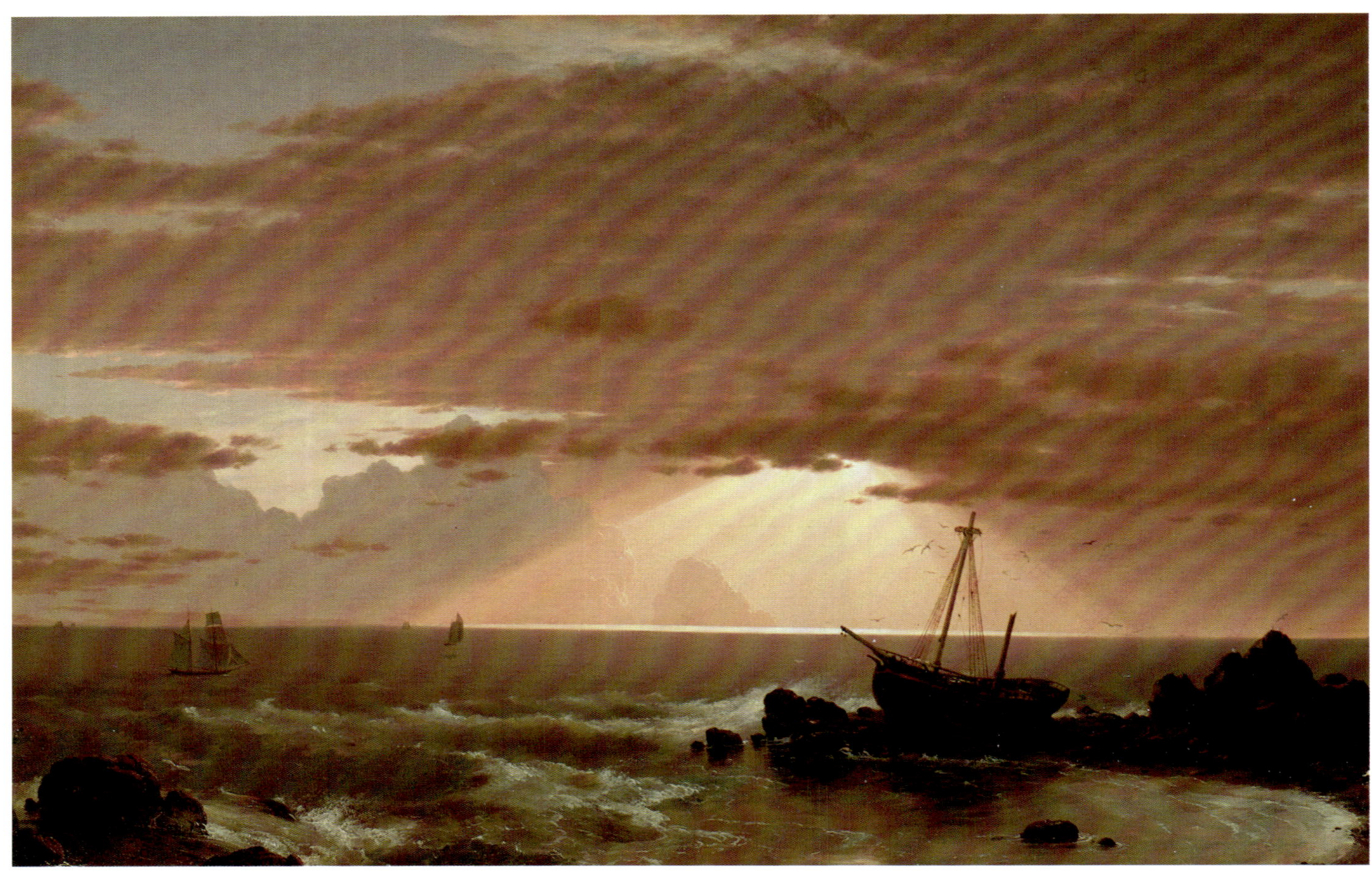

FIG. 42   Frederic E. Church, *The Wreck*, 1852, oil on canvas, 29¼ x 45¼". The Parthenon,
Nashville, Tennessee, Bequest of James M. Cowan, The Cowan Collection.

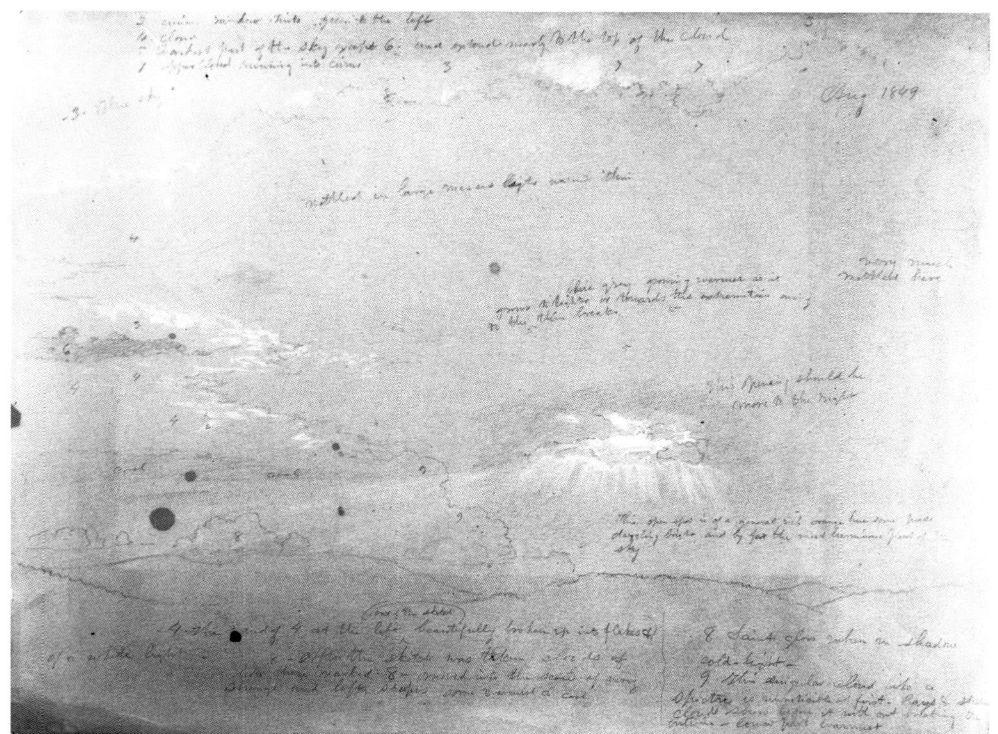

FIG. 43 Frederic E. Church, *Late Afternoon Over Walker Mountain, Vt.*, 1849, graphite on paper, 11⁷⁄₁₆ x 15⅜". Olana State Historic Site, New York State Office of Parks, Recreation and Historic Preservation, OL.1980.1430.

for his region, and that panorama of gorgeous effects, of which the clouds and the sun are the ruling powers."[72] In *Beacon* Church had not only depicted conventional associations and symbols of Protestant salvation, but had subtly shown the presence of the divine: "He is to show us in the splendid play of the light, and air, and clouds, that which we do not see, or seeing, do not perceive."[73] In their repose and solemnity Church sky-scape intimations of immortality represented for the first time the creator's presence in a light-filled firmament. Caught in its spell the "slight bestirring of sail in the offing, the surging of the sounding sea against the base of the beacon amidst the silent twilight, while above spreads that magnificent array of glowing clouds, and in the thickening distance of the murky horizon, shine a few golden bars of light—all these are features of this work that are deeply impressive."[74] A review in the *International Monthly Magazine* astutely recognized Church's developing ability not only to produce in the viewer's mind sensations of an actual site, but to associate abstract concepts within these realistic representations: "Why should he hope always to please those who have only a vague susceptibility of natural observation for their standard of criticism?"[75]

At its most commercially interested level of meaning the painting was surely appealing to the constituency that took it primarily as a vicarious substitute for actual travel. To this segment of the audience *Beacon* was a visual novelty for city dwellers seeking to escape the heat of summer, where "the gloom of gathering night breathes cool along the canvas."[76] In fact, the image was believed to be "worth almost as much in the sensations it produces, as a visit from the hot city in August to the still, cool sea-side, where, instead of the close confinement of brick wall and the little patch of blue seen between your neighbor's chimneys, the whole illimitable expanse of sky and ocean is opened to your astonished eyes."[77]

"Something Original and Striking": *The Wreck*

The following year Church's excitement about Maine and Mount Desert scenery led him to expand his summer sketching travels even farther north to include the Bay of Fundy. He began his 1851 trip at the Catskill Mountain House in July and then traveled north to Grand Manan Island at the Bay of Fundy, about eighty miles northeast of Mount Desert. He visited and sketched at Grand Manan for six weeks and on the return trip to New York made a brief stop at Mount Desert. The following year Church made another sketching trip to Grand Manan and ventured to north central Maine to the Katahdin Mountain wilderness region and possibly concluded his trip with another brief stop at Mount Desert, as he had done the summer before.[78] A major painting related to his experiences at Grand Manan and Mount Desert is *The Wreck* (fig. 42). It was critically acclaimed as a depiction in which "Mr. Church, this year, and the last, has shown himself the Poet."[79] Corresponding in size and related in its iconography to *Beacon, off Mount Desert Island* of the previous year, it, like its predecessor is a painting of dramatic sky, clouds, and the sea, intermingled with powerful associations of personal religious transcendence.

Church's dramatic image derived from several sources. Although Church spent six weeks at Grand Manan in 1851, *The Wreck* incorporates little of Grand Manan, some of Vermont in the effects of a twilight sky observed in 1849, and observations of the wrecked ship at Mount Desert in 1850. Church's August 1849 pencil drawing *Late Afternoon Over Walker Mountain, Vt.* (fig. 43) shows a circle of radiant light

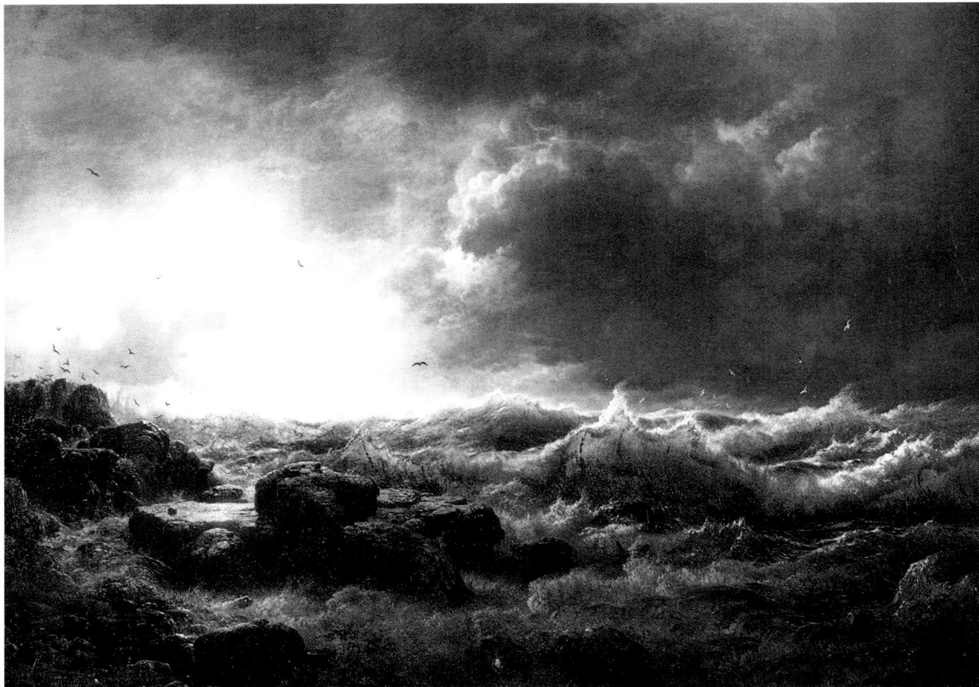

and similar cloud formations as in *The Wreck*. Two sketches with identical titles, *Beached Sailing Vessel, Mount Desert Island* (Olana), completed in August–September of 1850, bear obvious similarities to the wrecked schooner in the picture, including the vessel's rigging and tackle. The vessel's name was inscribed on the stern: *Joseph Ham Halifax NS.*[80]

Exhibited in 1852 at the National Academy of Design, *The Wreck* was singled out by George Washington Curtis as "one of the most popular pictures in the exhibition. It is of the same size and general character as his Beacon of last year, and is in no manner inferior to that." The young artist was "the first of our marine painters. Indeed we do not now recall any one who at all disputes the palm with him."[81] However, more than one reviewer found Church's painting "inferior." The art critic for the *Knickerbocker* noted "the sky is heavy and clumsy in arrangement; the sea weakly felt and deficient in force, though good in color; but the vessels are so sadly out of perspective as to destroy the keeping of the whole."[82] The critic for *The Albion*, disappointed that *The Wreck* did not in his opinion measure up to Church's previous work, stated that "he who has hit the public taste in one or two instances is not permitted to fall below the standard of his own setting up. Mr. Church does so in this present Exhibition." Despite this negative comment, he acknowledged that "still there is something original and striking in all that he [Church] paints."[83]

Artists' Competitions and Storm-Tossed Boats

The storm-tossed or wrecked ship was a popular subject in the nineteenth century, and Church surely saw Asher B. Durand's (1796–1886) *Shipwreck, Clearing Up After A Storm* (unlocated), which was also shown in the 1850 National

Academy exhibition. The critic for *The Albion* praised Durand's picture as having "more real poetry, and more feeling in this picture of a crippled and deserted ship, than any other in the exhibition."[84] Church could hardly have missed the distinction bestowed on Durand's shipwreck scene since he and the older artist were rivals for leadership among the New York landscape painters. To be sure, Church and Durand had both seen Andreas Achenbach's *Clearing Up, Coast of Sicily* (fig. 44). Its praise by critics and public alike may have surprised many New York artists, especially considering the criticisms of Cole's marine *View Across Frenchman's Bay* just a few years earlier (see fig. 23). According to one contemporary writer for the *American Art-Union*:

> *Church, Gignoux, and Hubbard have gone to the coast of Maine, where, it is said, that the marine views are among the finest in the country. None of these artists, we believe, have [sic] hitherto attempted such subjects. The exhibition of the magnificent Achenbach last year in the Art-Union Gallery seems to have directed the attention of our younger men to the grandeur of Coast scenery.*[85]

Church manipulated symbolic details in this painting of a wrecked ship much as he had done in *The Old Boat* and in *Beacon, off Mount Desert Island*. He was becoming known for his "remarkable perception of form, and a feeling of grandeur and gorgeous effect, rather more implied than expressed."[86] The rocks at the right foreground resemble those Church sketched at Grand Manan. Curtis praised the foreground effects, the "surf in the foreground combing over the ledge and sliding heavily up the strip of beach, with that cool, crisp, salt complexion of sea water, is a masterly success." He was unequivocal: "The highest triumph we remark in Mr.

Church marines is the *solemnity* of the sea." Other painters successfully painted the incidents of "ocean character," but Church's "pictures have a broad and grave character—a meaning—a thought which elevates them from sea-pieces into works of art." Curtis praised Church's "fine detail, which no one surpasses. Whoever . . . saw some relic of the sea's fury drifting by or lodged among the rocks, and as he looked across the heaving waste felt in the gathering gloom its melancholy wail made visible, so that by sight and sound he was sympathetically enthralled—he has that feeling of pathetic solemnity in the ocean of which Mr. Church this year, and the last, has shown himself the Poet."[87]

Solemnity and Redemption

The sea and New England's coastline were essential for transportation, commerce, and military power during the formation of national identity, particularly for Anglo-Protestant elites whose fortunes and social position were often linked to trade and shipping. Both beautiful and dangerous, the rocky coastline was perceived as the route to business opportunity and as a continuing peril for travelers. Henry David Thoreau observed: "Before the land rose out of the ocean, and became dry land, chaos reigned, and between high and low water mark, where she is partially disrobed and rising, a sort of chaos reigns still, which only anomalous creatures can inhabit." For Thoreau this coastal zone of islands and submerged ledges was largely distinguished "as the enemy of ships and the stalking ground of death."[88]

Analogous to the suffering, turmoil, and disaster experienced by individuals, persecuted groups, and even nations, a ship at sea conjured up metaphoric expressions such as "ship of state."[89] Visual associations of the human condition, fear, pain, death, and claims of personal salvation, were communicated by the careful and deliberate manipulation of visual conventions that produced an accumulation of visual and verbal associations.[90] Several elements in *The Wreck* suggest a hopeful outcome in a Puritan world of predestination. Natural signs abound: The most obvious is the cross formed by the mast and spars of the wrecked schooner, which signifies Protestant notions of personal deliverance. Just beyond the ship's mast, sea birds circle, visual conventions that contribute further associations of salvation, ministered by natural spirits.

The sky offers the most distinct suggestion of redemption. It opens in a halo of light at the center, the sun casts light through clouds to the sea. The ship's bow points at and pierces the light. The cross of light is a celestial reflection of the cruciform shape of the spars on the wrecked schooner. In fact, the ratlines on the mast create a triangular shape, subtly reinforcing the rays of the light cross. This type of light was held by mid-nineteenth-century audiences to be the "most essential element of sublimity."[91] Church's continuing references to Cole's religious allegories are unmistakable.

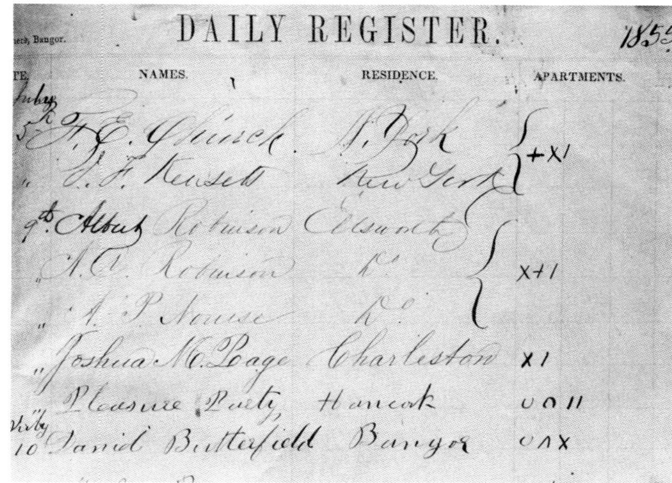

FIG. 45 *Agamont House Register, 1855*, 5 July 1855, entry "F. E. Church / N.York / J. F. Kensett / New York," Bar Harbor Historical Society.

A Summer Excursion: The Tracy Journal

Following his lengthy expedition to the tropics of South America in 1853, Church turned his attention again to the north, to Maine. He returned to Mount Desert in September of 1854, and the following year he spent much of the summer on the Island, although the 1855 visit was more about social events and perhaps Church's interest in some of the young women who accompanied the party that summer. For a short time he was accompanied by John F. Kensett (1843–1907), for the "Agamont House Register" records the signatures of both Church and Kensett on the same page (fig. 45).[92] Later, Church joined the company of a group of twenty-six travelers, including his two sisters, and Charles Tracy (1810–1885). Tracy was a railroad man, the personal advisor to J. P. Morgan, whom his daughter Frances later married. Another member of the party was Theodore Winthrop (1828–1861), Tracy's apprentice law partner, and a dashing bon vivant and aspiring author.[93] Tracy's journal of the trip documented the extended summer visit by artists, mostly from New York, to Mount Desert Island.[94] The group made their journey from New York to Boston where they boarded the *S.S. Penobscot* to Rockland, and from that point they traveled by small steamer bound for Southwest Harbor at Mount Desert. The party took over Daniel Somes's Tavern in Somesville during the month of August. Tracy's diary was later entitled, "The Log Book. Voyage from New York to Mount Desert, Stay There, and Return, July–August, 1855," and to it Church contributed a series of humorous illustrated vignettes of the party's visit (fig. 46).[95] The nineteen drawings comprise a slapstick running joke, mostly about "things that can and do go wrong." The series indulged Church's penchant for humorous personifications of dumb animals, boulders with faces, and a fantastical sea monster.[96]

FIG. 46 Charles Tracy, "The Log Book. Voyage from New York to Mount Desert Island,
Stay There, and Return. July–August, 1855," 22, 23, 55, 86. The Pierpont
Morgan Library, New York. Photo: David Krigsman.

Society, Courtship, Landscape Art

As the earliest record of such tourist trips to Mount Desert, the diary provides an important contemporary context. Tracy's description of the month's activities revealed among other things that for the bachelor Church this was both a sketching trip and social excursion. There were picnics and fishing, and both Winthrop and Church devoted much of their time to "entertaining" the group. Judging from Tracy's comments, in 1855 Church took sketching materials mainly when he wanted to share a laugh with his companions. Certainly he was solicitous toward two of the young ladies, his sisters, Charlotte and Elizabeth, and even more perhaps to Frances and Annie Tracy, to whom finished drawings are dedicated. Another possibility is Lucretia Titus, to whom Church later gave a small painting as a wedding present. None of these women became Church's wife however, because the next time he returned to Mount Desert, in 1860, a new bride of only two months accompanied him. A humorous drawing (fig. 47) from that later trip shows his petite new wife Isabel Mortimer Carnes standing bracingly on a rocky promontory whipped by winds and dashing surf while Church cowers in the rocks below. The inscription reads: "Mt. Desert/Time - two hours past dinner time— Isabel: —Oh Fred isn't it grand? I feel as if I never wished to go away— Fred: —Teeth Chattering — Y - y - y - e - e - s - s ver - r - r - ry -" Church's tolerance for cold winds and humid sea air had diminished drastically in less than a decade, and he would visit Mount Desert once again in 1862.[97]

Visitors and Islanders: A Tourist's Celebration

The Tracy group hosted a large celebration when the visit was nearly over, inviting many of the local Islanders who had supplied them, transported them, and entertained them. Mr. and Mrs. William Lynam were designated as guests of honor because for many years they had provided hospitality to artists and others and were guiding forces behind Mount Desert's increasing popularity among the leisured classes such as the Tracys. The whole dinner party numbered as many as eighty persons and was probably the earliest gathering of "tourists," artists, family and friends, and local residents. Tracy remarked of the Islanders that "of course they were all strangers to us, but we made ourselves very easy and soon all the houseful was in a state of sociality and happiness." Later in the evening "the table was made ready and with marching music we promenaded the company into the supper room." Each had their part in preparing the feast and "Mr. Winthrop had prepared a delicious lobster salad, and Mr. Church had cut out vegetable flowers to ornament the dishes." Tracy described at length the elaborate table setting in this remote Island settlement, which included "soft custard, the snowy-capped whipped cream, the fruits arranged for effect, the chandelier, the jellies, the cakes and the etceteras

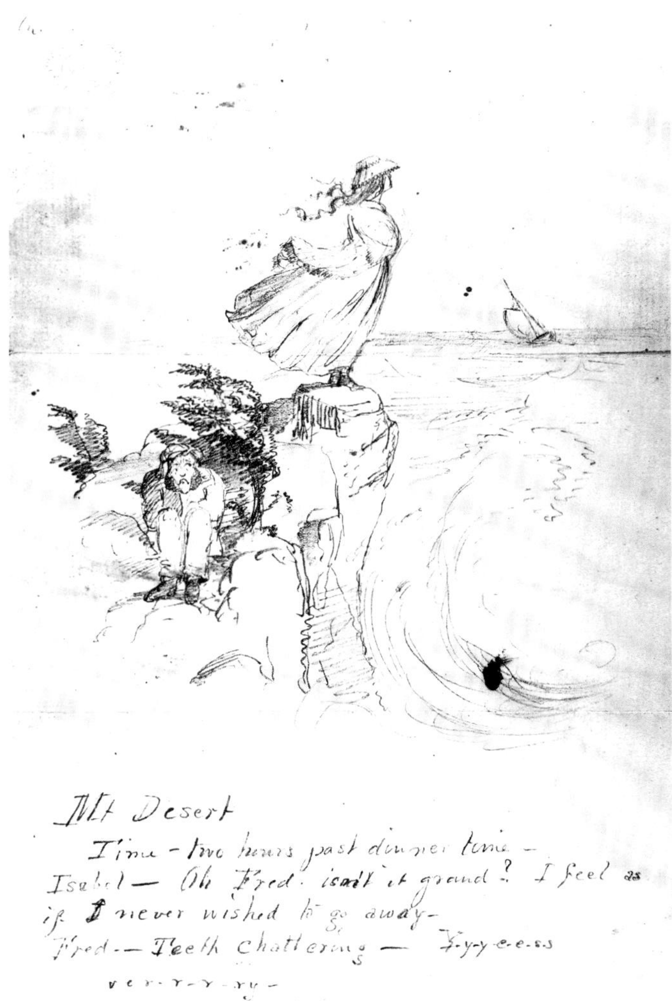

FIG. 47 Frederic E. Church, *Frederic and Isabel Church at Mount Desert Island*, c.1860–1862, graphite on thin white paper, 8 x 5″. Olana State Historic Site, New York State Office of Parks, Recreation and Historic Preservation, OL.1980.1603.

really made a pretty table. When it had been duly admired we fell to. The side tables gave duck and sandwiches."[98]

During the entire month the Tracys provided evening entertainment. The "piano is a standing resource and Mr. Church's capacity for entertainment is perfectly inexhaustible." At supper time the devilishly humorous Mr. Church entertained the party with a series of caricatures full of visual and verbal puns for which the artist was known. "Church proposed to paint arms of the party on the waggon, and suggested that it be a group—a pair of Fays, harnessed with Traces, pulling a Stone over a Church." Tracy, for his part, "proposed also a progressive picture of the party, coming here pale conservatives, and going away red Republicans: —a state of color to which they are fast approaching."[99]

An Acadian Scene

Later, in an emotional passage relying on the conventional rhetoric of tourist guides, Tracy provided details of an exciting excursion to Schooner Head. Reminiscent of the discovery rhetoric of early visitors at Yosemite or Yellowstone, Tracy described the scene as if the group was visiting a landscape garden. "Drawing near Schooner Head," he wrote, "the woods grew more open, the trees more broad and spreading, and the grass closer." Using for the first time the term that would be appropriated to name the national park sixty years later, Tracy remarked: "Here was an Acadian scene of the richest character. The open woods, the open grass fields, the meadow beyond, the ocean in the distance, and on the other side the great dark precipice, were enchanting."[100] About to arrive at Schooner Head, "the party straggling in, in waggons and on foot, and coming to the last opening were in ecstasy. . . . Every wave washes up and retreats by the side of our very steps."[101] Church recalled this scene as he planned a great picture of the rocky coast of Mount Desert Island that he eventually produced during one of the darkest moments of the Civil War.

NOTES

1. "The Fine Arts," *International Monthly Magazine* 3 (June 1851): 327.

2. Moses Foster Sweetser, *Summer Days Down East* (Portland, Maine: Chisholm Brothers, 1883), 125.

3. Clara Barnes Martin, *Mount Desert on the Coast of Maine: "Infinite Riches in a Little Room"* (Privately Printed, 1867; 4th ed., Portland, Maine: Loring, Short and Harmon, 1877), 33.

4. It is curious that Church waited six years to visit the Island when he knew of the scenery and was clearly enthusiastic. Why had Cole's new student not accompanied him on his 1844 journey? As speculated in Chapter 2, n. 16, perhaps because of his young age. Church was virtually the only student Cole would ever take. Cole died in 1848. Church may have reflected on his mentor's work and travels, reminding him of Cole's Mount Desert visit.

5. Frederic E. Church, "Mountain Views and Coast Scenery, by a Landscape Painter," *Bulletin of the American Art-Union* (November 1850): 130–1.

6. David C. Huntington, *The Landscapes of Frederic Edwin Church: Vision of an American Era* (New York: George Braziller, 1966), 30.

7. Church. "Mountain Views and Coast Scenery," 130.

8. Ibid.

9. Ibid.

10. Ibid.

11. Ibid.

12. Eleanor Jones Harvey, *The Painted Sketch: American Impressions from Nature, 1830–1880* (Dallas, Tex: Dallas Museum of Art; New York: in association with Harry N. Abrams, 1998), 154–97. John Wilmerding, *The Artist's Mount Desert* (Princeton: Princeton University Press, 1994), 95. See also Theodore Stebbins, Jr., *Close Observation: Selected Oil Sketches of Frederic E. Church* (Washington, D.C.: Smithsonian Institution Press, 1978).

13. Charles Tracy, "Log of a Voyage from New York to Mount Desert and Return, July–September 1855," 61.

14. Church, "Mountain Views and Coast Scenery," 130.

15. Ibid., 131.

16. "Art and Artists," *The Home Journal* (15 February 1851): 3.

17. Mary Bartlett Cowdrey, *American Academy of Fine Arts and American Art-Union Exhibition Record, 1816–1852,* (New York: New-York Historical Society, 1953), 72.

18. Ibid. The painting was sold at that time to S. W. Bridgham.

19. Gerald L. Carr, *Frederic E. Church Catalogue Raisonné of Works of Art at Olana State Historic Site* (New York: Cambridge University Press, 1994), 178–9, 273–4.

20. Harvey, *Painted Sketch,* 155.

21. Franklin Kelly, *Frederic Edwin Church and the National Landscape* (Washington, D.C.: Smithsonian Institution Press, 1988), 26–27.

22. Carr, *Frederic E. Church Catalogue Raisonné,* 170, no. 259, recto.

23. Martin, *Mount Desert on the Coast of Maine,* 36.

24. Ibid.

25. Hale, *The Story of Bar Harbor,* 137. It is interesting to note that the family stayed at the Lynam cabin while at Mount Desert.

26. Robert Carter, *A Summer Cruise on the Coast of New England,* first published, 1864 (Boston: Cupples and Hurd Publishers, 1888), 256–7.

27. Martin, *Mount Desert on the Coast of Maine,* 36.

28. Ibid., 17. The town of Bar Harbor was called Eden from 1796 through 1919 when the name was officially changed with the establishment of the national park. In 1796 the townspeople wanted to name the town Adams after Governor Samuel Adams, however, that name was already in use in Berkshire County. Samuel Eliot Morison, *The Story of Mount Desert Island, Maine* (Boston: Little, Brown, and Co., 1960), 77.

29. See Huntington, *Frederic Edwin Church,* for Church and the concept of the American Adam; see also R.W.B. Lewis, *The American Adam: Innocence, Tragedy, and Tradition in the Nineteenth Century* (Chicago: University of Chicago Press, 1955).

30. See Appendix for a list of paintings of Mount Desert and note especially those exhibited in Philadelphia.

31. Anna Wells Rutledge, *Cumulative Record of Exhibition Catalogues: The Pennsylvania Academy of the Fine Arts* (Philadelphia: The American Philosophical Society, 1955), 48. The painting was later owned by a Bar Harbor resident, Mrs. R. Armory Thorndike, who donated it to the Boston Museum of Fine Arts in 1986. See also Gerald L. Carr and Franklin Kelly, *The Early Landscapes of Frederic Edwin Church, 1845–1854* (Fort Worth, Tex.: Amon Carter Museum, 1987).

32. Church, "Mountain Views and Coast Scenery," 130.

33. Cowdrey, *National Academy of Design,* 80.

34. George William Curtis, "The Fine Arts: Exhibition of the National Academy, III," *New-York Daily Tribune,* 10 May 1851.

35. "Art and Artists," *The Home Journal* (10 May 1851): 3.

36. See J. Gray Sweeney, "A 'Very Peculiar' Picture: Martin J. Heade's *Thunderstorm over Narragansett Bay*," *Archives of American Art Journal,* 2–14; Gerald Eager, "The Iconography of the Boat in 19th Century American Painting," *Art Journal* 35, no. 3 (Spring 1976): 224–30; Lorenz Eitner, "The Window and the Storm-Tossed Boat: An Essay in the Iconography of Romanticism," *The Art Bulletin,* 281–90; and for earlier sources see Lawrence Otto Goedde, *Tempest and Shipwreck in Dutch and Flemish Art: Convention, Rhetoric, and Interpretation* (University Park: Penn State University Press, 1989).

37. See Paul D. Schweizer, ed., *The Voyage of Life by Thomas Cole: Paintings, Drawings, and Prints* (Utica, N.Y.: Munson-Williams-Proctor Institute, 1985); see also Ellwood C. Parry, *The Art of Thomas Cole: Ambition and Imagination* (Newark: University of Delaware Press, 1989), "Still a Youth in Imagination," 226–59.

38. See J. Gray Sweeney, "The Nude of Landscape Painting: Emblematic Personification in the Art of the Hudson River School," *Smithsonian Studies in American Art* (Fall 1989): 42–65.

39. William Cullen Bryant, ed., *Picturesque America: or the Land We Live In* (New York: D. Appleton and Company, 1872), 10.

40. Martin, *Mount Desert on the Coast of Maine,* 33.

41. Carr, *Frederic E. Church,* 186, no. 301 and 302. The title of the painting was given to it when it was discovered in 1883, after the inscription on the Olana drawing, no. 302.

42. Gerald L. Carr, "Frederic E. Church," Friends of Olana, Inc., Hudson, New York.

43. Church, "Mountain Views and Coast Scenery," 131.

44. Bryant, *Picturesque America*, 2.

45. "Mount Desert," *Harper's New Monthly Magazine*, 336.

46. Ibid., 323.

47. Martin, *Mount Desert on the Coast of Maine,* 19.

48. Church, "Mountain Views and Coast Scenery," 131.

49. "Art and Artists," *The Home Journal* (9 August 1851): 3.

50. Morison, *The Story of Mount Desert Island, Maine*, 37. Most of these vessels were part of the large fishing industry that made port at Bass Harbor, Cranberry Harbor, and Southwest Harbor.

51. Ibid., 38. Morison notes that prior to the beacon on East Bunkers Ledge, a light was positioned on Bakers Island in 1828, and on Mount Desert Rock in 1830. Also, in 1839, the Bear Island light went up to help navigation to both Eastern and Western Way.

52. The painting was sold at the American Art-Union sale in December, 1852. Cowdrey, *National Academy of Design*, 80.

53. "The Fine Arts: Exhibition at the National Academy," *The Literary World* 220 (19 April 1851): 320.

54. "The Fine Arts," *The International Magazine*, 327.

55. James Collins Moore, "The Storm and the Harvest: The Image of Nature in Mid-Nineteenth Century American Landscape Painting" (Ph.D. diss., Indiana University, 1974), 77.

56. Curtis, "The Fine Arts: Exhibition of the National Academy."

57. "Affairs of the Association," *Bulletin of the American Art-Union* (December 1851): 153.

58. Kelly, *Frederic Edwin Church and the National Landscape*, 37–42.

59. "The Fine Arts: Exhibition at the National Academy," 320.

60. Curtis.

61. For useful readings of *Beacon* and *The Deluge* see Kelly, *Frederic Edwin Church and the National Landscape*, 37–42. For typology see, Sacvan Bercovitch, *The American Jeremiad* (Madison: University of Wisconsin Press, 1978); Ursula Brumm. *American Thought and Religious Typology* (New Brunswick, N.J.: Rutgers University Press, 1970).

62. Curtis.

63. Goedde, *Tempest and Shipwreck in Dutch and Flemish Art*, 192.

64. See Goedde, 36; see also Sweeney, "A 'Very Peculiar' Picture," 8; and Eitner, "The Window and the Storm-Tossed Boat," 281–90.

65. Rev. William Holmes and John W. Barber, *Religious Emblems: Being a Series of Emblematic Engravings, with Written Explanations, Miscellaneous Observations, and Religious Reflections, Designed to Illustrate Divine Truth, in Accordance with the Cardinal Principles of Christianity* (Cincinnati, Ohio: John H. Johnson, 1851), frontispiece.

66. Holmes, and Barber, *Religious Emblems*, 25–26.

67. Ibid.

68. Sweeney, "Endued With Rare Genius," 64.

69. Curtis.

70. Ibid.

71. Thomas Cole, *Thomas Cole's Poetry*, Marshall B. Tymn, ed. (York, Penn.: Liberty Cap Books, 1972), 166.

72. "Twenty-Sixth Exhibition of the National Academy of Design," *Bulletin of the American Art-Union* 4 (1 May 1851): 23.

73. "The Fine Arts," *International Monthly Magazine*, 327.

74. "Twenty-Sixth Exhibition," 23.

75. "The Fine Arts," 327.

76. Curtis.

77. "Twenty-Sixth Exhibition," 23.

78. Kelly, *Frederic Edwin Church and the National Landscape*, 160.

79. George William Curtis, "The Fine Arts: Exhibition of the National Academy, IV," *New-York Daily Tribune*, 8 May 1852.

80. See Carr, *Frederic E. Church Catalogue Raisonné*, 184–5, no. 297–8. Carr calls the vessel in the drawings "cadaverous." See also Kelly, *Frederic Edwin Church and the National Landscape*, 62.

81. Curtis, "The Fine Arts: IV." The painting was sold to J. F. Stone. Cowdrey, *National Academy of Design*, 80.

82. "Exhibition of the National Academy," *The Knickerbocker* 39 (June 1852): 567.

83. "Fine Arts, The National Academy of Design - No. III," *The Albion* (8 May 1852): 225.

84. Kelly, *Frederic Edwin Church and the National Landscape*, 64, citing "Fine Arts, The National Academy of Design - No. III," *The Albion* (27 April 1850): 201.

85. "Chronicle of Facts and Opinions: American Art and Artists' Movement of Artists," *Bulletin of the American Art-Union* 89 (August 1850): 81. Cited in Kelly, 145, no. 55.

86. Curtis, "The Fine Arts: IV."

87. Ibid.

88. Henry David Thoreau, *Cape Cod* (1865; reprint, New York: Thomas Crowell, 1966), 81, quoted in John R. Stilgoe, "A New England Coastal Wilderness," *The Geographical Review* 71, no. 1 (January 1981): 50.

89. See Sarah Cash, *Ominous Hush: The Thunderstorm Paintings of Martin Johnson Heade* (Fort Worth, Tex.: Amon Carter Museum, 1994), 21–50.

90. See Eitner, "The Window and the Storm-Tossed Boat," 281–90. See also Goedde, *Tempest and Shipwreck*, 1–46; Gerald Eager, "The Iconography of the Boat in 19th Century American Painting," *Art Journal*, 224–30; Roger Stein, *Seascape and the American Imagination* (New York: Whitney Museum of American Art, 1975), 35–43; and John Wilmerding, *American Marine Painting* (Richmond: Virginia Museum of Fine Arts, 1976; Newport News, Va.: The Mariners' Museum, 1976).

91. Moore, "The Storm and the Harvest," 153.

92. The late Gladys O'Neil directed attention to the Agamont House guest book where Church and other artists signed on July 5; Jesup Memorial Library, Bar Harbor.

93. Church had expanded his travels in Maine to include Mount Katahdin in 1851 and again in 1856 with Winthrop. See Theodore Winthrop, *Life in the Open Air, and Other Papers* (Boston: Ticknor and Fields, 1863), 50.

94. George E. Street, *Mount Desert, a History*, Samuel A. Eliot, ed., 2nd rev. ed. (Boston: Houghton, Mifflin, and Co., 1926), 295.

95. Anne Mazlish, ed., *The Tracy Logbook: 1855, A Month in Summer* (Bar Harbor, Maine: Acadia Publishing Co., and Mount Desert Island Historical Society, 1997).

96. Gerald L. Carr, "Out on 'Rocks' and 'Peaks' all Day: Frederic Church and Mount Desert Island." Unpublished lecture, Bar Harbor Historical Society, July 1997, 10. Thanks to Gerald Carr for making available the text of his lecture which has been indispensable for this section on the Tracy Log, which Dr. Carr named.

97. Carr, *Frederic Edwin Church Catalogue Raisonné*, 270, no. 403.

98. Tracy, "Log of a Voyage," 68.

99. Ibid., 20, 47, 21–22.

100. Mazlish, *The Tracy Logbook*, 113.

101. Ibid., 49–51.

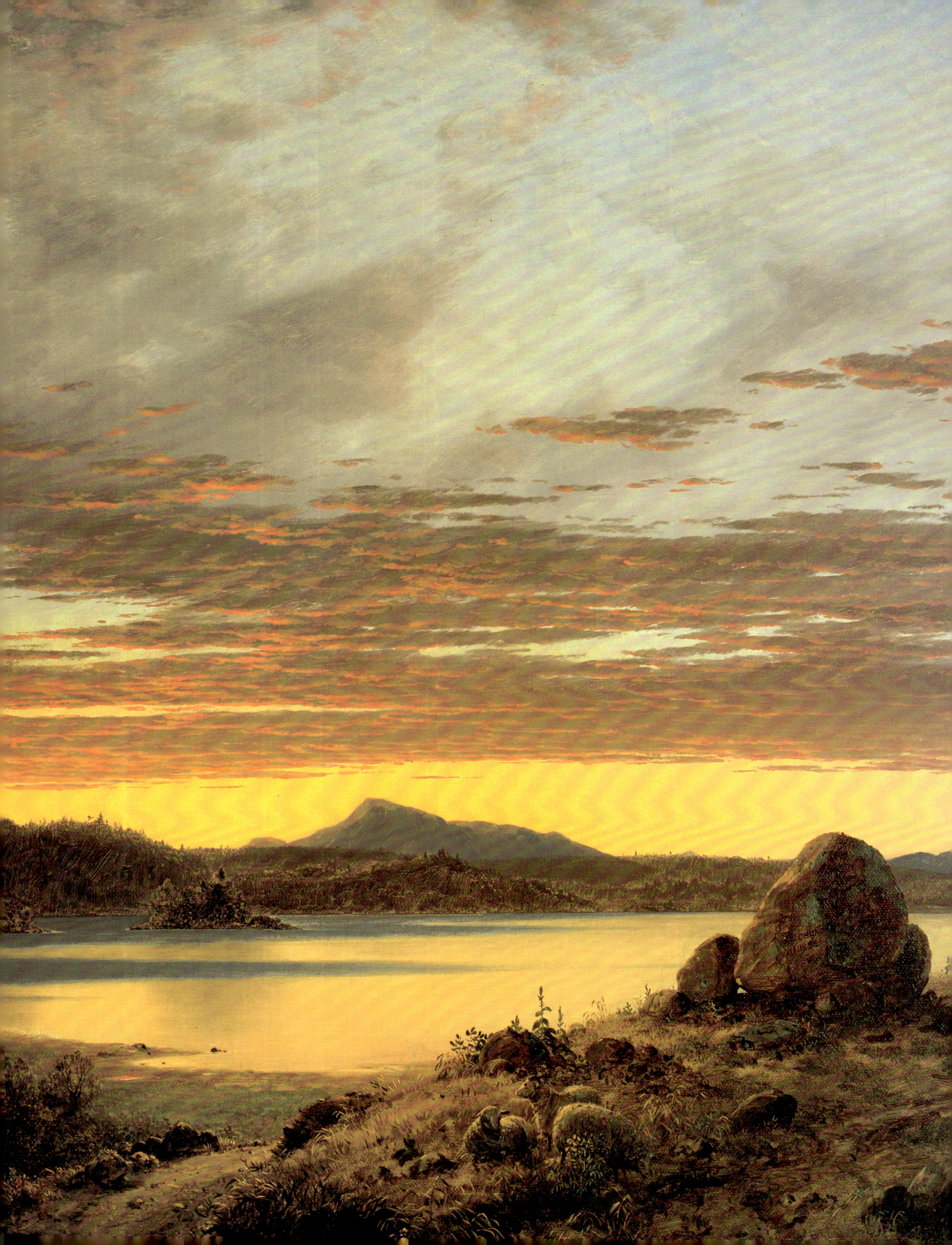

CHAPTER 4

The Enduring North: Mount Desert, Maine, and the Nation

In 1856, Church planned a trip to the remote wilderness interior of Maine and to Mount Katahdin. He had climbed Katahdin previously, in 1852, but failed to reach the summit. This time he would travel with his friend, the writer Theodore Winthrop, who had spent the previous summer with Church and the Tracy party exploring Mount Desert. The writer and the landscape painter planned to climb Mount Katahdin during the months of July and August when it was most accessible. On this trip into the North American continent's northernmost wilderness, Church witnessed several grand sunsets, and the mountain experience transformed the artist's conception of wilderness and his production of pictures.

Upon his return to New York Church set about producing *Sunset*, one of his most important paintings of Maine and of Mount Desert (fig. 48). Although the painting's early history is unclear, *Sunset* and the related oil study evidently held special importance for the artist. The picture's first appearance in the public record is a notice: Church exhibited it for sale in 1879. If he retained it, or repurchased it some time in the 1870s, as one scholar speculates, this was unusual. Church was besieged with demands for pictures, and eventually sold *Sunset* for two thousand dollars, a high figure for the time.[1] For these reasons, the picture received no known contemporary critical reception. This is compensated for by the fact that the painting was in Church's studio through the 1850s and 1860s when he was at his height as the nation's leading landscape painter, and that it would have been seen there by Winthrop as he wrote his narrative about the expedition to the great mountain. *Sunset* is now recognized as the major precursor image for Church's "great picture" of 1860, *Twilight in the Wilderness* (see fig. 113).

Origins of *Sunset*

The origins of *Sunset* can be traced directly to Church's September 1854 visit to Mount Desert. A rapidly executed pencil field sketch, *Sunset, Bar Harbor* (fig. 49), first recorded the dramatic sunset sky at Bar Harbor that would be incorporated in a finished oil study and eventually transferred to the exhibition-scale painting, *Sunset*, of 1856. Church's pencil drawing noted specific effects: "mottled clouds in regular ranks." To the left was "open sky" that led to "superb clear brilliant blue" and "exquisite warm blue." Sunset colors were "brilliant splendid orange" to "cooler green gold brilliant." The colors of the lower clouds were denoted by the number "4," which was identified in a legend at the bottom of the sheet as "illuminate with rich orange and leak [i.e. purplish-red] light/in parallel lines but dim compared with open sky/also broken with openings showing the cool bright sky/shadow tint brownish purple." He annotated rapidly the fleeting colors of sky reflected in water. They were in places "splendid silvery blue," elsewhere "duller and darker." Still other light effects were "superb clear brilliant blue/Exquisite warmlue [sic]."[2] Other notations give the time of day and weather. In one place Church observed "the water was ruffled by wind," while at the bottom of the sheet he wrote "2d Twilight." Second Twilight was that special moment Cole had written of in his long poem "The Lament of the Forest," when

The sun descended, and the twilight spread
Its soft empurpled wings; and that blessed hours,
When spirits stooping from the crimson clouds
Commune with man.[3]

Church's pencil sketch was reworked as a highly finished oil sketch perhaps in just a few hours or days after the artist had experienced the celestial sunset and while it was still vivid in his memory, *Sunset, Bar Harbor* (fig. 50). But Church laid the image aside for a year and a half to pursue expeditions to South America and explore other themes of the national landscape. Yet the production of the oil sketch would mark a turning point in Church's career.[4] Its brilliant color and the sharply defined forms of the massed ranks of clouds receding from the foreground to the distant horizon recall similarly painted passages in his *Beacon, off Mount Desert* (see fig. 37), but the study is far more venturesome with brilliant color, sweeping arcs, sharply receding diagonals, and broken horizontal ranks of clouds that seem to be processing across the heavens. The two small coastal schooners at anchor in the bay, and rows of fish stakes at the right subtly affirm a human presence of minute scale against the radiant canopy of the firmament. Like *Sunset,* the oil study *Sunset, Bar Harbor* was retained by the artist and was not exhibited.[5]

Wings of Angels, Hues so Wonderful

Sunsets and sunrises offered multiple associations to Hudson River School artists. Cole had written poetically, just a few months before Church had joined him in Catskill, of sunsets as, "the breath of God into free forms unearthly . . . hues so wonderful, so right and rare . . . and light and shadow strangely linked. . . . These are the wings of Angels I exclaimed!"[6] The many transcendental associations of sunset particularly interested Church. Through the 1850s Church developed the theme of sunset as a potent visual metaphor of the national landscape and an autograph of his personal style.[7]

The production of sunsets by landscape painters was the subject of an important article in *The Crayon* in September 1855, which Church would have read. It discussed three types of sunsets, giving special attention to "cirrus sunsets," which Church depicted in *Sunset.* Cirrus clouds produced sunsets "remarkable for repose, purity and delicacy of color, and serenity of light. . . . The colors the cirri assume at sunset, range from orange to the purist, faintest, golden yellow, with shadowed sides of pale amber. The tint becomes deeper and richer as the sun sinks." But color and tint were not enough: "In the most gorgeous sunsets the space and repose of the sky is no less remarkable than the brilliant color."[8] Gradually, Church transformed sunset allegories such as his early *Sunset, Short Arbiter 'twixt Day and Night* (Newark Art Museum), or the poetic pastoralism of his Cole-like *Mount Ktaadn* of 1853 (Yale University Art Museum), or his dramatic *Sunset,* 1856 (Albany Institute of History and Art), into landscapes in which man's presence is reduced and finally eliminated altogether.

To the Heart of New England's Wildest Wilderness

The disappearance of the figure, for the first time in *Sunset,* was a momentous conceptual achievement for Church. It required the most strenuous accomplishment—an expedition to the pure northern wilderness, a place without women, children, newspapers, and steamboats. Church and Winthrop traveled Down East to Maine's north woods, where they took manly pleasure in uncovering radiant sunsets of calm repose. After his journey to the mountain, Church returned to his New York studio where he completed *Sunset*, joining the view of Mount Desert and Mount Katahdin—his first truly national landscape. The image carried those few spectators privileged to see it in Church's studio far to the north, away from the madding city.

In late summer of 1856 Church and Winthrop began their hike across the Maine wilderness. "We both needed to be somewhere near the heart of New England's wildest wilderness. We needed to see Katahdin," Winthrop wrote emotionally.[9] Winthrop's vigorous, highly masculinized account of the trip was published posthumously as *Life in the Open Air* in 1863. The two men were, by the time of this wilderness trip, good friends, having spent the previous summer at Mount Desert with the Tracy party in pursuit of ladies and Island scenery. Their experience of Maine's vast interior wilderness deepened their bond. After the pair returned to New York he soon became an intimate of Church's studio in the new Studios Building on Tenth Street, often watching the painter at work on his easel. They discussed topical issues—politics, art, and the importance of wilderness for the nation. Winthrop's prose reflected these intense conversations with Church, whether they were held around the camp fire, or later in the studio.

Manly Life and the Artist-Soul

These literary and visual artist-explorers of Maine's scenery were looking for brilliant sunsets and great mountains. Winthrop observed, "[Church] has an eye for sunset. That summer's crop had been very short, and he had been for sometime on a starvation-allowance of cloud magnificence. We therefore halted by the road-side, and while I committed the glory to memory, Iglesias [Church] entrusted his distinct memorial to a sketch-board." A few minutes later, "Clouds, that donned brilliancy for the fond parting of mountain-tops and the sun, now grew cheerless and gray." The party paused momentarily to observe the devastation wrought by over-cutting the wilderness. "Maine has two classes of warriors among its sons—fighters of the forest and fighters of the sea," Winthrop noted of the economic interdependence of coastal Maine with the vast forested interior wilderness. "Only by the aid of the woodmen can the watermen build their engines of victory. . . . Foresters float down timber that seamen may build ships."[10] Winthrop decried the lumbermens' relentless campaign to find and cut the largest old-growth white pine trees, leaving behind the rest. What this meant was that the lumbering practices of the time had cut down every white pine, and all that remained were spruce, beech, birch, cedar, fir, and hemlock.

Church and Winthrop at that point in their expedition were already "manly men of the woods," breathing "nature as an Amreeta [Amaretto] draught, is it anything less than the *summum bonum?* 'Yet some call American life dull.' 'Ay, to dullard!' ejaculated Iglesias." "Manly men need the wilderness and the mountain," Winthrop thought, and "Katahdin is the best mount in the wildest wild to be had on this side of the continent." He saw that it was "all that [Church], connoisseur of mountains, had promised." [Church] fancied he "might see the visible, and hear the musical, and be stirred by the beautiful. These, truly, are not far from the daily life of any seer, listener, and perceiver; but there, perhaps, up in the strong wilderness, we might be recreated to a more sensitive vitality. . . . The diviner the power in any artist-soul, the more distinctly is he commanded to get near the divine without him."[11]

Wilderness Restaurant Ragmuff

A little steamboat dropped off Church and Winthrop at the end of Moosehead Lake. "As we started, so did the steamboat. The link between us and the inhabited world grew more and more attenuated. Finally it snapped, and we were in the actual wilderness." The border between the "actual wilderness" and civilization became an essential idea in Church's *Sunset*. Winthrop's narrative affected the persona of an explorer, or of a pioneer, including encounters with Indians: "This aboriginal meeting was of great value; it helped eliminate the railroad." Winthrop gloated, "we were to camp somewhere, 'anywhere out of the world' of railroads." For dining at the wilderness "Restaurant Ragmuff," Church acted the role of chef, preparing a feast of "woodland fare." Later that evening "we two solaced ourselves with scorning civilization from our [wilderness] vantage-ground. We were beyond fences, away from the clash of town-clocks, the clink of town-dollars, the hiss of town-scandals. As soon as one is fairly in camp and has begun to eat with his fingers, he is free," Winthrop exclaimed delightedly.[12]

A Little Giant

The production of poetic imagery and visual emblems of personification were widespread in landscape painting, and particularly strong with artists influenced by Cole. Church relied upon anthropomorphic conventions throughout his career, from the writhing, gesticulating trees and uplifted rocky faces in his early *Hooker and Company* (Wadsworth Atheneum) to the personifications in his pictures of Mount Desert's coastal scenery.[13] *Sunset* also deployed anthropomorphic conventions, although modified and transformed as part of a new expressive language of personal and national significance.

The artist and the writer cultivated fantasies of pursuing and subduing the distant mountain and seeing sunsets. Consequences of this masculine quest could emerge unexpectedly. One day the duo stopped at "a shady nook, just off Katahdin's reflection in the river, while Iglesias sketched." Winthrop informed his reader: "I, analyzing my view, presently discovered a droll image in the track of a land-

avalanche down the front [of Katahdin]. It was a comical fellow, a little giant, a colossal dwarf, six hundred feet high, . . . out of his head grew two misdirected skeleton legs, 'hanging down and dangling.'" The countenance was long, according to Winthrop, "elfin, sneering, solemn, as of a truculent demon, saddish for his trade, an ashamed, but unrepentant rascal." The figure in the side of Katahdin had other notable attributes for the dreamy-eyed Winthrop, now days from the nearest hotel or bar: "He had two immense erect ears, and in his boisterous position had suffered a loss of hair, wearing nothing save an impudent scalp-lock." Was he, Winthrop asks, "the guardian imp, the legendary Elf of Katahdin, scoffing already at us . . . and warning that he would make us unhappy, if we essayed to appear in demon realms and on Brocken heights without initiation?"[14]

Winthrop indulged the common rhetorical device of personifying nature, seeing in the random forms of a geological accident a face or perhaps a figure. Such personification may seem laughable, almost trivial to modern spectators who have lost the codes for reading this representational convention, but it was essential to nineteenth-century landscape painters and tourists. Writers such as Winthrop were also conversant with this method of constructing associations to enrich visual narratives, and understood that it was accessible to elite and popular audiences who held common anthropocentric ideas about the natural environment.

Ascent of Mount Katahdin

The party was not the first by any means to explore the mountain. At their base camp near the foot of Katahdin "a rough lean-to had been constructed by our Boston predecessors." A day was spent in camp fishing before ascending Katahdin. "We longed for the nervy climb," Winthrop wrote. The summit was encircled with clouds, "still we plodded on, following a path blazed by the Bostonians . . . and we grumblingly thanked them." "Mountains, too, are very stationary, —always at their post," Winthrop observed. "A mountain can be studied like a picture. . . . Purple precipice, blue pyramid, cone or dome of show, it is a simple image and a positive thought." The problem the party found was that the view *of* Katahdin was better than the view *from* Katahdin. "It is a vague panorama, a mappy, unmethodic maze of water and woods, very roomy, very vast, very simple . . . quite monotonous." The disappointment was palpable, "Maine's face thus exposed, has almost no features; there are no great mountains visible." Yet, "far away on the southern horizon we detected the heights of Mount Desert, our old familiar haunt." The sight reminded the party of "intimations of immortality." They stood on the heights "studying the pleasant solitude and dreamy breadth of Katahdin's panorama for a long time." From the overlook, they could see "far and wide, like a master of realms, [who] knows that the world is his."[15]

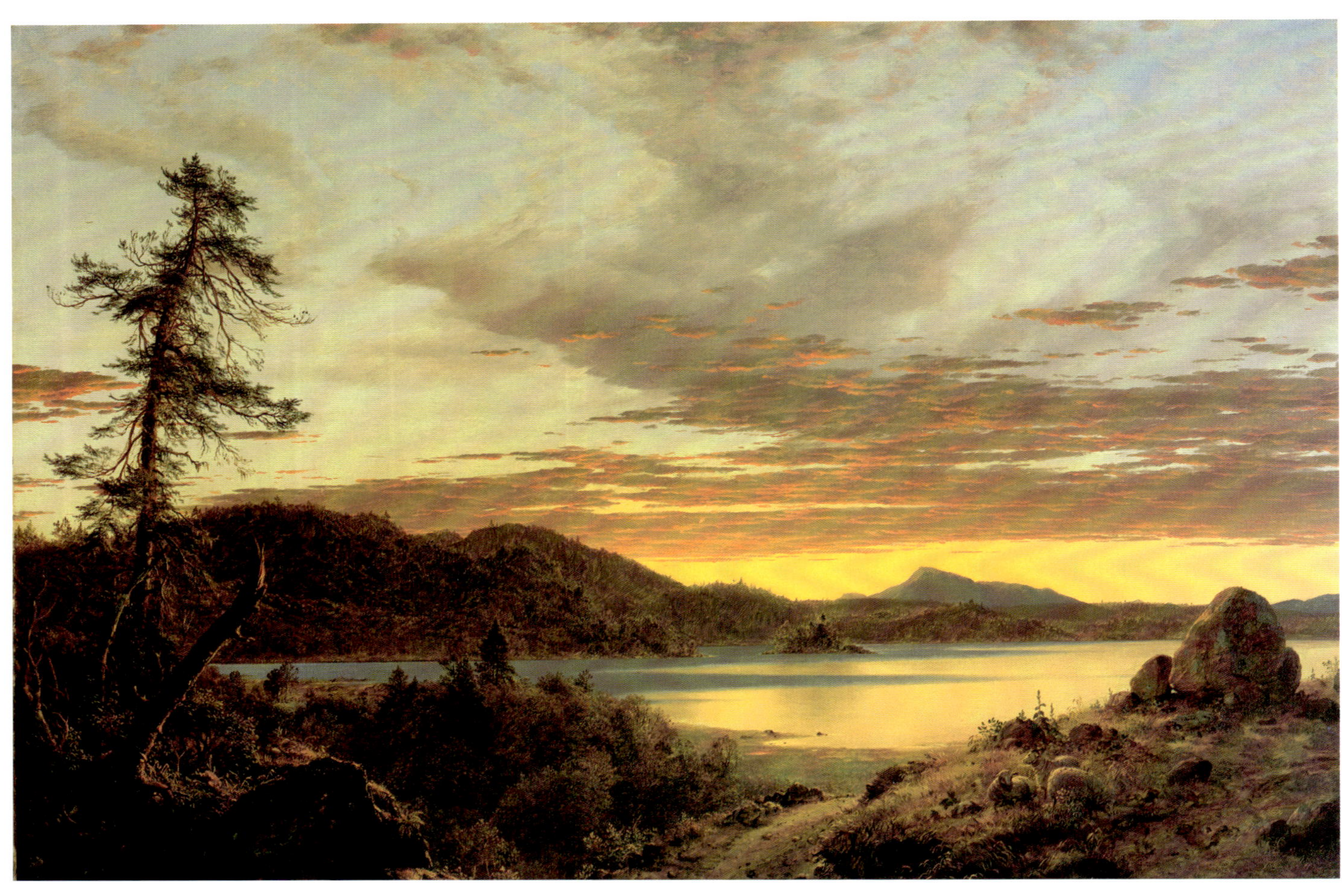

FIG. 48 Frederic E. Church, *Sunset,* 1856, oil on canvas, 24 x 36". Munson-Williams-Proctor
Institute Museum of Art, Utica, New York, Proctor Collection, PC.50. (detail p. 72)

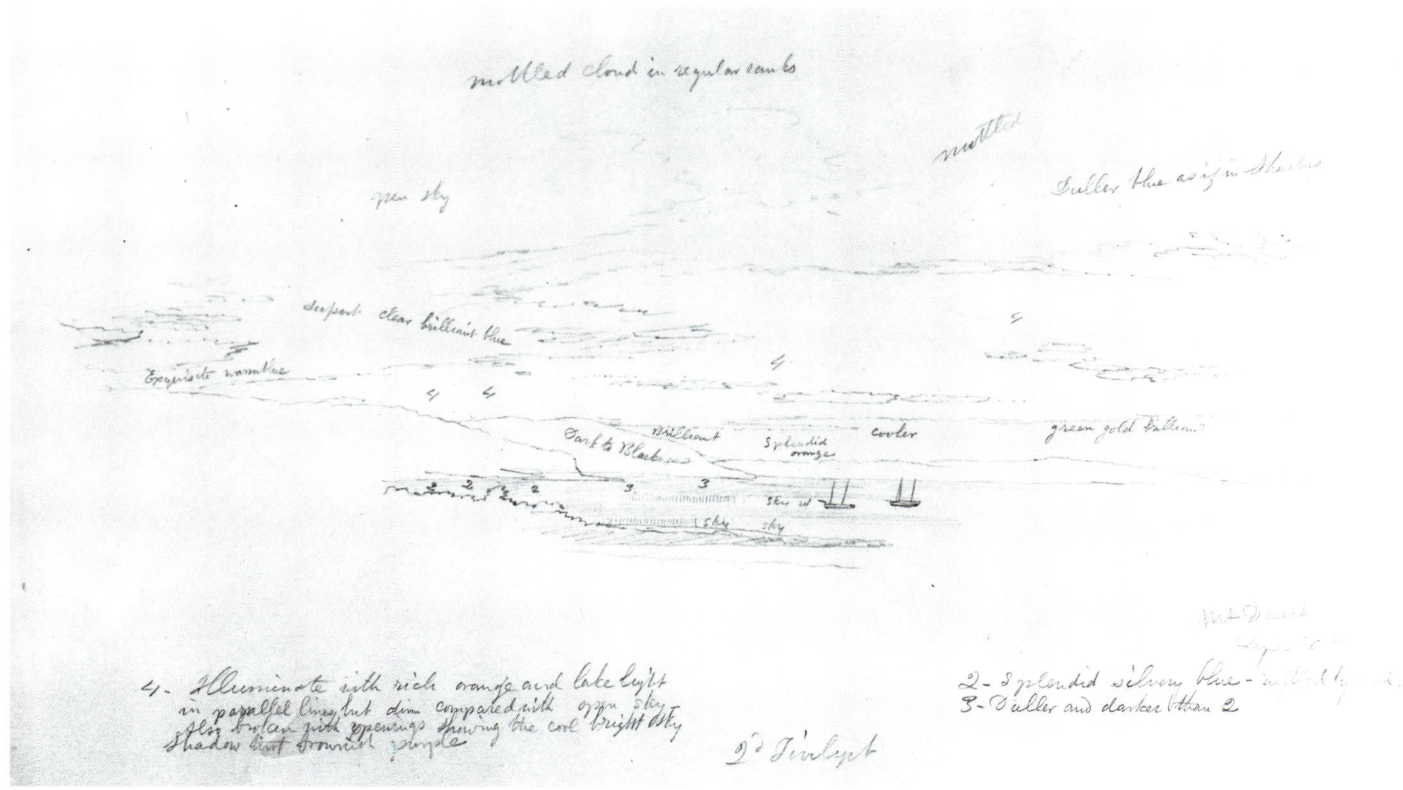

FIG. 49 Frederic E. Church, *Sunset, Bar Harbor,* 1854, graphite on tan paper, 9¹¹⁄₁₆ x 16¹³⁄₁₆". Olana State Historic Site, New York State Office of Parks, Recreation, and Historic Preservation, OL.1980.1448.

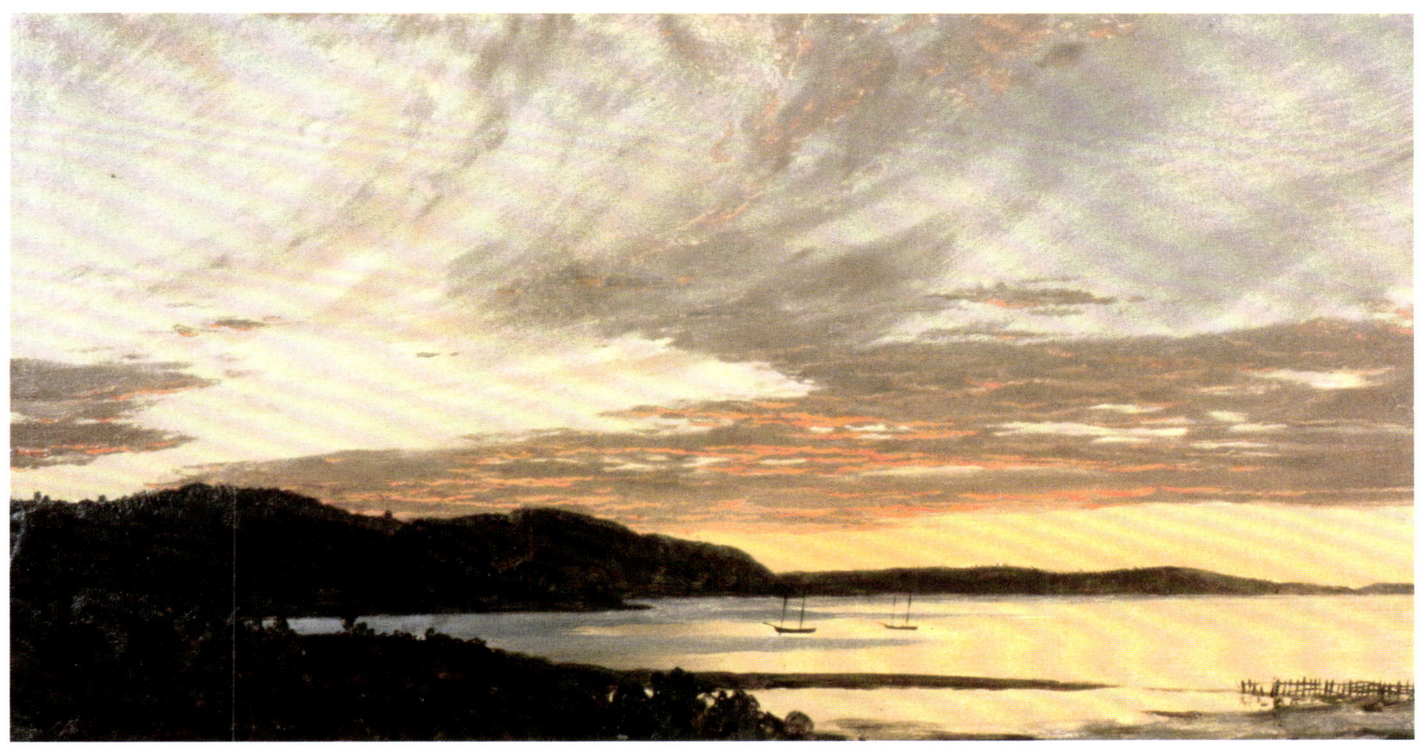

FIG. 50 Frederic E. Church, *Sunset, Bar Harbor,* 1854, oil on canvas mounted on board, 10⅛ x 17¼". Olana State Historic Site, New York State Office of Parks, Recreation, and Historic Preservation, OL.1981.72.

Cabalistic Ciphers

On their return to civilization Church and Winthrop glimpsed the mountain's grand form on the horizon, "one great upright pyramid like this was worth a continent of groveling acres." Katahdin, that sublime personification of power, "watched us well. Sometimes he would show the point of his violet gray peak over the woods." As the party turned homeward a radiant twilight was observed. "Just before sunset, from beneath a belt of clouds evanescing over the summit, an inconceivably tender, brilliant glow of rosy violet mantled downward, filling all the valley." Then, Winthrop's description turned more solemn: "The violet purpled richer and richer, and darkened slowly to solemn blue, that blended with the gloom of the pines and shadowy channeled gorges down the steep [mountain side]." In a passage that Cole would have approved, Winthrop described the celestial chorus and painted a word-picture of the great peak that Church would include in *Sunset*:

> *The peak was still in sunlight, and suddenly, half-way down, a band of roseate clouds, twining and changing like a choir of Bacchantes, soared around the western edge and hung poised above the unilluminated forest at the mountain-base; light as air they came and went and faded away, ghostly, after their work of momentary beauty was done.*

Church "did not fail to pencil rapidly the wondrous scene." When he had finished "his dashing sketch of this glory, so transitory, he peppered the whole with cabalistic cipher, which only he could interpret into beauty." These cabalistic ciphers were the extensive notations on color, value, and light effects on Church's pencil sketch. The sunset experience, said Winthrop, was one of "the transcendent moments of Nature, unseen and disbelieved by the untaught."[16]

Return to Civilization: Women, Children, and Politics

Their return to civilization was marked by Winthrop's observation: "What could society do without women and children?" The men of the small village, "like all American men in the summer before a Presidential election, wanted to talk politics." Late on the eighth day since Church and Winthrop were dropped off in wilderness by the departing steamboat they reached the lumber mill called Oldtown near Bangor and the nearby railhead from New York. Winthrop concluded his narrative with the nostalgic reflection that these were "eight days crowded with novelty and beauty, and fine, vigorous, manly life."[17]

On his return to his studio in New York, Church set about painting an image that would summarize his experiences of Maine. He had already won great success with his *Beacon* and *The Wreck* and other pictures of the region. But now he directed his production of images toward a continental vision of the nation, with its beginning in New England. The two foot by three foot painting on his easel merged memories of his just-completed trip to Katahdin with earlier images of sunsets at Mount Desert. At the picture's core was the memorable Mount Desert sunset that Church had painted in the small and highly finished oil study, *Sunset, Bar Harbor,* now intensified by memories of experiences he had shared with Winthrop.

Sunset, the Picture

Church selected a standard exhibition-size canvas for the image he was conceiving, a size often used for pictures intended for sale to wealthy patrons for private enjoyment in the best-decorated parlors, or private picture galleries. The size meant it was neither a "great picture," painted on a theatrical scale, nor an oil study. The visual drama of *Sunset* would derive from its radically new, and highly masculinized representation of pure northeastern wilderness. Church's eight days beyond the pale of civilization had been a transformative experience. Now, he eliminated the human figure altogether, sharing the rare privilege of witnessing a rapidly disappearing scene of wilderness splendor.

In a conceptual and artistic *coup*, Church transposed the scene of sunset over saltwater from his sketches of *Sunset, Bar Harbor,* into his new, larger image of continental Maine. Minor adjustments were made, such as omitting the sailing vessels and other evidence of maritime activity that were in the study. Otherwise, Church preserved the basic form of the oil sketch virtually intact in the large canvas. The viewer is positioned outside the frame of the picture, as if he is standing on the slight rise with a simple road in the center foreground, behind some large boulders. From that raised position the landscape sinks into gray darkness, appearing to subside as a celestial canopy blazes with luminous light. On the distant horizon, Katahdin's majestic pyramidal form rises, sphinx-like, its summit almost touching the radiant canopy.

Undwarfed by Any Rival

In joining two images and the two separate experiences Church produced a grand new visual metaphor for the nation as resplendent wilderness, "a lovely being in perfect toilet." *Sunset* is the visual recollection of an experience shared by Church and Winthrop in pure, manly wilderness, "the best mountain in the best wild." It was a continental image of North America stretching metaphorically from Mount Desert in the "eastern" foreground to the distant mountain rising its great head on the western horizon. Winthrop and Church experienced just such a glorious sunset during their week together in the open air, although Church relied upon the earlier sunset from Mount Desert to intensify the idea. Winthrop described the scene as a "landscape of vigorous simplicity, easy to comprehend." By twilight the grass slope of the old farm was "ripened" and the "oval lake was blue

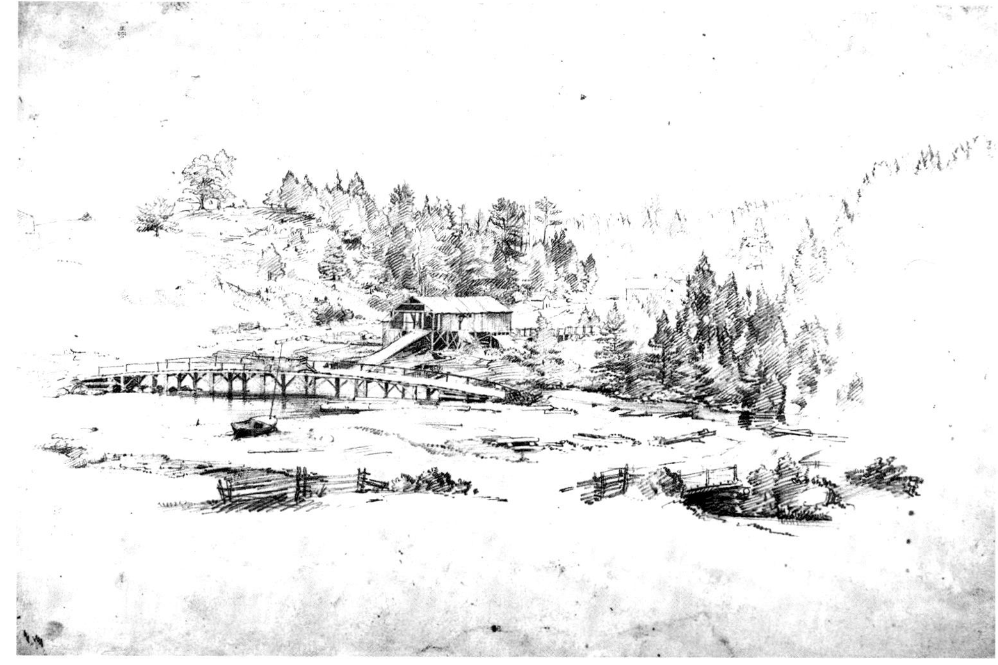

FIG. 51 Frederic E. Church, *Lumber Mill at Mount Desert Island,* 1850, graphite, gouache, and chalk on gray-green paper, 10¼ x 15". Olana State Historic Site, New York State Office of Parks, Recreation, and Historic Preservation, OL.1980.1610.

and calm, shadows of the western hills were growing over it, but flight after flight of illumined clouds soared above, to console the sky and the water for the coming of night." In a long passage that might be a gloss on the "effect" of *Sunset,* Winthrop wrote about the scene the two men shared and that Church painted on his two foot by three foot canvas:

> *Furthermost and topmost, I saw Katahdin twenty miles away, a giant undwarfed by any rival. The remainder of the landscape was only minor and judiciously accessory. The hills were low before it, the lake lowly, and upright above the lake and hill lifted the mountain pyramid. Isolate[d] greatness tells. There were no underling mounts about this mountain-in-chief. And now on its shoulders and crest sunset shone, glowing. Warm violet followed the glow, soothing away the harshness of granite lines. Luminous violet dwelt upon the peak, while below the clinging forest were purple in sheltered gorges, where they could climb nearer the summit, loved of light . . .*
>
> *Meanwhile, as I looked, the quivering violet rose higher and higher, and at last floated away like a disengaged flame. A smoldering blue dwelt upon the peak. Ashy-gray overcame the blue. As dusk thickened and stars trembled into sight, the gray grew luminous.*[18]

Landscape into Earthscape

The late Church scholar David C. Huntington saw *Sunset* as a product of a new openness following Church's trip to Maine and his experiences in South America. It represented an emerging outlook of the United States as a transcontinental nation, despite political fears that the Union itself might be dissolved. In *Sunset,* as Huntington first observed, Church changed landscape into earthscape.[19] Through close attention to the manipulation of foreground details, which he was at liberty to invent according to the aesthetic conventions of the period so long as he maintained the appearance of "truth of nature," Church ingeniously reordered conventional ideas of wilderness. His tree is but a ragged evergreen, perhaps a lowly spruce; it is the only tree standing in the immediate foreground. Silhouetted against the dying light, its branches are devoid of the graceful symmetry of the beautiful, drooping Claudian elm that Church painted in his earlier 1853 painting *Mount Ktaadn* (Yale University). In *Sunset,* the tree is a tough, sinuous specimen whose endurance and tenacious life is answered by the storm-blasted giant, broken off just below it.

Church's predecessor, writer and naturalist Henry David Thoreau, who trekked through the Maine woods three times from 1846 to 1857, had already discovered that the loveliest and most sought after tree in Maine, the great white pine, was virtually extinct. The white pine had towered over other trees in the northern forest, and its fine grain and knot-free wood made it sought after for lumber. A Maine forest after a lumbering campaign, Winthrop declared, is "like France after a *coup d' état*: the *bourgeoisie* are prosperous as ever, but the great men [the white-pines] are gone."[20]

By the early 1850s when Church first visited the Penobscot region in search of Mount Katahdin the white pine had largely been scouted out and selectively cut, leaving lumbermen only the less desirable species of spruce and fir. Church had carefully drawn the buildings of a lumber mill at Mount Desert in 1850, showing his interest in the operations of the tree cutters; his interest in these incursions of industry into wilderness areas was sustained in several other drawings of "mills" (fig. 51). Church's disappointment at not seeing the majestic tree is strongly suggested in Winthrop's chapter "The Pine-Tree," where the pair's disdain for the rapacious practices of Maine lumbermen is clear. "Down goes his Majesty Pinus I., three centuries old, having reigned fifty years high above all his race," Winthrop declared. "A little fellow with a little weapon had dethroned the quiet old king."[21] With the pines gone, lumbermen had turned to the spruce by the mid-1850s. By the end of the 1850s, spruce had replaced white pine as the most heavily cut tree. Knowledge of this lumbering practice helps explain Church's selection of the weathered spruce that stands in the last patch of wilderness in the wilderness. It inhabits the perilous border (for trees) between civilization and wilderness. It is the last of its type—a memento of American natural history, vestige of a virgin wilderness.

Save for the gaze of the viewer, *Sunset* is a landscape absent of man, although his work and animals are plainly evident. Nature is the great actor here, as David C. Huntington often observed. Following the conventions of emblematic personification, the rocks in the right foreground take on a special aura of meaning. Church was by this point in his career a master of subtle inflections of brush stroke, and the inscription of carefully encoded messages in nature was his forte. Observed carefully, the largest rock is positioned in such a way as to expose the side of a great stone head that looks out, directing the spectator's gaze, toward the distant mountain and sunset. Its profile is obscured, but the modulation of paint suggested to viewers with discerning perceptions a great Native American head, perhaps with smaller Indian "children" at its side. These inanimate actors are the lost Indians that Church and Winthrop encountered on their expedition to Katahdin, emblems of true wilderness.

The Manly Intimacy of *Sunset*

The most difficult aspect of interpreting Church's *Sunset* is determining what precisely it was the artist articulated about the national landscape, and about himself, at the deepest levels of visual association and emotion. Each age and each generation sees in works of art what is most meaningful to its own needs and interests. When considered from a post-modernist perspective the strong masculinization that lay behind the production of *Sunset* emerges as a useful perspective. In a key passage Winthrop mused on the artist's and the writer's relationship to nature, to a virgin landscape in perfect repose at sunset. Like Church, Winthrop at times personified the landscape as feminine, and the viewer or narrator as masculine. Winthrop wrote that they spent the day in the deepest wilderness, "all day poetry and music. Mountain airs bent and blunted noonday sunbeams. . . . All was untouched, unvisited wilderness, and we the first discoverers . . . for civilization had been here only to cut [white] pines, not plant houses." But it is "never lonely with Nature," Winthrop declared. Gazing at Church's *Sunset*—with its inviting recession of color into the deep space occupied by the mysterious mountain—does not invoke a feeling of loneliness either. Without "unnatural men or unnatural beasts," Winthrop exclaimed, "she [Nature] is capital society by herself."

And so we found her, —a lovely being in perfect toilet, which I describe in an indiscriminating, masculine way, by saying that it was a forest and river and lakes and a mountain and doubtless sky, all made resplendent by her judicious disposition of a most becoming light. Iglesias and I, being old friends, were received into close intimacy. She smiled upon us unaffectedly, and had a thousand exquisite things to say, drawing us out also, with feminine tact, to say our best things, and teaching us to be conscious, in her presence, of more delicate possibilities of refinement and a tenderer poetic sense. So we voyaged through the sunny hours, and were happy.[22]

Almost half a century ago, Henry Nash Smith, one of the founders of the discipline of American Studies, explored the cultural importance of grand agrarian metaphors including notions of the "virgin land." Since then feminist scholars have expanded and deepened awareness of how gendered notions of nature can be.[23] In a very real, even visually explicit way, Church's *Sunset* took the artist and the handful of his personal friends and patrons who saw it in his studio to the representational border of the virgin land, inviting their gaze upon a place of such beauty that it could only be gendered female. Perceiving such "tenderer" sentiments in a painted reproduction, or even better in an actual wilderness experience, presupposed the existence of a binary, yet highly masculinized viewer. These were real men whose own identity was affirmed by "close intimacy" with the startling detail and brilliant clarity of the representation of the glowing goddess. An earlier generation of art historians might have disregarded such rhetoric. But today, scholars are more sensitive to decoding deep emotional associations, enabling a better understanding of how such complex images functioned in Church's time, with their multiple levels of meaning: local, regional, national, political, and personal.

A New England Picture for 1863

In 1863 Church produced one of his most powerful paintings, *Coast Scene, Mount Desert* (fig. 52), an image of light breaking through sunrise mist over a rocky New England coast. More than a decade spent visiting and sketching the Island inspired the image. The visits were: Church's recent expeditions with the Tracy party, his visits in 1860 and 1862 with his new wife, Isabel, and his memorable journey with Theodore Winthrop. The death of Winthrop during the first year of the Civil War, and the pervasive uncertainty and turmoil of the devastating years of 1861 and 1862, provided cultural and political background for Church's production of what would be his next-to-last exhibition-scale painting of Island scenery. In the image Church represented associations of struggle and triumph with issues of national importance and of personal loss.

The picture was first shown at the National Academy of Design in 1863, where it was already listed as in the collec-

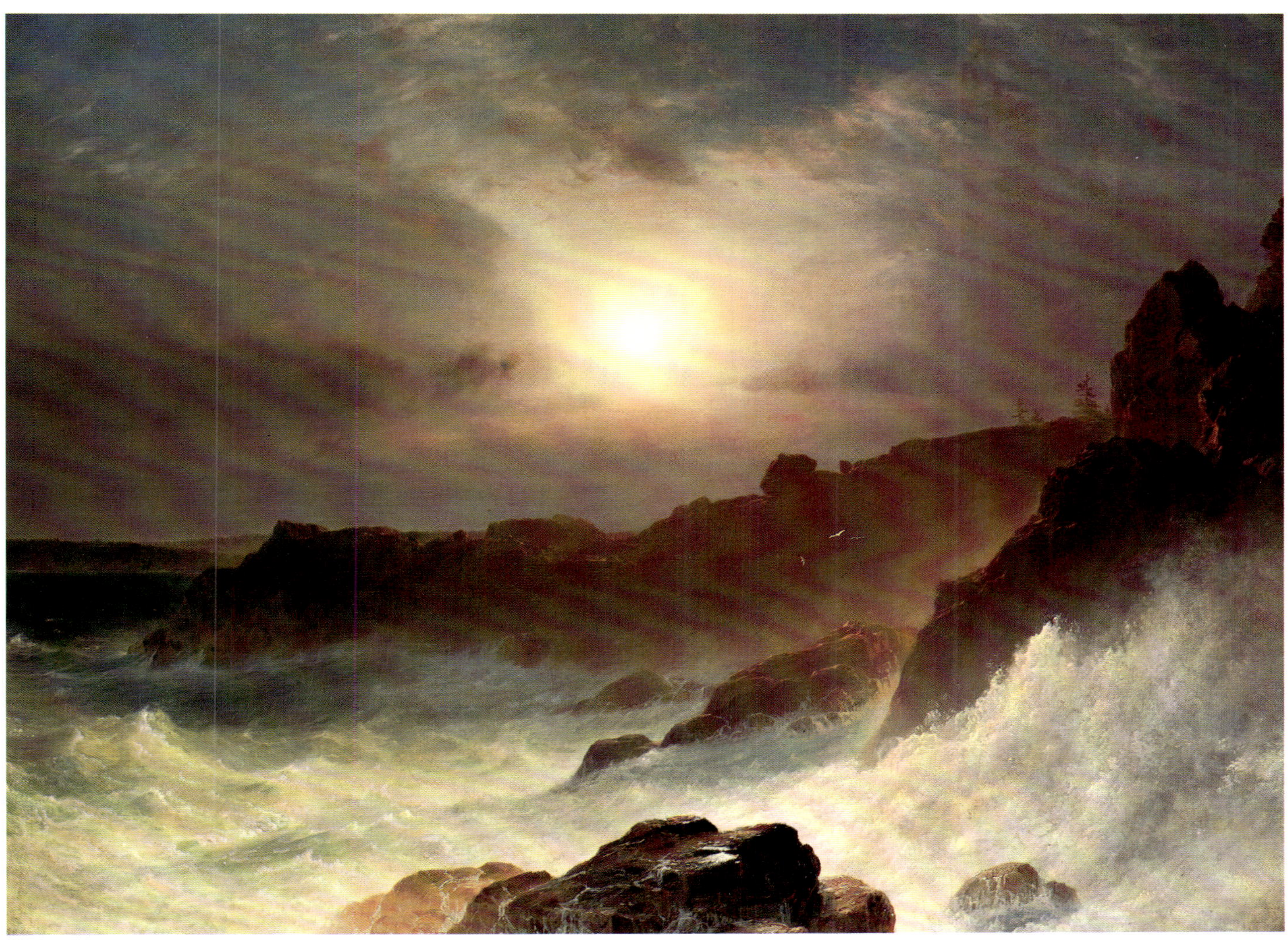

FIG. 52   Frederic E. Church, *Coast Scene, Mount Desert (Sunrise off the Maine Coast)*,
1863, oil on canvas, 36 x 48¼". Wadsworth Atheneum, Hartford, Bequest of
Mrs. Clara Hinton Gould.

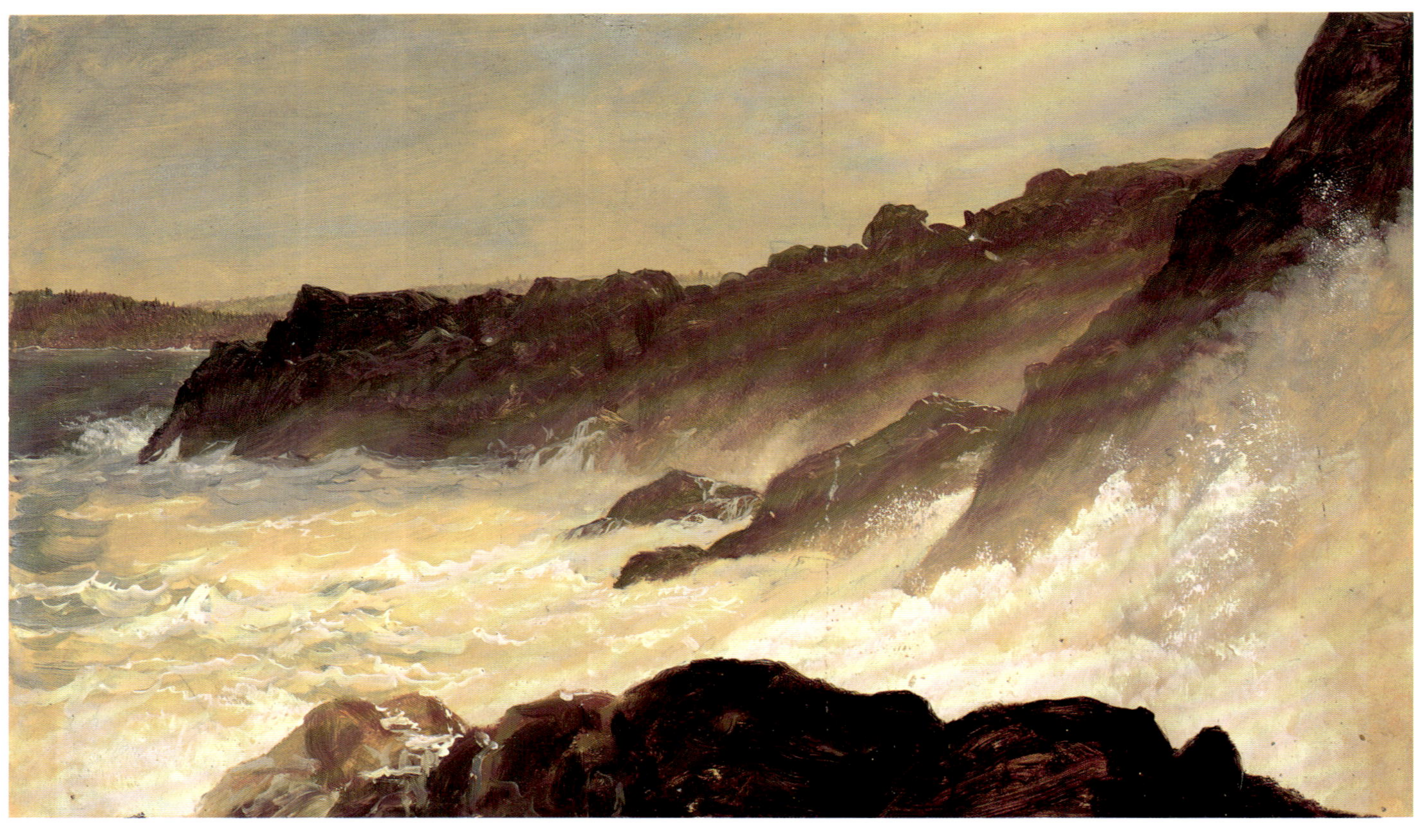

tion of Marshall O. Roberts, one of New York's wealthiest new money entrepreneurs, an elite collector of American landscape paintings, and one of the North's most notorious war profiteers.[24] At the time, Roberts, along with A. T. Stewart, one of the City's leading Republicans and staunch Unionists, was Church's most lavish patron and supporter. The picture was exhibited in 1864 at the Albany Sanitary Fair, a fund raiser for wounded Union soldiers of the Civil War.[25] *The New York Times* noticed the picture on exhibition at the National Academy. The "sun is seen struggling through a vapory sky and vaguely illumining craggy shore. The dashing water looks too much like rock, and the distant cliffs have too much of the unsubstantial quality of water. But the picture is effective, and is most worthy of its distinguished author. It is another offspring of the mist mania."[26] Clearly the painting carried political symbolism, but how precisely was it to be understood?

Sunrise, Maine Coast

Throughout the 1850s Church had repeatedly expressed enthusiasm for seeing great waves crash against Mount Desert's rocky shore. Charles Tracy's diary on 9 August 1855 recorded that "at dinner-table Mr. Church announced his design of going today to Schooner Head, to see the beating of the storm on the rocky shore . . . and the wild precipice there."[27] As early as 1850 Church was excited by "the pleasure of seeing some immense waves" on the Island's eastern

shore, although "the amphibious islanders scarcely looked at them, saying they were nothing." The artist was excited about the "stirring sight, to see the immense rollers come toppling in, changing their forms and gathering in bulk, then dashing into sparkling foam against the base of old 'Schooner Head,' and leaping a hundred feet into the air."[28]

The scene depicted is difficult to locate exactly, and in the details of its foreground the image is certainly a "composition," although it resembles, in places, the east side of Mount Desert, near Schooner Head. Church very closely followed his elongated oil sketch *Surf Pounding Against Rocky Maine Coast* (fig. 53), introducing only slight but important modifications from the study image. He reduced the size of the foreground rock, moved the middleground farther back, increased the vertical proportion and expanded the sky, imbued the rocks at right with expressive presences, and added an early morning sunrise through a mist at the very center of the composition. Another oil sketch completed in 1862, *Sunrise, Coast of Maine* (Olana), was probably painted on Church's short stop that year at Mount Desert, and depicts a sunrise centered over open ocean and rocks at the right foreground, with warm vaporous coloring as is found in *Coast Scene, Mount Desert.*[29]

Fierce, Frolicsome, Reckless, Mad Waves

Church's picture shows great waves crashing against an unyielding rocky shore. At the center foreground a single prominent rock appears to function as a microcosm of the towering crags beyond. Church depicted a similar type of foreground rock in his 1857 picture *Niagara* (fig. 54) that served the same compositional function. Both were small but unmistakable details, painted with a very high degree of finish, and placed prominently in the immediate foreground. Their visual function was to introduce on a small scale comparisons to similar objects glimpsed in the distance which are vast, sublime. Church had noted the wild quality of the Mount Desert waters, the "pulsations of old Ocean," that "cause us no small excitement." He wrote that there was "no such picture of wild, reckless, mad abandonment to its own impulses, as the fierce, frolicsome march of a gigantic wave." And although he "tried painting them, and drawing and taking notes of them, [we] cannot suppress a doubt that we shall neither be able to give actual motion nor roar to any we may place upon canvas."[30] The microcosm of water and rock in the foreground is suggestively repeated many times on the craggy peninsula in the middle distance and the great headland. At the right, passages of rock appear as suggestive profiles, impassive, unmoving, rock heads—silent witnesses to the unceasing tumult of wave and water. Church's primeval wilderness is a New England vision of America much as his ancestors in the Massachusetts Bay Colony and Connecticut might have imagined it. The unmoving rock of New England encounters the futile march of waves, crashing endlessly on the shore. Church had finally, with *Coast Scene,* painted a picture of the march of waves, "with the peculiar yeasty waves and lurid glow incident to a dry autumnal storm in north-ern latitudes. It is one of those November or late October mornings; the sun glows red through a murky sky."[31]

Geological Parables for a War-Weary Nation

Church painted *Coast Scene* during the middle years of the Civil War. As in other pictures completed around this time he made a subtle reference to a nation conflicted upon itself in war. More than that, he transformed the scenery of Mount Desert into a type of geological parable, a proverb drawn from texts of stone.[32] As the sun fights with the mist for supremacy, and the pounding waves attempt to undermine the rocky shore, the observer from the position on the foreground rock witnesses this struggle of opposing forces, the symbolic associations, and ultimately the supremacy of light and redemption.

Church immersed the viewer into the essence of Maine's coastal wilderness. The spectator is thrown into the picture without a firm place to stand except the Rock of Ages, positioned at the very brink of the "mad abandonment" of these waves. Citing an unidentified critic, Tuckerman observed that here "is magnificent force in the sea; we give ourselves up to enthusiasm for it, regarded as pure power; when it dies its final death in mad froth and vapor, tossed quite to the top of the beetling barrier crags on the right foreground, we feel ourselves in an audacious actual presence, whose passion moves us almost like a living fact of surf."[33]

A Fine Recklessness of Color

Church relied upon light as he had done successfully before to express sentiment and the ultimate associations of his pic-

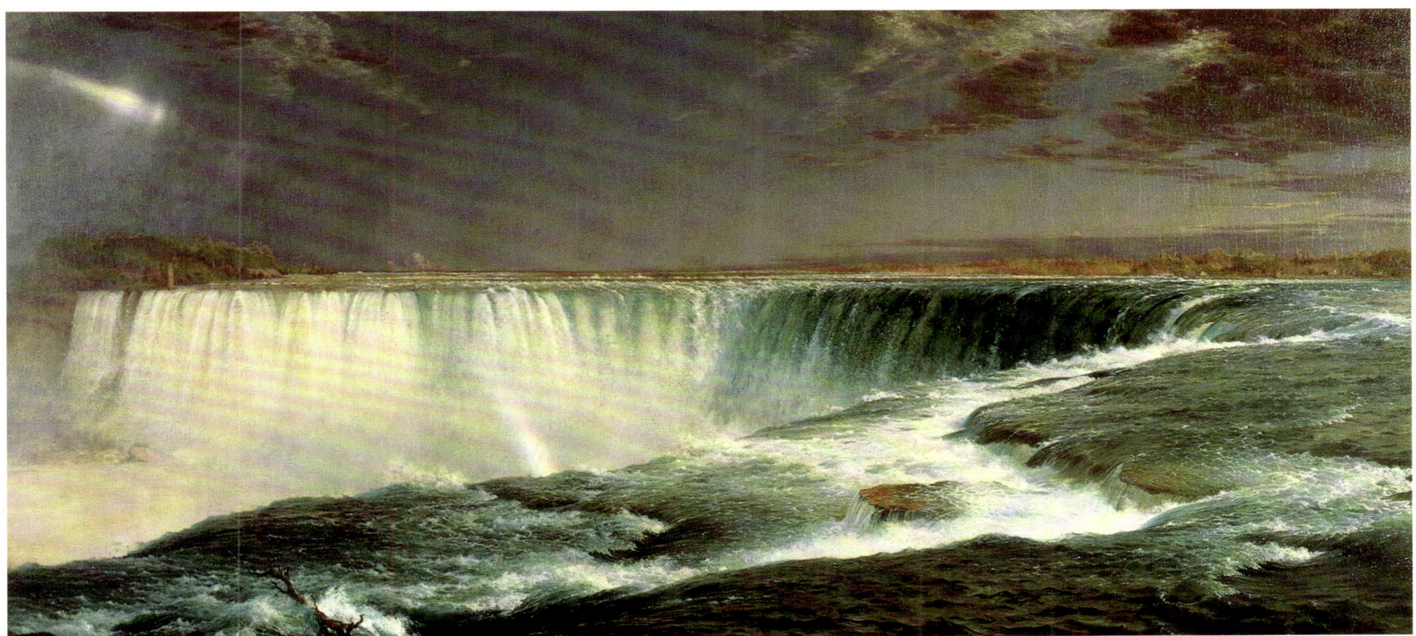

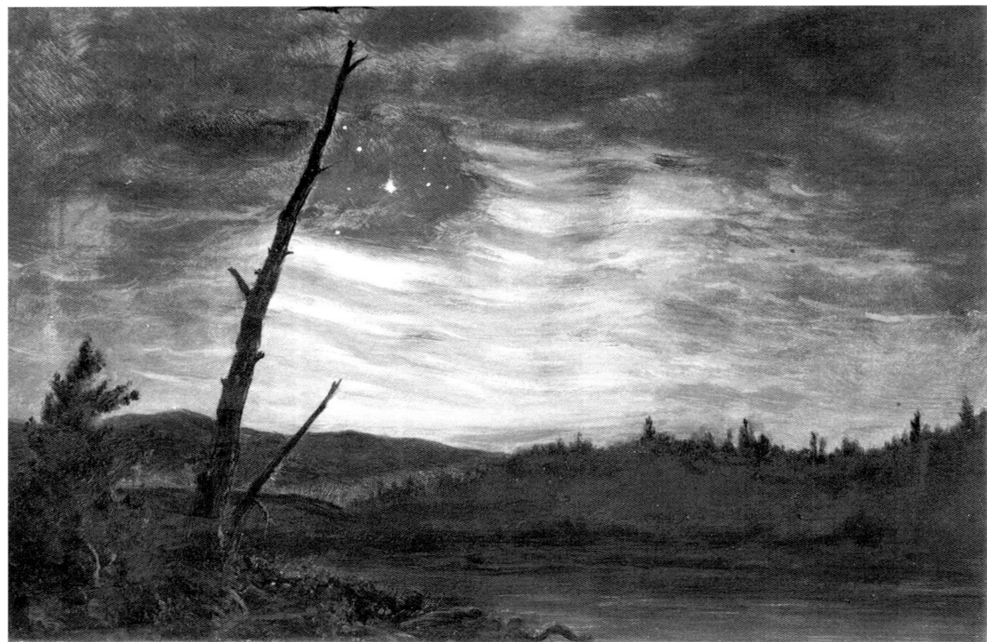

ture. Light's importance for Church was noted by Tuckerman, who praised the picture strongly: "We value the light's effects separately, and the fine recklessness of color by itself, among the best instances of Church's power."[34] Tuckerman introduced his lengthy discussion of *Coast Scene* by noting "among the characteristic works of this artist is a fantastic but genuine sky-study, widely circulated at the outbreak of the Civil War. . . . *Our Banner in the Sky,* whereby an ingenious yet natural sun-emblazoned cloud-study, the folds of our national banner . . . are delineated with effective truth" (fig. 55).[35] Sunset was a moment particularly fraught with associations of "hope" and "promise."[36] Church's representation of light could produce feelings of sublimity, holding the viewer in awe, and as such were widely accepted as expressions of sentiments of divinity and transcendence. The critic for the *Independent* admired the painting, especially the brilliant "white disk" of the sun emerging from behind a "bank of vapory clouds. . . . It fairly made the eyes wink to look at it."[37] By placing the sun at the center of the composition, Church made light a powerful unifying force, and created one of his most impressive cruciforms of light. It was not the first time the artist had reused the luminous cross iconography that Cole had first introduced in his 1845 painting *The Cross in the Wilderness* (Musee Louvre).

A year before he painted *Coast Scene,* Church produced *Cotopaxi* (fig. 56). In that painting he developed a similar imagery for representing through visual metaphor a titanic struggle between light and darkness, between the hopeful disk of the sun burning through a dark cloud of South American smoke and destruction. Recent studies of *Cotopaxi* have demonstrated its complex iconographic program, and its relationship to contemporary social and political discourses and geographical knowledge. Rhetoric similar to that used to discuss *Coast Scene* was also applied to *Cotopaxi's* "forms of strange fantasy . . . behind which the burning disk of the sun appears, new risen, glaring around with a lurid fiery light. . . . It is a scene of strange solemn magnificence . . . in these vapors of various kinds there are magical feasts of the pencil."[38] Tuckerman was emphatic about Church's depiction of light in his South American paintings: "Seldom has a more grand effect of light been depicted than in the magnificent sunshine on the mountain of a tropical clime, from his radiant pencil. It literally floods the canvas with celestial fire, and beams with glory like a sublime psalm of light."[39] In *Cotopaxi,* "the newly-risen sun flares with a lurid fire through its thick volumes."[40]

Although no conclusive documentary evidence can confirm the interpretation, Church scholar David Huntington's reading of *Cotopaxi* insists that it is a work where as he phrased it, "Upon land and water the sun 'god of day' burns a cross: God and Son of God live in Nature."[41] Yet *Cotopaxi's* direful scene of an exploding volcano throwing out "bombs" was the antithesis of the luminous light and rocky repose of *Coast Scene,* painted a year later when the war was finally beginning to turn in favor of the North. Both pictures shared at their core a Civil War iconography that resonated with Church's earlier cruciform symbolism, and provided that most essential of sentiments during war, "hope." *Coast Scene,* like *Cotopaxi,* is filled with the radiant promise of a cross of light, a symbol that would have been understood as "a natural allegory of ultimate restoration of order out of chaos."[42] Huntington observed that a painting such as *Cotopaxi* or *Coast Scene* accomplishes in visual terms what the "Battle Hymn of the Republic" and the Gettysburg Address accomplish in speech. They offered enduring visual metaphors of hope for New Yorkers weary of war. Tuckerman noted approvingly of *Coast Scene,* "there can be no doubt of the transcendent ability wherewith the waves and coast are portrayed."[43]

Twilight: End of an Era

In April 1865, with the Civil War drawing to a close and himself recalling personal tragedy, Church completed what would be his last picture of the Island. He titled it *Twilight: Mount Desert Island, Maine* (fig. 57). A poignantly expressive picture, *Twilight* evokes emotions of deep exhaustion resonating with the psychic wounds of the North and with the devastating loss of Church's two young children. His son and daughter had died of diphtheria less than eight days apart in March of 1865.[44] The artist finished the picture the next month, just before the end of the Civil War on May 26. It was exhibited at the National Academy in 1865 under the title *Twilight* where it garnered mixed reviews, many critics failing to understand its complex symbolism, and finding it merely a weak picture.[45]

Church stated in a 7 July 1864 letter to his friend and patron, railroad entrepreneur William H. Osborn, that "I have commenced a picture, four feet long, which includes a fine twilight effect which I made a sketch of from nature some weeks ago."[46] In the letter the artist seems to express a hesitancy about the work and a pressing need for funds: "I intend the picture for England according to your kindly expressed desire. I hope to make a good thing of it—certainly I shall try. . . . It would be of great service to me if I could [sic] a fair price for it. For my expenses are greatly increased and my engagements for the next season are of the green-back-ache kind."[47] Church composed a view across Frenchman Bay from just south of Bear Brook at the northern spur of Champlain Mountain. Egg Rock is barely discerned as Church emphasized the darkening foreground and melancholy sky. In the distance "a stretch of land forms the opposite shore of the bay, and terminates in a bold, rocky mass just where the bay opens into the sea."[48] These are elevations on Schoodic Peninsula. Church exaggerated Schoodic Head, or perhaps substituted the form of Schoodic Mountain, which is several miles north on the mainland.

A Want of Harmony

The mood of malaise was immediately noticed when the picture was exhibited at the National Academy of Design. An unidentified reviewer for *The Albion* stated:

> *Mr. Church has become so great a man that one wonders, perhaps unreasonably, that every work from his easel is not a masterpiece. Certainly, his Twilight, no. 310, cannot be so called. It is a landscape made up of broken foreground, a lake, and distant hills, over which a thunderstorm impends. The hues of the setting sun are nearly absorbed by the lurid clouds, save in the upper sky, where cloudlets of orange—that ought to float, but don't—are brilliantly tinted. These latter tints, to our eye, are so laid in, that they resemble chalk more than oil-color, and thereby produce a want of harmony throughout.*[49]

A reviewer for *The New York Evening Post* was no less critical. Church's *Twilight* was "dull and false in the color of the landscape, with cloud forms delicately and truly drawn, [although] a passage of color and effect just above the horizon that is admirable and true." The picture was not a "masterpiece," but at least it was not "common and vulgar."[50]

In contrast to *Sunset* or *Twilight in the Wilderness,* with their sharply defined clouds and brilliant sky, Church's 1865 *Twilight* has a diffuse sky that appears vague and undefined, wanting harmony, although there was repose after a storm. The powerful optimism of the earlier pictures, particularly *Coast Scene, Mount Desert,* completed just two years earlier, gives way to the solemn reddish-green sky. In the foreground a large flat rock is highlighted in the cheerless glow, like

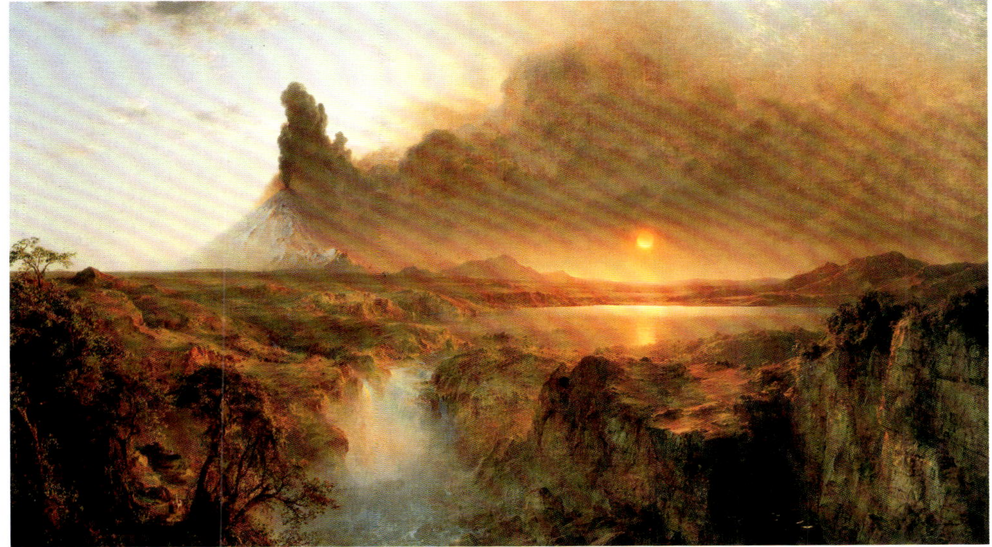

FIG. 56 Frederic E. Church, *Cotopaxi*, 1862, oil on canvas, 48 x 85". The Detroit Institute of Arts, Founders Society Purchase, Robert H. Tannahill Foundation Fund, Gibbs-Williams Fund, Dexter M. Ferry Jr. Fund, Merrill Fund, Beatrice W. Rogers Fund, and Richard A. Manoogian.

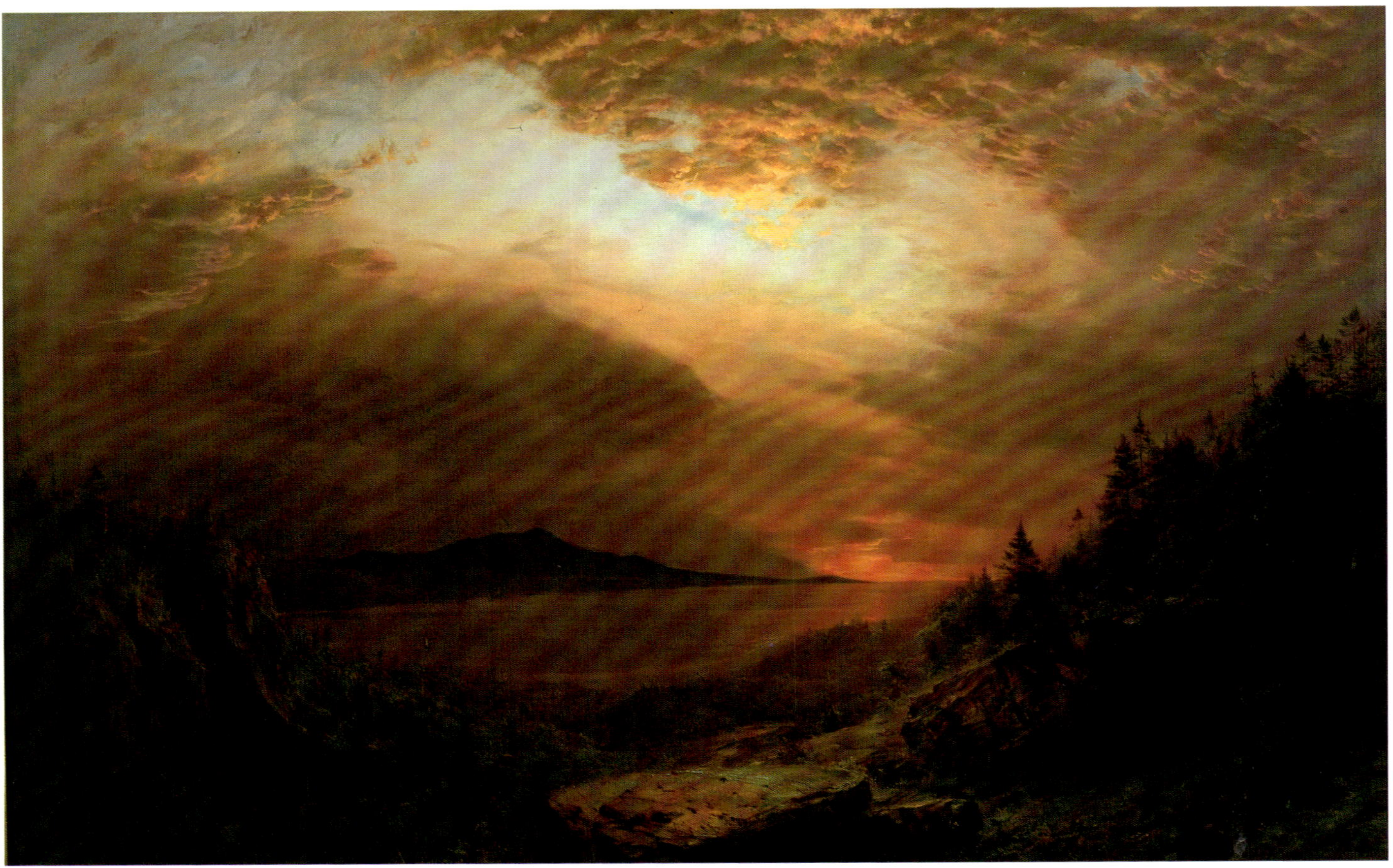

FIG. 57   Frederic E. Church, *Twilight: Mount Desert Island, Maine*, 1865, oil on canvas, 31¼ x 48½".
Washington University Gallery of Art, St. Louis, Gift of Charles Parsons, 1905.

some ancient sacrificial altar. At the right, a small deer comes down to drink. Martin's Island guide book mentioned "there are deer, as one might suppose, in these large forests, protected as they have been from the ravages of the wolves by their separation from the mainland."[51] A pencil and ink drawing, *Studies of Deer*, dated 1865 (Olana), is clearly related to the painting's production, showing a deer in the same position as the animal approaching the stream in the right foreground.[52] It is a figure that recalls the drinking deer in Thomas Cole's *Desolation*, the last picture in the series *The Course of Empire*. In that series, the drinking deer symbolizes the renewal of life after the devastation of war and civil strife. In light of Church's admiration for Cole's work, in particular *Desolation*, it is evident that the deer performs a similar symbolic function in *Twilight*. In the distance a small white sail on the water of the bay suggests another of Cole's series, *The Voyage of Life*, with its controlling metaphor. The image of a vessel, distant, small, perhaps nearing the end of its voyage after a storm, carried associations with ideas of the end of life's voyage, an idea that was very much on Church's mind after the death of his children, and much in the mind of a nation mourning its war dead. To the right, large rocky pinnacles repeat in vague, disturbing forms the personification of nature, playing out their role as actors in the vitalistic life of nature.

In little more than two decades, painted and printed images by Church, Cole, and Doughty represented Mount Desert to the nation as a desirable place to visit. Other artists soon followed their lead, and by the 1870s the Island was a popular destination for other artists from New York. With contributions to the cultural work of Cole and Church, following the Civil War, Mount Desert rapidly emerged as a popular summer destination for well-to-do tourists and summer visitors from Boston, New York, and Philadelphia. The artists' role in this impressive cultural and economic transformation was formally recognized as early as 1872. Cole was named "the pioneer" at Mount Desert, but it was through Church's pictures "seen in the exhibitions of the National Academy . . . that Mount Desert has become so popular as a watering-place."[53]

NOTES

1. Franklin Kelly, *Frederic Edwin Church and the National Landscape* (Washington, D.C.: Smithsonian Institution Press, 1988), 88–94; see also Gerald L. Carr, *Frederic E. Church Catalogue Raisonné of Works of Art at Olana State Historic Site* (New York: Cambridge University Press, 1994), 217, no. 2. The picture was listed in the exhibition catalogue as owned by Church. *The New York Evening Post,* 25 March 1879.

2. Carr, *Frederic Edwin Church Catalogue Raisonné*, 215–6, no. 351; see also no. 350.

3. Thomas Cole, "The Lament of the Forest," in *Thomas Cole's Poetry*, Marshall B. Tymn, ed. (York, Penn.: Liberty Cap Books, 1972), 108. Church could have read the poem in the *The Knickerbocker* (May 1841): 516–9.

4. Carr, 216–7, no. 252.

5. Ibid., 87.

6. Cole, "On a Sunset Sky," October 4, 1843, in *Thomas Cole's Poetry*, 141.

7. See Kelly, *Frederic Edwin Church and the National Landscape*, passim.

8. W. Splbester, "Sunsets," *The Crayon* 2, no. 8 (26 September 1855): 191–2.

9. Theodore Winthrop, *Life in the Open Air, and Other Papers* (Boston: Ticknor and Fields, 1863), 50.

10. Winthrop, *Life in the Open Air,* 10. Winthrop never refers to Church by name, coining the nickname "Iglesias," a reference to the Spanish term "Iglesia" (church), made to sound like a Latin name by adding a final "s."

11. Winthrop, 66, 59, 50–51.

12. Winthrop, 59, 62, 62, 62, respectively as quoted.

13. J. Gray Sweeney, "The Nude of Landscape Painting: Emblematic Personification in the Art of the Hudson River School," *Smithsonian Studies in American Art* (Fall 1989): 42–65.

14. Winthrop, 88.

15. Winthrop, 99, 99, 53, 102, 102, 103, 104, respectively as quoted.

16. Winthrop, 107, 107, 108, 108, 108, respectively as quoted.

17. Winthrop, 115, 115, 119.

18. Winthrop, 76, 76–77.

19. David C. Huntington, *The Landscapes of Frederic Edwin Church: Vision of an American Era* (New York: George Braziller, 1966), 76.

20. Winthrop, 20–21. See Geoffrey Paul Carpenter, "Deforestation in Nineteenth-Century Maine: The Record of Henry David Thoreau," *Maine History* 38, no. 1 (Summer 1998): 2–35.

21. Winthrop, 22.

22. Winthrop, 84, 85.

23. For images and metaphors of nature as female see: Annette Kolodny, *The Lay of the Land: Metaphor as Experience and History in American Life and Letters* (Chapel Hill: Univ. of North Carolina Press, 1975); idem, *The Land Before Her: Fantasy and Experience of the American Frontier, 1630–1860* (Chapel Hill: Univ. of North Carolina Press, 1984); Sam Gill, *Mother Earth* (Chicago: Univ. of Chicago Press, 1987); Carolyn Merchant, *Ecological Revolutions: Nature, Gender, and Science in New England* (Chapel Hill: Univ. of North Carolina Press, 1989); idem, *The Death of Nature: Women, Ecology, and the Scientific Revolution* (San Francisco: Harper and Row, 1981); Robert Mugerauer, "Hermeneutic Retrieval: American Nature as Paradise," in *Interpreting Environments: Tradition, Deconstruction, Hermeneutics* (Austin: Univ. of Texas Press, 1996), 57–116.

24. Maria Naylor, *The National Academy of Design Exhibition Record, 1861–1900* (New York: Kennedy Galleries, 1973), 160. The picture was purchased by Marshall O. Roberts, who also owned Church's 1853 *Mount Ktaadn* (Yale University Art Gallery). Roberts's wealth was acquired through his investments in the railroad and steamship lines—the Erie and Lackawanna Railroad and his own steamship company. He had capitalized on America's vision of Manifest Destiny by seeing the commercial possibilities of undeveloped areas. Lillian B. Miller, *Patrons and Patriotism: The Encouragement of the Fine Arts in the United States 1790–1860* (Chicago: University of Chicago Press, 1966), 157–8; Eric Foner, *Politics and Ideology in the Age of the Civil War* (New York: Oxford University Press, 1980).

25. Franklin Kelly, Stephen Jay Gould, James Anthony Ryan, and Debora Rindge, *Frederic Edwin Church* (Washington, D.C.: National Gallery of Art and Smithsonian Institution Press, 1989), 165. The association of the Union cause may have been hinted at during the exhibition of the painting.

26. "The National Academy of Design," *The New York Times*, 24 June 1863.

27. Charles Tracy, "Log of a Voyage from New York to Mount Desert and Return, July–September 1855," 69, 73.

28. Frederic E. Church, "Mountain Views and Coast Scenery, by a Landscape Painter," *Bulletin of the American Art-Union* (November 1850): 131.

29. See Carr, *Frederic Edwin Church Catalogue Raisonné*, 284, no. 414.

30. Church, "Mountain Views and Coast Scenery," 131.

31. Henry T. Tuckerman, *Book of the Artists: American Artist Life Comprising Biographical and Critical Sketches of American Artists, First Published 1867* (reprint, New York: James F. Carr, 1967), 372.

32. David C. Huntington, "Church and Luminism: Light for America's Elect," in John Wilmerding, *American Light: The Luminist Movement 1850–1875* (Princeton: Princeton University Press, 1989), 180.

33. Tuckerman, 372.

34. Ibid.

35. Ibid.

36. David C. Huntington, "Frederic Edwin Church, 1926–1900: Painter of the Adamic New World Myth" (Ph.D. diss., Yale University, 1960), 318.

37. *The Independent* 15 (18 June 1863): 6.

38. "Mr. Church's Pictures," *The Art Journal* (December 1865): 688.

39. Tuckerman, 378.

40. Tuckerman, 379.

41. Huntington, *The Landscapes of Frederic Edwin Church,* 16.

42. Katherine Manthorne, *Creation and Renewal: Views of Cotopaxi by Frederic Edwin Church* (Washington, D.C.: Smithsonian Institution Press, 1985), 50.

43. Tuckerman, 372.

44. The best source for details on these events is Carr, *Frederic Edwin Church Catalogue Raisonné,* 283–9, no. 423, 414.

45. Naylor, *The National Academy of Design*, 160; Franklin Kelly, *Frederic Edwin Church and the National Landscape*, 162.

46. Frederic E. Church to William H. Osborn, 7 July 1864, Church Papers, Olana State Historic Site, Hudson, New York.

47. Ibid.

48. William M. Bryant, "Review of The Loan Exhibition at Crow Museum," *The Western* (1881): 418.

49. "Fine Arts: The National Academy of Design: Fourth Notice," *The Albion (*3 June 1865): 261.

50. "National Academy of Design," *The New York Evening Post*, 31 May 1865.

51. Clara Barnes Martin, *Mount Desert on the Coast of Maine: "Infinite Riches in a Little Room"* (Privately Printed, 1867; 4th ed., Portland, Maine: Loring, Short and Harmon, 1877), 22.

52. Carr, *Frederic Edwin Church,* 289, no. 422. Carr notes that the deer were drawn near the end of Church's work on *Twilight*, some "probably from animals observed on the grounds of his farm."

53. "Mount Desert," *Harper's New Monthly Magazine*, 324.

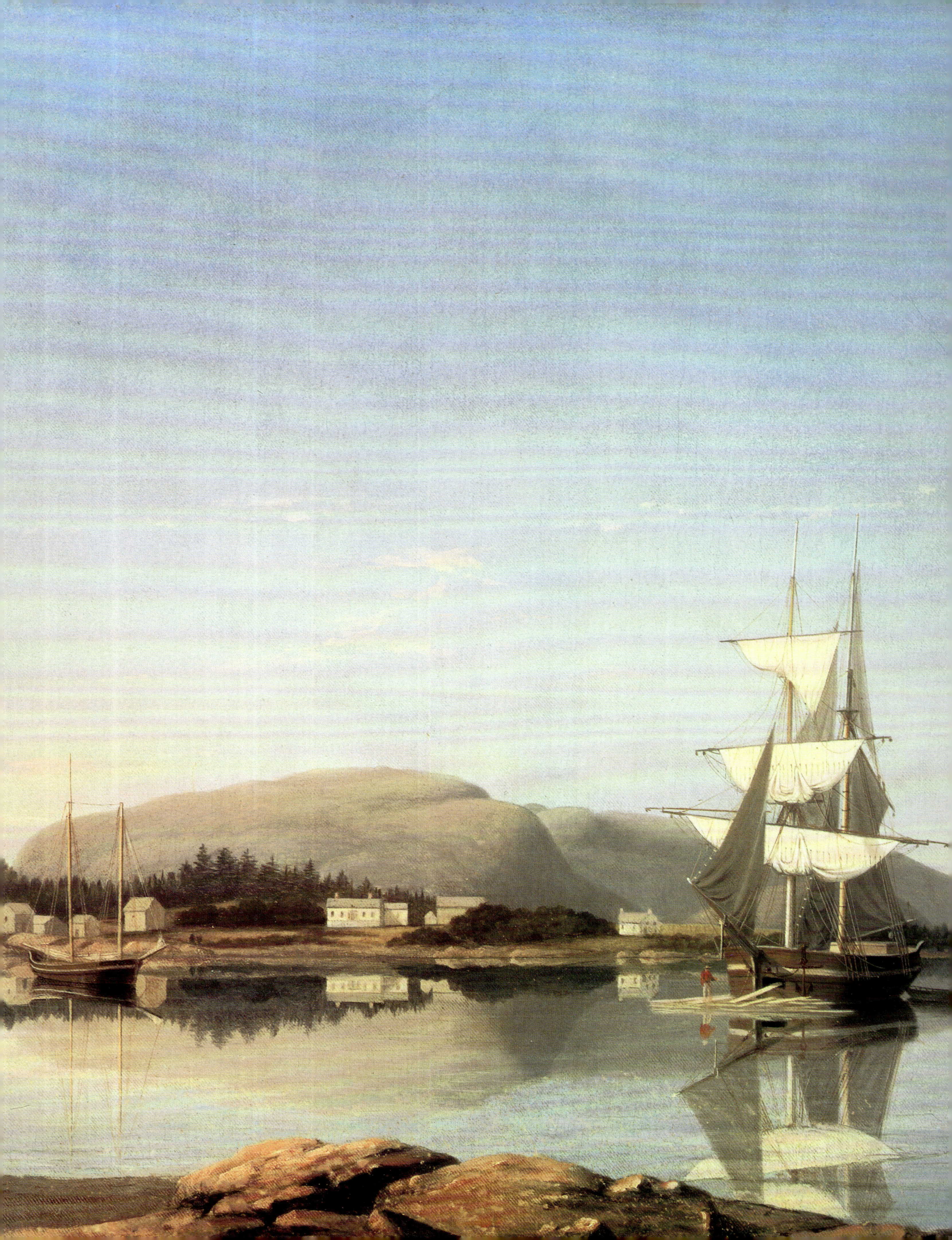

CHAPTER 5

So Grand and Beautiful

The discovery of Mount Desert's coastal and mountain scenery by Doughty and Cole, followed by Church's critically acclaimed paintings of the 1850s, stimulated Island interest amongst East Coast artists. Gloucester artist Fitz Hugh Lane traveled to the Island as an early yachtsman to record its picturesque maritime activity during the same decade. He was followed by William Stanley Haseltine (1835–1900), Sanford Robinson Gifford (1823–1880), and Jervis McEntee (1828–1891) who painted panoramic views of sea and mountains during the Civil War. They were attracted to Mount Desert because they hoped to sell paintings of Island scenery in the art market (see Appendix). By the 1870s, many other artists visited Mount Desert to paint, and as they did the Island also emerged as a major summer resort area for wealthy cultural elites.

Fitz Hugh Lane: Cruising Artist

The summer of 1850 marked the first trip to Mount Desert for Fitz Hugh Lane (1804–1865). At mid-century Lane was comparatively little-known, although he is regarded today as a central figure in American landscape painting. He exhibited in Boston and Gloucester, and only occasionally in New York at the American Art-Union. Since he worked in relative isolation in Gloucester, Lane was only distantly influenced by Cole and developments in landscape painting by artists of the Studios Building on Tenth Street. In contrast to Cole, Church, Gifford, or McEntee, and many others, Lane's pictures received little contemporary comment in the press. However, Lane did have important patrons who were well connected in the New York art market; because of this, and his visits to Mount Desert, he recast his art in response to his experiences in Maine and the art market conditions that emerged during the 1850s.

An artist of Cole's generation, Lane was forty-four when he first visited Maine. He was descended from a family of mariners—his father was a sail maker—and while growing up in Gloucester, Massachusetts, he observed maritime life and the intricacies of the fishing industry. Like Cole, Lane was an artistic autodidact who began his career producing prints. Perhaps because of childhood illness Lane walked with a crutch, and was most comfortable traveling in and painting on boats. Lane often sketched scenes while at anchor or while cruising offshore. Lane's early paintings combined his interests in commerce, trade, and history, with a seascape vision bathed in calm, clear light. Unlike Cole, however, he was not "discovered" until the mid-twentieth century when he was included in a group of artists termed "luminists."

Mr. Lane's Genius

The longest notice Lane received in Boston newspapers was his 1865 obituary in *The Daily Evening Transcript*. It considered his death "a national loss as [far] as art is concerned." His paintings were praised for their *"perfect accuracy* in all the details of marine architecture and thought and true natural position on the canvas and complete equipment of vessels." It was Lane's faithfulness in the delineation of vessels that "procured him orders [for paintings] from the largest ship owners of New York and Boston, who did not consider their country rooms (and even their parlors sometimes) furnished, without one of Lane's paintings of some favorite clipper."[1]

Lane scholars argue that the experience of Maine transformed the artist's mature work.[2] Around 1855, in his most significant works resulting from these visits, the ostensible subjects of the artist's canvases, ships and mariners at work or at rest, were increasingly subordinated to dramatic, light-filled landscapes. These changes in personal style may be explained by an increasing interest in the work of New York artists during the early 1850s, especially the paintings of Church that dominated the New York art market. The writer of Lane's obituary noticed his growing interest in landscape:

In 1848 Lane accepted an invitation from his friend and
patron, the yachtsman Joseph L. Stevens, Jr., to join him in
a sail to Castine, Stevens's parents' home. Although they did
not visit Mount Desert on that trip, their cruise along the
mountainous coastline, and Castine's proximity to the Island,
stimulated their interest in future visits. Visual material of
great maritime interest could be found around the Island,
with its extensive lumbering and fishing industry, and its
shipping fleets. Stevens often cruised with friends and rela-
tives, exploring scenic spots along the New England coast in
late summer. Lane joined him on these cruises in 1850, 1851,
1852, 1855, and 1863.[4]

Active in art and literary organizations and deeply interested in historical study, Stevens served as secretary of the
American Art-Union in New York and the Western Art-
Union. Lane, evidently influenced by Stevens, became the
unofficial town historian in paint on canvas, and began to
record local buildings and sea vessels at Gloucester.[5] A letter
from Stevens to a Mr. Mansfield reveals Stevens's relationship to Lane and his years spent in dedicated support of the
artist's interests. He wrote, "I was with him on several trips
to the Maine coast where he did much sketching, and sometimes was [sic] his chooser of spots and bearer of materials
when he sketched in the home neighborhood . . . for his physical infirmity prevented his becoming an outdoor colorist."[6]
He also avidly promoted Lane's work, and may have urged
the artist to exhibit two paintings that resulted from their
trip together at the American Art-Union the next year. Neither received critical review, although as recent scholarship
has noted, *Twilight on the Kennebec* (Private Collection), with
its dramatic Church-like sunset, demonstrated a more
intense vision of a traditional maritime wilderness soon to
pass into history with the arrival of the steamboat.[7]

"So Grand and Beautiful"

In 1850, Lane and Stevens learned by hearsay of the
"remarkable and picturesque range of mountains, fine harbors, and beautiful sound, that even abating liberally for
enthusiastic exaggeration, we were certain of being amply
repaid for a sail of fifty miles each way." They were excited
to see this "supposed barren and desolate place" that paradoxically could "boast of scenery so grand and beautiful as
to be unsurpassed by any on the whole American coast."[8]
Lane's group was aware that other artists were present on
the Island. In fact, "Champney and Kensett were then in
another part of the island and we have reason to believe that
Church and some others were in the immediate vicinity."[9]
There is no evidence that Lane and Church met, but the coin-
cidence of their arrival at the same moment suggests how
fields of cultural production stimulated artists in two entirely
different contexts (Church from New York, Lane from
Gloucester) to travel to Mount Desert, representing the mountainous, coastal, and maritime scenery for urban audiences.

After arriving by sea in 1850, Stevens described the
Island's impressive scenery, in the series of articles he wrote
for the *Gloucester Daily Telegraph,* as "a grand sight
approaching Mount Desert from the westward, to behold the
mountains gradually open upon the view." As they neared,
the view of the mountains transformed, "assuming an infinite diversity of shapes, and it sometimes requires no great
stretch of imagination to fancy them huge mammoth and
mastodon wading out from the main."[10] Entering Eastern
Way "toward the close of as lovely an afternoon as summer
can bestow," they began their sail to Somesville at the head
of Somes Sound and were introduced to views that "exceeded
all expectations." He added that "just as the sun was setting
we encamped opposite the settlement, at the entrance of the
miniature bay, on an island well wooded and covered with a
profusion of berries."[11] Lane shared Stevens's enthusiasm for
the scenery and translated it into one of his earliest pictures
of Mount Desert, completed in 1850: *Bar Island and Mount
Desert Mountains from the Bay in Front of Somes Settlement*
(Erving and Joyce Wolf Collection).

Entrance of Somes Sound from Southwest Harbor

In 1852 Lane visited the Island for a third time, and that
year produced one of his most complex early paintings of
Mount Desert, *Entrance of Somes Sound from Southwest
Harbor* (fig. 58), a light-filled view of the harbor and surrounding mountains. A drawing by Lane, *Duck Harbor*,
recorded the party aboard the sloop *Superior*—"F. H. Lane,
artist / W. H. Tilden, J. L. Stevens, jr., G. F. Tilden, S. Adams, jr.
Companions / Sloop Superior, Getchel, Pilot from Castine."[12]
Stevens's guests aboard were again cruising to Mount Desert,
where they could engage in local maritime lore and enjoy the
mountainous scenery from the perspective of the water. Lane
recorded the appearance of Southwest Harbor, its residents
and their work, and the particular types of ships that pas-
saged from the port. Stevens's sensitivity to Lane's desire to
find scenery for sketching often dictated the location at which
he anchored his yacht. One such stop was made with a
"beautiful prospect to wonder at and admire, now wafted

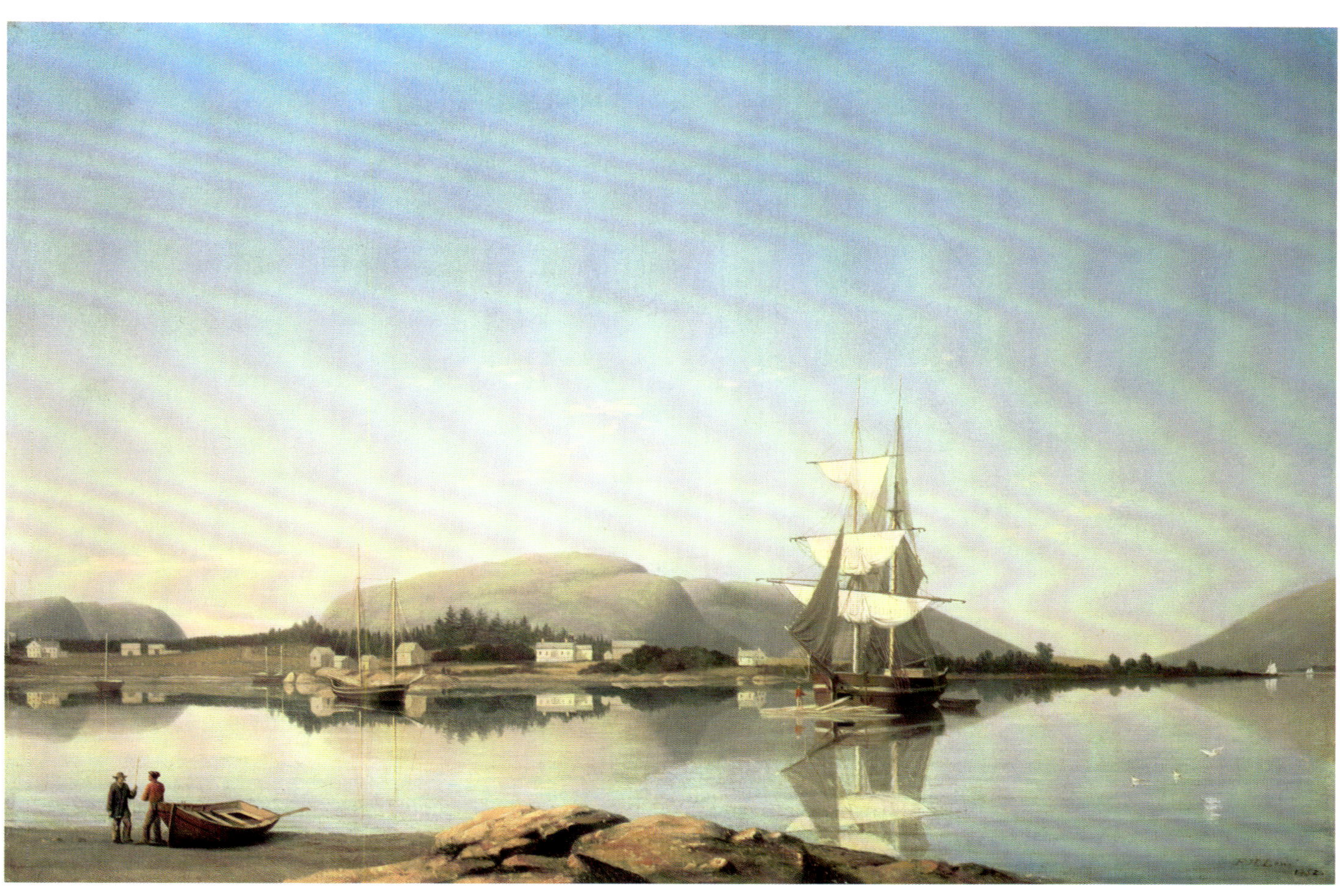

FIG. 58   Fitz Hugh Lane, *Entrance of Somes Sound from Southwest Harbor,* 1852,
oil on canvas, 23¾ x 35¾". Anonymous loan. (detail p.88)

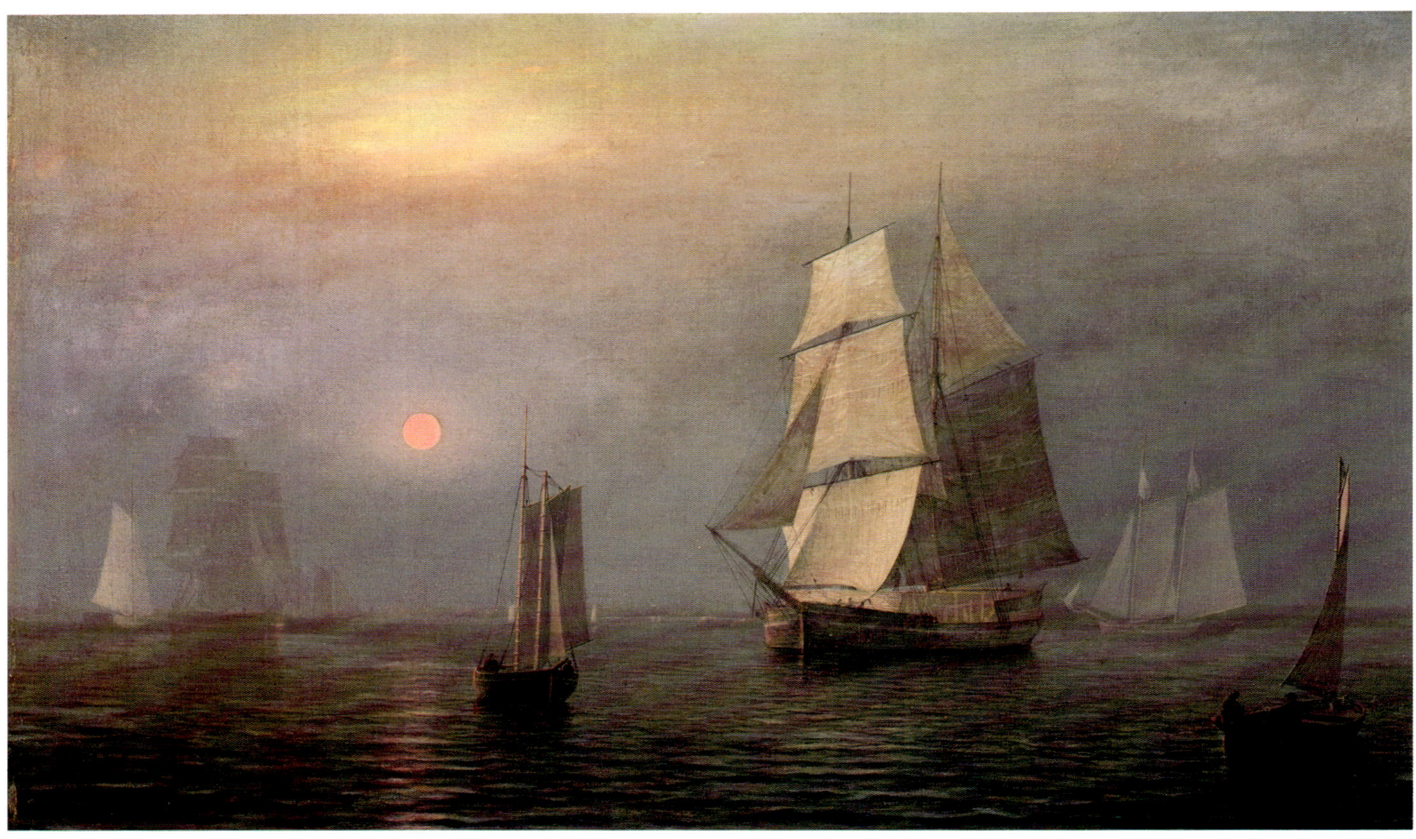

FIG. 59   Fitz Hugh Lane, *Shipping in Down East Waters,* 1854, oil on canvas, 17¾ x 29¾".
The Farnsworth Art Museum, Museum Purchase, 1960.

along by light winds, then entirely becalmed for a time, we were slowly carried into Southwest Harbor."[13] They did not land at Southwest Harbor but anchored west of it, giving Lane a view of the harbor and Somes Sound on the right and the mountains in the background.[14]

Back in his Gloucester studio he completed a virtually topographical view, depicting the buildings and vessels of the harbor scene. The finished painting was based on two deck sketches, *West Harbor* & *Entrance of Somes Sound,* and *Southwest Harbor, Mount Desert* (Cape Ann Historical Society), produced on the 1852 trip. He had recorded the settlement at Southwest Harbor and the mountains surrounding Somes Sound on two pages of his sketchbook. The lack of a foreground in *Southwest Harbor* indicates that it was taken from the deck of Stevens's sloop. Southwest Harbor's dramatic location at the center of the water-born tourist activity on Mount Desert interested Lane, and its special visual appeal was heightened by its dramatic approach to "a great gorge seven miles into the heart of the island. . . . An intervening point concealed the entrance until we had nearly approached it, and the sails passing before us disappeared as if by enchantment."[15] Southwest Harbor boasted "an uninterrupted view up Somes' Sound. This beautiful sheet of water, pronounced by critics the most picturesque in America, is a deep indentation nearly bisecting Mt. Desert Island."[16] Elaborating on his deck sketches, Lane enhanced the scene by balancing a mirror image of the settlement reflected in the

waters of the harbor, and by giving more than half of his canvas to the sky. Adjusting his perspective to eliminate most of the mountain at right, he focused on the harbor and its maritime activities.

Hermaphrodite Brig as Figure

Lane placed a Maine lumber schooner on this sheet of glasslike water. This type of vessel was sometimes referred to as a "hermaphrodite brig," or half brig, or even "packet brig" because of its adaptation to coastal economic and sailing conditions. Because the vessel is not present in his field sketches, its appearance in the painting and its central position announce its importance as a primary "figure" of Lane's visual narrative. In this case, her sails hang loosely, drying in the sunlight, and cargo is being loaded; perhaps she is preparing to sail on the next tide, or with the wind. He depicted the turning blocks, ratlines, stays, and running rigging with an accuracy that would have been approved of by yachtsmen such as Stevens. Lane demonstrated his attention to minute details in the particular way he represented the anchored vessel: taking on freshly sawn lumber that has been floated out to her on a "raft" and is being stowed below through a "lumber port" in her bow.[17] The discovery, cutting, and marketing of lumber interested educated visitors who often lamented the loss of the great wilderness forests of the north. Lane's painting *Shipping in Down East Waters* showed brigs laden to the gunnels with cargoes of finished lumber

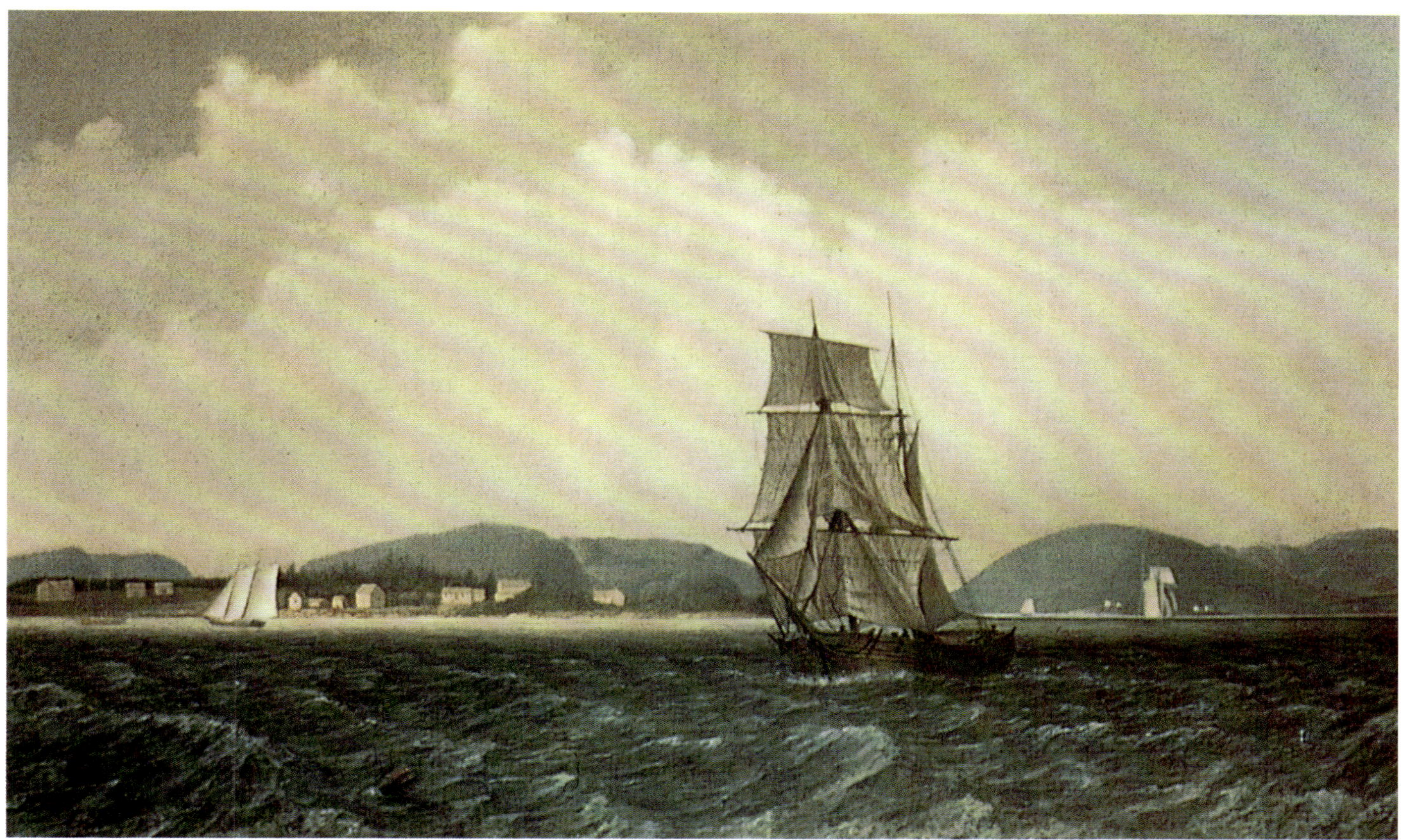

FIG. 60   Fitz Hugh Lane, *Off the Coast of Maine, with Desert Island in the Distance,* c.1850s,
oil on canvas, 20 x 33". Collections of the Shelburne Museum, Shelburne, Vermont.

products (fig. 59). In *Entrance of Somes Sound,* he also noted a typical "Down East" fishing and coastal boat in the middle distance, the "Pinkney," with its curiously upturned stern.

In the foreground of *Entrance of Somes Sound,* two picturesque figures, one in a red shirt, stand conversing next to a pulling boat or perhaps a "Captain's Gig." Lane arranges the oar of their beached boat to point toward the action on the brig, where another red-shirted figure draws the eye toward the ship, everything in absolute stillness save for the loading of cargo. Lane adjusted the landscape slightly by subtly manipulating the mountains in the background, whose "breadth and scope, in grace of outline and varied forms and color, [are] not excelled any where upon the island."[18]

Off the Coast of Maine, with Desert Island in the Distance

Lane also derived a companion painting from his 1852 trip: *Off the Coast of Maine, with Desert Island in the Distance* (fig. 60). While *Entrance of Somes Sound* depicted a brig in calm waters, at anchor, the related image showed a loaded brig under full sail, heading out to sea in a fair breeze. Recent scholarship on Lane's work has emphasized that despite his physical disability Lane was an excellent seaman. He invariably depicted ships under precise control, displaying what seems today to be an almost esoteric evidence of seaman-like handling.[19] His early training in printmaking, with its strong emphasis on graphic linearity, served this interest, allowing him to depict the exact movements of vessels in a precise manner. For the dedicated yachtsman or veteran master mariner, seeing a ship in "action," under full sail, or even in repose in port, was as exciting as gazing from the summit of a mountain was to the lover of landscape scenery.

Backing Her Sails

In *Off the Coast of Maine, with Desert Island in the Distance,* Lane represented a common maneuver on vessels with square fore-sails. In tacking, the sails are "backed" as the vessel comes around to catch the wind from a new direction. Lane captured the moment when the ship comes "about" and the square fore-sails are turned, and the wind blows them back into the rigging for a moment as the clumsy sails are hauled around by the crew to catch the wind. These maneuvers required large crews, which eventually made square-rigged ships obsolete when enterprising Yankee shipowners developed new types of schooner-rigged vessels. An alternative reading of the ship's maneuver suggests that she has backed her sails to stop forward motion, after discharging a pilot. In this scenario, the small schooner-rigged vessel in the left with the sun falling brightly on her sails may be the recently departed fast pilot boat.

In landscape paintings, clothing and other details provided important visual cues about the social or cultural function of the figural representations. Similarly, in marine paintings vessels were cast as chief protagonists, as dramatis

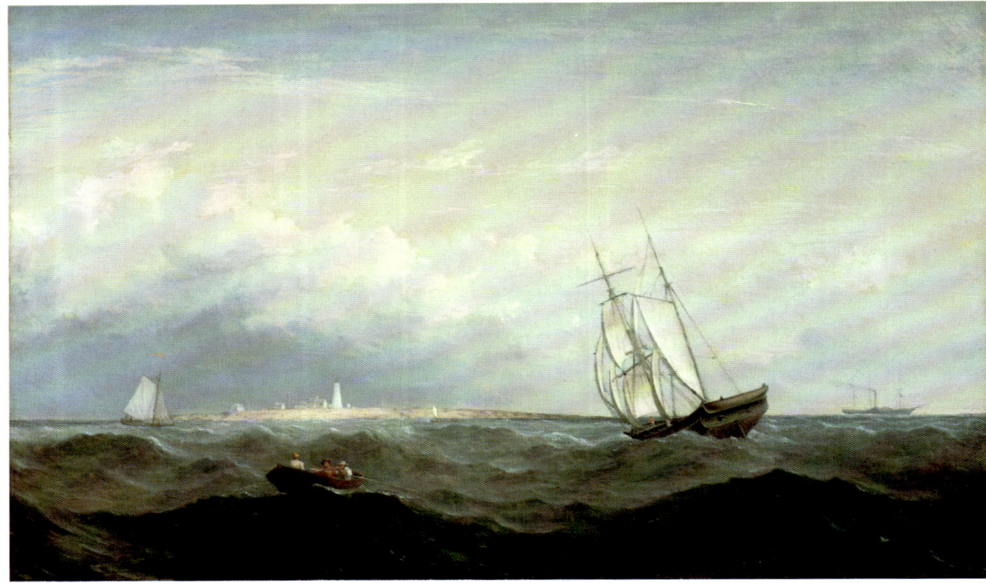

personae. As in many of his paintings, Lane here represented a nostalgic image of a lifestyle and a traditional type of sailing vessel that was rapidly disappearing. In the distance the swelling forms of Mount Desert provided a backdrop for Lane's visual drama of sailing vessels and displays of old-fashioned Yankee seamanship.

To the Desert Rock Lighthouse

Lane's and Stevens's enthusiasm for yachting was boundless, and they decided to cruise to the famed, remote lighthouse on Desert Rock that Doughty had painted nearly two decades earlier. Lane made deck sketches that eventually led to an exhibition-size painting, *Northwesterly View of Mount Desert Rock,* 1855 (fig. 61). In a long passage, Stevens described the visit and Lane's participation:

> We started with a fresh breeze for "Mount Desert Rock" 18 miles distant—it was rougher than we had yet had it—being a considerable swell but we got on finely—with the exception of George being sea sick—which however we comfort him with the opinion that it will do him good—About noon we arrive[d] at the Rock. . . . we spent a couple of hours most pleasantly rambling about the Rock examining a wreck of a Sch[ooner] that was lately cast away there—watching the seas dash up on to the windward side—as a Fin Back Whale dash[ed] every now and then into Shoals of Herring which almost surround the rock. . . . we felt that we should enjoy two days there—but as we had proposed to reach Somes Sound that night we had to tear ourselves away—Mr. Lane took two sketches while there.[20]

Lane inscribed one of those sketches with "North Westerly View of Mt. Desert Rock, taken from the deck of the Sloop Superior at anchor." In the painting Lane depicts a packet brig running on a broad reach in a fresh breeze in the right foreground, while at the left a smaller sloop, like the one Lane was aboard, stands off the dangerous rock, its sails luff-ing as it plows into a head sea, perhaps to drop its anchor and its sails. In the immediate foreground Lane includes a detailed pulling boat, called a "peapod," with three salty looking figures aboard. The boat is the type that would be lowered from the sloop to carry parties such as Lane's and Stevens's ashore to visit the Rock. The slight figure at the stern with a red-and-white striped shirt and red seaman's cap may be self-referential, perhaps Lane's memoir of his adventure of going ashore to visit the lighthouse in a fair sea. In the distance stands the gleaming white tower of the lighthouse with its outbuildings. The wrecked schooner that Stevens described and that Lane's drawing depicted was removed from the painting.

The most important actor in Lane's maritime narrative is found at the extreme right. In the distance, a single- stack, extreme-speed, side-wheel steam vessel is seen on the horizon. Her black, clipper hull and distinctive vermilion funnel identify her as a Cunard steamer probably on a transatlantic run heading from Halifax, Nova Scotia, to Desert Rock Lighthouse on the great circle route, before bearing south toward Boston and New York. For Lane and Stevens, dedicated yachtsmen and sailors, mechanized ships such as this represented the future of navigation, and simultaneously their presence foreshadowed the demise of sail. By the mid-1850s sailing vessels and the rich maritime ways of life they supported would eventually pass away, becoming anachronistic pleasures for leisured yachtsmen who could afford the nostalgia needed to "go cruising."

Poetical Elements: *Off Mount Desert Island*

The intense, almost topographic verisimilitude of Lane's *Entrance of Somes Sound,* or the drama of seamanship involved in a visit to Desert Rock Lighthouse, contrasts with the more complex and nuanced images Lane began to produce in the mid-1850s. *Off Mount Desert Island* (fig. 62), completed in 1856, provides an example.[21] In 1855 Lane made a

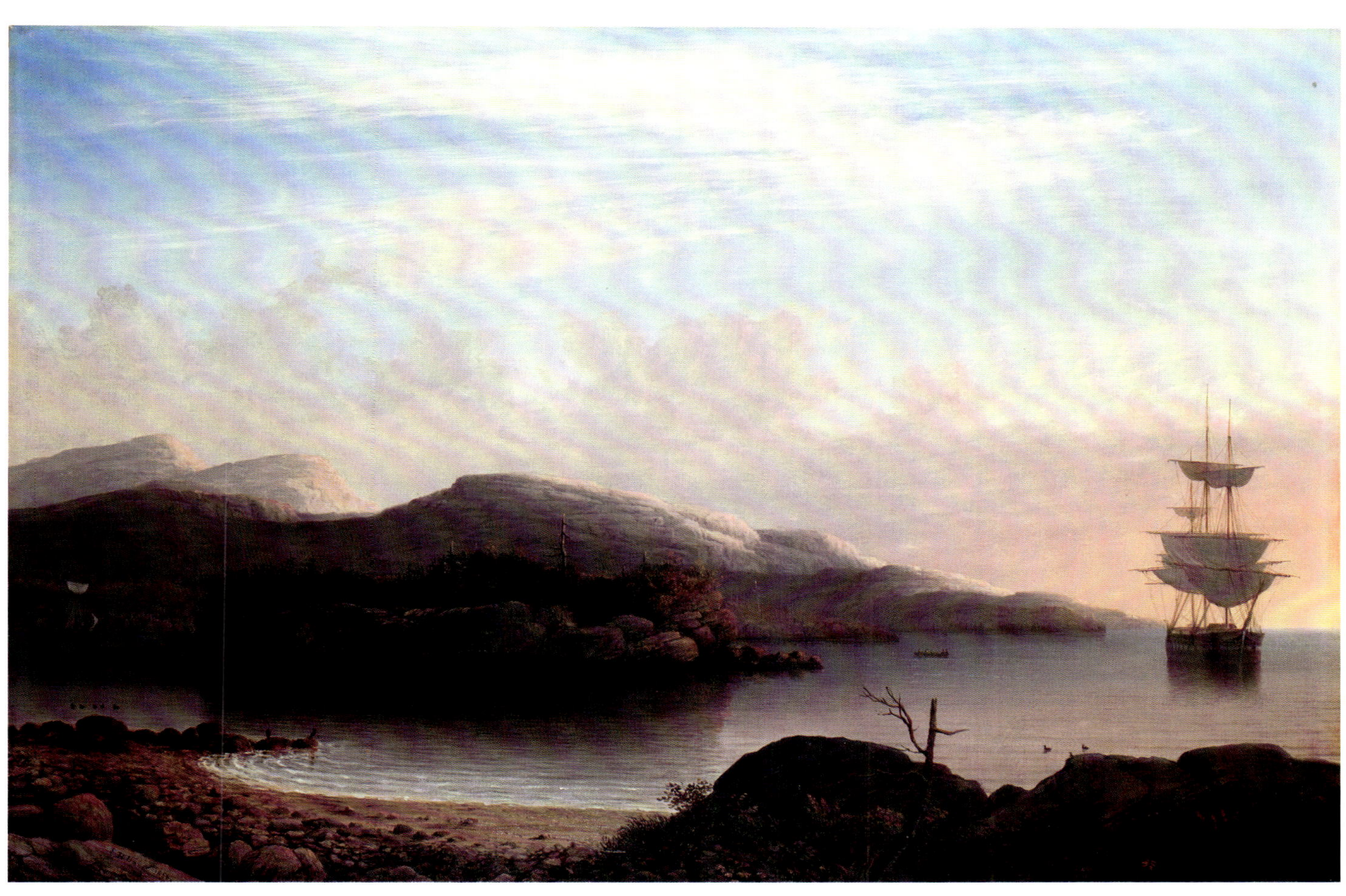

FIG. 62   Fitz Hugh Lane, *Off Mount Desert Island*, 1856, oil on canvas, 22³⁄₁₆ x 36⁷⁄₁₆".
Brooklyn Museum of Art, Museum Collection Fund, 47.114.

more extended trip along the Maine Coast with Stevens. After sketching at Camden and Owl's Head, they sailed for Mount Desert, and this time Lane's sketching focused on Southeast Harbor, Somes Sound, and Northeast Harbor. Clarence Cook, the art critic of the weekly New York newspaper *The Independent*, praised Lane's recent work in his 7 September 1854 column and urged him to send pictures "to New-York for exhibition. It could not fail to make an impression, and to call forth criticism. A finer picture of its class was never in the Academy." Cook, who was to become one of New York's most powerful art critics, wrote: "Mr. F. H. Lane, whose name ought to be known from Maine to Georgia . . . in knowledge, feeling, and skill, has had no rival, certainly in America, and I doubt if more than two abroad."[22]

Cook had not always held Lane in such high esteem. In fact his review continued: "four years ago, I was doubtful if I should find in Mr. Lane the poetical element that must be a constituent in the artist's mind." He felt that Lane's early pictures had "something in them too hard and practical to permit enthusiastic admiration: the water was salt, the ships sailed, the waves moved, but it was the sea before the Spirit of God moved upon the face of the deep." "Lane knows," Cook wrote, "the name and place of every rope on a vessel; he knows the construction, the anatomy, the expression—and to a seaman every thing that sails has expression and individuality—he knows how she will stand under this rig." Indulging the mariner's linguistic habit that personified ships as female, Cook in effect critiqued Lane's highly masculinized early images—a man's world of seamen and yachtsmen, where women and poetic sentiments seldom made an appearance except as figureheads or vessel names. Cook declared that he "missed in them the creative imagination of the artist."[23]

Lane heeded the critic's advice: dramatic effects of light are strongly present in *Off Mount Desert Island,* they introduce a new, more poetic, imaginative sentiment to the picture. Departing from his usual topographic subjects, the view appears to be a composite of scenery from Mount Desert, and probably not a specific place. Lane had by this time perhaps traveled to New York with Stevens and encountered the work of artists active in the city, particularly the most celebrated painter of the time, Church. This experience and Cook's critique stimulated Lane to review his technique and expand his conceptual horizons, even daring to compete in his own way with the "boy genius." Church's powerful yet subtle images, filled with symbolic meaning, may have suggested to Lane new approaches to supplying the "creative imagination" that Cook had urged. He also could have drawn upon many other examples, such as Gifford whose interest in calm scenes of tranquility were consistent with Lane's approach. *Off Mount Desert Island* represents Lane's awareness of how he could build more complex and interesting visual narratives through the production of "sentiment." Marine detail is subordinated here to the representation of effects of transparent light.

Hanging Her Gear

While adding imagination and sentiment to please critics and to make his art more competitive, Lane still looked to the life of the sea in ships. His patrons' emphasis on factual detail could not entirely overshadow his new interests in producing a more cosmopolitan, sophisticated style of painting. In *Off Mount Desert Island*, a large three-masted ocean-going vessel stands at anchor in the cove, enveloped in purple mist. She is "hanging her gear," or drying her sails, perhaps having taken some weather recently. A Captain's Gig carrying several tiny figures heads to the island, or to visit the smaller brig anchored farther back in the serene cove. The larger vessel is silhouetted, with all Lane's fidelity to detail, in the purple-rose light whose tints illuminate the mountaintops, and perhaps pleased a patron who appreciated the successful artistic merging of fact and sentiment.

Drawing on the full range of Anglo-American artistic conventions that he had become aware of in the work of the leading New York artists, Lane included a standard gestural tree in the foreground, a surrogate witness to the absolute serenity and silence of the scene. The tree's branch directs the spectator's gaze from the foreground beach to the small island in the middle distance where a solitary tree catches the last rays of sunlight. Clarence Cook described a scene like this in his 1854 review of a picture that preceded *Off Mount Desert Island,* but which is unlocated today. His words indicate how a leading art writer perceived Lane's painting. "The time is sunset after a storm. The dun and purple clouds roll away to the south-west, the sun sinks in a glory of yellow light, flooding the sea with transparent splendor. Far away in the offing, hiding the sun, sails a brig fully rigged, a transfigured vision between the glories of the sky and sea."[24] By the mid-1850s Lane had probably encountered the transcendentalism of Emerson, perhaps in lectures in Gloucester or Boston, and he had definitely absorbed Church's Calvinist ideas of representing transcendence visually.

Off Mount Desert Island dramatically demonstrates Lane's rapid development as an artist increasingly connected to the main field of national art production centered in New York. Lane's images were probably not as important in stimulating scenic tourism at Mount Desert as were Cole's and Church's, although for a small group of wealthy yachtsmen, Lane's views of maritime life were just as exciting as the scenes Tenth Street Studios artists painted. A scholar recently described Lane's paintings as "articles of commerce, whose value and meaning depended on the circumstances in which they were produced and of the visible world they recorded."[25] The metropolitan field of cultural production,

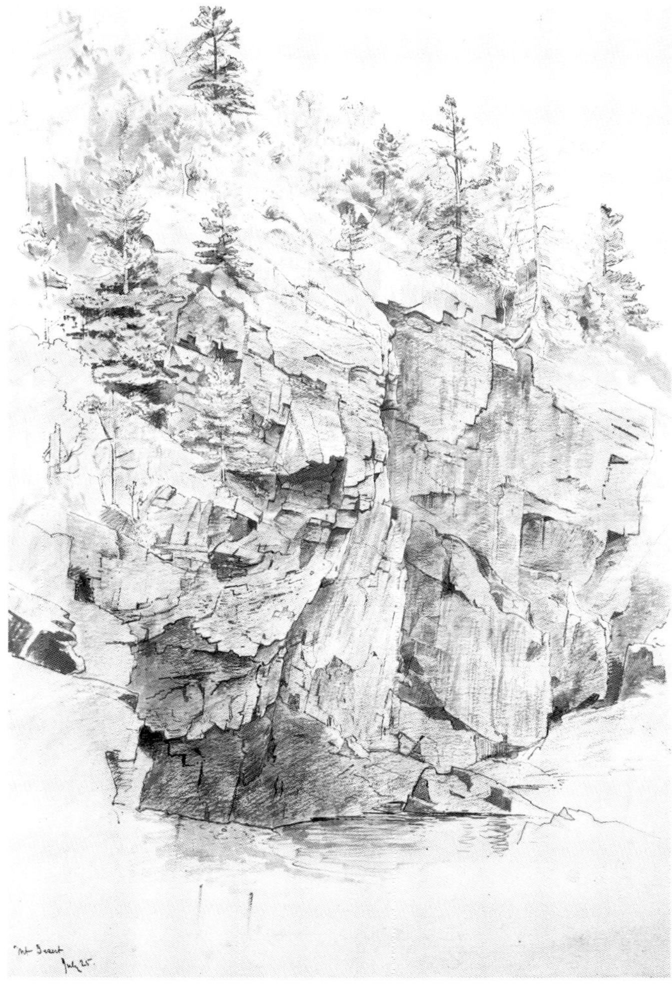

FIG. 63   William Stanley Haseltine, *Rock Wall, Near Otter Cliffs, Mt. Desert*, c. 1859, pen and black ink, watercolor, graphite, on heavy off-white wove paper, 22 x 14¹⁵⁄₁₆". Cooper-Hewitt, National Design Museum, Smithsonian Institution/Art Resource, NY, 1953-155-2.

with its competitive practices and demands, greatly influenced regional artists such as Lane.

William Stanley Haseltine

A resident of the Studios Building, William Stanley Haseltine realized the opportunity awaiting artists at Mount Desert after seeing Church's paintings. He decided to visit Maine, and arrived in the summer of 1859 with another Studios Building companion, Charles Temple Dix (1838–1873), who would also become noted for his marine paintings, but whose career was soon to be interrupted by service in the Union Army where his father was a general. Both men came from "good families." Haseltine's family traced its lineage back to 1637; his father was a wealthy Boston Brahmin, able to support his son's education at Harvard, where he was taught by Henry Wadsworth Longfellow, and perhaps studied natural history with Louis Agassiz. It was at Harvard that his lifelong interest in geology began. Agassiz was the most popular lecturer at Harvard, and his intellectual rigor and passion excited Haseltine and his classmate Henry Adams, who said

that Agassiz's lectures on the Glacial Period had more influence on his intellectual development than the rest of his college instruction altogether. It may have been around this time that Haseltine developed an interest in another emerging seaside resort, Nahant, where Agassiz took his students to study glaciation. After his visit to Nahant, Haseltine produced a series of paintings of the abraded rocks of the peninsula, battered like those of Mount Desert by the violence of the sea.[26]

Upon graduation in 1854, Haseltine decided to pursue a gentleman's career in art, and moved to Dusseldorf in 1855. He quickly mastered the meticulous drawing techniques and conventions of "objective" representation practiced at the Academy. Haseltine had the special advantage of working in the studio of Andreas Achenbach, whose marine paintings created and opened a new market for the genre when they were shown in New York (see fig. 44). Haseltine traveled with Achenbach to the coast of southern Italy in 1858, practicing his technique with pencil sketching, wash drawings, and the production oil sketches. This trip provided him with subjects for the many pictures he eventually exhibited. Upon his return from Italy in 1859, Haseltine settled in New York. Handsome, wealthy, well connected, and personable, he soon gained entrance into an elite company of artists. *The Crayon* reported that Haseltine "returned to a city with art prosperity. . . . Leutze, Haseltine and Whittredge have taken studios in the Tenth st[Street] Building, Bierstadt and others are looking out for studios elsewhere; the studio-building being as full as a Broadway Omnibus on a rainy day. A new studio building would be a splendid investment for some capitalist."[27]

Portraits of Rocks

Haseltine's and Dix's visit to Mount Desert from New York can be dated by their registration on 9 July 1859 at the Agamont House in Bar Harbor, and from inscriptions on numerous drawings and several oil sketches produced by Haseltine. The visit resulted in a suite of drawings that demonstrated Haseltine's technical mastery of graphic media according to the conventions of the Dusseldorf Academy. These drawings were executed from mid-July to early August. A representative example of Haseltine's personal style of close observation drawing is apparent in *Rock Wall, Near Otter Cliffs, Mt. Desert* (fig. 63), dated 25 July 1859. Haseltine, with his interest in geology, staked his claim to a position in the field of landscape painters by painting rocky seacoasts. As a student he had become interested in modern ideas of geology, and would have agreed with art critic John Ruskin's notion that a representation of a geological specimen could be scientifically accurate, and could also reveal the hidden truths of creation. Haseltine's *Rock Wall* drawing is a fine example of what Ruskin would have accepted as "truth to nature." Its rendering of light and shadow, and the intri-

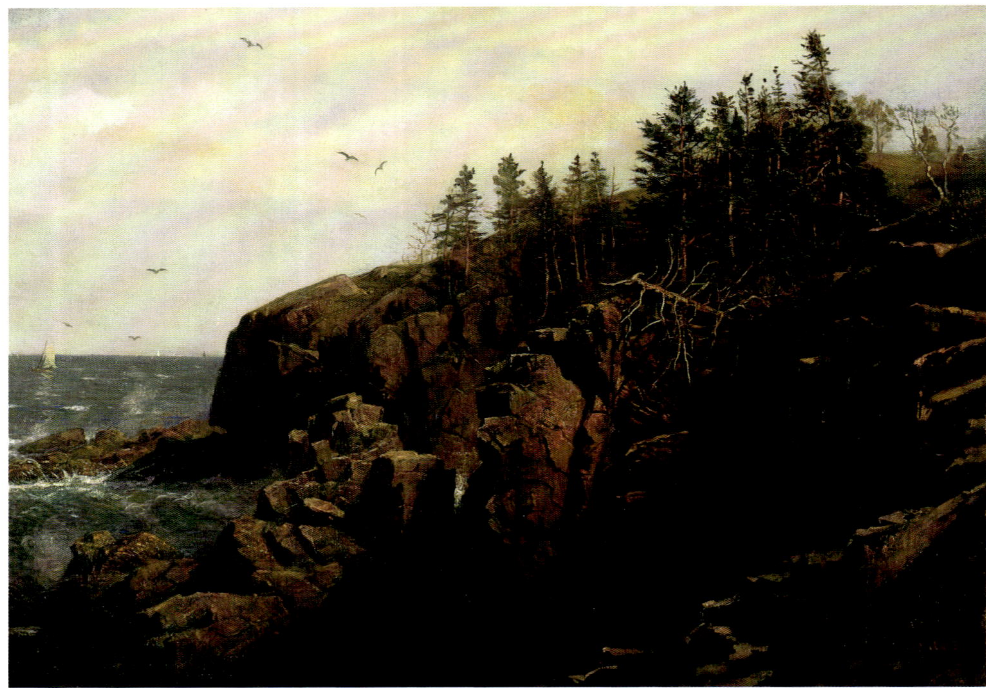

cate strata of rock could be read by a geologist. Tuckerman noted approvingly: "Few of our artists have been more conscientious in the delineation of rocks; their form, superficial traits, and precise tones are given with remarkable accuracy. His pencil identifies coast scenery with emphatic beauty . . . rock-portraits set in deep blue crystalline of the sea."[28]

During his tour of the Island Haseltine produced plein-air sketches in oil; an example is *Rocks and Pine, Mount Desert Island, Maine* (fig. 64), inscribed "July 31, 1859." At first glance this is a finely executed sketch, most likely finished back in the studio from one of Haseltine's preparatory drawings or field sketches. With the competitive pressure placed on New York artists on the eve of the Civil War, painters tried to establish a hold on the art market. Everyone sought to imitate the enormous success of Frederic Church, and Haseltine was no exception. He and Dix were eager to demonstrate that they could produce original and imaginative marines that would excite national enthusiasm for northern coastal views. The enterprise was a success, and by 1867 Tuckerman recognized Haseltine's expertise. "There is a history to the imagination in every brown angle-projecting slab, worn, broken, ocean-mined and sun-painted ledge of the brown and picturesque-heaped rocks, at whose volcanic birth and the antiquity of man . . . appeal to the lover of nature for recognition or reminiscence."[29] Evidently these images were complex for contemporary viewers, with "a history of the imagination" etched in the rock faces. When late-twentieth-century viewers examine *Rocks and Pine, Mount Desert Island, Maine*, they may see only a close

description of geologic fact, but in Haseltine's time the landscape was a field of vital presences and rich associations. After 1859, and the sensational publication of Charles Darwin's theories, deistic interpretations that continued to privilege an anthropocentric view of the landscape were increasingly discredited, and Haseltine's turn, in the early 1860s, to an ever more scientifically rigorous conception of rocks, reflected this fundamental shift in attitudes.

Rocky Reminiscences: Severity Predominant

In his studio Haseltine confronted the question of how to translate his field sketches and his memory into paintings that could be exhibited and sold to buyers in New York or Philadelphia. The impending secession of Southern states and the prospect of war implanted an uncertainty in the air. The "Domestic Art Gossip," a popular column in *The Crayon*, reported in December 1860 that, "Notwithstanding the political commotion, the art world pursues the even tenor of its way. Artists are now busy in their studios with the harmonies of nature, not its discords. We cannot help but think that the general cultivation of artistic feeling and perception would be of great political advantage."[30] In 1860 Haseltine exhibited "#87. Mount Desert" at the Philadelphia Academy of the Fine Arts, although the picture had already been sold before the exhibition opened.[31] The next year he exhibited two paintings of Maine in New York at the National Academy of Design: *A View from Mount Desert,* and a work entitled *Iron Bound—Coast of Maine* (Private Collection). *A View from Mount Desert* (fig. 65) is an impressive example of an exhi-

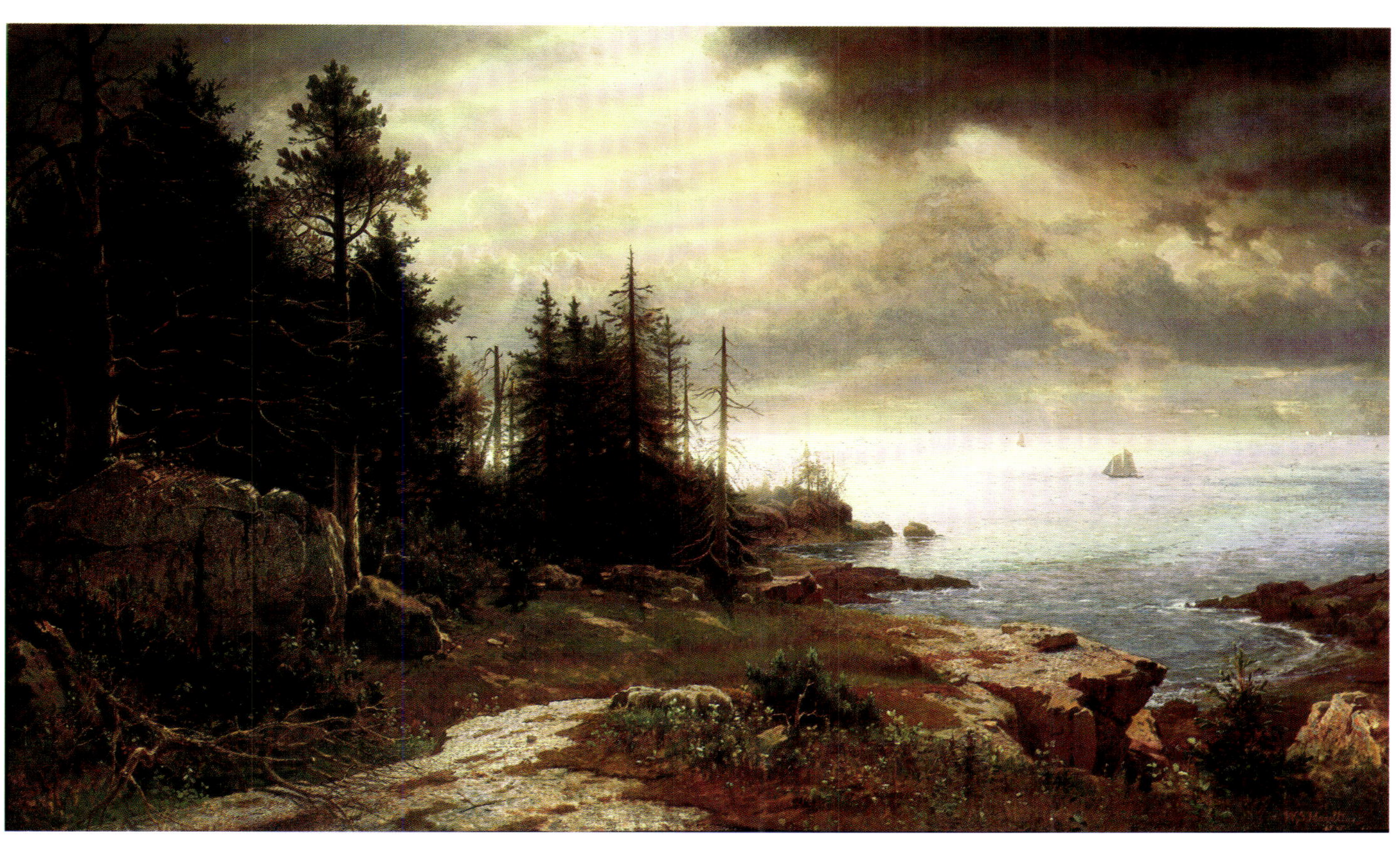

FIG. 65 William Stanley Haseltine, *A View From Mount Desert*, 1861, oil on canvas, 30 x 50".
Private Collection, Photograph Courtesy of D. Wigmore Fine Art, Inc., New York.

bition-size painting executed for an affluent buyer, a work that might have sold for around one hundred to two hundred dollars in its time.

How Haseltine's painting of Mount Desert was received or understood during the war years is suggested by a review of *Indian Rock,* exhibited in 1863 at the Academy. The critic thought that,

> *Every Inch of his "Indian Rock" tells a story in the most idiomatic language of nature. The staircased mass of red granite bears reminiscences all over it of a fiery birth and trial through cycles under the Thor hammer of the sea. If the water were at its wildest we question whether more oceanic force could be suggested than speaks from the sharply fractured, chinked and square-blocked mass of finely variegated stone. In the same picture the harmony between the dun sky and deep-green sea in its shadow is quite admirable.*[32]

Painted in the style of Achenbach and the Dusseldorf Academy, which Albert Bierstadt was also popularizing around that time with his paintings of the far West, *A View from Mount Desert* presents the Island and its rocky coast as a rugged yet accessible wilderness where great vistas await the viewer and visitor. In the distance Haseltine produced a misty sky of the type that would make him sought after by European and American collectors. A solitary figure strolls along the open rocky cliffs; his gaze, like that of the spectator, surveys a luminous sea with the sails of coastal schooners silhouetted against the white light. A radiant sky, suggestive with requisite sentiments of transcendence, complements the stillness of the scene, a perfect visual antidote to the unsettling news from the war fronts that year. Because of his scientific interests, Haseltine avoided the conventions of emblematic personification. Although occasionally practiced by Bierstadt, anthropomorphic symbolism was not a regular part of the Dusseldorf artistic practice, and Haseltine instead placed emphasis primarily on the play of light and its outlining effect on solid objects.

The Anglo-American newspaper, *The Albion,* praised it extravagantly, along with an Italian picture:

> *We pass on from Mr. Haseltine's* Amalfi *to his* Mount Desert Island, *no. 80, which has almost as much local characterization, or in other works is altogether a different affair, though also a coast scene. Pine trees and boulders, on a slope that edges away down to the sea, are combined with a wide ocean expanse which glitters in a very strong light peering forth from behind dark clouds. There is severity predominant and in keeping throughout, while the good drawing and the indescribable sense of air and space make this also an attractive picture. But let Mr. Haseltine beware of mistaking white pigment for light. It is an easy substitute, but passable only where the spectator is remote perforce and where effect alone is consequently studied.*[33]

The production of "sentiments" by the manipulation of light effects had many degrees and gradations, but it was an essential element in a successful landscape, especially when combined with exotic, remote, or dramatic scenery.

It is puzzling that, considering Haseltine's success with this Mount Desert subject, he produced so few paintings of the Island. The explanation may lie in the fact that the market for pictures of the Island was suddenly becoming saturated (see Appendix). Haseltine needed to establish a personal style, and rocks in all their variety and color were to be his forte. Yet this extreme specialization was fraught with uncertainty, not the least of which surfaced in an 1864 review of Haseltine's work. "Mr. Haseltine is threatened with . . . martyrdom to a specialty. . . . It is a great injustice to an artist to encourage him in one direction at the expense of versatility. Most of all when a speciality is not one of sentiment, but of subject-matter—rocks, water, and sky."[34]

The Best Sign of Appreciation

Patrons wanted landscapes of sublimity and rich historic associations in Achenbach's grand style, but the niche for wilderness views of Mount Desert was already occupied by the versatile and highly competitive Church. Instead Haseltine turned his attention increasingly to painting Italian scenery. In the same exhibition where he showed his scene of Mount Desert, Haseltine presented *Amalfi, Coast of Naples* (unlocated). It received a rave review that reinforced Haseltine's European orientation. "Take a seat. Shut out, if possible, what hangs above, below and around: and surrender yourself to the charm of a very fine sea-shore piece by a young practitioner, who is rising rapidly to a high place in his profession." Haseltine's picture has recently "put on it that best sign of appreciation—the little word, *sold*. The purchaser must be envied."[35]

The following year, 1864, one of Haseltine's paintings of Maine attracted a harsh review. The critic thought "the picture is very feeble, and does no sort of justice to the grand character of the rocks, and the sea is most lamentably tame. . . . He must abandon this pretty, neat way of treating rocks and surf, if he wishes to associate his name with the much-resounding sea. A rock is a solid body, capable of resisting the force of wind and water; it is not a semi-transparent structure of tissue paper which the flirt of a fish's tail would knock over; and the dash of the breaker is something more than the foam blown from a glass of weak beer."[36] Recent scholarly investigation has shown that Haseltine found in the rocky peninsula of Nahant both the subject and society he had been seeking. In those paintings he embedded aspects of American culture, "the social stratification (class structure), the popular fascination with geological science, and the defining political event of the era, the Civil War.[37] Haseltine's paintings were conflicted images for a conflicted era.

After the Civil War, Haseltine returned to Europe in 1865, and lived there permanently after 1867. He seldom visited the United States, and did not revisit Mount Desert again until 1893 and 1895. His personal style had by then changed, and he produced intimate pastorals with low horizons and close up views of tranquil water and lovely trees. His visit to the Island was by that time as much a social event as an artistic one. His daughter recalled:

> *Many of the residents of N.E. Harbor, the Bishop of Albany, the Gardeners, the Storys, the Forbes, the Huntingtons, Dr. Potter, Bishop of New York, were friends many years' standing and he was glad to link up with them again. Pierpont Morgan was up there in those waters with his yacht and, from entries in his diaries we know Haseltine often joined him.*[38]

Gifford and McEntee Visit

Sanford R. Gifford and his close friend from the New York Tenth Street Studios Building, Jervis McEntee, two other major New York artists, followed Cole, Church, and Haseltine to Mount Desert during the Civil War. Gifford and McEntee had personal and professional reasons for visiting the Island. Back from service at the front, Gifford needed a respite from Army duty and the anguish of personal loss. His brother Edward had been captured during the battle of New Orleans in 1863 during an extremely dangerous volunteer mission, yet had escaped by heroically swimming across the Mississippi. He later contracted typhoid and died. Gifford's other brother Charles had also been killed, at the outset of the war in 1861. McEntee desired to paint the same landscape his traveling companion and former teacher Church had painted. In that summer of 1864, Gifford and McEntee decided to go North to Maine. They had undoubtedly seen Church's impressive 1863 *Coast Scene, Mount Desert* (see fig. 52) at the Academy and perhaps even seen it in process on Church's easel in the Studio at Tenth Street. Gifford and McEntee had also heard about the Island from Studio-mates Haseltine and Dix who had visited a few years earlier, and who had been successfully producing pictures from their inventory of field sketches. The men wanted to see Mount Desert for themselves to assess its potential as scenery and also to escape from the heat of the city in July.

A Region of Patriots

Gifford and his sister left New York in July for a two-and-a-half month sketching tour of the northeast and New England, and Mount Desert. The Giffords were joined by Jervis McEntee and his wife in Boston, where the party proceeded north to the Island by boat. They spent three weeks, from July 14 to August 5, on the Island, including a glorious encampment at the summit of Cadillac Mountain in a rustic one room cabin. Gifford filled two sketch books with pencil drawings and notations. Like Cole and Church before him, Gifford sketched the Porcupine Islands, and Southwest and Northwest Harbors at Somes Sound (Collection of Sanford Gifford, M.D.).[39] The physical exertion of exploring the Island provided a good countermeasure to the background of frustration and dismay felt because of the immense toll of men and national treasure the war was consuming. Gifford's brothers' deaths must have weighed heavily as he escaped to the pure air and clear, crisp light of northern New England. His destination also had distinct patriotic overtones. His friend Edmund C. Steadman went to New England to summer, declaring "Goodbye New York. I go to a region where there are patriots still!"[40] Adding to these interests, Church's impressive painting of 1863, *Coast Scene, Mount Desert,* had made everyone aware by means of its grand visual metaphor that New England's bedrock was indomitable and enduring, when all else seemed to be reckless madness. That *Coast Scene* was sold to New York's premier collector may have also sparked Gifford's and McEntee's interest in capturing a few views of the Island wilderness.

Upon his return to New York Gifford began to make oil studies of the Island scenery. A reporter for the *Boston Evening Transcript,* after interviewing Church while at work in his studio, turned his attention to Gifford's recent productions. "Then we climbed another flight to Gifford's studio. Here we saw a number of charming coast studies, chiefly from the neighborhood of Mount Desert. These were very successful in the life and motion of the waves, and the effect of distance."[41] One of these pictures may be the 1864 painting *Rocks at Porcupine Island Near Mt. Desert* (fig. 66), which depicts dramatic cliffs, waves crashing against rocks, swirling sea birds, and massive rock faces that loom above the sea's surface.

The Artist Sketching at Mount Desert

The next year Gifford summarized the experience of Mount Desert in one of his most important paintings, *The Artist Sketching at Mount Desert, Maine* (fig. 67). It represents a popular tourist view from Cadillac Mountain with its "effect of distance." Gifford's picture is signed and dated 1865, a year after he visited, but incised in the wet paint is "Mt. [Desert]/ July 22, 1864," the exact date he experienced the scene. That moment of plein-air perception was recorded in an oil sketch entitled *A Sketch at Mount Desert, Maine*, 1864, (fig. 68), which in its turn may be based on two pencil sketches made on the spot of Otter Cove seen from Cadillac Mountain. One sketch is inscribed "Green Mt. Mt. Desert July 15th 64," and faithfully records the panoramic view depicted in the 1865 picture. On a sketch of Otter Cove Gifford had inscribed, "gradation of sea same as that of a mountain distance / Sails like constellations."[42] The combination of these drawings resulted in an oil study that may have

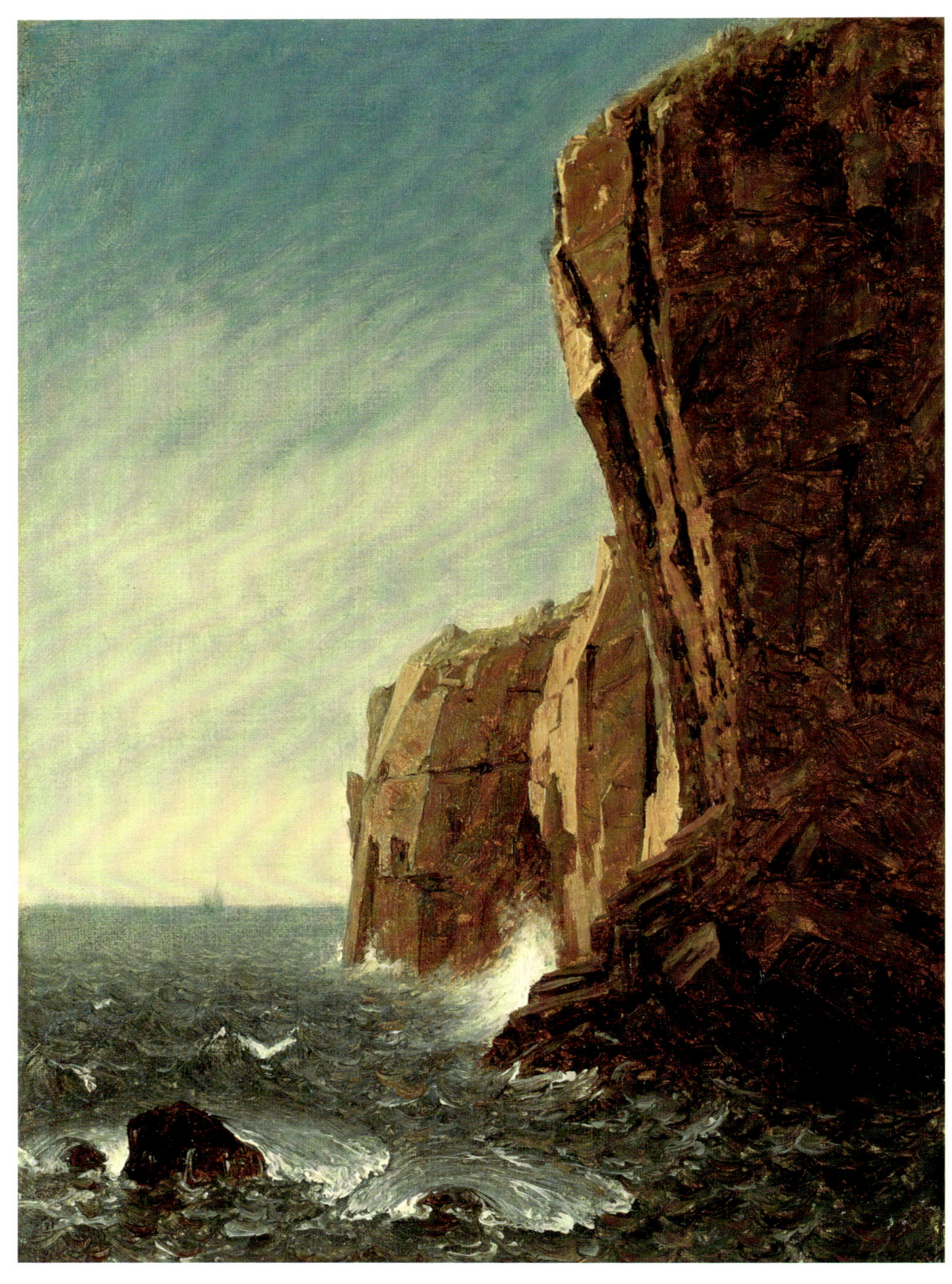

FIG. 66　Sanford Robinson Gifford, *Rocks at Porcupine Island Near Mt. Desert,* 1864, oil on canvas, 12½ x 9". The Farnsworth Art Museum, Museum Purchase, 1998.

been executed in the cabin during the week the party spent there, although the 1865 painting is clearly a highly finished production of the New York studio.

Self-Referencing Landscape

Gifford's studied image of the artist sketching at the summit of Cadillac Mountain was one of a handful of paintings that self-referenced the landscape artist as observer and producer of images. Thomas Cole had done it earlier in *The Oxbow* (Metropolitan Museum of Art), where the painter is shown at work on a sketch. In Gifford's picture an artist's work is glimpsed as if it were just completed. It is safely held in the cover of his portable sketch box. An artist with a full beard and white cap sketches the scene before him, which is also the same scene drying inside the sketch box. The picture within a picture invites perception of a moment shared between the artist and the spectator, who is invited to gaze upon the painting as if he were gazing on the scene itself, only to discover upon close observation that within one reproduction is another. This experience creates a sense of shared identity and intensifies the emotions of a special moment so remembered in the brilliant light and absolute repose of the picture. The image invites the spectator in an art gallery to join at the overlook with the artist sketching, to emphatically see in reproduction what he is seeing and has seen. The real "genius" of Gifford's painting was its subtle positioning of the spectator as a privileged "insider" sharing the creative experience of the artist, linking the gaze of the spectator vicariously with the artist's.

Although *The Artist Sketching at Mount Desert* was not recorded by Gifford in his 1874 list of "My Chief Pictures," it is today considered to be one of his most compelling images. Two years before Gifford completed his picture, the art critic for the *New York Times* commented on some of Gifford's pictures at the National Academy exhibition, naming them "superb specimens of the misty style which is just now so fashionable."[43] Similar to *Artist Sketching* in its representation of scenery from a commanding prospect, Gifford's *Kauterskill Clove* (Metropolitan Museum of Art), completed in 1862, was praised for the "mountain gorge, resplendent with the yellow sunlight of declining day." However, this reviewer added that "Mr. Gifford is a perfect master of the art of 'how not to do it.'" The critic urged "a little more botany and geology in the foreground of this picture is due to its otherwise transcendent merits." In fact, compared to other pictures, "there are neither rocks nor trees in this exhibition so badly painted as those which disfigure the foreground of this picture."[44]

Gifford may well have responded to such criticisms, for *The Artist Sketching* is carefully rendered with a crisp, highly detailed delineation of the foreground. The writer of a *Harper's* article commented on the "strong foregrounds to the pictures, which vary, and as you move in the center of this magic circle, the hard gray rocks lie all around in masses of brilliant light and deep shadows of violet and of green where the foliage of fern and brake grows from the crevices of the rock."[45] Yet within this depiction of nature is a rock formation that evokes Church's anthropomorphic profiles in *Coast Scene, Mount Desert* (see fig. 52). McEntee, probably the artist shown working in the picture, had been Church's student in 1850 and 1851, and there must have been discussion of the use of this sort of emblematic visage, since McEntee also employed it in his work occasionally. These stony profiles appear to look beyond the lone artist in the foreground to the wide vista, already an acknowledged tourist view.

Gifford's situation exemplified the response of New York artists during the Civil War. His military service, personal experience of the war at the front, and loss of his brothers and friends, made him acutely conscious of national civil violence. He responsed not with paintings of heroic action, but images of "inaction"—restful landscapes enveloped in mist and golden vapor. Among the most frequently used terms to describe the sentiments of Gifford's paintings of the early 1860s are the words "repose" and "radiance." A long article in the high culture magazine *The Round Table* for December 1863 on "American Genius as Expressed in Art" described Gifford as a painter who "alone has given us something approaching the magnificent, the opulent, and the intense in nature." Kensett was "lyrical," Church was "purely intellectual," while Gifford's works of that year possessed "the emotional element: they are pervaded with fervid feeling and seem more like the products of an impassioned nature than the works of any man in American art or literature."[46]

Anti-War Art and Mist Mania

Gifford's work was among the most emotional responses to the Civil War, and it was couched in a personal style that might be termed today "anti-war," in part because it deliberately avoided images of war or even hints of war, focusing instead on scenes with transcendent associations. Nevertheless, the "anti-war art" of the Tenth Street Studios was produced with an eye to its sale, and the overt lack of expression against war was less a comment on patriotism than it was an assurance of retaining art's hard-won cultural status as a visual palliative.

Jervis McEntee was also deeply involved in the production of scenic landscapes. Like Gifford, McEntee's melancholy, misty skies and autumnal tints represented a new more "poetic" direction for American landscape painting that had emerged with the mysterious "mist mania" of 1862–1863, and which would gather momentum after the Civil War. McEntee produced a highly finished oil sketch of the view from the summit of Cadillac Mountain, commanding a sweep of sea, shore, and sky (fig. 69). A solitary eyewitness, an

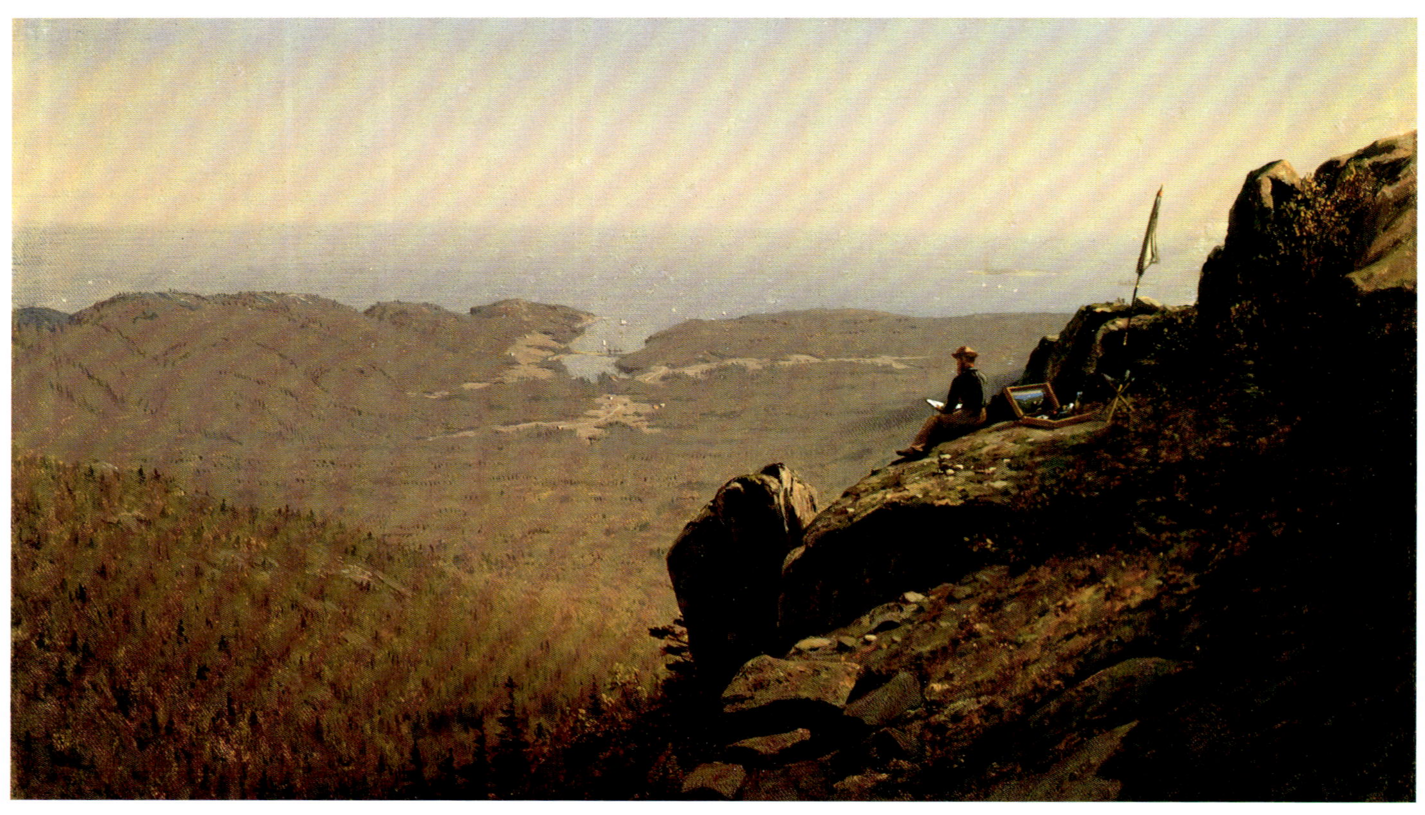

FIG. 67   Sanford Robinson Gifford, *The Artist Sketching at Mount Desert, Maine*, 1864–1865,
oil on canvas, 11 x 19". Collection of Jo Ann and Julian Ganz, Jr.

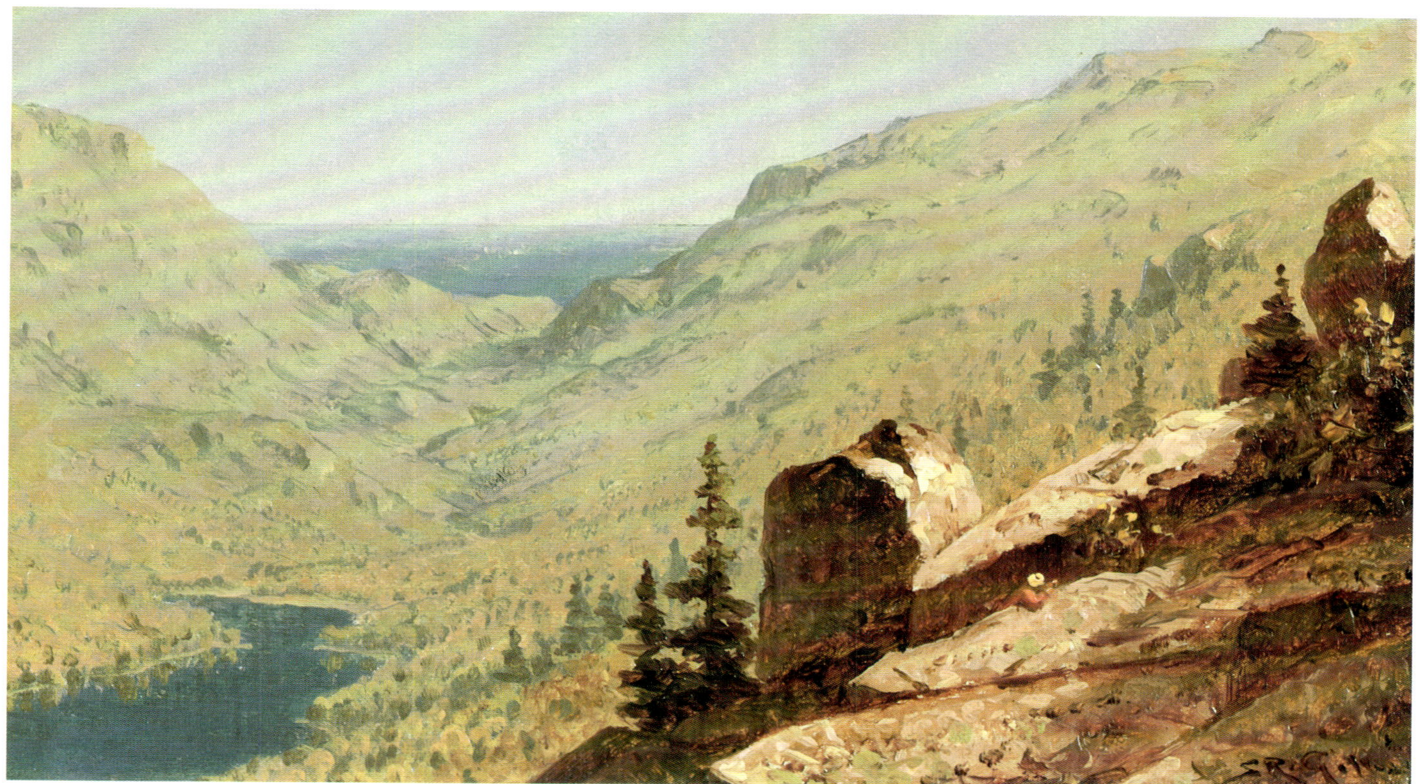

FIG. 68   Sanford Robinson Gifford, *A Sketch at Mount Desert, Maine,* 1864, oil on canvas,
7 x 12". North Carolina Museum of Art, Raleigh, Purchased with Funds from the
State of North Carolina.

artist, perhaps the lanky figure of Gifford in this case, reclines on the smoothly eroded rocks. His recumbent figure and turned-away head invite spectators to join in gazing at the distant scene and misty, vaporous atmosphere. A steamer passing far out at sea leaves a faint trace near the point where sea and sky merge. *Harper's* also noted the peculiar effect of sea and ships that seemed to sail in the sky:

> *Stand and gaze to the south, and see at your feet little villages hugging close to the golden belt of shore which divides the iron-gray land from the azure of the sea; and then, still looking seaward, you raise your eyes slowly in the effort to find some sort of lines which will mark the perspective, and, save little dark specks, which are mighty vessels going to and fro, you perceive a wide, measureless expanse of blue, melting off into delicate gray, and then, looking higher and higher, until you meet the blue once more away up in the zenith.*[47]

For artists such as Gifford and McEntee the grand panoramic view's repose and its calming silence, far removed from the deadly violence of war, might have resonated with concerns of the moment for an imperiled ship of state, the Union, during that fateful summer. The sheer exultation at the panoramic view and the pleasure at being far from the killing fields must have been a transcendent moment for both artists.

Grand—Almost Overwhelming

Gifford's and McEntee's images are classic examples of the "magisterial gaze." Sweeping panoramic views were often designed to suggest associations of expansionism, but could carry other associations as well.[48] Another analysis suggests that by establishing a specific historical position, or local context for a scene, the gaze of spectators could be cued to produce a variety of ideological inflections. In his Island guide, Lapham described this construction of the panoramic gaze prescribing the kind of emotional experience tourists were expected to have. It was "grand—almost overwhelming. Here one gets a birds' eye view of more than three-fourths of the entire island, including its harbors, bays, coves, sounds, lakes, ponds, mountains, forest, farms and villages; also of several towns on the mainland, numerous islands along the coast line, and a broad expanse of ocean." Language is inadequate, Lapham declared, "to express the beauty and variety of the scenes here opened to view, and the emotions they awaken cannot be told in words; the impressions they make upon the mind are indelible, and remain as an unfading memorial of a most delightful and enjoyable occasion." In fact, "the two grandest objects in nature, high mountains and a boundless ocean, here occupy the same horizon, and no earthly view can be more absorbing."[49]

By 1865 a trip up Cadillac Mountain was a required destination on the tourist itinerary. Transportation was abundant for the Cadillac Mountain ascent, the "so-called 'mountain wagons,' such as are in general use all about the White Mountains" were especially recommended before the railway was built.[50] *Picturesque America's* essay noted that Cadillac Mountain could also boast of suitable lodging: "A cottage, originally built by the United States Coast Survey, stands on the extreme top of the mountain, and affords satisfactory

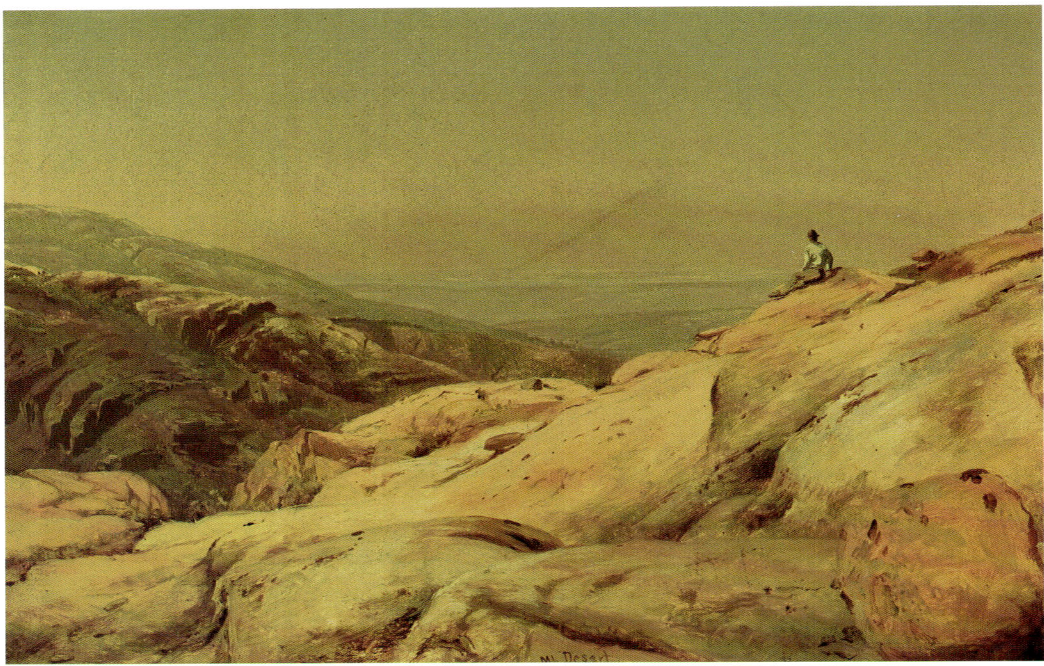

FIG. 69 Jervis McEntee, *On Mount Desert*, 1864, oil on canvas, 10¾ x 15⅞". Private Collection.

accommodation for the tourists."[51] Earlier, Martin's guide noted the Green Mountain House where food was now served at the "small but comfortable cottage where one may dine or spend the night." Martin added "the rude track up which long ago the belongings of the Coast Survey were dragged, has been replaced by a very tolerable mountain road. A trifling toll is charged, to keep it in repair.[52] Tourist culture and its attendant commercial aspects were quickly apparent. By 1886 an even more convenient means to the summit was popularized. "By far the largest number prefer to go by the regular conveyance furnished by the Green Mountain Railway which is by carriage to Eagle Lake, thence by steamer up the lake to the base, then by railway to the summit," Lapham explained.[53]

Moses Sweetser's 1883 travel guide elaborated on the now acclaimed tourist view seen from Cadillac Mountain that so excited Church, Gifford, McEntee, and a host of other artists and tourists. Sweetser described the view as "magnificent, and includes leagues on leagues of open sea, the gem-like outer islands, the long levels of Frenchman's Bay, the great mountains from Interlaken Hill to Katahdin, and bits of Eagle Lake and Somes' Sound." The new route to the summit was an astounding success and "five thousand persons visit this peak every year; and now that the route has been made at once easier, cheaper, and more interesting, the number will greatly increase."[54]

After the Civil War, rapid advancements in transportation, first by steamboat then by railroad, accelerated an unprecedented transformation of a wilderness area into a major tourist destination. Many later artists visited the Island to paint scenery, but the work of the first generation of artists led by Cole was completed. When commercial and private development seriously threatened the Island's scenic wilderness character, preservationists emerged. They quickly acknowledged the vital role landscape artists played. The artists "drew and painted, and what was most important, sold their paintings. By doing this they told just that group which could afford long summer vacations of the beauties of Mount Desert in general and of the ocean side of Bar Harbor in particular."[55]

NOTES

1. W. B., "The Late F. H. Lane, Marine Artist," *Daily Evening Transcript,* 19 August 1865.

2. John Wilmerding, *The Artist's Mount Desert* (Princeton: Princeton University Press, 1994), 45–46. See also John Wilmerding, *Paintings of Fitz Hugh Lane* (Washington, D.C.: National Gallery of Art, Harry N. Abrams, New York, 1988).

3. W. B., "The Late F. H. Lane."

4. John Wilmerding, *Fitz Hugh Lane 1804–1865: American Marine Painter* (Salem, Mass.: Essex Institute, 1964; reprint, 1967), 15.

5. When Lane died Stevens executed his estate, and was key to the safekeeping of Lane's drawings, now in the Cape Ann Historical Society. Frederic Alan Scharf, "Fitz Hugh Lane: Visits to the Maine Coast, 1848–1855," *Essex Institute Historical Collections* 98 (April 1962): 112.

6. Joseph L. Stevens, Jr., Boston, to Mr. Mansfield, Gloucester, 17 October 1903, Cape Ann Historical Society, quoted in John Wilmerding, *Fitz Hugh Lane* (New York: Praeger Publishers, 1971), 51.

7. Franklin Kelly, "Lane and Church in Maine," in Wilmerding, *Paintings of Fitz Hugh Lane*, 1988, 132–4.

8. Joseph L. Stevens, Jr., *Gloucester Daily Telegraph*, 17 September 1850, quoted in Wilmerding, *Fitz Hugh Lane*, 1971, 53.

9. Ibid., 54.

10. Ibid., 53.

11. Ibid., 53–54.

12. Wilmerding, *Fitz Hugh Lane*, 1971, 62.

13. Scharf, "Fitz Hugh Lane," 117.

14. Ibid., 116.

15. Stevens, *Gloucester Daily Telegraph*, quoted in Wilmerding, 1971, 53.

16. W. B. Lapham, *Bar Harbor and Mount Desert Island* (New York: Liberty Printing, 1886), 43.

17. See Eric A. R. Ronnberg, Jr., "A Few Words About this Picture," *Invention and Technology* 4, no. 2 (Fall 1988): 15–20. I appreciate clarification of vessel details from John Arrison, librarian/archivist, Penobscot Marine Museum, Searsport.

18. "Mount Desert," *Harper's New Monthly Magazine* 45, no. 267 (August 1872): 324–5.

19. See Eric A. R. Ronnberg, Jr., "Fitz Hugh Lane: A Storm, Breaking Away, Vessel Slipping Her Cable, 1858," in *Twelve American Masterpieces* (New York: Spanierman Gallery, 1998); and "Imagery and Types of Vessels," in Wilmerding, *Paintings of Fitz Hugh Lane*, 1988, 61–106. See also, John H. Harland, *Seamanship in the Age of Sail* (London: Conway Maritime Press, 1984).

20. Quoted in Wilmerding, *Paintings of Fitz Hugh Lane*, 1988, 54.

21. Lane completed two oils of Mount Desert in 1856: *Off Mount Desert Island* and *Sunrise on the Maine Coast* (Private Collection). Wilmerding, *Fitz Hugh Lane*, 1971, fig. 70.

22. Clarence Cook, "Letters on Art - No. IV," *The Independent* (7 September 1854), quoted in William H. Gerdts, "'The Sea is His Home': Clarence Cook Visits Fitz Hugh Lane," *The American Art Journal* 17, no. 3 (Summer 1985): 49.

23. Ibid., 47-49.

24. Ibid., 49.

25. Elizabeth Garrity Ellis, "Cape Ann Views," in Wilmerding, *Paintings of Fitz Hugh Lane*, 1988.

26. Rebecca Bedell, "Haseltine, Agassiz, and the Rocks at Nahant," *Nineteenth Century* 14, no. 1 (1994): 3–9; see also Marc Simpson, Andrea Henderson, Sally Mills, *Expressions of Place: The Art of William Stanley Haseltine* (San Francisco: The Fine Arts Museums of San Francisco, 1993); and Helen Haseltine Plowden, *William Stanley Haseltine: Sea and Landscape Painter, 1835–1900* (London: Frederick Muller, Ltd. 1947).

27. "Sketchings: Domestic Art Gossip," *The Crayon* (November 1859): 349.

28. Henry T. Tuckerman, *Book of the Artists: American Artist Life Comprising Biographical and Critical Sketches of American Artists, First Published 1867* (reprint, New York: James F. Carr, 1967), 556–7.

29. Tuckerman, *Book of the Artists*, 557.

30. "Domestic Art Gossip," *The Crayon* 7, no. 12 (December 1860): 353.

31. Anna Wells Rutledge, *Cumulative Record of Exhibition Catalogues: The Pennsylvania Academy of the Fine Arts* (Philadelphia: The American Philosophical Society, 1955), 94.

32. "The National Academy of Design," *The Evening Post*, 13 May 1863.

33. "Fine Arts: National Academy of Design," *The Albion* (10 May 1862): 225.

34. "Art and the Century Club," *The Round Table* 1, no. 9 (13 February 1864): 139.

35. "Fine Arts: National Academy of Design," 225.

36. "Fourth Artist's Reception," *New York Daily Tribune*, 26 March 1864.

37. Bedell, "Haseltine, Agassiz, and the Rocks at Nahant," 3.

38. Plowden, *William Stanley Haseltine*, cited in Wilmerding, *The Artist's Mount Desert*, 1994, 120, no. 23.

39. Ila Weiss, *Poetic Landscape: The Art and Experience of Sanford R. Gifford* (Newark, N.J.: University of Delaware Press, 1987), 100.

40. Edmund C. Steadman and George M. Gould, *Life and Letters of Edmund Clarence Steadman* (New York: Moffat and Yard, 1910), 1:342.

41. "Art and Artists in New York," *Boston Evening Transcript*, 17 November 1864.

42. Weiss, *Poetic Landscape*, 246.

43. "The National Academy of Design," *New York Times*, 24 June 1863.

44. Ibid.

45. "Mount Desert," *Harper's New Monthly Magazine* 45, no. 267 (August 1872): 337.

46. "American Genius as Expressed in Art," *The Round Table* (26 December 1863): 21–22.

47. "Mount Desert," *Harper's*, 336–7.

48. Albert Boime, *The Magisterial Gaze* (Washington, D.C.: Smithsonian Institution Press, 1991), 1–2.

49. Lapham, *Bar Harbor and Mount Desert Island*, 36.

50. "Mount Desert," *Harper's*, 336.

51. William Cullen Bryant, ed., *Picturesque America: or the Land We Live In* (New York: D. Appleton and Company, 1872), 14.

52. Clara Barnes Martin, *Mount Desert on the Coast of Maine*. "Infinite Riches in a Little Room" 4th ed. (Portland: Loring, Short, and Harmon, 1877), 17.

53. Lapham, 36.

54. M. F. Sweetser, *Summer Days Down East* (Portland, Maine: Chisholm Brothers, 1883), 127.

55. Richard Walden Hale, Jr., *The Story of Bar Harbor* (New York: Ives Washburn, Inc., 1949), 127.

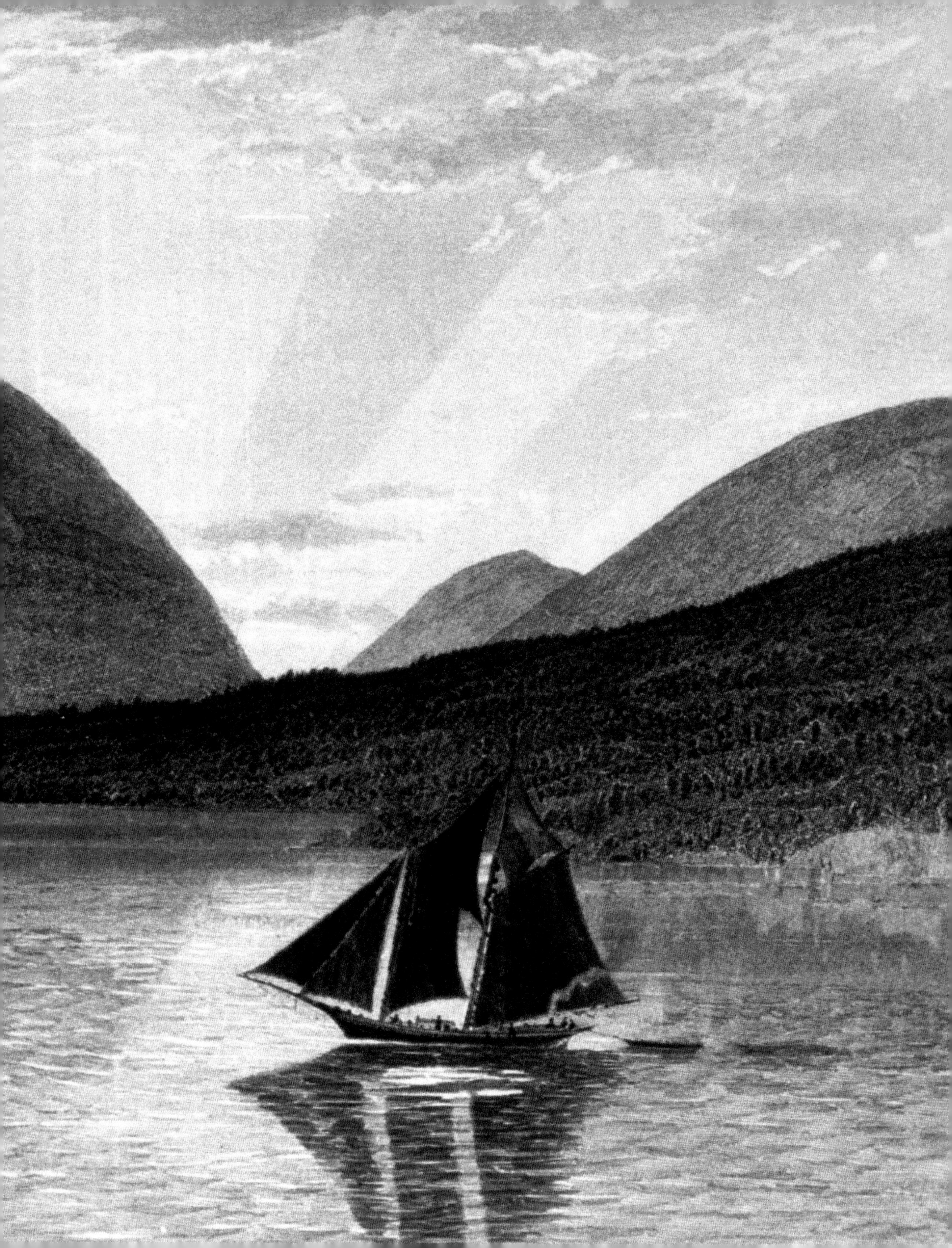

CHAPTER 6

Prospecting for Scenery

Interest in Mount Desert among the metropolitan upper class in the Northeast resulted from the work of New York landscape painters. In the decades after the Civil War a number of artists took the tourist's pilgrimage to Mount Desert, usually "prospecting" for opportunities to boost sales of their landscapes in the city. The achievements of these second generation and even third generation artists to the continuing reaffirmations of tourist culture is traced in John Wilmerding's *The Artist's Mount Desert.* Tourist culture at Mount Desert was promoted on the idea that proper appreciation of Island scenery necessitated seeing it as an artist might, an idea that was deeply implicated in the inception of Acadia National Park. At the end of the nineteenth century Mount Desert scenery became a geographical and a cultural commodity.

The contributions of the artists who explored Mount Desert before the Civil War, making it and themselves famous, was noted as early as the 1872 when writers in *Harper's New Monthly Magazine* endorsed the desirability of Mount Desert as a destination, based on the paintings of Church and Cole. Other writers and local historians observed the phenomenon as well. In 1886 W. B. Lapham stated that artists "F. E. Church and others . . . who had found their way across from Southwest Harbor by way of Somes' Sound, and who, attracted by its marvelous scenery, had remained here for the purpose of transferring some of its unique views to canvas . . . soon made the locality familiar to the residents of the large cities and summer travel soon began to gravitate toward the eastern part of the Island." Lapham insisted that this process was the "beginning of Bar Harbor as a seaside resort."[1]

After 1865 the influx of summer visitors at Mount Desert was unprecedented, such that, "of all the numerous nooks and corners on the North Atlantic coast which have become famous as seaside resorts, there is none whose growth has been more rapid than that of Bar Harbor."[2] The period 1866 to 1872 saw Bar Harbor transformed from a small settlement into a major resort; by 1887 the town had become a major destination.[3] The official *Colby's Atlas of the State of Maine* (fig. 70) for 1884 showed "Mount Desert and Adjacent Islands" with their original names, including "Eden," which became Bar Harbor when Island place names were changed in the early twentieth century to make them sound more cultured, historical, and "authentic." Because of the remoteness of the Island and the considerable cost of a long trip by sea, or later by railroad, "resorting" at Mount Desert was expensive, available mainly to those with ample discretionary funds and leisure time. These summer visitors escaped the heat, disease, and pressures of life in Northeastern metropolises, cities now filled with immigrants whose ethnic identity, languages, and customs seemed foreign to post-war Anglo-Protestants. At places like Mount Desert, Nahant, and Newport, they purchased respite from the rapidly changing urban and industrial society to which they often owed their privileged positions.[4]

Picturesque America

The commercial promotion of remote places such as Mount Desert after the Civil War was directly linked with rapid growth in transportation and the tourism industry. The publication of *Picturesque America; or The Land We Live In* resulted from this promotion. This multi-volume series of deluxe illustrated travel books, designed to present the scenic wonders of the nation from East to West and North to South, was published by Appleton's Company, a firm known for its dedication to the educational mission of culture because of its usefulness in "refining" the coarseness of American life. The redoubtable figure of pre-Civil War high culture William Cullen Bryant, editor of the influential newspaper the *New York Evening Post*, and doyen of American letters, edited and nominally directed publication of *Picturesque America.* His name lent unimpeachable authority, but Oliver B. Bunce prepared the actual letterpress, which was accompanied by elab-

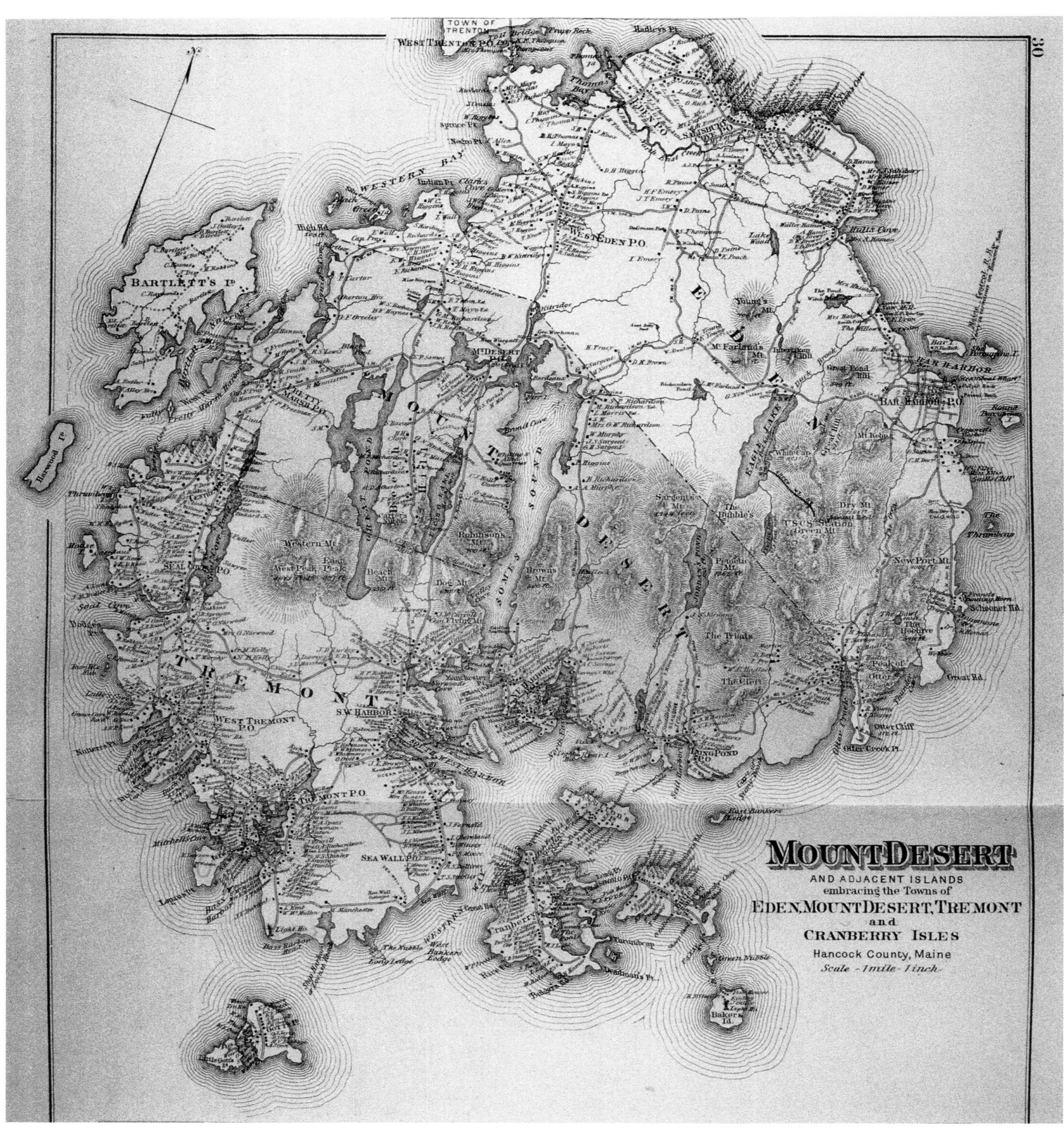

FIG. 70 "Mount Desert and Adjacent Islands," from *Colby's Atlas of the State of Maine*, Houlton, Maine:
Colby and Stuart, 1884–1900. Courtesy of the Osher Map Library, University of Southern Maine.

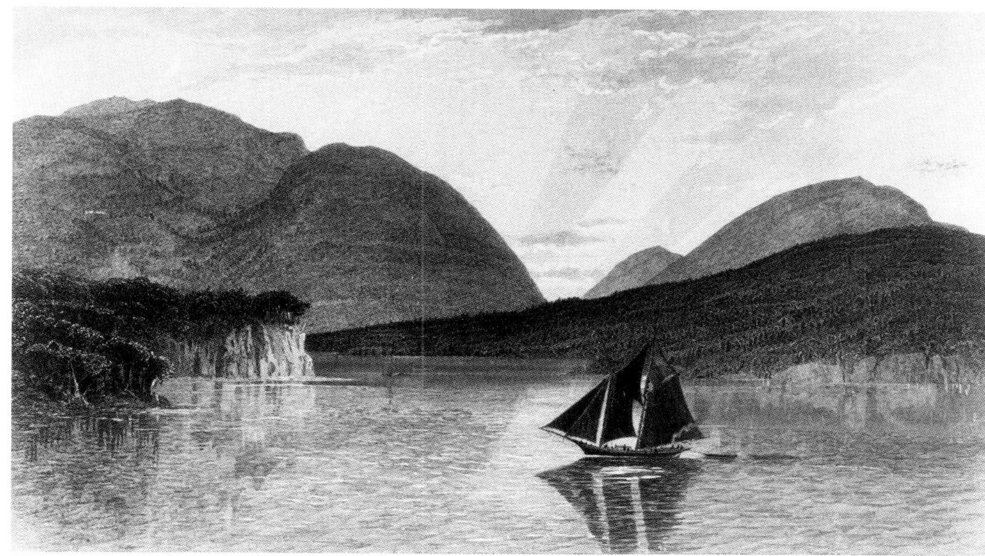

orate steel plate engravings commissioned from Harry Fenn and other American illustrators. Recent scholarly study shows how the production of *Picturesque America* was deeply entwined with nationalism and with the commodification of tourism.[5] The volumes linked the production of fine arts, in the paintings of Cole, Church, Gifford, Lane, and others, with the consumption of scenery by larger audiences of tourists after 1865.

Successions of Scenic Effects

Until the mid-1840s only schooners and fishing sloops plied the waters of the Island, as Cole, Church, and Lane experienced. By 1872 tourists virtually ignored these modes of travel; they preferred the certainty of steamboat service. The slow travel by sailing vessel, which had excited Lane and his yachtsmen patrons, and frustrated Cole and Church, was romantically recast by Fenn as the frontispiece image for *Picturesque America's* chapter on Mount Desert. It directly followed the book's first plate of the nation's most famous scenic place, Niagara Falls (fig. 71), offering a suggestive linkage. This frontispiece for Bunce's article depicted a lovely Maine schooner with all her sails set, ghosting along silently at the sacred moment of second twilight. The scene is a "tourist moment," when the rays of the setting sun emblazon the swelling profiles of mountain summits. Fenn's image induced nostalgia for a sailing way of life that no respectable, practical tourist heading North in 1872 would have considered, especially Bunce and Fenn who traveled to the Island on a steamboat. The touristic desire for nautical and "historical" experiences of old-fashioned sailing schooners would be resurrected as an exclusive tourist attraction in the later twentieth century: a fleet of "Down East" schooners, much like the one Fenn depicted, today cruises the waters around Mount Desert and Rockland.

Bunce constructed the accompanying narrative, promoting Mount Desert's attractions, around one essential assump-tion—that visitors would wish to see Island scenery with the eyes and mind of a landscape artist. This assumption informed almost every page of *Picturesque America*, and its ubiquitous presence demonstrates the centrality of conventions of landscape painting in the production of tourist culture after the Civil War. The volumes' many illustrations provided "texts" and visual stimulus to those with the inclination and wherewithal to actually make a visit, and were accompanied by narratives inviting arm-chair travel to the Island for those who could not afford a trip. The narrator's voice always assumed that the reader of *Picturesque America* shared a cultivated, educated taste for landscape scenery, and understood, or sought to understand, its conventions. The publication simultaneously offered advice on practical matters of concern to visitors: preferred views and reaching them, road conditions, and availability of accommodation.

The writer's account of the approach to Mount Desert is an example of this didactic style of travel narrative. It might have been an accompaniment for Fenn's frontispiece of an old-fashioned sailing vessel, or for one of Lane's later sentiment-filled images of sailing vessels at sunset, but with one difference—it was described from the deck of a steamboat.

The best view of the mountains [of Mount Desert] is from the sea. The steamer from Portland, which lands at Bar Harbor twice a week, approaches the island at noonday, when the landscape under the direct rays of the sun, possesses the least charm. . . . If it so chance, as it did the writer, that delays bring the steamer along the coast when the sun is sinking behind the hills, a picture of singular beauty is presented. The mountains then lift in gloomy grandeur against the light of the western sky, and, with the movement of the steamer, break every moment into new combinations of rare beauty. Now they lie massed, one against another, in long, undulating lines, now open into distinct groups . . . in a dissolving view that for an hour or more presents a superb succession of scenic effects, which the spectator watches with

East Eden, according to the outsider Bunce, was "built upon
a treeless plain, and consists for the most part of a group of
small white houses, rapidly extemporized for the accommodation of summer boarders." There were no trees, gardens,
or other "pleasant surroundings." Bunce gently mocked the
pretension of the name: "The place [East Eden] is as con-
spicuously inexact in its cognomen as the island itself is; one
wonders whether the notion of naming places by their con-
traries is a legitimate Down-East institution."[7]

After the tourist had found "himself satisfactorily domi-
ciled at East Eden," two purposes of special interest fill the
mind. "One is to explore the rocky shore and the other is to
climb Green Mountain [Cadillac], and enjoy the superb view
from its 'thunder-smitten brow.' These respects to the scenery
of the island having been paid, his subsequent purpose is
likely to be fishing and boating."[8] The "amenities" for yachtsmen did not escape the notice of the promoters of scenery:
"The bays, inlets, and sounds of the coast of Maine afford
superb resources for the yachtsman. . . . There is a vast area
of inland-sea navigation, which, with infinite variety of scene,
gives ample space for boating. A yachting-party might spend
the summer delightfully threading the mazes of this 'hun-
dred-harbored Maine.'"[9]

No Indifferent Half Glance Will Suffice

Bunce carefully outlined the most important sites for scenic
experiences such as the great cliffs named The Ovens, which
Fenn illustrated in a full-page print entitled "The Cliffs
Near the Ovens" (fig. 72). These rocks "contrast happily with
the rocks on the sea-front of the island in possessing delicious quiet and repose. . . . The shores here supply almost
exhaustless material for the sketch-book of the artist."[10]
Fenn's illustration depicted a group of tourists arriving at
low tide. In the foreground a fashionably dressed lady and
gentleman admire the rocks. "To this spot pleasure seekers
come in great numbers. It is a favorite picnic-ground for the
summer residents of East Eden, whose graceful pleasure
boats give animation to the scene. . . . The cliff, crowned with
its green forest, makes up a picture of great sweetness and
beauty." The great painter, the sea, had painted the rocks "in
various tints of rare beauty . . . such as would delight the
eye and tax the skill and patience of a painter to reproduce."[11]
Fenn's patience may have been limited, but his skill in
employing the conventions of emblematic personification was
considerable. He suggestively personified many of the rocks
at The Ovens, adding layers of associations with "sermons
in stone."

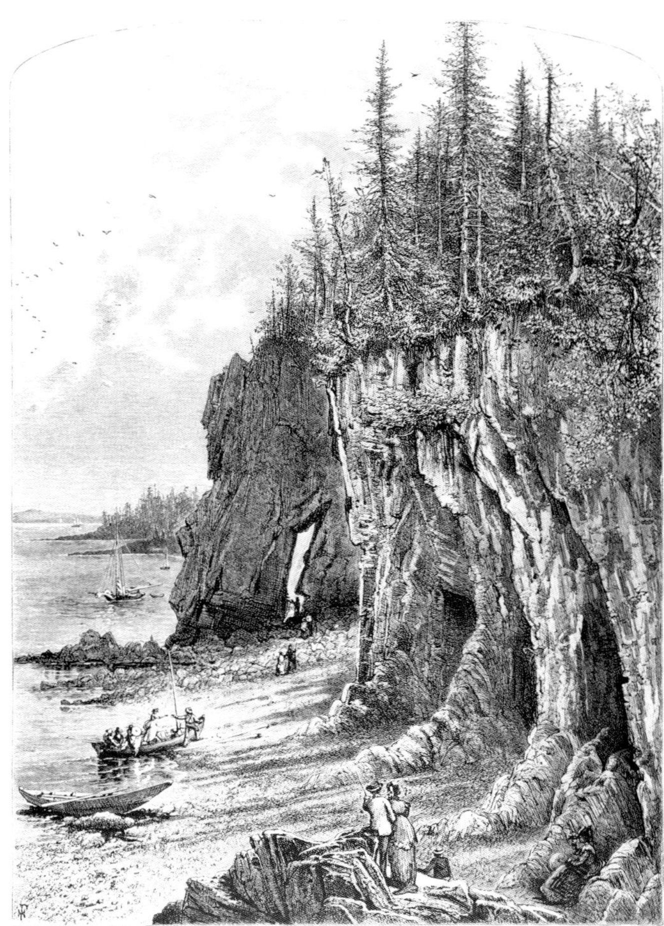

FIG. 72   William Cullen Bryant, ed., *Picturesque America: or the Land
We Live In*, New York: D. Appleton and Company, 1872, "The
Cliffs Near the Ovens," 5.

To properly grasp the beauty of nature and to understand
its sacred texts in rock, mountain, and sea required the correct geographical and conceptual point of view. The meaning
of a scene or the ability to interpret a picture sometimes
depended on this. "It is often a matter of search to discover
the point from which an object has its best expression, and
probably only those of intuitive artistic tastes are enabled to
see all the beauties of a landscape, which others lose in igno-
rance of how to select the most advantageous standing-
place."[12] In a passage that resonated with an art writer's
praise of Church's ability to show viewers "that which we do
not see, or seeing do not perceive," Bunce wrote: "To the cold
and indifferent, Nature has no charms; she reveals herself
only to those who surrender their hearts to her indifference,
and who patiently study her aspects. The beauty of any object
lies partly in the capacity of the spectator to see it, and partly
in his ability to put himself where the form and color impress
the senses most effectively." Not one man in ten "discerns
half the beauty of a tree or a pile of rocks, and hence those
who fail to discover in a landscape the charm others describe
in it should question their own power of appreciation rather
than the accuracy of the delineation." The rocky coasts of
Mount Desert "must be studied with this appreciation and
taste, if their beauties are to be understood. No indifferent
half glance will suffice." Bunce advised visitors or readers to

"go to the edge of the cliff and look down; . . . sit in the shadows of their massive presence; study the infinite variety of form, texture, and color, and learn to read all the different phases of sentiments their scarred fronts have to express. When all this is done, be assured you will discover that 'sermons in stone' was not a mere fancy of the poet."[13]

Sights to suit the fancy of poets, artists, or ministers abounded on Mount Desert according to *Picturesque America*. There were birch woods that "filled any artist with delight, and especially the painter [Worthington T.] Whittredge, whose birch-forests are so famous."[14] From the repose of The Ovens to the sublimity of the seaward side of the Island a dramatic change was evident. Schooner Head and Great Head were the next designated sights on Bunce's itinerary that included places where the sea's wild fury could be fully admired. "Visitors to Mount Desert but half understand or appreciate its wonders if they do not visit the cliffs in a storm." Relying on the war metaphor that Church had so effectively used in his *Coast Scene, Mount Desert* (see fig. 52), "at such times they cast themselves against the cliffs with a violence that threatens to beat down the rocky barriers . . . at other times the ceaseless war they make upon the shore seems to be one of defeat." The waves strike in "full, sweeping charge upon the rocks, but hastily fall back, broken and discomfited, giving place to fresh and hopeful levees, who repeat the first assault, and, like their predecessors are hurled back to defeat." At Great Head the sublime effect was pronounced. "It is a bold, projecting mass, with at its base deep gashes worn by the waves. A view of its grim, massive front is obtained by descending a broken mass of cyclopean rocks . . . where at low tide, the cliff towers above you in majestic mass."[15] Fenn's image of "Great Head" (fig. 73) deployed the full convention of emblematic personification. The rock's "grim massive" visage is formed by merging a profile view and a frontal view in a fragmented facial construction that twentieth-century cubists might have conceived. Tiny figures of tourists clamber about the foreground rocks while on the horizon, enveloped in fog, the sails of a passing vessel recall Cole's painting of *Frenchman's Bay, Mount Desert Island, Maine* (see fig. 22) with its excited tourist gazing at the spectacle of rock, sea, and air.

Artists "Squattin' and Fussin'"

In the same year that *Picturesque America* appeared, *Harper's Magazine* published a lengthy article about the Mount Desert scenic attractions. "Cole was the pioneer here, as he was in our landscape art, and he had a host of followers. One day Church, when prospecting upon the island, made the discovery of Bar Harbor. The next year, and for I do not know how many years afterward, he took a party of friends to the same place." Over the course of time, the article continued,

Church's pictures of scenery at Mount Desert were seen in the exhibitions of the National Academy. At one time and another most all the noted artists have followed on sketching tours, and it is chiefly by this means, in the first instance, that Mount Desert has become so popular as a watering place. . . . Now, most of the visitors to Mount Desert, even the prosaic folk, go prepared to enjoy the picturesque, the beautiful, the sublime.[16]

In other words, the tourist was already prescribed to find and see the approved scenes that famous artists had selected for them.

The locals were not so impressed. In an exchange with Abraham Somes—the landlord of the Somes Mount Desert Tavern, the oldest hotel on the Island, in Somesville—the *Harper's* narrator inquired about making arrangements to see the great headlands of the Sound by boat. "It's the scenery we wish to see," was the inquiry to Somes, who was "also town-clerk, postmaster, and I know not what else besides." The reply from the elderly innkeeper, who had greeted Cole and Church, the Tracys, and many later artists and tourists who had followed their path, was amusing. "Yes, I know, its what them artist men come here fur. But what it amounts ter, after all their squattin' and fussin', I don't

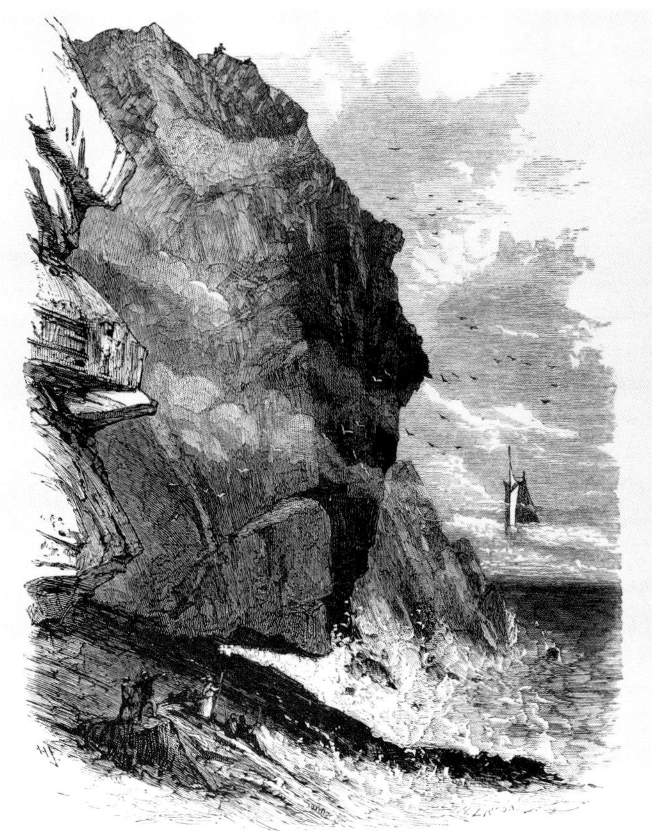

113

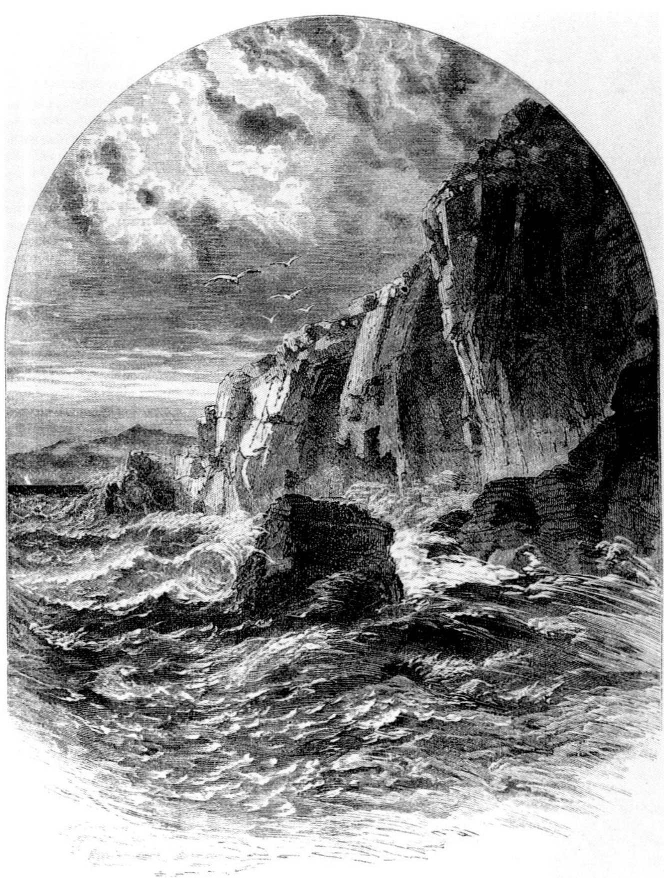

FIG. 74 "Mount Desert," *Harper's New Monthly Magazine* 45, no. 267 (August 1872), "Cliffs on Bald Porcupine," 329.

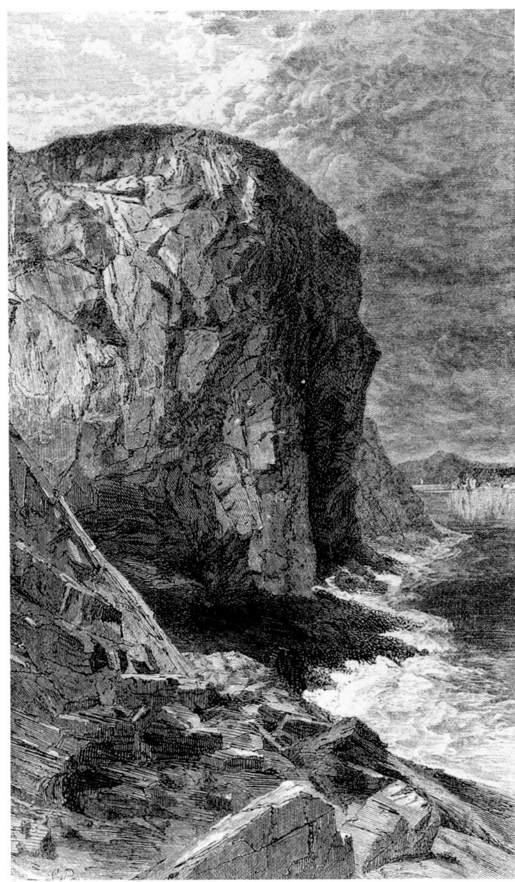

FIG. 75 "Mount Desert," *Harper's New Monthly Magazine* 45, no. 267 (August 1872), "Great Head," 333.

know." Later, as they were being rowed to a scenic place by one of the Island boatmen, the attitude of the locals to the tourists momentarily broke the surface decorum of the narrative, as the boatman observed that the reason visitors come is "'cause we're handy to the Bluenoses."[17]

Celebrated Artists' Hotels

Selected scenes and views were required for *Harper's* readers as they had been for *Picturesque America's* arm-chair travelers. The rocky coast with its great prospects and overlooks was a favorite, and "Cliffs On Bald Porcupine" and "Great Head" were illustrated in the article (fig. 74, and fig. 75). "Here the massive cliffs lift their bald front high in the air, as if to challenge the wildest, most furious assaults of wind and wave. . . . Monstrous waves [are] lifted up by some mighty hand and cast furiously against the cliff."[18] The de rigueur tour of the Island was punctuated by a new sight, the "Lynam Homestead." The house itself was not particularly picturesque, and "the surrounding country side is bleak and bare, while an old wind-swept and withered tree in the yard give the place a look of loneliness and neglect." But, the article asserted, "it is the artistic associations of the old house which will make it most celebrated, for within its walls have been gathered many of the names most celebrated in American art—Cole, Church, Gifford, Hart, Parsons, Warren, Brown, Colman, and others."[19] By the early 1870s the Lynam

House was enshrined as the veritable "artists' hotel" at Mount Desert, although it was long out of use. Associations of the early artists who had first explored and painted the Island were already part of the mythology of Mount Desert's emergence. In spite of its long acknowledged associations with celebrated American artists, the Lynam house was eventually pulled down.

By the 1880s new artists, many from New York, came to the now popular Island with hopes of attracting wealthy patrons who summered or visited.[20] Xanthus Smith (1839–1929), an unofficial artist-in-residence on the Island during the 1880s and 1890s, first visited around 1867, but the year for which substantial documentation exists is 1877, when he sketched the rugged eastern shore.[21] Smith practiced his profession as a hotel artist at the Claremont Hotel in Southwest Harbor, where the register shows that he was there in 1883, 1884, 1885, 1886, 1887, 1889, 1890, and 1892–1895. As a memento of one of his summers there he produced a small painting of the hotel for its owner, which still hangs there today (fig. 76). The figures on the hotel porch, and other figures by the water suggest the leisured life of the summer boarder.

Scenic Tourism: Steamboats and Railroads

The arrival of dependable steam navigation in the late 1850s marks the moment when Mount Desert became a regular

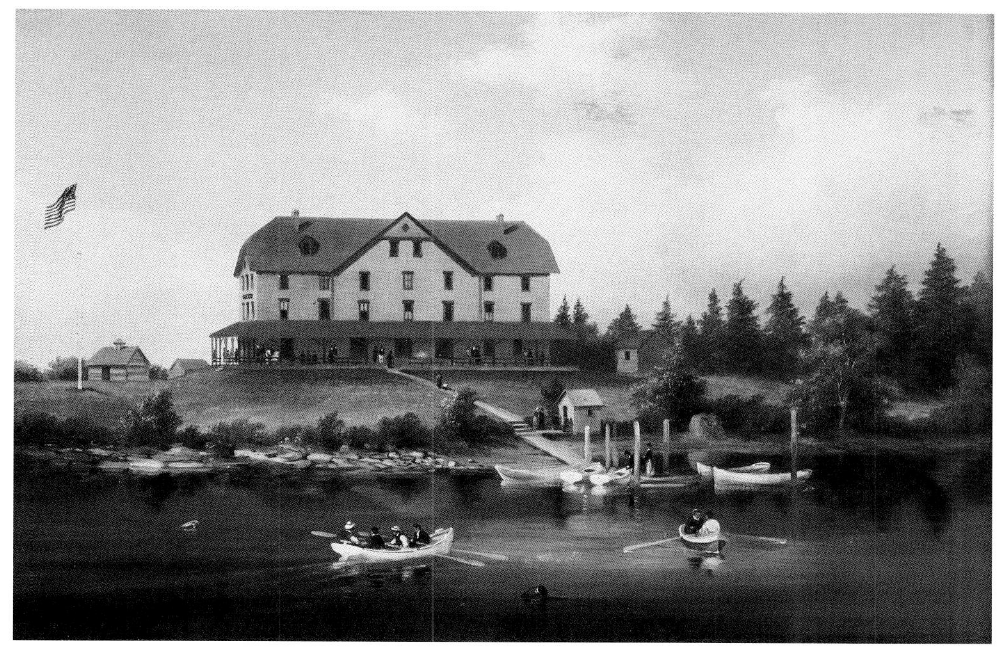

tourist destination. Entrepreneurs quickly responded to the new market for mechanized transportation (fig. 77). As early as 1846, the Hancock and Washington Steam Navigation Company built the steamer *T. F. Secor.* It traveled the Belfast, Ellsworth, and Bar Harbor route and was one of the first steam-powered passenger vessels to call at Mount Desert. It connected northern points with the "Boston Boat" at Belfast.[22] The steamer *Rockland* that regularly stopped at Southwest Harbor in the 1850s added Bar Harbor to its run after 1857, after Tobias Roberts erected his wharf at the end of main street to accommodate large steamers. A narrator in *Picturesque America* observed that the "steamer from Portland, which lands at Bar Harbor twice a week, approaches

the island at noonday."[23] In 1879 the *Mount Desert,* affectionately dubbed the "Old Mounty," began regular runs between Rockland and Bar Harbor.[24] Also in 1879 faster steamers such as the *City of Richmond* and the *Lewiston* began calling at Bar Harbor. Making only one stop at Rockland, the overnight express-boat service left Portland at 11:00 in the evening and arrived at Bar Harbor at 9:30 the following morning. This route had the "advantage of enabling one to view the grand scenery which is unfolded from every side from the time Rockland is left until Bar Harbor is reached."[25]

Clara Martin's guide book traced the improvements and the various routes available to passengers by the late

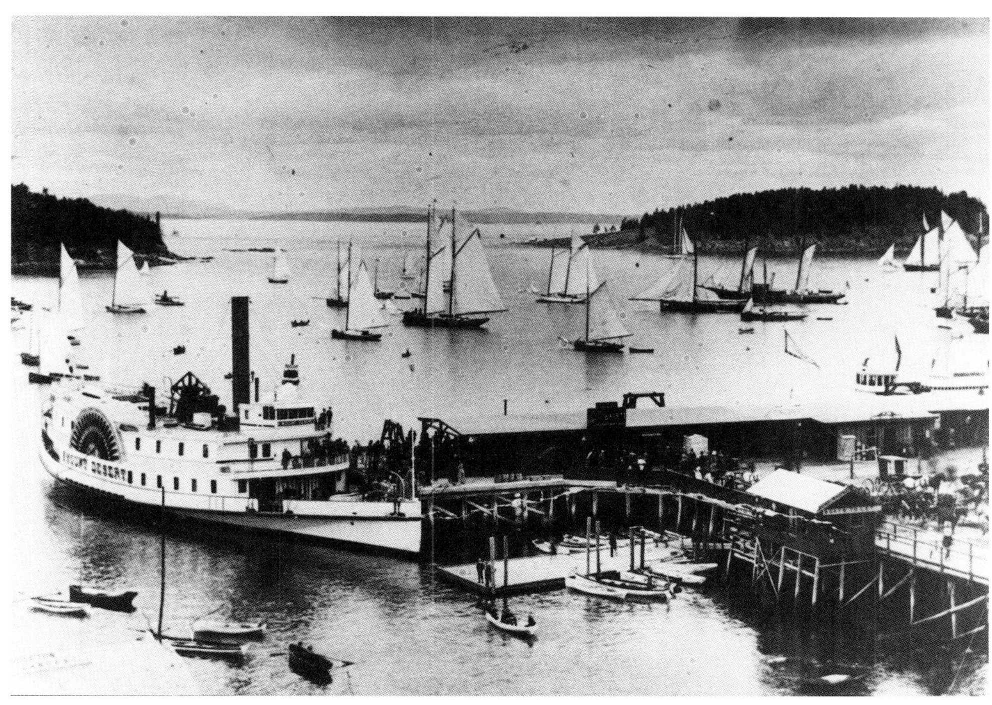

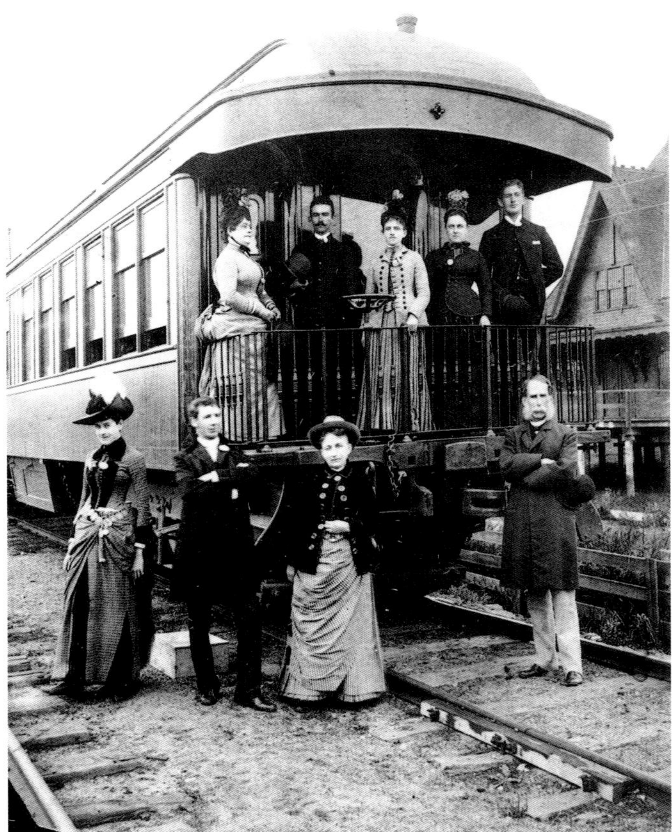

FIG. 78 *Bar Harbor Express*, c.1880s. Photograph Courtesy of the Bar Harbor Historical Society.

1860s—all-land (rail and stagecoach), all-water (steamer and schooner), and a combination of rail and steamer, or rail and schooner, connecting at Portland or Rockland.[26] She believed that the most popular and picturesque route to the Island was by steamboat from Portland. *Picturesque America* and *Harper's* provided their readers with similar information. Always eager to increase tourism Clara Martin added that "it was the opening of this route which made Mount Desert the popular resort that it is. So long as but one stage a week connected it with the outside world, only a few artists or leisurely tourists traveling with their own horses found their way to its marvels."[27] The stagecoach from Bangor to Mount Desert took eight hours; however, for the unhurried traveler "this gives you a drive of some fifty miles over superb roads through a picturesque country."[28]

The arrival of the railroad signaled the end of the reliance on sea travel and stage coach, and greatly accelerated the development of tourism on the Island.[29] In 1884 the forty-two mile Mount Desert Branch of the Maine Central Railroad lead to a surge that "more than quadrupled" the number of visitors.[30] This was an "all-rail route to within eight miles of the Bar Harbor wharf, and safe ferry boats always in waiting to convey passengers across the intervening space, known as Frenchman's Bay."[31] Lapham detailed the speed in which the journey from Boston could be made. Passengers could "leave Boston in elegant palace cars at nine o'clock in the

morning and before eight the same evening they can be at their hotel or cottage at Bar Harbor." If a passenger preferred a morning arrival they could "leave Boston at seven o'clock in the evening by sleeping cars, arrive in Bangor at five-thirty the following morning and at Bar Harbor at eight-thirty."[32]

On 29 June 1885, the Bar Harbor Express made its first run from Boston to Bangor to connect with the Mount Desert Branch (fig. 78). In fact, the "day train during the excursion season is a fast express, and makes the distance between Boston and Bangor, including all stops in less than eight hours."[33] The demand for rail passage to the Island was so great that in 1887 the express "limited" the number of stops "by using track water pans at three points, so that the train's steam engines could take water on the run."[34] In addition, newer and faster engines and lighter Pullman cars were used, all making the Bar Harbor Limited one of the fastest express trains in America. In 1901 a traveler could board the Express in New York City and arrive at the Mount Desert Ferry wharf in one day. In 1917 tourists from as far away as Washington, D.C. could reach the Mount Desert Ferry in about twenty hours. There was such demand that "Pullman cars were run directly to the ferry from Washington, Baltimore and Philadelphia, so that the western (and southern) terminus of the Express had in reality been moved to the nation's capital."[35] The automobile spelled the end of the Bar Harbor Express, which made its final run in 1960.

From Boarding Houses to Hotels

In a development that paralleled the improved transportation, local hoteliers eagerly accommodated the increasing number of travelers visiting the Island. Small modest boarding houses quickly gave way to palatial hotels. The Agamont House (fig. 79) was the first hotel at Bar Harbor, built in 1855 by the enterprising Tobias Roberts; its register is a veritable who's who of pre-Civil War visitors. After building a small boarding house in 1866, David Rodick enlarged his house in 1875 to accommodate 275 tourists (fig. 80, and fig. 81). The last expansion to his Rodick House in 1882 resulted in an impressive six-story hotel with four hundred rooms that claimed to be the largest hotel in Maine (fig. 82). Several other hotels were built at Bar Harbor from 1869 to 1892: The Rockaway, The Newport Hotel, The Louisburg, Grand Central, Belmont House, West End, Marlborough, The Porcupine, DeGregoire Hotel, and others.[36] By 1873, Bar Harbor had fifteen hotels and at the height of the hotel era, around 1887, Mount Desert could boast of seventeen at Bar Harbor, two at Seal Harbor, five at Northeast Harbor, and six at Southwest Harbor.[37]

The accommodations and food still left something to be desired in the early 1870s. *Harper's* complained about the beds in a manner that was reminiscent of Church's annoy-

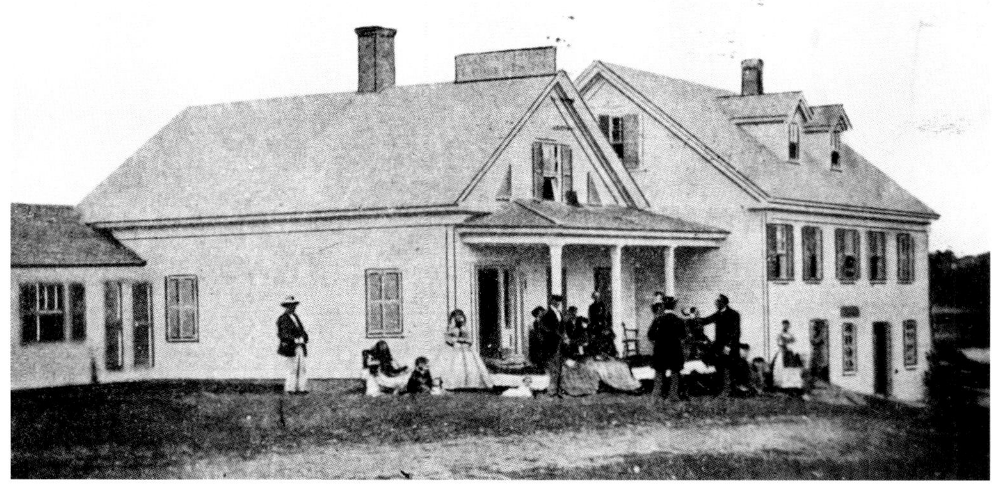

FIG. 79 *Agamont House,* c. 1860s–1870s, Mount Desert. Photograph Courtesy of the Bar Harbor Historical Society.

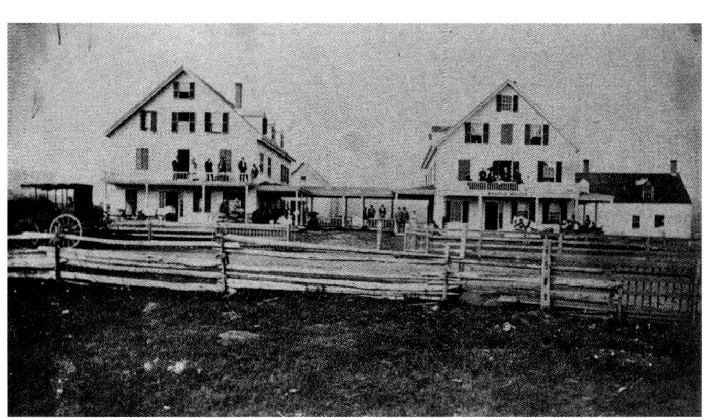

FIG. 80 *Rodick House,* built c.1866, Mount Desert. Photograph Courtesy of the Bar Harbor Historical Society.

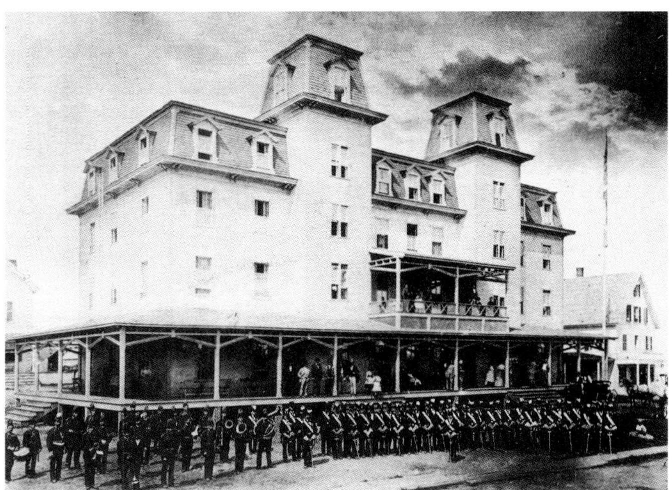

FIG. 81 *Rodick House,* built 1875, Mount Desert. Photograph Courtesy of the Bar Harbor Historical Society.

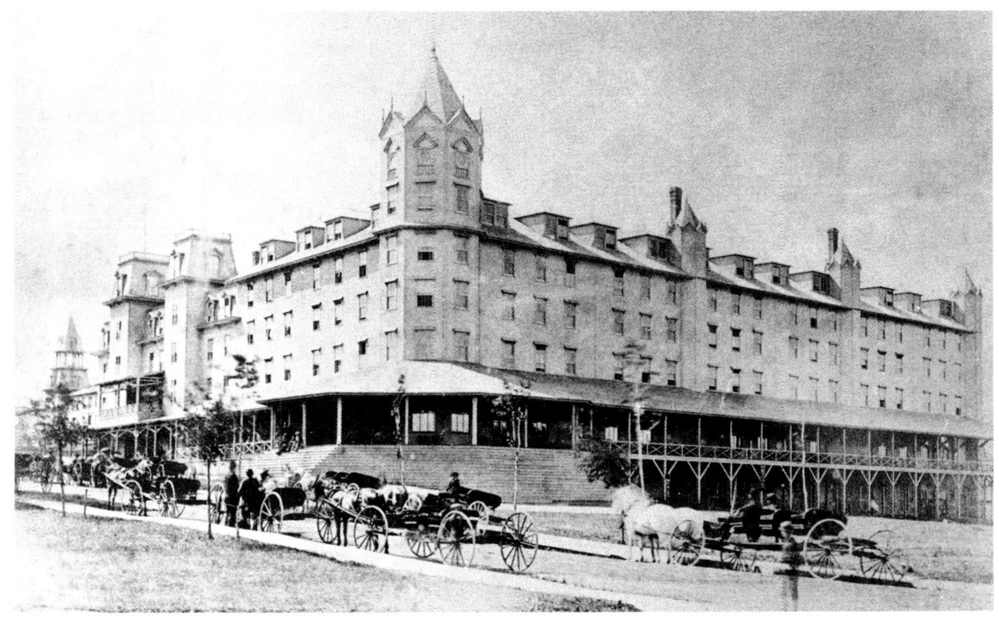

FIG. 82 *Rodick House,* built c.1882, Mount Desert. Photograph Courtesy of the Bar Harbor Historical Society.

ance with fleas. "The beds, however, remained as hard and lumpy as ever, and, though not a downy couch, you must bear with it until the Mount Desert landlords overcome their prejudices against hair mattress, or until some civilized hotelkeeper arrives there, and starts a healthy competition."[38] The food situation in 1872 did not fare better. "When one sits down at a Mount Desert table, the memories of Parker's beefsteak, or Delmonico's Poulet a l'Espagno, to say nothing of the luxuries of the home table, come thronging sumptuously before him to banish what little appetite remains." The hotel diet is "perhaps satisfying to the intellectual Bostonian, who seeks that food that stimulates and adds to the brain; but the more sensuous New Yorker, or the rearing tearing half horse and half alligator of the West, must have beef, fowl, and mutton."[39] But it was the matter of lobsters and scenery that was most unpleasant. In fact Bar Harbor's emergence as the dominant port and leading town on the Island may owe much to the lowly lobster. The writer for *Harper's* objected strongly to the odor and ugliness attendant to the lobster canneries at Southwest Harbor in 1872, preferring Bar Harbor for its cleaner fisheries. "The lobster business may be a profitable branch of industry, but . . . they are [lobsters] neither romantic nor poetical. . . . Just as [visitors to Mount Desert] are about to be ushered into this new world of romance and delight, [that they are] met upon the threshold by thousands of lobsters, raw, boiled, cooked, and canned, is discouraging, to say the least."[40]

The Grand March of Cottagers

While the hotels grew in number and size, their success laid the foundations of their subsequent decline. Edwin Lawrence Godkin (1831–1902), a long-time summer resident, considered the summer boarder at the great hotels to be "often, if not generally, the cottager's superior in culture, in acquirements, and in variety of social experience. He does not board because he likes the food, but simply because it enables him to live in the midst of beautiful scenery." The boarder represented a type of intellectual culture. For fully fifteen years after its discovery Bar Harbor, Godkin wrote, was "frequented exclusively by a very high order of boarders, and probably has been the scene of more plain living and high thinking than any other summer spot on the seacoast. It was, in fact, remarkable at one time for an almost unhealthy intellectual stimulation through an almost exclusively fish diet."[41]

Often, however, a boarder at one of the hotels was captivated by the scenic charms of the Island and decided to provide the domestic comforts enjoyed in the city. Members of America's wealthiest families built summer "cottages" at Mount Desert during the boom period of the 1880s, allowing them to entertain freely during the high season. Each larger and more ostentatious summer villa demonstrated the status of its owner. The permanent residents were increasingly

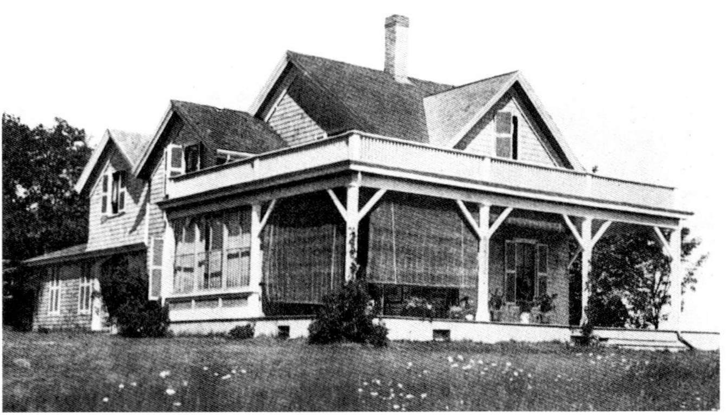

FIG. 83   House of Alpheus Hardy, *Birch Point,* built 1868, Mount Desert. Photograph Courtesy of the Bar Harbor Historical Society.

forced out, selling their land for cottage sites to city outsiders. Summer hotel boarders who did not construct cottages were also excluded socially, and as more land fell into private hands many favorite scenic sites were closed. Godkin shared the frustrations: "dislodgement along our coast and in our mountains of the boarder by the cottager is to-day the great summer tragedy of American life." He believed that the "worst of it . . . is that this is not the expulsion of the inferior by the superior race."[42]

Thirty-Thousand Dollar Lots

The building of the summer cottages signaled the gradual decline of the great hotels as centers of social life on Mount Desert. Highly ritualized social protocols developed around the life of extreme consumption in these great houses with their staffs of maids, butlers, and other domestic servants. Increasingly, private parties replaced general gatherings and exclusive clubs were preferred to the simpler pleasures of the buckboard rides, hikes, and picnics that had entertained Church, Winthrop, and members of the Tracy group. As the summer boarder was forced out, or became a cottager, the grandiose hotels became less popular and one by one most were closed, or were replaced in the twentieth century by motel chains. The cottagers who followed the summer boarders were wealthier and were aggressive in privatizing the finest views for themselves. As this occurred the tourist culture of the Island underwent a decisive class change.

The "cottagers" represented the highest class of society. They were often America's new industrialists and financiers, men made wealthy beyond any previous measure from war profits and the emergence of industrial monopolies. The Island also continued to attract members of New England's old money. Both groups found in Mount Desert a place remote enough, exclusive enough, and cool enough in the hot summer months, to become a destination on the "summer tour." According to Godkin, "the future at all our leading seashore places, in truth, belongs to the Cottager, and it is really useless to resist him. His march along the American coast is nearly as resistless as that of the hordes who issued from the plains of Scythia to overthrow the Roman Empire."

This cottager "moves on all the 'choice sites' without haste, with the calm and remorselessness of the man who knows that the morrow is his." Godkin noticed that this was the "growing passion, or fashion, if any one likes to call it so, of Americans to live in their own houses, both summer and winter." He not only singled out the wealthy but all segments of the American society. This "growing passion" was quickly "taking possession of all classes, from the New England mechanic, who puts up his shanty or tent on the seashore, to the millionaire who builds his hundred-thousand dollar villa on his thirty-thousand dollar lot."[43]

Recreation and Neurasthenia

In 1869 Alpheus Hardy from Boston became the first cottager, building "Birch Point," a modest dwelling by later standards (fig. 83). He lead a list of cottagers that eventually included the Fords, Vanderbilts, Rockefellers, Astors, Carnegies, Proctors, Stotesburys, and Mrs. William Morris Hunt, widow of the artist. Godkin, a dispossessed "victim" of the cottagers, expounded on their domination. "The Cottager has become to the boarder what the red [squirrel] is to the gray, a ruthless invader and exterminator." After building his cottage "caste has been established . . . the community is now divided into two classes, one of which looks down on the other."[44] He continued:

More cottages are built, with trim lawns and private lawn tennis grounds, with "shand-gaff" and "tennis-cup" concealed on tables in tents. Then the dog-cart with the groom in buckskin and boots, the Irish red setter, the saddle-horse with banged tail, the phaeton with two ponies, the young men in knickerbockers carrying imported racquets, the girls with banged hair, the club, ostensibly for newspaper reading, but really for secret gin-fizzes and soda-cocktails, make their appearance with a number of other monarchal excrescences.[45]

The newspaper publisher, Joseph Pulitzer, was Mount Desert's most sensational cottager, and the kind of monarchal figure that Godkin deplored. Pulitzer leased "Chatwold" (fig. 84) in June 1893, and bought the mansion the following year. An eccentric personality, Pulitzer promptly set about rebuilding his "Tower of Silence," to help soothe his nervous exhaustion and insomnia. The Tower was also his heavily insulated bedroom, which rotated on ball bearings. Pulitzer's compound also boasted the first heated swimming pool at Bar Harbor. These improvements assuaged his neurasthenia, a common ailment—perhaps akin to today's chronic fatigue syndrome—that affected America's overworked men of business. Neurasthenia required all manner of restorative cures and rests. Recent scholarly analysis shows that neurasthenia was perceived as a signifier of refinement, a cultured response to the stress of modern life, or a sign of old-fashioned values. Whatever its exact cause, it was an illness that helped cottagers such as Pulitzer justify their multi-million-dollar investments in vacation homes, where they could escape from or come to terms with the radical cultural and economic changes that were reshaping American society after the Civil War.[46] John Stewart Kennedy, another member of the New York elite set, built

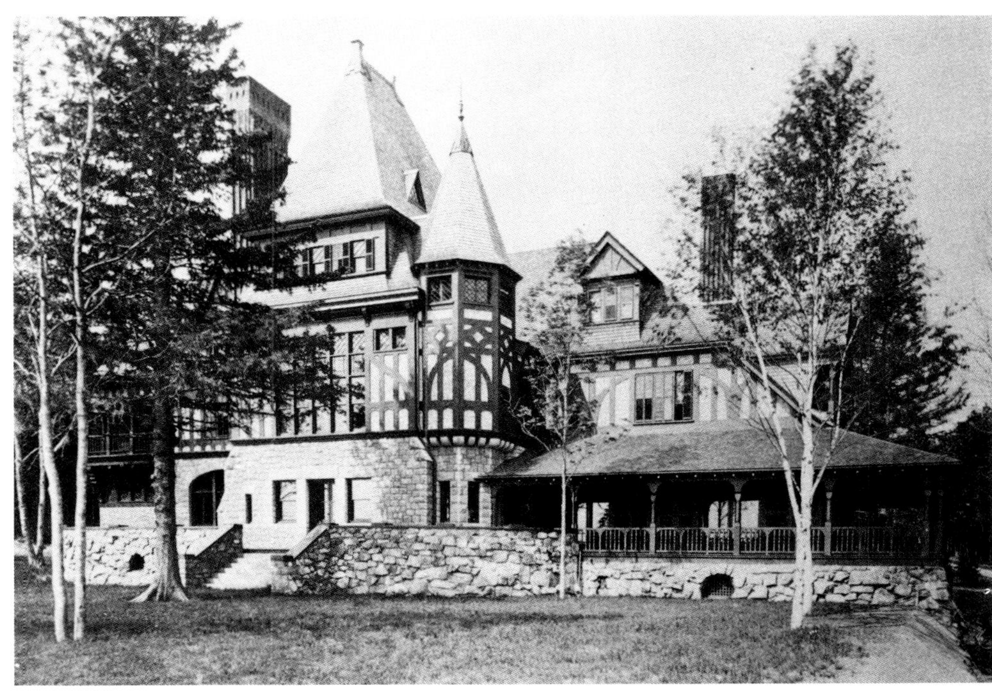

FIG. 84   House of Joseph Pulitzer, *Chatwold,* before 1893, Mount Desert. Photograph Courtesy of the Bar Harbor Historical Society.

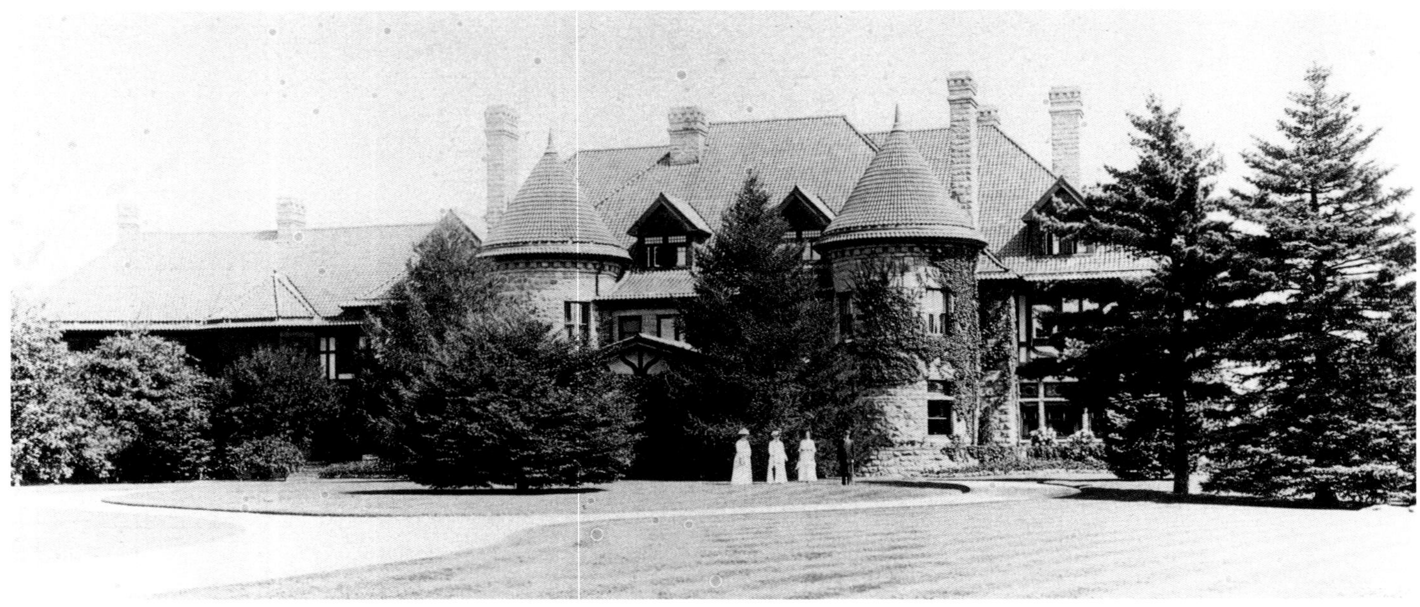

FIG. 85   Rowe and Baker for John S. Kennedy, *Kenarden Lodge,* built 1892, Mount Desert.
Photograph Courtesy of the Bar Harbor Historical Society.

his "Kenarden Lodge" (fig. 85) in 1892 at a cost of two hundred thousand dollars. The cottage was designed by Rowe and Baker of New York City and had its own electric generating plant. A banker and major stockholder in western railroads, Kennedy strongly supported Island preservation.

Along with the cottagers came a proliferation of social clubs, beginning in 1874 with The Oasis Club (fig. 86). Renamed the Mount Desert Reading Room after incorporation in 1881, the club's stated mission was "literary and social culture." Yet, "under the Maine prohibition law, most of the 'Reading' was done through the bottom of a glass."[47] The many other private recreational clubs included the Mount Desert Canoe Club and Bar Harbor Swimming Club. The Kebo Valley Club (fig. 87, and fig. 88), which still exists today as a golf club, was dedicated to the blue-blooded sport of

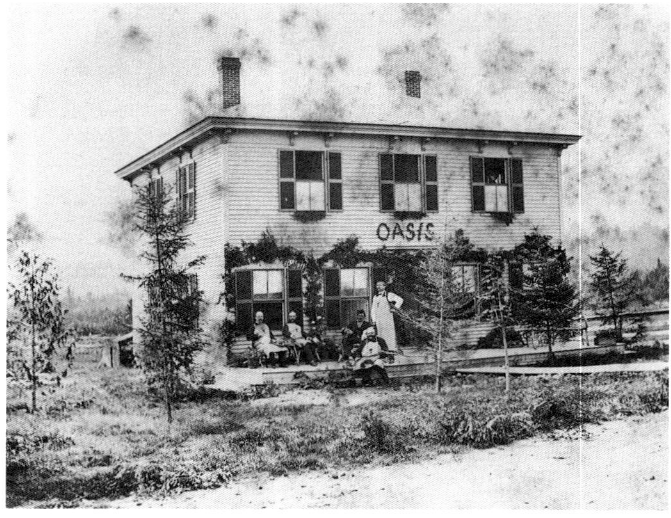

FIG. 86   *The Oasis Club,* 1874, Mount Desert. Photograph Courtesy of the Bar Harbor Historical Society.

horse racing in 1889. A portion of the clubhouse enclosed a small theater and a restaurant, while the surrounding grounds encompassed a baseball field and lawns for croquet and tennis.[48] The Robin Hood Park (fig. 89), purchased in 1898 by Colonel Edward Morrell of Philadelphia, had its beginning in 1890 as Newport Race Track. In its heyday the audience boxes "which only contained eight folding chairs, were sold for the three-day period for $500 to finance the event."[49] Exclusivity defined these clubs, and only recently have outsiders and local residents been allowed to join.

Cog Railways to the Overlook

As tourism to Mount Desert increased through the 1870s, an enterprising entrepreneur from Bangor, Frank Clergue, decided that a cog railway to transport tourists quickly and easily to the summit of Cadillac Mountain would be profitable. During construction of the railway the old survey building and hotel on the summit was used for boarding workmen (fig. 90). Shortly after the cog railroad was completed the old hotel was remodeled to accommodate fifty guests with a restaurant that could seat one hundred (fig. 91). A broadsheet advertising the new establishment linked its attractions solely to the "extensive and beautiful view" (fig. 92). Clergue kicked off the 23 June 1883 opening of the Green Mountain Railway with a publicity campaign (fig. 93). The Bangor *Mining Journal* compared the new railroad at Mount Desert to the line up Mount Vesuvius. Passengers of the railway were first conveyed from Bar Harbor by "horse-drawn 'barge'" to Eagle Lake. From there the steamer "Wauwinnet" delivered them at the foot of Cadillac Mountain where they boarded the railway for the dramatic ride to the summit. The railway was prosperous the first year but the contender for transport, the buckboard, had proved to be adequate and the railway ceased operation in 1893.[50]

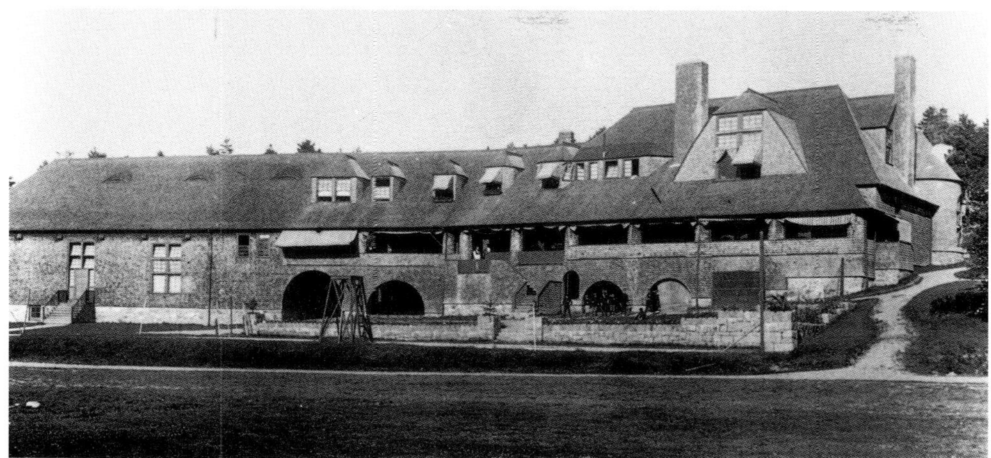

By 1890 Bar Harbor had become one of the nation's most important places for the wealthy and socially prominent of the Northeastern United States. During this period Mount Desert almost replaced Newport, Rhode Island, as the summer social capital of the United States. For those who could afford such a life, Mount Desert was part of the grand tour of resorts that began with Palm Springs, Florida, in the winter, Newport in the Spring, Mount Desert in the summer, the Berkshires in early fall, and White Sulfur Springs in the late fall.[51] The famed financier, J. P. Morgan, anchored his sleek yacht *Corsair IV* (fig. 94) in Bar Harbor every season. His wife Frances was photographed in front of the "artists' hotel," the Lynam House, with George Dorr in the 1920s (see fig. 20). Morgan came ashore to purchase pollack from the local fishermen; he did not like lobster. His vessels, all named *Corsair,* were floating "cottages," complete with the latest technology and comforts. The ostentatious lifestyle of America's aristocrats began to decline in the 1920s, due in part to the personal income tax introduced in 1913, the stock market crash of 1929, and the Great Depression. The final blow to the cottage lifestyle came in 1947 with a devastating fire that ravaged seventy-two out of 220 cottages along the eastern side of the Island. Most of the great mansions were never rebuilt.[52]

Cordon of Invaders versus the "Money Kings"

At the time the cottagers were in their heyday, in the 1880s, the first calls for conservation or even preservation began to be heard. Mount Desert was fast "surrounded by a cordon of invaders, and the time will come when all the land bordering on or near the sea, will be cut up into houselots."[53] Godkin noted that because of the "love of the seashore among the vast population of the Mississippi Valley, whose wealth is becoming great, for whom long railroad journeys have no

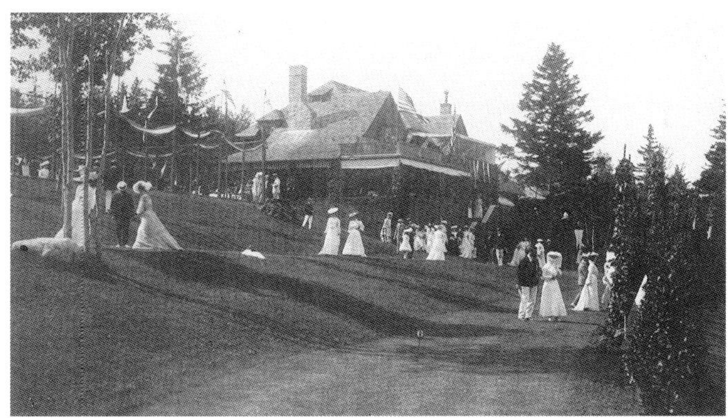

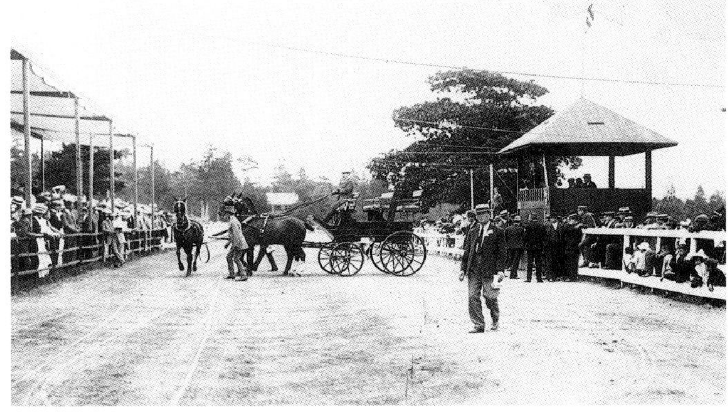

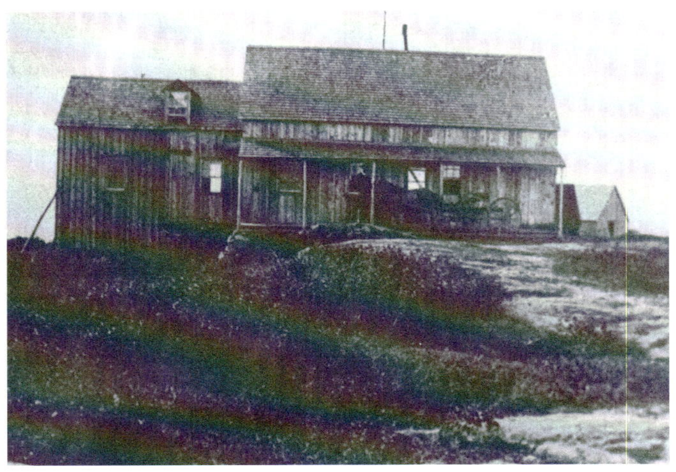

FIG. 90   *Hotel on Green Mountain*, c.1875, Mount Desert. Photograph Courtesy of the Bar Harbor Historical Society.

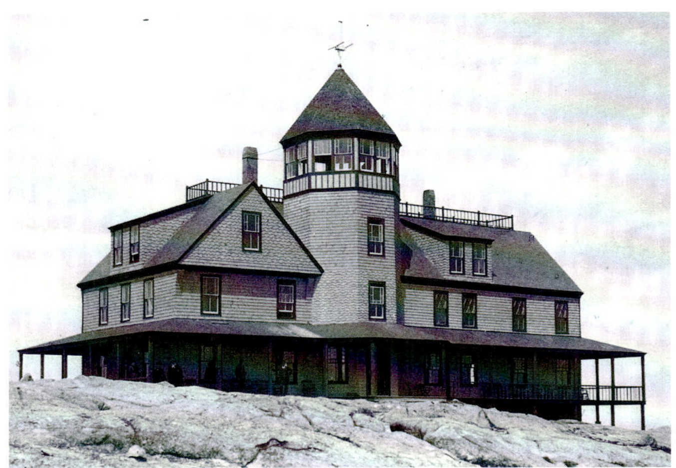

FIG. 91   *The Summit Hotel on Green Mountain,* c.1886, Mount Desert. Photograph Courtesy of the Bar Harbor Historical Society.

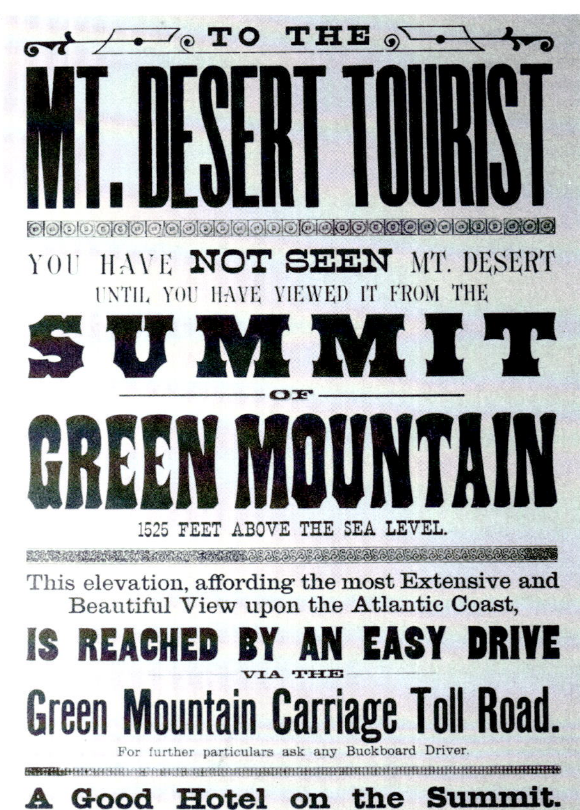

FIG. 92   *Broadsheet Advertising Summit Hotel,* c.1883–1887, Mount Desert. Photograph Courtesy of the Bar Harbor Historical Society.

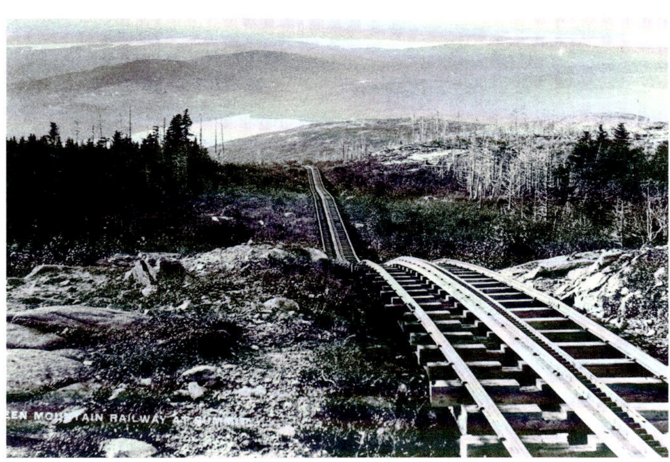

FIG. 93   *Track of the Cog Railway on Cadillac Mountain,* c.1883–1887, Mount Desert. Photograph Courtesy of the Bar Harbor Historical Society.

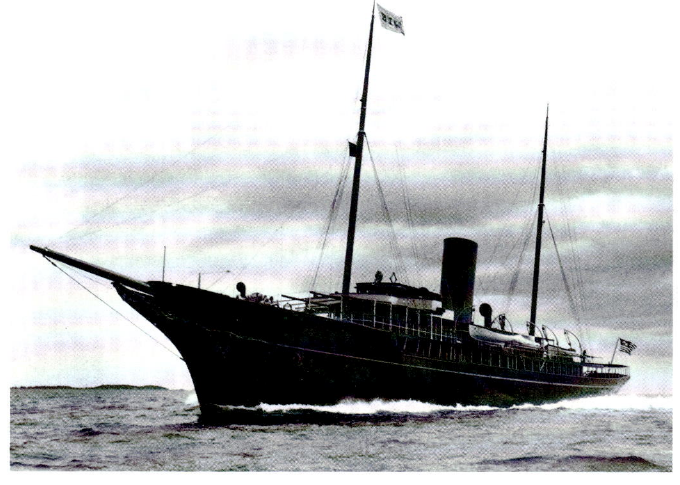

FIG. 94   *J.P. Morgan's Corsair IV Underway during Sea Trials*, c.1920. Photograph Courtesy Maine Maritime Museum, Bath, Maine.

terrors . . . [they] are likely now to send their thousands every year to compete with the "money kings" of the East for the best villa sites along the coast."[54] It was already clear as early as 1880 the Island was no longer the wilderness that Cole and Church had represented.

Speculative land companies tirelessly promoted Mount Desert property. The Bar Harbor Land Company had been formed as early as 1883, and after the Bar Harbor Express began its runs in 1887, real estate speculation flourished with a vengeance. At least thirteen offices operated at one point.[55] The Mount Desert and Eastern Shore Land Company published a report titled *Description of Mount Desert Island and the Magnificent Property of this Company*. The publication claimed that "the natural attractions of White Mountains, Newport, Adirondacks, Atlantic City, and other well-known seashore and mountain resorts are all concentrated within the property." In fact, "five hundred of these lots are now ready for the market." The company invited investors to join in the speculation because those who purchased "now will realize handsomely from the inevitable advance in price which must result from the early completion of the proposed roads and improvements which will render these lands accessible and available."[56] Lapham astutely summed up the skyrocketing land values: "Landscape which twenty years ago was a barren waste, and almost worthless, has been transformed. . . . Land has advanced in price a thousand fold, and choice building lots will command almost any sum asked."[57]

Mount Desert's rapid over-development in the 1890s threatened the exclusivity and elite lifestyle of the wealthiest "cottagers." From this group emerged concerns about protecting the Island from further real estate development. George B. Dorr, a wealthy bachelor from Boston and the sole heir to a great textile fortune, emerged as the movement's leader. Dorr's family had built a summer home at Bar Harbor in 1868 and as a long-time cottager he devoted his life to protecting the Island. Another leader was Charles W. Eliot, the thirty-seven-year-old president of Harvard, who traveled many times to Frenchman Bay and Bar Harbor, sailing along the Maine coast attempting to specify Champlain's route for his friend, historian Francis Parkman.[58]

Years later, as emeritus President of Harvard College, Eliot organized a private meeting at Seal Harbor on 13 August 1901, inviting wealthy friends and leaders of local improvement groups to discuss ways of protecting Mount Desert. Dorr became vice president and executive officer of the corporation. Among the moneyed men at the meeting were John S. Kennedy, the New York banker, and powerful railway executive George Vanderbilt. Eliot proposed that a corporation be instituted for the preservation of the major scenic sites on the Island. Its purpose would be to preserve the remaining wilderness beauty for public enjoyment. They formed The Hancock County Trustees of Public Reservations,

and in January 1903 a charter was obtained from the Maine legislature recognizing the public aims of the corporation with tax-free status. The corporation was patterned after the Massachusetts Trustees of Public Reservations, which had been organized by Eliot's son, Charles.[59]

The Right Development of Mount Desert Island

In 1904 Eliot privately printed a pamphlet titled *The Right Development of Mount Desert Island* that outlined the goals of the trustees—holding and improving for public use land which had scenic, historic, or other valuable characteristics. Eliot's perspective was that of an outsider, a summer resident. He stated clearly what his class wanted: "The beautiful conformation of the island itself, the availability for sailing and fishing . . . and the roughness and wildness of its hills and shores. . . . The greater part of the island has never been inhabited or cultivated." He also made it clear that the Islanders, the insiders who resided year round, derived their support "almost exclusively from the summer residents." Eliot took a broad perspective, embracing both cottagers and boarders, but adamantly excluded "excursionists." These were the unwashed masses that frequented a "Coney Island or a Revere Beach."[60] Eliot thought:

> *Is a cottage population more desirable than a hotel or a boarding-house population; and, if the cottage population is the more desirable, are the very rich cottagers the most valuable, or is a mixture of the rich with professional people and other people of moderate means more likely to promote the interests of the permanent population? Or would throngs of excursionists be more valuable than cottagers or boarders by the week at hotels? The last question may be confidently answered in the negative; because there are no large cities near Mount Desert to afford an adequate supply of excursionists.*[61]

To accomplish these ambitious objectives Eliot thought that large tracts of land should be purchased and returned to the public. He urged every resident to treat the Island as if it were a public park, and believed that future development of Mount Desert should be based on principals of landscape design and conservation as advocated by Frederick Law Olmsted and others.[62] Eliot summarized the groups' other objectives: "What needs to be forever excluded from the island is the squalor of the city, with all its inevitable bustle, dirt, and ugliness. Not even the appropriate pleasures and splendors of city life should be imitated at Mount Desert."[63] Over the next few years donations of land were made to the corporation and Dorr secured the financial assistance of John S. Kennedy to complete the acquisition of important parcels. Later Rockefeller made substantial donations of property to the preserve. By 1914 the association had six thousand acres in one continuous area, mostly comprising mountain peaks and a few remaining wilderness areas.[64]

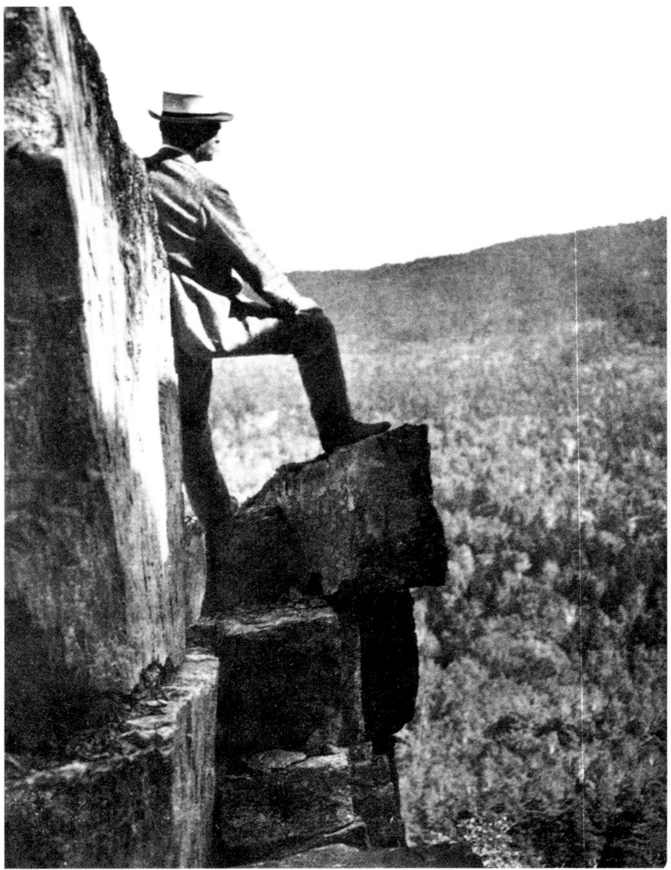

George B. Dorr, c.1920, Mount Desert. Photograph Courtesy of the William Otis Sawtelle Collection and Research Center at Acadia National Park.

Dorr, later named the "Father of Acadia," assumed ever greater responsibility in the group's efforts (fig. 95).[65] In order to permanently safeguard the preserve during the next decade Dorr and Eliot orchestrated a campaign to create the national park. One element of their strategy was the publication of two articles in the July 1914 issue of the *National Geographic Magazine*. Eliot's essay, "The Need of Conserving the Beauty and Freedom of Nature in Modern Life," and Dorr's "The Unique Island of Mount Desert," underscored the need to preserve the historic, ornithologically and botanically rich Island, while providing a much needed and highly desirable recreational and educational wilderness environment for the public.[66] Eliot pointed out that the "powers of the national government have thus far been exerted to these conservation ends chiefly in the Far West." He sharply recommended that it would be "just and highly expedient that these beneficent powers should now be exerted in the East." He reasoned that "manufacturing industries occupy the major part of the population and the destructive effects of city life have long been manifest."[67] Dorr's article singled out the Island's special attributes, its history, the trustees' intended donation of the land to the government as a "gift to the nation." This will "create a wild park . . . saved to future generations as it has been to us."[68] Thus began the process of surmounting the many political and legal obstacles that Dorr and his supporters were to face.

A Park That Fronts Up to the Sea

The first step toward the goal of a national park designation was the donation of the already acquired lands to the Federal Government and the formation of the Sieur de Monts National Monument on 8 July 1916. The next phase involved establishing that the monument lands were fully worthy of national park status. This effort was handled by Dorr, whose political influence and persistence is evident in a letter from U.S. Secretary of the Interior, Franklin K. Lane, to House of Representatives Chairman, The Honorable Scott Ferris. Dated 15 May 1918, this correspondence summarized the arguments Dorr and Eliot had agreed upon as grounds for preserving Mount Desert as a national park. In his letter Lane emphasized Mount Desert's historic value: "Champlain first landed on this coast, and the French had a station here years before the landing of the Pilgrim Fathers." He cited the picturesque aspects that the artists first discovered, and asserted that "scenically, its impressive headlands give Mount Desert the distinction of combining sea and mountain." Lane's third point, conservation, held that "the value of the proposed park can hardly be overestimated" because throughout the Island are "exhibits of scientific interest as well as beauty. . . . This was the first part of the continent to emerge from the prehistoric sea." Lane stressed not only geologic study but ornithologic since "all of the conditions for a bird sanctuary in the east seem to be here fulfilled." His last rationale for park status was the recreational possibilities "giving pleasure in the summer months to hundreds of thousands of people living east of the Mississippi River." Thus, he reasoned, "developed as a national park in the interests of all the people, this reservation will become one of the greatest of our public assets."[69]

Two weeks later, Lane reiterated his position in a statement issued at the Subcommittee hearing before the Committee on Public Lands, House of Representatives. He stated that the Island "is a true park area in the highest sense, totally different from any other . . . that fronts upon the sea." In a convincing conclusion Lane exclaimed what many already knew: Mount Desert is "one of the oldest and most important recreation areas upon the Continent—the New England Coast. . . . The lands constituting the monument have been of over 60 years the object of resort from all the great eastern cities, from southern ones extending to New Orleans, and central ones to St. Louis."[70] Also on behalf of Mount Desert, Theodore Roosevelt addressed the same hearing. Emphasizing what he believed to be the single most crucial point, the ex-President stated that Mount Desert "is our one eastern national park and gives for the first time to the crowded eastern city population of the country the opportunity to share directly and immediately in the benefits of our national park system."[71]

Mount Desert was granted national park status on 26 February 1919. It operated under the name of Lafayette

National Park until 7 January 1929 when Congress passed another bill authorizing the acceptance within the park of lands lying off the Island proper, and authorizing a name change, to Acadia National Park.[72] At this time many of the original names for mountains were changed to reflect historical association or to commemorate the individuals who played pivotal roles in the establishment of the park. The town of Eden was renamed Bar Harbor, Asticou Hill became Eliot Mountain, Little Brown's Mountain became Parkman Mountain, and Dry Mountain was renamed Dorr Mountain.[73]

Mr. Rockefeller's Roads

The automobile first appeared on the Island in 1913. Eliot and Dorr had initially wanted to ban the car, but this proved impossible.[74] In 1917, John D. Rockefeller, Jr., who had owned a summer home at Seal Harbor, "The Eyrie," since 1910 (fig. 96), proposed to build and maintain an extended "horse-road system." He envisioned carriage roads and walking paths that would provide access to recognized sites of scenic beauty on Mount Desert and was granted permission to construct elaborate, engineered roads—for the exclusive use of horse and carriage on only his own land—at his own expense. Later, he was allowed to build roads on land deeded to the government. Between 1913 and 1940 he designed and built fifty-seven miles of scenic carriage roads.[75] Rockefeller ultimately became the greatest contributor to the park of both of land and money.[76]

There was some irony in Rockefeller's project because, as his granddaughter later wrote, "without the car, the family fortune that allowed Grandfather to help create Acadia National Park and build the carriage roads would not have existed, and yet Grandfather's roads were built in order to keep the car at bay."[77] Rockefeller's carriage roads and bridges were carefully designed to create "a combination of the natural landscape and the hand of humans." He intended to make more accessible the "beauties of nature while at the same time introducing the orderliness by which humans have attempted to make their seemingly chaotic world comprehensible."[78] Built in 1933, the "Stanley Brook Bridge" (fig. 97) is one of two triple Roman arch bridges, and like the sixteen other bridges built on the Island, was designed to be little noticed from the motor road above. "JDR Jr. had no intention of imposing a personal style or making a personal statement as a designer." He strived to "arrange the elements to reveal beauty, not to make a beautiful arrangement."[79]

The Legacy of Art

The energy and financial support of wealthy summer residents exemplified the convergence of art and culture, tourism, and social/political policy that produced one of the nation's most popular scenic locations. By the early twentieth century acceptance of the idea that artists were respon-

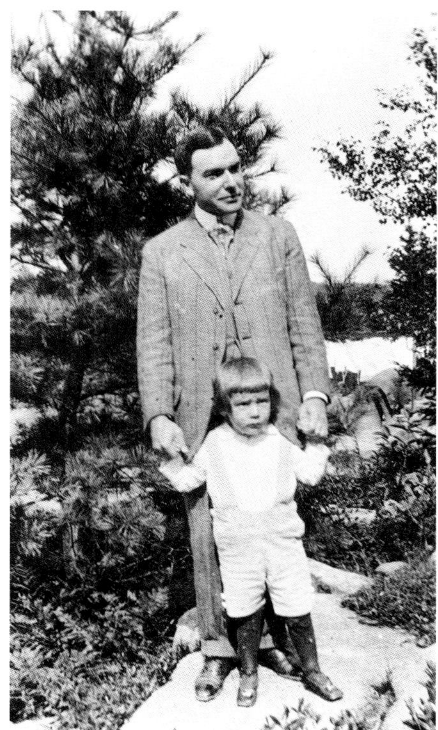

FIG. 96 *John D. Rockefeller, Jr., with son Winthrop at Seal Harbor, Maine,* August 1915. Photograph Courtesy of the Rockefeller Archive Center.

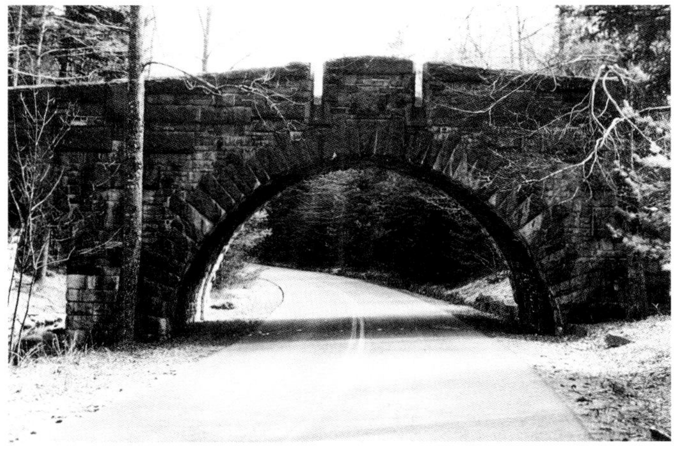

FIG. 97 John D. Rockefeller, Jr., *Stanley Brook Bridge*, 1933, Mount Desert. Photograph 1991, Courtesy of Pamela J. Belanger.

sible in great measure for the emergence of Mount Desert as a scenic place was thoroughly established. In 1911 a journalist writing for *The Century Magazine* observed that "Mount Desert was discovered about the middle of the last century by that famous group of American artists headed by Church and Cole."[80] Hale's Bar Harbor history acknowledged the artists who "drew and painted, and, what was most important, sold their paintings. By doing this they told just that group which could afford long summer vacations of the beauties of Mount Desert in general and of the ocean side of Bar Harbor in particular." Thus, tourism, the "new industry came to the Town of Eden."[81] By 1973, *Down East* magazine

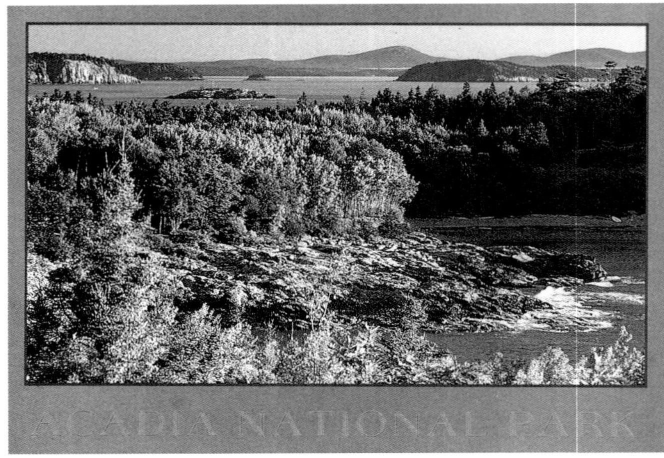

FIG. 98 *Frenchman's Bay and Acadia National Park,* postcard, CPS Inc. The Acadia School of Photography, Southwest Harbor, Maine.

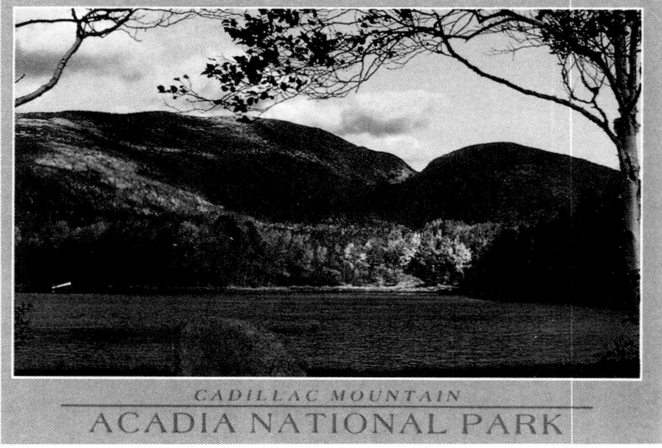

FIG. 99 *Cadillac Mountain, Acadia National Park from Otter Creek,* postcard, CPS Inc. The Acadia School of Photography, Southwest Harbor, Maine.

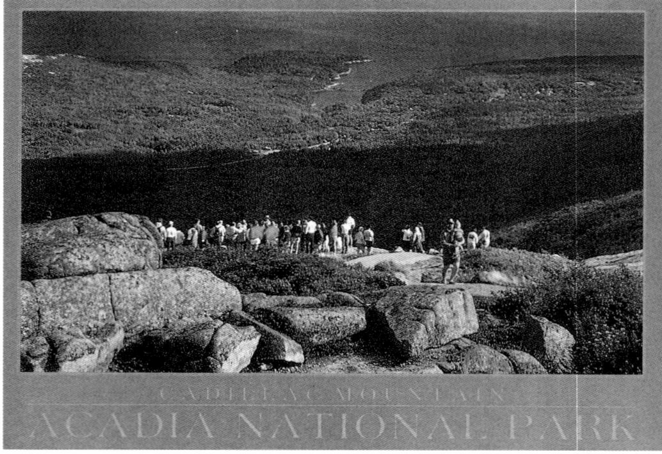

FIG. 100 *Looking to Otter Cove from Cadillac Mountain,* postcard, CPS Inc. The Acadia School of Photography, Southwest Harbor, Maine.

confidently asserted that "thirty years before the coming of the millionaire 'cottagers' in the 1870s–80s, Bar Harbor was 'discovered' by artists of the Hudson River School of landscape painters."[82]

The 1960s produced a new type of middle-class vacationer whose mobility radically changed Mount Desert. These visitors brought new attitudes toward nature and superficially resembled the type of boarder that had been excluded by the cottager seventy years before. Motor tourists expected the comfort and access of the motor hotel, and the tourist economy of the Island grew exponentially. At the same time the idea of wilderness achieved a new importance in the United States—it symbolized the idea of a pure and unspoiled environment, a powerful antidote to the stress, disillusionment, and existential anxiety of the Cold War.[83] At Acadia National Park, visitation numbers tripled from one million in the early 1960s to three million at the end of the 1970s, and reached nearly seven million in 1990.[84] The wealthy still come to their cottages, and the hotels flourish as never before. In addition to land-born tourists, Southwest Harbor and Bar Harbor, among many others, are crowded each summer with cruising sailors, yachtsmen who, following Lane's and Stevens's voyages, fill Island anchorages and marinas just as other tourists occupy hotels and campsites.

Unfortunately, the protection of Mount Desert as Acadia National Park now threatens its very existence. Environmental ethicists question whether viewing the environment as 'scenery' is only a veiled reformulation and commodification of nineteenth-century anthropocentrism and sentimentality.[85] Tourism may one day be viewed as another aspect of European colonialist practice. A leading tourism theory holds that a tourist attraction requires three things: a sight, a marker, and a tourist. Without markers a tourist site may be difficult or impossible to identify. Markers include postcards, travel guidebooks, and, most importantly for the period examined in this study, paintings, prints, travel books, and other visual and written materials. The tourist first hears about or sees a sight through a marker then responds to whatever directions are given to the site, described as "sight sacralization" stages. The stage termed "enshrinement" occurs when the area around a place becomes as much a "site" as the original attraction. The enshrinement of Mount Desert as one of the nation's most exclusive "sacred places" was, in its initial stages, a product of the cultural work of landscape painters who were also "enshrined" for their genius in representing the place.[86] As early as 1876 Mount Desert had become a site enshrined. No longer were the specific sites depicted in paintings and guide books solely attractive to visitors; the Island as a whole had become famous. The fame of artists such as Church, who linked his name to Mount Desert in hopes it would help him win fame and fortune, became a reason to visit the Island.

The complete residual impact of the process of cultural invention cannot be gauged accurately today. It is amusing, however to consider the semiotics of post-cards that are sold to tourists at Mount Desert. A recent printing of the popular card "Frenchman's Bay and Acadia National Park," replicates the view in Cole's *View Across Frenchman's Bay* (fig. 98). The sublime view of Cadillac Mountain in Church's *Otter Creek* is echoed in a postcard entitled "Cadillac Mountain, Acadia National Park, from Otter Creek" (fig. 99), while Gifford's image of Otter Cove from Cadillac Mountain is identical to the postcard view, complete with a group of tourists (fig. 100). Today, the places Cole, Church, Lane, and Gifford explored, and the views they painted in the 1850s and 1860s are mechanically converted into the commodity of photographic post-cards. Their very presence would not be possible without the Mount Desert that nineteenth-century artists invented.

NOTES

1. W. B. Lapham, *Bar Harbor and Mount Desert Island* (New York: Liberty Printing, 1886), 38, 3.

2. Lapham, *Bar Harbor and Mount Desert Island,* 3.

3. Richard Walden Hale, Jr., *The Story of Bar Harbor* (New York: Ives Washburn, Inc., 1949), 150.

4. See Ronald Takaki, *A Different Mirror: A History of Multicultural America* (Boston: Little Brown and Co., 1993); and Reeve Vanneman and Lynn Weber Cannon, *The American Perception of Class* (Philadelphia: Temple University Press, 1987).

5. Sue Rainey, *Creating* Picturesque America: *Monument to the Natural and Cultural Landscape* (Nashville, Tenn.: Vanderbilt University Press, 1994), 86–94.

6. Oliver B. Bunce in William Cullen Bryant, ed., *Picturesque America: or the Land We Live In* vol. 1 (New York: D. Appleton and Company, 1872), 2.

7. Bunce, in Bryant, *Picturesque America,* vol. 1, 3.

8. Ibid.

9. Ibid., 4.

10. Ibid., 6.

11. Ibid.

12. Ibid., 8.

13. Ibid., 10.

14. Ibid., 12.

15. Ibid., 8.

16. "Mount Desert," *Harper's New Monthly Magazine* 45, no. 267 (August 1872): 324.

17. "Mount Desert," *Harper's,* 339.

18. Ibid., 334.

19. Ibid., 331-2.

20. See John Wilmerding, *The Artist's Mount Desert* (Princeton: Princeton University Press, 1994), especially Chapters VII, VIII, 125–71.

21. Ibid., 144.

22. Vincent Short and Edwin Sears, *Sail and Steam: Along the Maine Coast* (Portland, Maine: Bond Wheelwright Co., 1955), 121.

23. William Cullen Bryant, ed., *Picturesque America: or the Land We Live In* (New York: D. Appleton and Company, 1872), 2.

24. Short and Sears, *Sail and Steam*, 159, 185.

25. Lapham, 13.

26. Clara Barnes Martin, *Mount Desert on the Coast of Maine: "Infinite Riches in a Little Room"* (Privately Printed, 1867; 4th ed., Portland, Maine: Loring, Short, and Harmon, 1877), 1–17.

27. Martin, *Mount Desert on the Coast of Maine*, 4.

28. "Mount Desert," *Harper's,* 338.

29. See Dona Brown, *Inventing New England: Regional Tourism in the Nineteenth Century* (Washington, D.C.: Smithsonian Institution Press, 1997); Richard R. Wescott, "Early Conservation Programs and the Development of the Vacation Industry in Maine, 1865–1900," *Maine Historical Society Quarterly* 27, no. 1 (Summer 1987): 2–13; Wolfgang Schivelbusch, *The Railway Journey: Trains and Travel in the 19th Century* (New York: Urizen Books, 1979); and William Leonhard Taylor, *A Productive Monopoly: The Effect of Railroad Control on New England Coastal Steamship Lines, 1870–1916* (Providence: Brown University Press, 1978).

30. Lapham, 9.

31. Ibid., 11. Several steamers operated by the Maine Central Railroad Company ferried vacationers from the Mount Desert Ferry in Hancock, Maine, to Bar Harbor: "Rangeley," "Moosehead," "Sappho," "Norumbega," and the "Sebenoa." See Short and Sears, 193.

32. Lapham, 11.

33. Ibid., 13.

34. "The Bar Harbor Express," *Yankee* 31 (August 1967): 139.

35. Ibid., 142.

36. For details on these and other hotels at Bar Harbor, see G. W. Helfrich and Gladys O'Neil, eds., *Lost Bar Harbor* (Camden, Maine: Down East Books, 1982), 84–105.

37. Samuel Eliot Morison, *The Story of Mount Desert Island, Maine* (Boston: Little, Brown, and Co., 1960), 47. A complete list of hotels at Bar Harbor in 1873 is found in Hale, *The Story of Bar Harbor*, 142.

38. "Mount Desert," *Harper's,* 326.

39. Ibid., 327.

40. Ibid., 325.

41. Edwin Lawrence Godkin, *Reflections and Comments: 1865–1895* (New York: Charles Scribner's Sons, 1896), 300–1. In fact, the classical revival Building of Arts was constructed in 1908. Created as a focus of artistic and intellectual activity at Bar Harbor, several members of the Boston Symphony Orchestra performed during the summer. There were also theater performances such as "Midsummer Night's Dream." See Owen Johnson, "The Building of Arts at Bar Harbor," *The Century Magazine* 76 (August 1908): 676–8.

42. Godkin, *Reflections and Comments*, 299–300. For an extended discussion on the development of a summer resort see Godkin's chapter "The Evolution of the Summer Resort," 295–308.

43. Ibid., 306–7.

44. Ibid., 298.

45. Ibid., 299.

46. See Tom Lutz, *American Nervousness 1903: An Anecdotal History* (Ithaca, N.Y.: Cornell University Press, 1991).

47. Morison, *The Story of Mount Desert Island, Maine*, 49. In 1881, when the club had changed its name and its status, it also moved from its initial small cottage to a new building designed by William R. Emerson. Later, with membership sharply down, the clubhouse was sold to the Maine Central Railroad. In 1924 the building along with a pier

was leased to the Bar Harbor Yacht Club. During World War II the building served as naval quarters, and from 1950 on, it became part of the Bar Harbor Hotel. See Helfrich and O'Neil, *Lost Bar Harbor,* 116–7; and Hale, 169–170.

48. Helfrich and O'Neil, *Lost Bar Harbor,* 114–5.

49. Ibid., 118.

50. Hale, 157–160.

51. See Cleveland Amory, *The Last Resorts* (New York: Harper, 1952), 23; and George E. Street, *Mount Desert, a History*, ed. Samuel A. Eliot, 2nd rev. ed. (Boston: Riverside Press Cambridge; New York: Houghton, Mifflin Co., 1926), 281. For additional details on Bar Harbor and Mount Desert during its height as a social resort see Herbert J. Seligmann, "Bar Harbor-From Eden to Tourism," *Down East* 4 (August 1957): 24–29, 45–46; Nan Cole, "Personal Glimpses of Bar Harbor's Lush Era," *Down East* 15 (July 1969): 22–47, 81–83, 87–89; and Margaret F. Hammel, "Bar Harbor's Great Cottages," *Down East* 19 (June 1973): 58–63.

52. Hammel, "Bar Harbor's Great Cottages," 61. For more on the 1947 fire see Joyce Butler, *Wildfire Loose, The Week Maine Burned,* 2nd ed. (Camden, Maine: Down East Books, 1979).

53. Lapham, 38.

54. Godkin, 307.

55. Hale, 161–2.

56. Charles Lewis, *Mount Desert and the Eastern Shore Land Company: Description of Mount Desert Island* (Privately printed, 1889), 16.

57. Lapham, 6.

58. Hale, 19.

59. George B. Dorr, *The Story of Acadia National Park* (Bar Harbor, Maine: Acadia Publishing Co., 1985), 51–52.

60. Charles W. Eliot, *The Right Development of Mount Desert Island* (Privately printed, 1904), 1.

61. Eliot, *The Right Development of Mount Desert Island,* 6–7.

62. See Eliot, *The Right Development of Mount Desert Island,* 1–14; and Street, *Mount Desert, a History*, 300–1. For a discussion of landscaping of a distinctly Italian flavor see Phil M. Riley, "Adapting the Italian Villa to the Maine Coast," *Country Life in America* 24, no. 4 (August 1913): 27–31.

63. Eliot, *The Right Development of Mount Desert Island*, 13.

64. George P. Dorr, Ernest Howe Forbush, and M. L. Fernald, "The Unique Island of Mount Desert," *The National Geographic Magazine* 26 (July 1914): 77.

65. See Dorr, *The Story of Acadia National Park,* 5–20.

66. Charles W. Eliot, "The Need of Conserving the Beauty and Freedom of Nature in Modern Life," *National Geographic Magazine* 26 (July 1914): 67–73; and Dorr, Forbush, and Fernald, "The Unique Island of Mount Desert," 75–89.

67. Eliot, "The Need of Conserving the Beauty and Freedom of Nature in Modern Life," 73.

68. Dorr, Forbush, and Fernald, "The Unique Island of Mount Desert," 77.

69. Luther S. Winsor, *Acadia National Park: A Study of Conservation Objectives Relating to its Establishment and Boundary Adjustments* (Washington, D.C.: U.S. Department of the Interior, 1955), II-1, II-2.

70. Winsor, *Acadia National Park: A Study of Conservation Objectives Relating to its Establishment and Boundary Adjustments*, II-3.

71. See Dorr, *The Story of Acadia National Park*, 69.

72. The first land addition to the park outside the Island proper was the southern portion of Schoodic Peninsula. For more on this addition and further detail on the formation of the park see Winsor, *Acadia National Park: A Study of Conservation Objectives Relating to its Establishment and Boundary Adjustments*, 7–18, 20–23; and Dorr, *The Story of Acadia National Park,* 22–76.

73. Parkman Mountain was named after historian Francis Parkman. Other mountains whose names changed after the park was established were:

Newport, to *Champlain*
Bauld, Green, to *Cadillac*
Brown's, to *Norumbega*
Jordan, to *Penobscot*
Robinson, to *Acadia*
Dog, to *St. Sauveur*
West Peak, to *Bernard*

74. For a history of automobile touring in America from 1910 through the 1950s see Warren J. Belasco, *Americans on the Road: From Autocamp to Motel, 1910–1945* (Cambridge, Mass.: MIT Press, 1979).

75. For more on the Rockefeller roads and the complications that arose in the construction and the controversy between summer residents who felt Mount Desert should be left as wild as possible and those who believed like Rockefeller that the beauties of the Island should be made available see George B. Dorr, *Acadia National Park: Its Growth and Development* (Bangor, Maine: Burr Printing Co., 1948), 14–24; and Ann Rockefeller Roberts, *Mr. Rockefeller's Roads* (Camden, Maine: Down East Books, 1990), 55–108.

76. For other conservation efforts by Rockefeller see Nancy Newhall, *A Contribution to the Heritage of Every American: The Conservation Activities of John D. Rockefeller, Jr.* (New York: Alfred A. Knopf, 1957).

77. Roberts, *Mr. Rockefeller's Roads*, 4.

78. Roberts, 128. For Rockefeller's work with nationally known landscape architect, Beatrix Farrand, see Roberts, "Landscaping Roads with Beatrix Farrand: 'Better Done Than Anything I Could Do,'" in *Mr. Rockefeller's Roads*, 126–34.

79. Roberts, *Mr. Rockefeller's Roads*, 6.

80. Robert Haven Schauffler, "Unique Mount Desert," *The Century Magazine* 82, no. 4 (August 1911): 478.

81. Hale, 127.

82. Hammel, "Bar Harbor's Great Cottages," 59.

83. The National Wilderness Preservation System was enacted 3 September 1964. This marked a change in the concept of preservation, from simply defending a particular wilderness area from development, to a more generalized and abstract idea of the wilderness.

84. Assistance with visitation records has been provided by The Acadia National Park Service. The Park currently uses a new method to calculate visitation, which results in the 1998 visitation number to be just over three million. There has been no decrease in visitors to Mount Desert Island, this new measure accounts only for those who enter the Park officially.

85. See William Cronon, ed., *Uncommon Ground: Rethinking the Human Place in Nature* (New York: W. W. Norton, 1995), especially "Reinventing a Common Nature: Yosemite and Mount Rushmore—A Meandering Tale of a Double Meaning," 379–408; Michael Frome, *Battle for the Wilderness* (New York: Praeger Publishers, 1974), 93, see also pages 70–104; and Roderick Nash, *Wilderness and the American Mind* 3rd ed. (New Haven, Conn.: Yale University Press, 1982).

86. Georges Van Den Abbeele, "Sightseers: The Tourist as Theorist," *Diacritics* 10, no. 4 (Winter 1980): 4. See also Dean MacCannell, *The Tourist: A New Theory of the Leisure Class* (New York: Schocken Books, 1976).

An "*Indomitable Explorative Enterprise*":
Inventing National Parks

J. GRAY SWEENEY

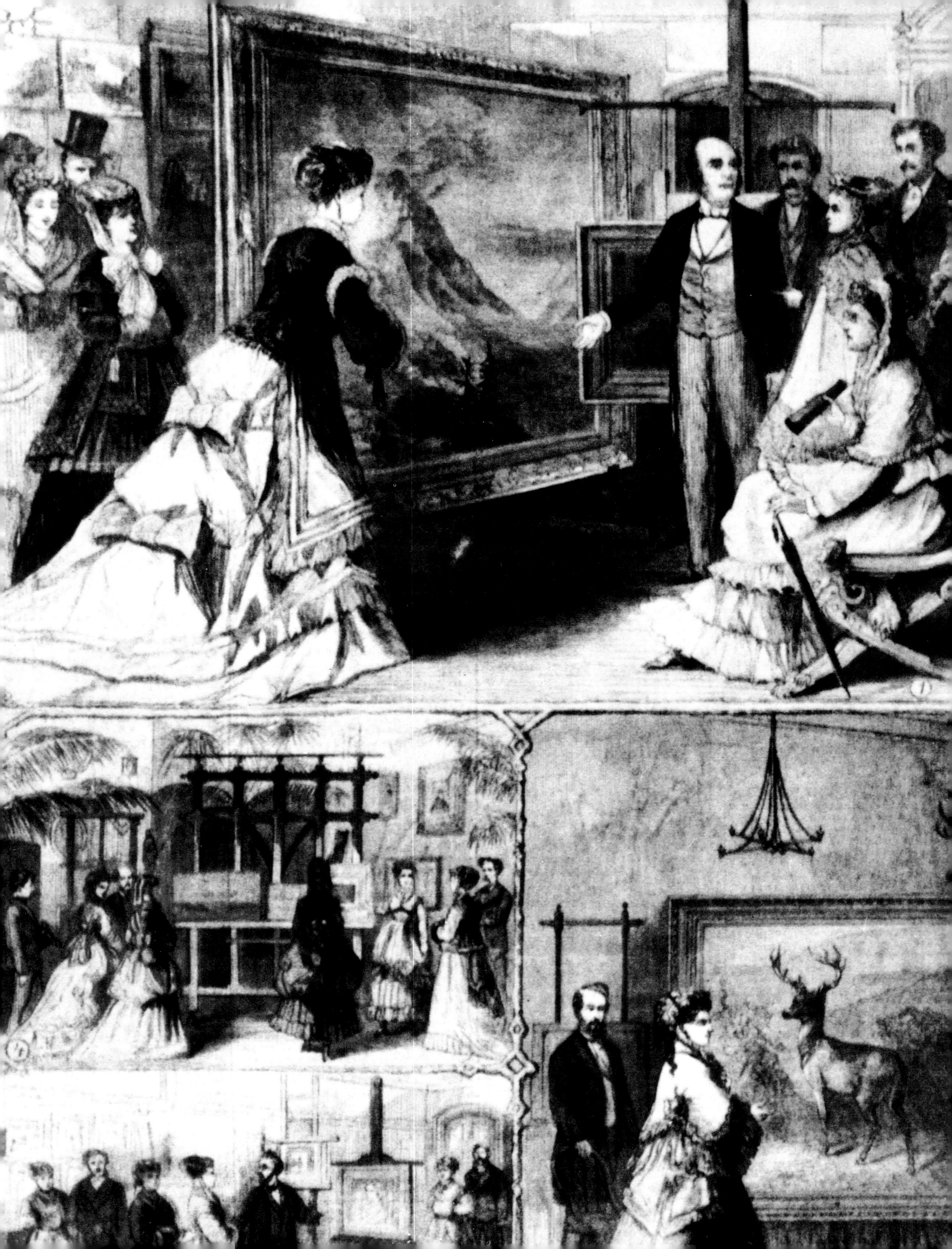

An "Indomitable Explorative Enterprise": Inventing National Parks

Viewed from a broad historical perspective, the invention of Acadia National Park resulted from social and cultural processes that also included the establishment of the other major National Parks at Yosemite Valley, the Yellowstone Region, and the Grand Canyon in Arizona. In an unprecedented historical transformation, wilderness landscapes in the western United States, and a remote rocky island on the Maine Coast, became geographical sites of enormous economic importance. Today these places are meccas for tourists in search of "scenery" primarily because of the work of visual artists—artist-explorers. How did this happen? What conceptual framework might be proposed to help explain underlying reasons for this remarkable historical change in which landscape painting played a leading role?

Artist-explorers helped incorporate wilderness landscapes into American society: as Acadia National Park in Maine, and in remarkably similar ways as the now popular parks in the far West. Explorer-artists discovered, selected, and represented places in the natural environment seldom before seen by white people. Their significance reached its peak in nineteenth-century America. The images they produced ranged in importance from grand theater-scale landscapes that were acquired by the national government, or by the country's wealthiest men, to plein-air oil and watercolor sketches. Their images sometimes included topographical drawings and illustrated maps that might be useful to settlers or for military operations. Typically, artist-explorers reported back to metropolitan centers of culture and commerce as authentic, believable, often "official" agents. Illustrated reports of their explorations were published by a government eager to open new lands to settlement.

In nineteenth-century America many "unofficial" artists gained fame with their travels to the far West, abroad, or "Down East" to Maine. In the United States a handful of sites that were first identified by these exploring-artists became national parks.[1] Other sites, such as the Hudson River, the Catskills, Niagara Falls, the White Mountains, and the Adirondacks, were enshrined in the national con-

sciousness as prime attractions for a public in search of scenery.[2] Still others, even more remote and exotic—South American mountain ranges or Arctic icebergs—excited the popular imagination.

West, East, and War

Yosemite Valley became the first place in the world to be "saved" as a wilderness landscape park, in 1864. A nation convulsed by a devastating Civil War, and weary of military carnage and political turmoil, gratefully received this "gift." For Northeasterners, the remote Yosemite, as seen in the paintings of Albert Bierstadt during the 1860s, was an inspiring symbol of natural purity and national promise deferred by war (fig. 101). An act of Congress in 1872 established the Yellowstone Region as the world's first "National Park." Images of these places excited Northeasterners, and wilderness scenery, especially Mount Desert, became some of the country's most valuable natural commodities.

The promise of the West seemed unlimited, mostly because so little was known about it, and few had actually seen it. Albert Bierstadt and Thomas Moran, considered the greatest landscape painters of the period, gained fame by feeding the growing appetite for images of the West. Bierstadt's paintings of Yosemite were instrumental in its becoming a national park. Thomas Moran, sometimes referred to as "the father of the national parks," played a key role in opening the Yellowstone and the Grand Canyon. Moran epitomized the American explorer-artist; he successfully embodied a type whose origins trace back to the Renaissance. Moran's great paintings of Yellowstone, the Grand Canyon, and The Mountain of the Holy Cross represented these western sites that he claimed as a triptych of national scenic shrines.[3] Congress purchased two of the large canvases and hung them in the Statuary Hall of the Capitol as official icons of national pride (fig. 102).

Frederic Edwin Church, the most successful artist-explorer of the period, prepared the way for Bierstadt's and Moran's successes in painting the West. Like adventurers, Church

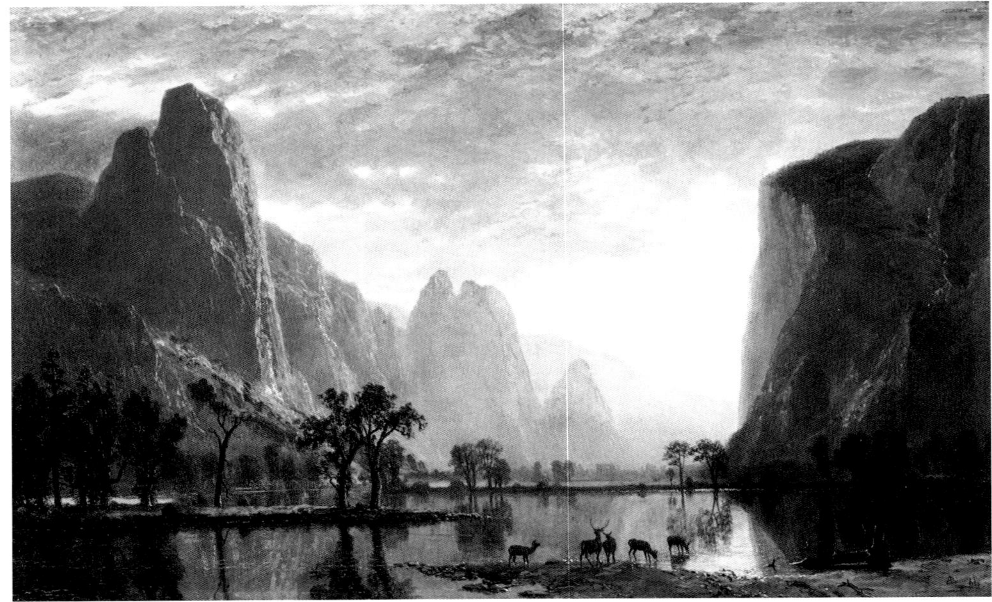

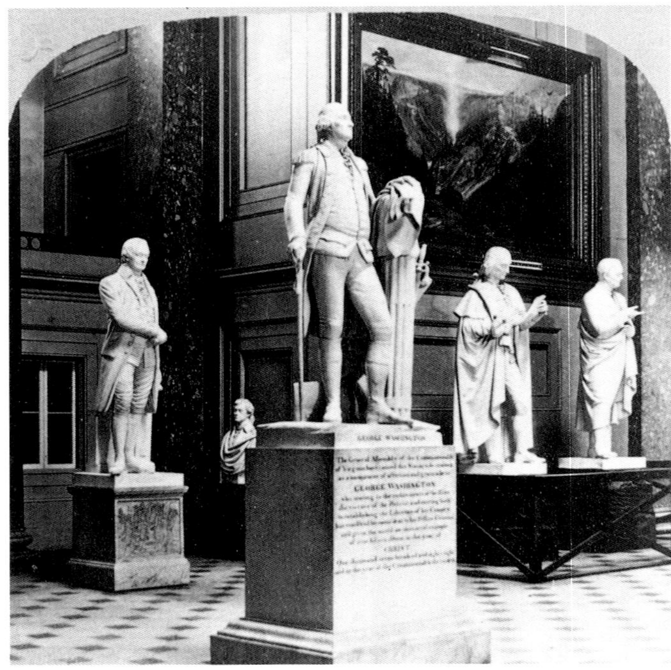

FIG. 102 Charles Bierstadt, *Moran's* Grand Canyon of the Yellowstone *in the U.S. Capitol,* 1872. Stereograph from the Collection of Merl M. Moore, Jr., Washington, D.C.

and his teacher, Thomas Cole, explored and painted Mount Desert in the 1840s and 1850s and together they also promoted many other scenic places in the Northeast through their paintings. Church's images made the Island a major scenic destination, although it still lacked official designation as a national park.

High Mindedness and Popular Taste

Only three decades ago, art historian Barbara Novak dismissed the images produced in this field of culture, referring to them as "Hollywood spectaculars," and "parodies of high-mindedness and a magnification of popular taste."[4] They fascinate cultural historians today precisely because they were once so popular and exerted such wide influence. Their revived popularity and value in today's art market are potent reminders of a continuity of social, political, and economic interests that surround these artifacts of American history. Museum exhibitions celebrate Bierstadt, Moran, and Church as original artistic "geniuses," and biographies reveal the deep social and cultural process that unfolded historically through these individuals. An understanding of the reception of the artists' work also proves fruitful, allowing a recognition of their active contributions to producing the shape and texture of history and to building their own reputations. By considering the social, political, economic, and institutional outcomes, and by examining how paintings by artist-explorers were implicated in larger fields of power, it is possible to consider the production of this art without reliance on conventional formalist models for interpreting art history.

In addressing these issues, a further question emerges: What underlying social and cultural processes led to the establishment of the national parks, West and East? What might these processes tell historians about developments in visual culture in the United States? The principal artist-explorers enjoyed unprecedented popular appeal and financial success because they were part of a field of visual culture in New York City. It comprised individual artists, dealers, patrons, and other groups or institutions with "interests" in landscape painting.[5] Yet another issue remains, how precisely did these "fields of visual production" compound with the larger economic, political, and institutional "fields of power" to produce the first national parks, scenic tourism, and a self-proclaimed national school of art? What conventions of visual representation actually performed this valuable cultural work? The questions are important because the

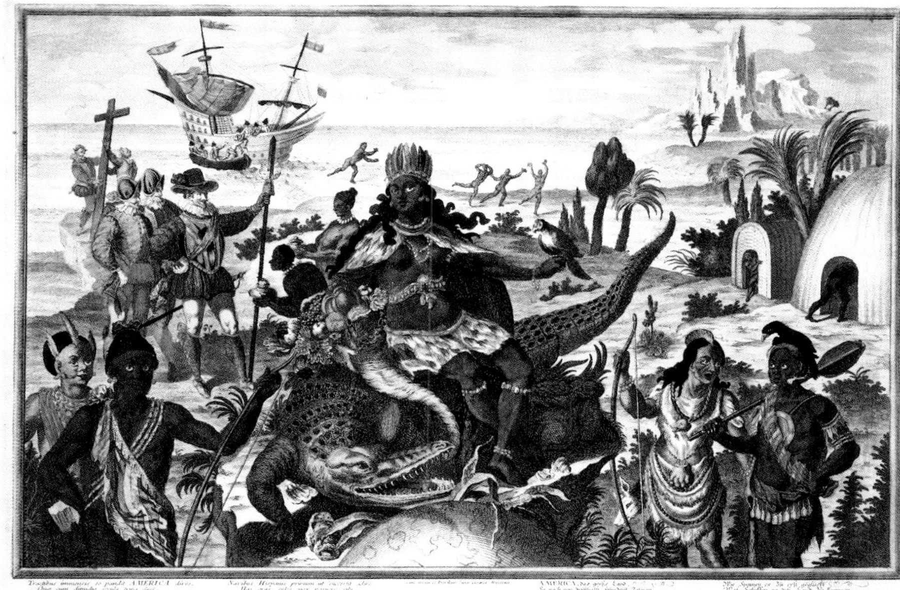

FIG. 103 Gottfrid Berhard Goetz, *America*, Agusburg, c.1750. Photograph Courtesy of the John Carter Brown Library, Brown University.

consequences of nineteenth-century artist-explorers' contributions continues to regulate consumption of wilderness environment as scenery at national parks today.

ARTIST-EXPLORERS AND THE INVENTION OF NATIONAL PARKS

The cultural work of artist-explorers first gained importance early in the sixteenth century when Europeans began colonial expansion on a global scale. Visualizing, controlling, and promoting their overseas colonies required images, usually accompanied by written accounts. The work of explorer-artists assumed special importance for emerging nation states. Explorer-artists were among the first to make contact with new worlds and new peoples and to report on their experiences. In its historical origins, exploration art and the force of conquest remain unmistakably linked.

The French colonist Jacques Le Moyne de Morgues in Florida and the English settler John White in Virginia were the first explorer-artists of North America. Their paintings of the natives of their colonies in the second half of the sixteenth century exhibited characteristics that became more sharply defined as the practices of exploring-artists became more specialized. Le Moyne and White idealized unknown places and peoples, making them appear exotic, desirable, or demonic. The dissemination of explorer-artists' images relied on close collaboration with publishers. The Flemish entrepreneur Theodore DeBry purchased their works and published them, with much acclaim and profit.

By the seventeenth century, European artists and travel writers reported back regularly to emigrants eager to accept the adventure of America's promise. The New Worlds were marvelous possessions, and Europeans represented them in literature and art as colonialist constructions that were at once provocative and savage. Europeans conquered the New World by force-of-arms, and the brutality and destruction are implicated in highly gendered ideas of masculine identity and power that are now the subject of lively scholarly study and debate.[6] The European ideal of the Americas as an eroticized and passive female possession appears in the German allegory *America* from the middle of the eighteenth century (fig. 103). Columbus's discovery of "America" is symbolized by an African-Indian queen with a parrot in hand, enthroned upon an alligator in the foreground. She offers the new world's riches to the Europeans. In the distance landscapes that no European had yet seen are represented as Edenic, beckoning, and conveniently empty.

Imperialism and Enlightenment rationalism led European states to commission artists to accompany exploring parties sent forth to claim new territories; upon return, the reports and images they produced provided impetus for further exploration and colonization. The English painter William Hodges sailed with Captain Cook on his voyages of discovery to the South Seas, and created a sensation in London with his paintings and prints of remote yet alluring locations in the Pacific Ocean. Momentum gathered in the eighteenth century for European colonial expansion and with it came an outpouring of images produced by a variety of artists to accompany commentaries by travel writers. Written texts still predominated as a means of communicating the importance of new lands. Eagerness for news of these exotic places stimulated the production of prints, illustrated maps, and guide and travel books that provided increasing quantities of visual information for European colonists.[7]

Exploration and National Expansion

By the early nineteenth century, as the United States expanded westward across the continent, the importance of artist-explorers dramatically increased. The young nation claimed an imperial future. Spurred by notions of Manifest

Destiny in the 1850s, its most zealous nationalists urged an empire stretching from the Atlantic to the Pacific. Exploration was the first instrument of this aggressive ideology in an age enthralled with explorers as heroes. Artists eagerly accompanied expeditions to unknown places in the far West, to the Catskill Mountains, the Adirondacks and White Mountains, or traveled independently Down East to Mount Desert, in search of beautiful, sublime, and picturesque scenery. The elaborately wrought images they produced employed the prevailing conventions of art and thinly disguised a purpose not ultimately different from the earliest images of explorer-artists—facilitating appropriation of territory by imposing a compelling visual order on its representation.[8] For artists the far West was pure opportunity: "It is in our border life alone that we can find the material for national development as far as literature and art are concerned," declared the art writer Henry T. Tuckerman.[9] He was called the "American Vasari" because he wrote the first comprehensive art history of the period. Gazing at their cunningly crafted representations, a viewer could see into the past and the future simultaneously. Representations of western landscapes merged pleasing anticipations of future national mastery with emotions of nostalgia for a rapidly disappearing past. Images of these remote landscapes produced what recently has been termed an "Empire of the Eye."[10]

From the financial and political capitals of New York and Washington, parties of government-sponsored explorers set forth to describe, visually document, and topographically survey the western landscape. Immigrants followed this vanguard to take possession of the land by "settlement." By the 1850s artists regularly accompanied these expeditions. Although their position was at times an informal one, this did not lessen the value of their images. Even simple sketches made by soldiers were prized by an eastern public anxious for information about remote wilderness landscapes, and eager for any visual evidence of opportunity. No visual artist accompanied the most renowned expedition of the early nineteenth century, the Lewis and Clark Expedition. Yet so amazing were its accounts that the necessity of artists accompanying future expeditions revealed itself immediately.[11]

Early American Artist-Explorers

The first official American artist-explorer was Titian Ramsey Peale, youngest son of the famous artist-naturalist and museum impresario, Charles Wilson Peale of Philadelphia. Titian R. Peale went West in 1819–1820, accompanying Major Stephen H. Long's expedition, the first expedition to assert federal claims to the lands west of the Mississippi. Peale and another artist, Samuel Seymour, fulfilled their commission by documenting what the exploring party encountered, particularly the flora and fauna of the West. Seymour's images displayed a "geological imagination" that enabled them to function on several levels of meaning. They were topographic documentation of what the explorers experienced, metaphors for nationalism, and occasionally personifications of the landscape.[12]

George Catlin, predecessor of Bierstadt and Moran, helped advance the cultural importance of the artist-explorer. The ambitious Catlin traveled up the Missouri River into the far West in 1832–1834 to paint Native Americans.[13] He hoped to profit by producing a touring "Indian Gallery" that would exhibit the paintings of his discoveries. Catlin's canvases, shown to acclaim in the East and in Europe, were the first substantial body of images to promote the West. Catlin also produced elaborate contexts for these images, ranging from tableaux vivants, to books and paintings that were shown as part of his traveling Indian show, to displays of actual natives in costume with authentic cultural artifacts, although often white actors played the Indians. In one of his many conceits about Native Americans, Catlin provocatively called for a national park to protect Indians and preserve their way of life. "What a beautiful and thrilling specimen for America to preserve," Catlin wrote, ". . . a nation's park containing man and beast in all the wild freshness of nature's beauty."[14] When the government finally established national parks it was not to "save" Indians or buffalo, but to serve other commercial and political interests. A few years after Catlin's trip West, Karl Bodmer, a Swiss artist, explored the upper Missouri with an aristocratic patron, Prince Maximilian of Wied-Neuwied. The Baltimore artist Alfred J. Miller also painted the West as he traveled with Scotsman Captain William Drummond Stewart on a hunting expedition to the Rocky Mountains. The production of images by these and other artists during the 1830s and 1840s helped to increase the lure of the West in the crucial decade before the Civil War.[15]

During the 1850s, a few official artist-explorers joined government expeditions surveying the West. As part of their commissions they published reports of what they had seen on their explorations. These excited partisan groups in the North and South were vying for control of the route of a proposed transcontinental railroad. The landscape painter Henry Cheever Pratt and the scholar-artist John Russell Bartlett accompanied the U.S.-Mexico Boundary Survey in the early 1850s through the Southwest. Their images were produced as part of one the largest and most expensive government expeditions following the conquest of vast territories from Mexico.

Bartlett, the official Boundary Commissioner, had wanted Thomas Cole to accompany him, but the artist died unexpectedly in 1848. Bartlett turned to Cole's long-time associate and good friend, Pratt, who had visited Mount Desert with Cole in 1844. The arid desert landscapes of the Southwest proved as difficult to incorporate into the aesthetic conventions Pratt and Cole relied upon as they would for

Thomas Moran two decades later. The illustrated report that Bartlett published, along with numerous other more elaborate volumes produced at government expense through the 1850s, stimulated a wide variety of commercial, political, and cultural interest in the Southwest and its many opportunities.[16]

During the 1850s, parties of explorers traveled West to survey rivers, wagon roads, and potential routes for the Pacific railroad. American artists, engravers, and printers of that period used government subsidies and produced the reports that resulted from these surveys. The artists whose field images were the basis of these publications were not always the principal beneficiaries of this government largess. The production of lavishly illustrated official volumes, some with costly colored engravings, stimulated further popular demand for visual evidence of the "Great West." That need was met, in part, by "Indian Shows" and the many travel guides with illustrations that adapted and recycled motifs developed by artist-explorers for government reports. John Mix Stanley in Detroit, Michigan, painted the far West and its inhabitants for a touring Indian Gallery that imitated Catlin's successful example. The Prussian artist Balduin Möllhausen accompanied the expedition of Lt. Joseph C. Ives to explore the Colorado River, producing more dramatic images of the arid desert. The Canadian artist-explorer Paul Kane traveled to the Pacific in search of images of the West and natives. Both Kane and Stanley hoped to sell their collections to the Congress, but failed.[17]

Albert Bierstadt and the Yosemite Valley

Albert Bierstadt, the most important western artist-explorer who specialized in landscapes, first traveled West in 1859 as part of Frederick W. Lander's U.S. Government sponsored surveying party exploring the Rocky Mountains. He returned to New York to build an impressive career depicting the West. Bierstadt appeared at just the right moment in the late 1850s, when national interest in the West was at a fever pitch. One of the first professionally trained New York based artists to supply images of the West, he was recognized by the leading art magazine *The Crayon*. "The scenery of this section of our territory," its editors declared, "has for a long time been a matter of curiosity to lovers of landscape, who have been excited and yet not satisfied by the vague and contradictory reports of explorers. Through the better expressions of the brush we can now form some idea of it, Mr. Bierstadt's pencil being too true too powerful to be questioned."[18] Yet Bierstadt, a latter-day explorer, only reached the foothills of the Rockies on his first expedition, and did not even visit Yosemite until 1863, after he saw photographs of the valley by California landscape photographer Carleton Watkins in a New York gallery. Bierstadt's dramatic paintings of the Rocky Mountains and Yosemite came at exactly the right time. The Civil War temporarily diverted national energy from west-

ward expansion. A great yearning existed to keep the promise of the West alive, and Bierstadt capitalized on this with a prolific production of paintings of western scenes, particularly Yosemite Valley. The New York public enthusiastically received these works.

Bierstadt's enormous popularity resulted from the adept way that he exploited the expectations and desires of the nation. In this ability he resembled his model and rival Frederic Edwin Church, the other leading explorer-artist of the period. Tuckerman thought that Church carried the "indomitable explorative enterprise of the New England mind into landscape art." Both Church and Bierstadt "have explored distant regions for characteristic and fresh themes."[19] Church first gained national and then English celebrity with his 1857 painting *Niagara* (see fig. 54). It represented the great national scenic spectacle so realistically that it was described as "Niagara with the roar left out." Just two years later, Church unveiled another great picture, *The Heart of the Andes*. With these triumphs Church became an artistic celebrity in New York.[20]

That same year Bierstadt began his production of western paintings in direct competition with Church. He represented the western wilderness as if it were an inviting natural landscape park, a beautiful garden-like place created by man instead of by nature. He did not realize that Native Americans had practiced selective horticulture, resulting in an appearance of human intervention—a common misperception. Thomas Starr King wrote upon seeing the Yosemite, "It was difficult to believe that we were in the aboriginal wilderness. For miles, we would ride up a gentle slope, undisturbed by stones, upon which it seemed that thousands of dollars had been spent in clearing the underbrush, and given the flowers field to sport and revel." Bierstadt specialized in painting "the natural 'parks' which nature has bestrewn the American Occident—scenes which, when man first bursts upon them, amaze him by their appearance of preparation and deliberation culture."[21] His images satisfied a desire to believe that the West, and Yosemite more specifically, were great national symbols of prosperity and hope.[22]

In 1864, the nation's leading landscape architect, Frederick Law Olmsted, drafted a bill to preserve Yosemite Valley. President Abraham Lincoln quickly signed it into law. The bill passed easily since no opposing commercial or private interests sought the California valley. In his report Olmsted stated:

> It was during one of the darkest hours [of the Civil War] when the paintings of Bierstadt . . . had given to the people on the Atlantic some idea of the sublimity of the Yosemite . . . that consideration was first given to the danger that such scenes might become private property and through false taste, the caprice or requirements of some industrial speculation of their holders, their value to posterity be injured.[23]

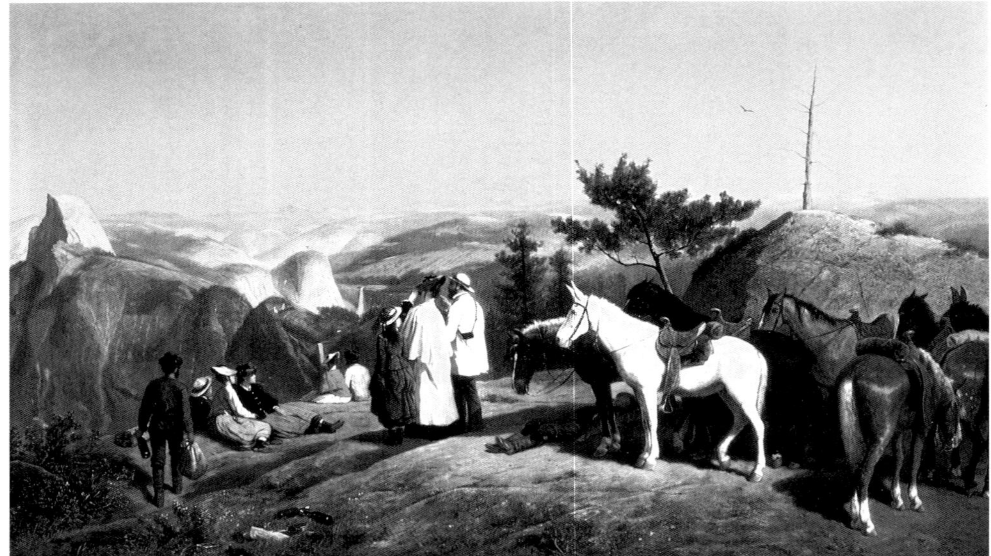

FIG. 104 William Hahn, *Yosemite Valley from Glacier Point,* 1874, oil on canvas, 27¼ x 46¼". California Historical Society, San Francisco, Gift of Albert M. Bender.

Geographical Turf

For a time Bierstadt's Yosemite paintings were wildly successful with the press and public. He soon vied for the title of "Monarch of Landscape Painters" with Church. In this competition Church had advantages: his more adventurous travels took him to South America twice in search of volcanoes; and he explored wilderness closer to home, traveling to remote parts of Maine, including many trips to Mount Desert. Church's "great pictures," such as *Niagara*, and *Twilight in the Wilderness*, were more original than Bierstadt's in their manner of execution and conceptualization, although they frequently concerned similar issues that Bierstadt capitalized upon, particularly a national obsession with Manifest Destiny. Church preceded Bierstadt in the creation of the great picture, but Bierstadt's staking of his claim by producing great pictures of the West effectively preempted Church from also working that territory. Thus Church decided to reinforce his claims on the Northeast and other wilderness scenes.

Church, the son of New England's Puritan elite, never overcame his distaste for his rival sufficiently to undertake a trip to the West. In 1888 he lauded the Great East, noting that it was the enterprise, energy, brain, and cash of the East that made the West. Church and Bierstadt were locked in a competitive relationship in the New York art market. The places each chose *not* to explore and paint speak of an informal, probably unexpressed self-regulating division of territory—of geographical turf. A critic for the magazine *The Round Table* noted the common perception that "Mr. Bierstadt's name is now associated with the Rocky Mountains and that of Mr. Church with the Andes." By 1868, Bierstadt so dominated the Rockies and Yosemite that the critic could note jocularly that Bierstadt had already "copyrighted nearly all the principal mountains."[24]

Bierstadt never visited Mount Desert or the Maine Coast, although he painted and sketched extensively in the Northeast. Thomas Cole first painted Mount Desert for the New York audience, and then it was claimed by Church, Cole's

self-anointed artistic heir, who produced major pictures of Island landscapes during the 1850s and 1860s. The competitive stakes Church and Bierstadt held in the New York art market directly circumscribed the range of geographical locales in which they could paint. Such self-imposed limitations did not trouble other artists, however. Church's and Bierstadt's fame was so great the places they discovered quickly attracted other artists. Louis R. Mignot and Martin Johnson Heade attempted to improve their standing by traveling to South America, while William Bradford followed Church's lead and ventured to the arctic in search of icebergs.[25] Many landscape painters followed Bierstadt's successful example, traveling West to paint scenery and natives. Worthington Whittredge, John F. Kensett, Sanford R. Gifford, Jervis McEntee, and other artists who worked or lived in New York City traveled West to exploit the scenic potential of the region, as each hoped to discover the next Niagara, or Yosemite, or Yellowstone, and to connect the fame of the place to their name in hopes of gaining an increased share of the art market.

Tourist Art and Tourist Manners

After 1869 a trip to the West shortened in time from months to days on the recently completed transcontinental railroad. A proliferation of prints and illustrated guides heavily promoted the Yosemite Valley, in particular. From Bierstadt's studio in New York flowed a steady production of paintings of Yosemite. Other artists followed his example, flourishing by supplying the national demand for images of the nation's western Eden. At his studio at the entrance to Yosemite National Park, California landscape painter Thomas Hill could paint views of the valley virtually on demand for visitors. He was euphemized as the "artist in waiting to the Yosemite." Hill's career exemplifies how images produced by Bierstadt in New York resulted in tourism at the Yosemite Park, which in turn produced a new market for local artists who also supplied paintings on the spot for California visitors. Hill is an example of the circulation of cultural production—an artist whose position in the field was directly stimulated by Bierstadt's creation of new markets for tourist art in the East.[26] There were many such followers of Church at Mount Desert in the 1870s and 1880s.

The excitement and boredom of travelers—in pursuit of the western scenic overlooks that Bierstadt and others popularized—is the subject of a humorous picture of 1874 produced by San Francisco artist William Hahn (fig. 104). Consuming "approved" scenery at the newly established national parks meant the dutiful rehearsal of conventional sentiments of appreciation and awe. Hahn captures the gaze and gestures of tourists practicing tourist manners: the tourist family members clutch their guidebooks, their field glasses, and wear fashionable attire for a proper scenic experience. The family group contrasts with the distracted lovers in the left foreground and the bored guides who are fast asleep under their pack horses, having seen the view many times. The rhetoric and imagery of guidebooks reclaimed for visitors the designated prospects that the artists represented in paintings.

Thomas Moran and the Yellowstone

After the Civil War, interest in the West that had been deferred during the conflict was renewed with a vengeance. The Far West was finally opened by the railroad in 1869, unleashing new rounds of government-sponsored exploring and surveying parties that completed the exploration of the region. In 1871, a party led by the geologist and western promoter Ferdinand V. Hayden, accompanied by landscape painter Thomas Moran, entered the Yellowstone Region. Just a year earlier, a company of soldiers had reconnoitered the area and returned with some crude sketches of strange geological formations. Moran had reworked these sketches for publication and resolved to reach the area himself. On arrival, the explorers were overwhelmed (fig. 105). Yellowstone exceeded all their expectations, appearing to imitate art with its riots of brilliant colors, fantastic geologic shapes, and cultivated park-like appearance.

The explorers returned to the East determined to "save" the Yellowstone from reckless commercial exploitation. The politically astute Hayden immediately began a promotional campaign, starting with an article in *Scribner's*. He urged, "Why will not Congress at once pass a law setting it apart as a great public park for all time to come, as has been done with the not more remarkable wonder, the Yosemite Valley?"[27] Moran's on-the-spot sketches and watercolors, and photographs by the expedition's official photographer William H. Jackson, were shown to Congress, where they created a sensation. "They did a work which no other agency could do and doubtless convinced every one who saw them that the regions where such wonders existed should be carefully preserved to the people forever," wrote one participant.[28] After intense lob-

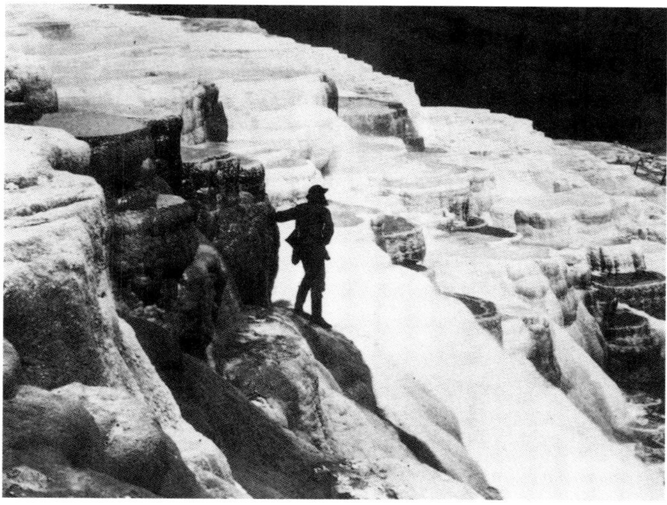

FIG. 105 William H. Jackson, *Thomas Moran at the Mammoth Hot Springs, Gardener River*, 1871. Photograph Courtesy of the Thomas Moran Biographical Art Collection, East Hampton Library.

bying by railroad interests, an act of Congress proclaimed Yellowstone a National Park on 2 March 1872. By the spring of that year Moran completed his large *Grand Canyon of the Yellowstone* and arranged its installation in the Capitol (fig. 106). After further lobbying it was purchased by Congress for ten thousand dollars. The painting became the official icon of America's first national park. Soon after, Moran began adding a "Y" to his monogram signature: to denote his association with the place he became known as Thomas "Yellowstone" Moran.

Capitalizing on newly found fame, and seeking a fresh supply of western landscapes to increase his competitive position, Moran accompanied famed explorer-scientist John Wesley Powell to the recently discovered Grand Canyon of the Colorado River in the Arizona Territory in 1873. Powell's government exploring party had first descended the Colorado by boat in 1869. This trip in 1873 was Moran's second "break." At the Yellowstone he had claimed a vast scenic territory, and now in the Southwest he would again identify himself with another scenic wonder. Hastening back to New York, Moran began a new painting of the South Rim of the Canyon that was intended as a companion to the Yellowstone picture. *Chasm of the Colorado* was also purchased by Congress (fig. 107).

Businessmen who ran the railroads were eager to employ Moran's images of the scenic splendor of the West to promote their routes, and they soon realized their power to stimulate tourist interest in visiting these places. With his western images Moran quickly became a formidable rival to both Bierstadt and Church, and he maintained a solid position in the field, enjoying popular admiration and patronage into the second decade of the twentieth century, long after Church was forgotten and Bierstadt had gone bankrupt.

The Commerce of Scenery

Works produced by artists, especially those who claimed to have discovered a celebrated place and whose paintings bore witness to its beauty or sublimity, carried cultural value based

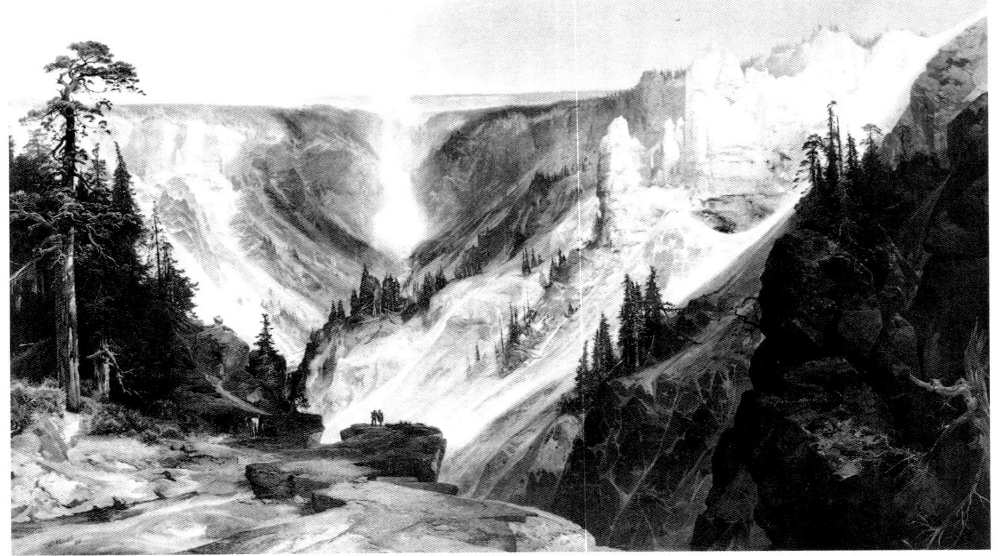

on a perception of disinterestedness. The cultural work of the explorer-painters was always performed in the name of art and science, for public good, not for private gain. The appearance of such disinterestedness by landscape painters essentially masked art's service to other agendas. Yet this disinterestedness was an illusion, because, for example, Thomas Moran could not have traveled to the Yellowstone without financial backing from Jay Gould's Northern Pacific Railway. The railroad's corporate agents, who by that time included *de facto* the leader of the Yellowstone expedition, F. V. Hayden, lobbied Congress to designate Yellowstone as a national park and to purchase Moran's great paintings for the Capitol. For the railroad's managers these were business expenses and Moran's art served as advertising. Moran's later production for the Santa Fe Railroad of paintings and prints of the Grand Canyon, and of the Southwest, followed a similar pattern.[29]

Paintings of Mount Desert were often hung with images of the far West at the Annual Exhibitions of the National Academy of Design, and reproductions in illustrated magazines increased popular interest in these exceptional places. In their paintings of the Island, and of American scenery more generally, Cole and Church self-fashioned themselves to make it appear as if they acted solely out of concern for higher artistic, cultural, and national interests, just as Bierstadt and Moran would do with their representations of Yosemite and Yellowstone. However, it is evident that privately they understood how the images they produced directly supported the emerging industry of tourism, and that these two seemingly dissimilar fields of production—one of the high art visual culture of the reigning artist-explorers and the other of mass tourism—had many interests in common.

Even the conservative Cole, scholars recently have observed, understood the value of the emerging tourist industry to art producers, although he complained about it.[30] The artist-explorers were never apologetic. Church's letters about Mount Desert that appeared in the *Bulletin of the American Art-Union* urged the construction of accommodations. While

Church lacked only the imprimatur of "official" to add institutional esteem and governmental honor to his images, he relied on and refined the channels that Bierstadt and Moran used to reach a popular audience. These included special exhibitions, mass circulation magazines, newspapers, and travel guides, many illustrated with wood-block and lithographic reproductions.[31] Travel books such as *Picturesque America* made Mount Desert, along with Yosemite, Yellowstone, and the Grand Canyon, better known. These travel books were the not-too-distant ancestors of a still proliferating genre of glossy illustrated travel magazines.

Cultural Work of Artists

The cultural work begun by Thomas Cole and carried forward by Frederic Edwin Church, Sanford R. Gifford, John Frederick Kensett, and other artists who later painted Mount Desert was a more drawn out variation on the process of cultural and economic transformation through which western sites became parks. A major difference between the western parks and Mount Desert was their remoteness. The distance between the western parks and the East buffered the immediate exploitation of natural resources, which were often claimed to be valueless, hence their residual value as scenery. The *only* evident natural resource at Mount Desert, aside from lumber and fishing, was scenery. Comparative proximity to major metropolitan centers proved to be its greatest advantage. Geographical realities also affected differences in the historical process: the time from the discovery of Yellowstone until it became a national park was only two years, while more than half a century passed between Cole's and Church's visits and the establishment of Acadia National Park.

The fact that land in the West was publicly owned enabled the creation of parks by Congressional decree, but establishing a national park at Mount Desert, where much of the land had already passed into private ownership, required nothing less than the efforts the richest man in the United States, John D. Rockefeller, Jr. Rockefeller invested great

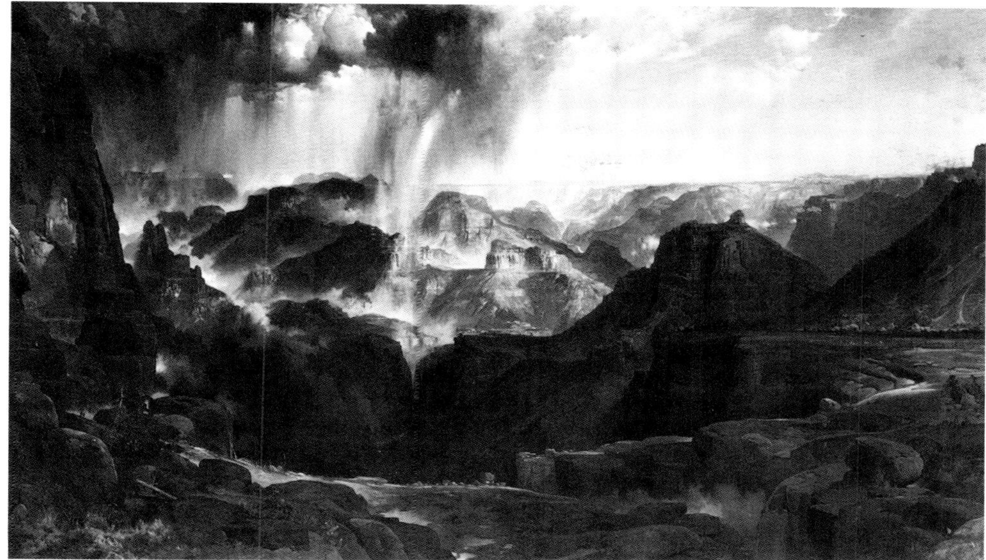

sums in maintaining the Island as a preserve for others of his class, and his massive construction program of carriage roads and bridges furthered aristocratic leisure. Consummating the process initiated by Cole and Church, Rockefeller converted some of his immense economic capital into the cultural capital of a new national park designed to preserve scenery and an elite style of life.

PRODUCING PERSONAL STYLE

Why were American landscape painters who helped invent the first national parks so popular, and why were they rewarded as the highest paid visual artists of the Civil War era? The great pictures of Church, Bierstadt, and Moran, and reproductions of them, stimulated both cultured and popular audiences by championing national agendas of expansionism and, later, tourism. But that alone does not fully explain what it was about these artifacts of mid-nineteenth century visual culture that gave them power to engage the imagination of the nation and reward their makers so richly. To understand this it is necessary to look more closely at the field of visual cultural in New York and the artistic conventions involved in the production of art during this period.

The "boom and bust" economy of the young nation experienced a rapid phase of expansion during the decade before the Civil War. New York became the nation's largest and wealthiest metropolis, the financial and trade center of the nation, and hub of its new railroad network. With unprecedented urban growth, financial opportunities for producers of visual arts in the city dramatically increased. In 1867 Tuckerman noted approvingly that every year since 1850, "the demand and supply [for art] have constantly expanded."[32] By the early 1860s, a critical mass of artists, patrons, dealers, and art writers had emerged. Dramatic manifestations of this growth included a new Tenth Street Studios Building for artists and the rise of influential commercial galleries and art dealers specializing in selling Amer-

ican art. "Art, like everything else here, is in a transitional state," Tuckerman observed. "European travel, the writings of Art-commentators, clubs, and academies, the biographies of artists, lectures, more discriminations, a love of collecting standard engravings, the reciprocal influence in society of artists and amateurs . . . are evidence of progressive intelligence among us."[33] These individuals, organizations, and institutions comprised the first field of market-driven visual culture production in the United States.

Demands for an increased supply of art resulted in a new emphasis on producing freshness, imagination, and originality. Achieving these elusive qualities became the essence of developing personal style. After the nineteenth century the importance of personal style expanded enormously, reaching a culmination with the modernist painters of the mid-twentieth century. The development of a personal style in mid-nineteenth century New York was no less important, and may have taken on a special urgency in the United States because of "the inequality of productions" that Tuckerman and others observed. "The variations in ability or merit in the results of individual art[ists] are unparalleled. We can sometimes hardly realize that the same hand is responsible for so wide is the interval between . . . the best and worst pictures."[34] However, the search for artistic originality was easier in the United States, Tuckerman believed, because the lack of long-established traditions and conventions of art production provided the American artist with an advantage over his European counterpart. The absence of routine helped artists escape the "tyranny of conventionalism." "When a painter really expresses what is in him, and not what the public *fiat* approves, or famous limners have made manifest for ages, he is sure to be attended to if there is a spark of artistic feeling in his nature."[35]

The leading explorer-artists were successful because of their ability to produce art that provided original and convincing visual constructions of national identity. This often meant the simultaneous representation in a single landscape

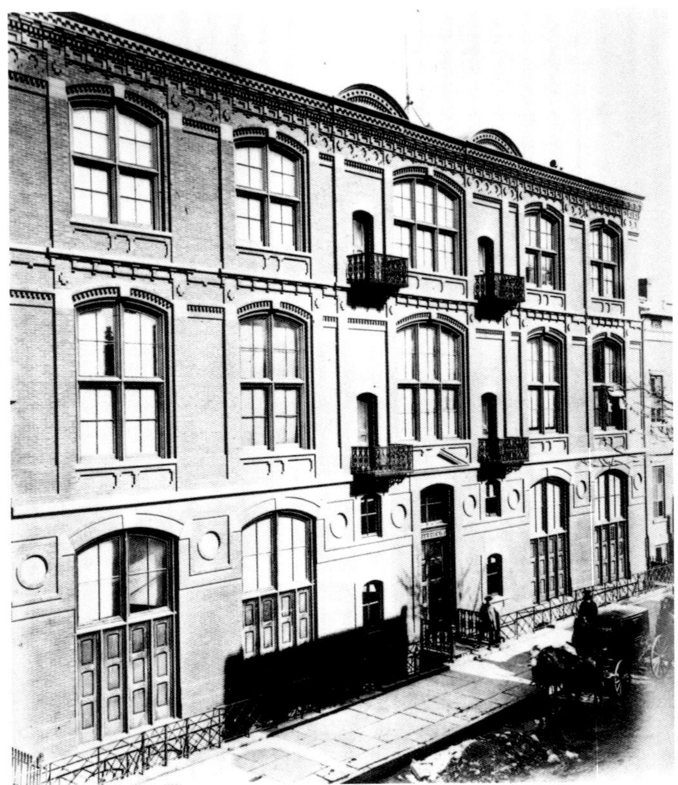

of nostalgic memories of the past and optimistic dreams for the future. The West was the ideological locus of these cultural and social expectations. Enthusiasm for explorers who could lead national expansion intoxicated Northeasterners, and New Yorkers in particular. During the 1850s representations of historical figures such as Daniel Boone offered prospects of sales in the city for artists William Ranney and George Caleb Bingham. Their historical landscapes depicted the famed, long-dead explorer as "the Columbus of the Woods," a heroic pathfinder leading settlers westward. In Bingham's famous image Boone became an American Moses marching chosen people through the wilderness to a promised land, and simultaneously became a device to help assimilate the West as a region into a national economy and culture.[36] After annexing vast territories from Mexico, the spoils of war, the last pockets of "unknown land" beckoned for final exploration before the West could be penetrated by railroads. In the decade before the Civil War, bitter, even violent controversy erupted over the issue of expansion of slavery to western territories. Californian John C. Fremont, one of the most prominent exploring heroes of the empire, ran for President in 1856 as the first anti-slavery western Republican. The production of images to support this imperial national agenda was a sure route to patronage and recognition in a society that believed its artists free of the tyranny of conventionalism. "Who," Tuckerman asked, "in this land of railroads and elections stands apart rapt in solemn visions such as absorbed of old a Dürer or an Angelo?"[37]

Becoming an explorer, whether visual or literary, and sending back letters to newspapers from beyond the frontier was, by the end of the 1850s, a well-worn path. Catlin demonstrated as early as the 1840s that exhibitions of western images produced good financial results. By the 1860s this had been refined into the production of a single great picture that could dramatically present the results of explorations to exotic, unknown places to large numbers of spectators.[38] Tuckerman thought that landscape painting was "destined to achieve new triumphs in our time" because it would render "the grand, beautiful, and unfamiliar aspects of nature, only accessible at great cost of fatigue and exposure, and even peril of life and limb."[39] In an expanding field of cultural production and consumption, marked by the emergence of art journalism, illustrated magazines, and mass circulation newspapers, good money could be made by discovering special places and producing a "hit." Accompanied by an explanatory brochure and commercial advertising, these elaborate visual promotions offered assurances of profits, although paradoxically, for producers of high art who aimed at attracting elite patrons, feigning a certain disinterest in the *business* of art was advantageous.

Generally, artists of the Hudson River School labored dutifully to appear as solid, respectable businessmen of art. They sought social recognition as industrious, qualified professionals, and feared the labels of craftsmen or tradesmen. They seldom cultivated the image of dandies or Bohemians creating "art for art's sake" (that would come later, in the Gilded Age). Their biographies demonstrate just how remarkably successful they were in occupying leading positions in the field precisely because of the astute ways they self-fashioned their personal styles and artistic personas to match their audience's expectations. The fact that exploring-artists of the Hudson River School gained such enormous popularity and commanded such high prices for their work foreshadowed the extreme commodification of art production today.[40]

The social and cultural conditions that allowed this momentary confluence of high art conventions and popular reception could not last. By the end of the century, the peculiar dance of high art with money had all but rejected the idea that good art could also be popular. Scenic landscape parks for masses of tourists were one social outcome of this historical moment. For the field of visual production the emergence of superstar artists in a free-market competition was a comparable cultural transformation of enduring importance. That they all gained fame as explorers was essential for their construction in Tuckerman's history of American art.

The Field of Visual Culture in New York

The expanding field of visual culture in New York centered itself in the now-famed Tenth Street Studios when the building opened in January 1858 (fig. 108).[41] It was built specifi-

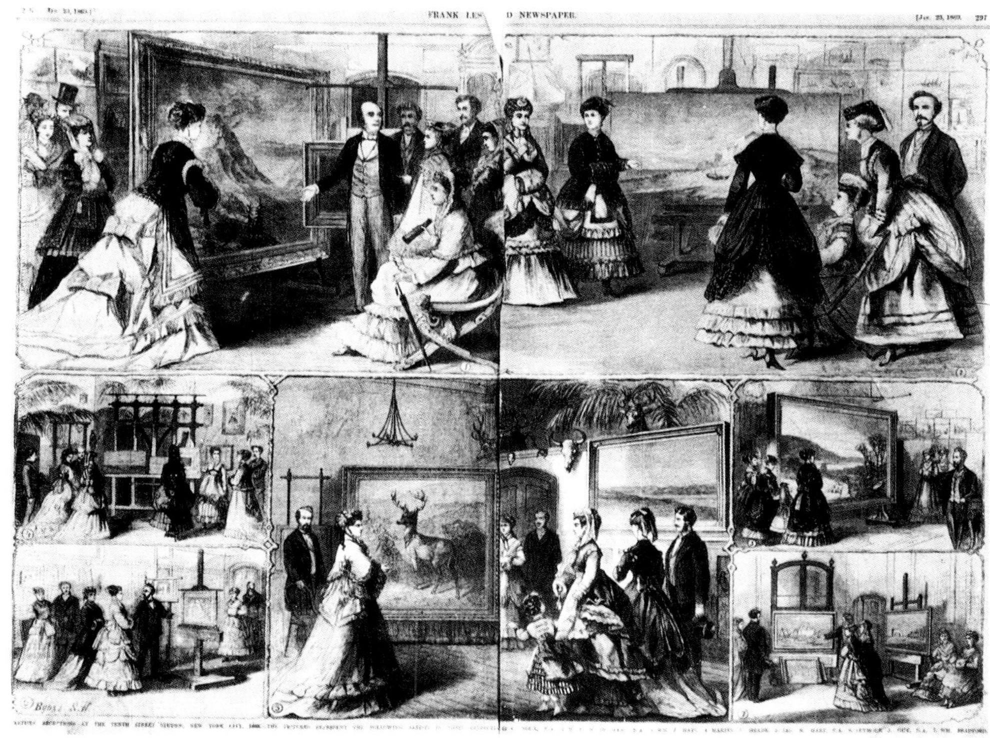

FIG. 109 *Frank Leslie's Illustrated Newspaper,* 29 January 1869, "Artists' Reception at the Tenth Street Studios." Photograph Courtesy of the Museum of the City of New York. (detail p.130)

cally to serve artists in producing, exhibiting, and selling their work, and was the first building of its kind in the United States. At a coveted Studios building address on 51 West Tenth Street, Church, Bierstadt, Sanford R. Gifford, Worthington Whittredge, Emanuel Leutze, Martin J. Heade, William J. Hays, Jervis McEntee, and many others unveiled their latest creations. The builder of the Studios, James Boorman Johnston, was the brother of railroad tycoon John Taylor Johnston, a leading New York art collector, and a major patron of modern art produced by landscape painters active in the City. He represented the powerful new-money elites who emerged just before the Civil War. At the Studios Building every room was rented to what became the "who's who" of New York artists. With his connections John Taylor Johnston was especially well positioned to acquire examples of their best work.

Crowds often gathered at the building's large exhibition gallery for artist's "receptions," prompted both by newspaper advertising and critical coverage (fig. 109). In one memorable event in 1863 large crowds of spectators gathered at the Studios Building to view Bierstadt's *Rocky Mountains.* At nearby commercial art galleries, such as Goupil's Gallery, and later Williams, Stevens, Williams and Company, thousands paid "two bits" admission to see Church's *Niagara Falls,* or *The Heart of the Andes.* The productions of artists returning from expeditions to the West or other exotic places prompted similar exhibitions at other galleries around the city such as William Schus's Broadway Gallery, Leeds and Company, Snedicor's Gallery, Avery's Gallery, the Dusseldorf Gallery, and later Knoedler & Co. Tuckerman gloated, "The increased value of Art, as a commodity, and of its appreciation as an element of luxury, if not of culture, is evinced by the statis-

tics of the Picture trade in the commercial metropolis [over the last twenty-five years]."[42]

A few of the most acclaimed images presented to the public at these receptions and commercial exhibitions were painted on a very large scale. After they had served their initial function as spectacles for a mass audience, they were eagerly sought by newly wealthy "gentlemen," such as Johnston, or railroad builders William H. Osborn and LeGrand Lockwood. Their financial interests in national progress rewarded them with profits sufficient to afford such prestigious luxury goods, and their mansions were grand enough to display them (fig. 110). Tuckerman observed wryly: "The sudden prosperity of an imperfectly educated class, who with little discrimination, and as a matter of fashion, devote a portion of their newly acquired riches to the purchase of pictures; and as our artists have of late established a certain social prestige, friendly influences are not found wanting to secure their liberal patronage." The emergence of a class of self-made men who desired art for its cultural prestige, and a middle class with leisure to visit art exhibitions and the discretionary funds to acquire reproductions was another result of a strengthening of the field of cultural production. "In fact," Tuckerman stated, "the entire relation of Art to the public has changed within the last ten years: its products are a more familiar commodity; studio buildings, artist-receptions, auction sales, the influence of the press, constant exhibitions . . . have greatly increased the mercantile and social importance of Art."[43] Often spectators with leisure and funds were encouraged to leave the city; they became scenic tourists after seeing exhibitions, or reading travel magazines with illustrations of the nation's scenic places by its famous explorer-artists.

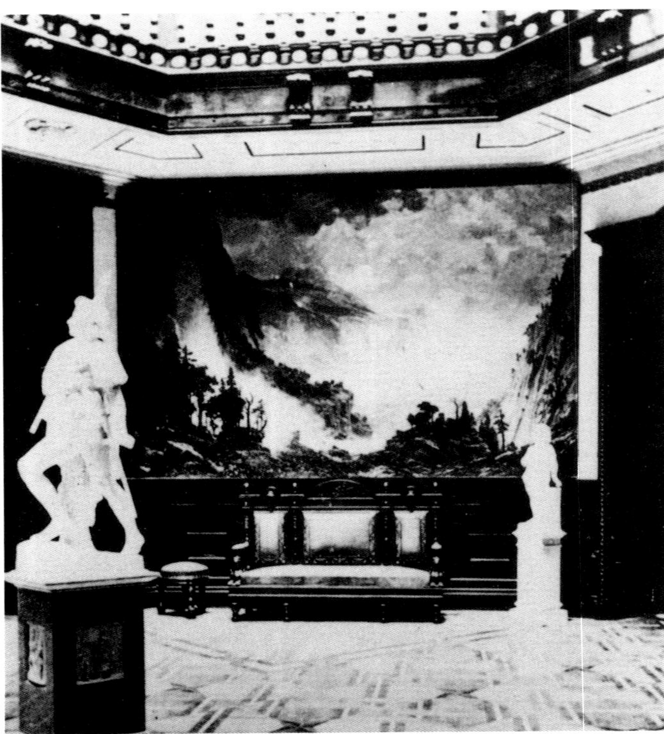

"Our Men of Fortune" and A Company of Artists

The reward for most landscape painters, even in the best of economic times, was hard-earned patronage. Jervis McEntee observed in 1876: "We are more and more impressed by the fact that we shall ultimately have to get some dealers to interest themselves in our work or we shall sink out of sight."[44] To achieve success in New York City, especially if the artist could not claim a Niagara Falls, a Yosemite, or Yellowstone as his own artistic territory, it became increasingly important to fashion a personal style because the market for art in the City was highly competitive. A vogue for high status works by European academic artists and particularly "Old Masters" (many of which were fakes) further depressed the demand for modern art, and was frequently complained about in *The Crayon*. While Church, Bierstadt, and later Moran sold "great pictures" for ten thousand dollars and sometimes more, most artists received around one hundred dollars for their paintings. Newspaper reviews of exhibitions and auctions are full of accounts of painters who vied for patrons and press attention—many little-studied or collected today. In a candid moment, Tuckerman noted, "few [artists] are prompted by disinterested enthusiasm . . . the spirit in which most of our artists work is that of trade rather than of poetry or exalted perception."[45] But for those few who succeeded and were accepted in the clubby, mostly male, National Academy of Design or the elite Century Association, there was academic distinction and the privileges of a brotherhood of artists, and consideration in an emerging national art history. For the great men of landscape paint-

ing, Church and Bierstadt, and to an extent later Moran, there was financial success: social position, grand homes, and travel.

The fields of economic production, with the expansion of railroads, trade, and manufacturing in the 1850s, generated new art patrons, some with great wealth. The development of mass circulation newspapers and illustrated magazines indispensably strengthened the field of visual arts production. The publications needed illustrations, and mass audiences were reached through their advertisements. Prospects of both elite and popular patronage stimulated visual artists to reconsider how the fine arts, and particularly landscape painting, could serve various cultural interests while maintaining an appearance of disinterest in money. One faction of artists led by John Durand and James Stillman, who edited *The Crayon,* urged a more private kind of intimate art form, and they eschewed the large public productions that characterized artist-explorers' work. Asher B. Durand's *Letters on Landscape Painting* advised aspiring artists to first seek their own personal truth in depicting nature, avoiding becoming a "mere imitator, a mannerism." A great fear was that too obvious an interest in making money could degrade art, "perverting it to the servility of mere trade."[46] Durand's conservative and elitist views asserted that professional artists who served in the calling of Art needed to claim a transcendent purpose. But Durand, who supported himself engraving bank notes early in his career, also recognized the necessity of providing soothing or "entertaining" pictures for "our men of fortune." "To the rich merchant or capitalist," Durand wrote, ". . . on his return home, after completion of his daily task of drudgery—his dinner partaken, and himself disposed of in his favorite arm-chair, with one or more faithful landscapes before him, and making no greater effort than to look into the picture instead of on it. . . . many a fair vision of forgotten days will animate the canvas, pleasant reminiscences and grateful emotions will spring up at every step, and care and anxiety will retire far behind him."[47]

Superstar Artists

After 1848, the unfortunate example of Cole's last unfinished and perhaps unsalable series, *The Cross and the World*, made the community of artists painfully aware that while ministers were eager to extol religious and allegorical pictures, buyers found them wanting in regard to removing the "care and anxiety" that Durand would later refer to in his *Letters*. Younger artists, some of them ambitious immigrants like Bierstadt and later Moran, realized that religious or historical paintings simply lacked potential for great commercial success. By the mid-1850s landscape painting had become the best choice for artists aspiring to make a career in New York. Church's impressive early successes stimulated regional painters as far away as Cincinnati, Ohio, where the

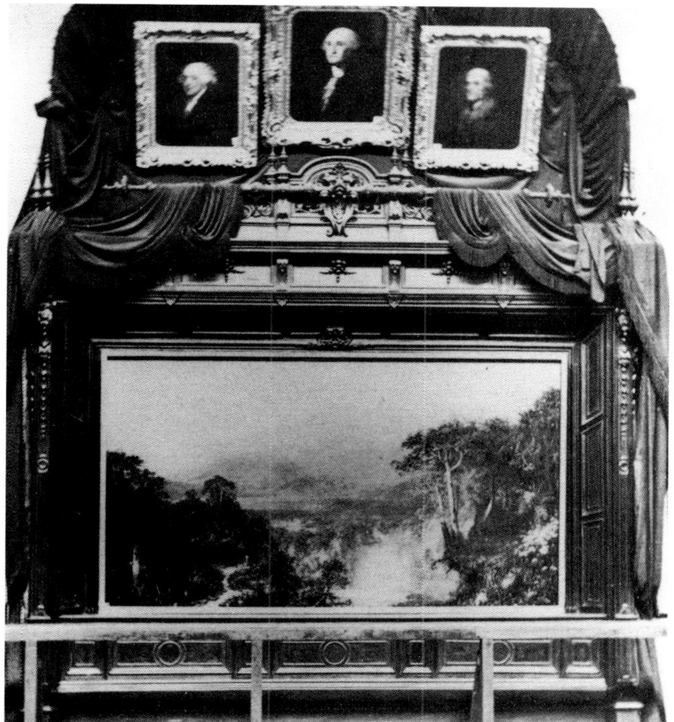

African-American landscape painter, Robert Duncanson, painted his own epic landscapes in the grand manner.[48]

An extreme example of the competitive self-fashioning process occurred early in Church's career. In 1848, immediately following Cole's death, Church moved to position himself ahead of Asher B. Durand, a long-established, older artist. Church audaciously preempted the more conservative Durand by swiftly producing his brilliant memorial painting, *To the Memory of Cole* (see fig. 34), a year before Durand completed his homage to Cole, *Kindred Spirits* (Collection New York Public Library).[49] Soon, Church was hailed as a genius. His actions and the promotion of the picture by his first dealer, George Washington Austen, were highly controversial, and, later, some of Austen's inventory was mysteriously slashed.[50] Church's youthful maneuvering around the older, more conservative Durand continued with his savvy marketing decision not to exhibit his great pictures at the National Academy of Design, where their impact was diluted. He would show them only at solo touring exhibitions which he and his dealers controlled. This self-promotion insulted Durand further, and the feelings between the two artists became so strained that when John Durand wrote of his father's life and career he did not even mention Church.[51] The upshot of this early head-to-head competition for the leading position in the field was that the elder Durand became president of the National Academy of Design, while the younger Church went on to gain fortune and fame.

Church quickly perfected techniques of staging elaborate exhibitions of his "great pictures" in commercial spaces. Cole had promoted his series, such as the *Voyage of Life*, in a similar way, but on a smaller scale. Church, the Puritan businessman's son, understood the value of effective mass promotion. Following his lead, later explorer-artists installed their works in exhibition galleries equipped with special lights and filled with visual "props," including tropical vegetation or Indian artifacts. These theatrical devices were supplemented by printed guides written by leading art critics, travel writers, and adventurers, such as Theodore Winthrop, Fitz Hugh Ludlow, and Louis Noble. The consummate self-promoter, Church quickly grasped the sales advantage of producing dramatic pictures of new places each year, including the Northeastern wilderness of Maine, South American jungles and volcanoes, icebergs of the Arctic, the mournful Vale of St. Thomas in Jamaica, the ruins of Greece, and views of Jerusalem and the Holy Land.[52] Church's relentlessly competitive New England spirit, his artistic discipline and talent, coupled with an aggressive grasp of his market, provided him with a powerful competitive advantage until rheumatism crippled his painting hand. Because of his limited output, his market suffered a postwar collapse. Like other artists of the school, he cultivated a serious, business-like public demeanor, although privately he could be engagingly congenial and devilishly humorous.

Exciting a Nation

Following Cole's lead, Church claimed Mount Desert as a major subject, exploring it thoroughly and painting it often. He defined his geographical territory as continental North and South America, although competition with Bierstadt deflected him from exploring the American West. Church's trips to South America in 1853, and again in 1857, were precedent-setting explorations inspired by Alexander Von Humboldt's multi-volume book *Cosmos*. The famous German naturalist pointed out the natural resources and scenic opportunities awaiting landscape painters in South America. Church's first expedition was made with Cyrus W. Field, one of the nation's most ambitious capitalists and the man who laid the first transatlantic telegraph cable. The commercial potential of South America fascinated Field. Church's paintings would document the continent and arouse support for Field's enterprises. Church's trips resulted in numerous paintings of South America, including *The Andes of Ecuador* (Reynolda House Museum) of 1855. Its success was instrumental in building Church's reputation as the nation's premier painter-explorer of the tropics.

In 1859, Church capped a decade-long promotion of his reputation, which had begun with his memorial painting to Cole, when he exhibited *Heart of the Andes* in New York to unprecedented acclaim (fig. 111). Crowds eagerly paid to view the super-real spectacle of tropical wonder and promise. "Mr. Church" became the nation's first artistic celebrity. The pic-

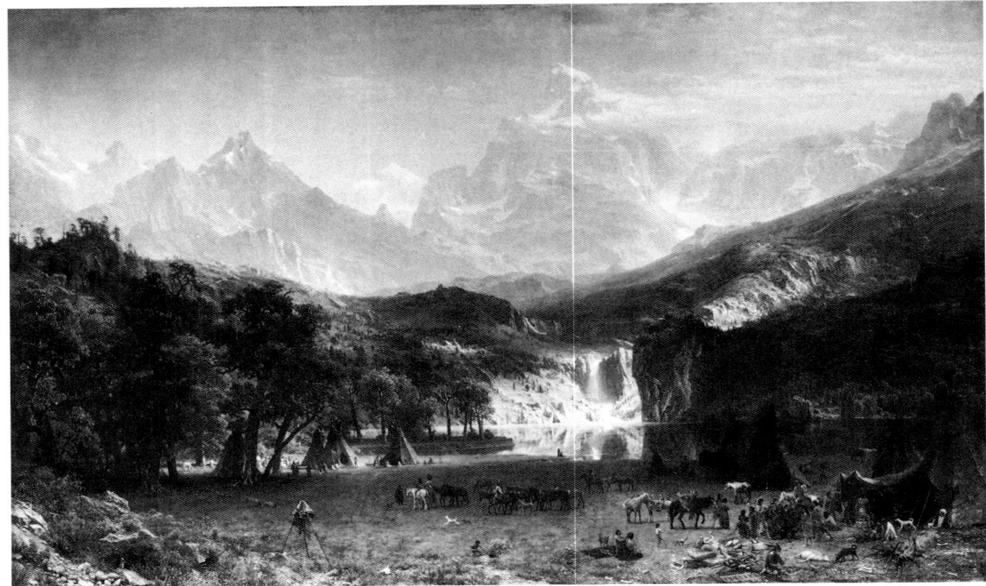

FIG. 112 Albert Bierstadt, *The Rocky Mountains, Lander's Peak,* 1863, oil on canvas, 73½ x 120¾". The Metropolitan Museum of Art, Rogers Fund, 1907.

ture then went on a two-year tour to England and the north-eastern United States. Today, spectators experience Church's *Heart of the Andes,* or Bierstadt's *Rocky Mountains,* at the Metropolitan Museum of Art, in a decontextualized environment. Their original meanings must now be historically recovered. In the case of Church's picture, the special trompe l'oeil frame designed to exaggerate the illusion of a window opening into a vast panoramic space has been reconstructed. It provides a feeling of the way in which spectators in 1859 encountered the image, although the *The Albion* found it "Barnumesque and altogether objectionable. . . . We hope Mr. Church will not subject himself to the charge of resorting to a showman's device. . . . Artifice does not fraternize with Art!"[53] Visitors were advised to bring opera glasses to simulate the effect of observing the scene from a great distance. Church's aggressive self-fashioning through the 1850s resulted in more hard feelings among other artists, but his success bred numerous imitators as competitors moved to appropriate his innovative methods. Yet, Church's success in the field was soon challenged by Bierstadt, just as Bierstadt himself would, in his own turn, find Thomas Moran a powerful rival a decade later.

Rivals in the Field

In 1860, at a Tenth Street Studios reception, Bierstadt exhibited his first large western picture from Lander's 1859 expedition, the now unlocated *Base of the Rocky Mountains: Laramie Peak.* Practically overnight he became a new darling of the press. His debt to Church was obvious. "The chain of lofty mountains are [sic] worthy of Church, and the flora of the valley, display the minute handling of that master," the *New York Herald* observed of Bierstadt's picture.[54] Bierstadt staged an elaborate reception at the Studios where he displayed Indian objects and even buffalo robes in his rooms, making one reporter think he had entered an Indian trading post. Two years later, in 1863, he exhibited his own "great

picture," *The Rocky Mountains*, *Lander's Peak* (fig. 112). Its enormous popular success demonstrated how thoroughly Bierstadt had incorporated Church's refinements in controlling the reception of his "great pictures" with press releases, pamphlets, engravings, and tours. Bierstadt boldly and aggressively bid for public recognition, and he succeeded beyond expectations, demonstrating just how important the West remained for New Yorkers during the depths of the Civil War. Deliberately capitalizing on the nation's preoccupation with war, Bierstadt named the central peak of his European-looking mountains after Lander, who provided him with the opportunity to explore the West, and whose heroic death in military action in 1861 remained fresh in public memory. When Bierstadt's audience gazed upon this complex image they could feel that the sacrifice of men like Lander was worth the cost for "the nation's future greatness is somehow dimly seen in the great West. This picture is a view into the *penetralia* of destiny as well as nature."[55] Bierstadt's own pamphlet was more direct, expressing the anticipation that on the foreground plain depicted in the picture, "a city, populated by our descendants, may rise, and in its art-galleries this picture may eventually find a resting place."[56]

In 1864 the great pictures of the two rivals, Church and Bierstadt, went "head-to-head" when *The Rocky Mountains* was shown together with *The Heart of the Andes* at New York's Metropolitan Art Fair, an event staged to raise funds for the U.S. Sanitary Commission for wounded Union soldiers. Bierstadt cleverly managed to have his picture hung directly opposite Church's and he also presented an Indian Show with a "Monster Wigwam." The moment was a triumph for both artists, although Bierstadt may have won the contest since he had in only a few years fashioned himself as Church's peer. The comparison was invidious in the end for both men. A reporter for the *Times* observed, "Neither of them looks so well here as when seen by themselves and surrounded by all the appliances of the skilled picture-hanger."[57]

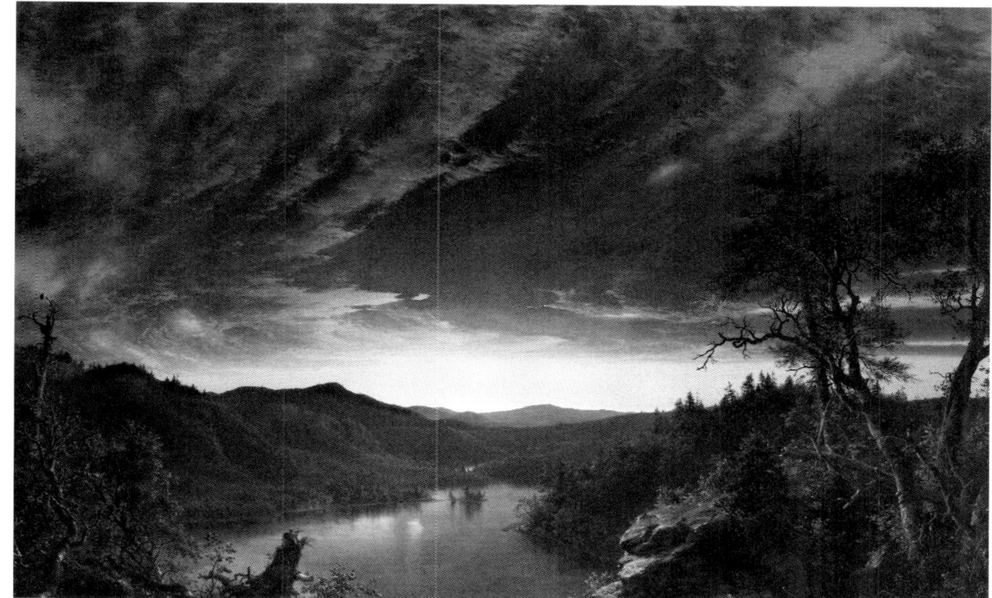

FIG. 113 Frederic E. Church, *Twilight in the Wilderness*, 1860s, oil on canvas, 40 x 64". © Cleveland Museum of Art, 1998, Mr. and Mrs. William H. Marlatt Fund, 1965.233.

The Competition of 1860

While Bierstadt was exploring the Rocky Mountains with Lander, Church spent the summer of 1859 sailing the sub-Arctic in search of icebergs, the subject of his next great picture. When he learned of Bierstadt's success with his western pictures, he postponed work on *The Icebergs* (Dallas Museum of Fine Arts), turning instead to what a critic called his "American sky-landscape."[58] Bierstadt had just rented a studio on Tenth Street where Church was already established, and the two painters simultaneously rushed to complete new pictures for the 1860 season. Bierstadt finished first, exhibiting his *Base of the Rocky Mountains* by the end of March at the Studios Building and later at the National Academy of Design Annual Exhibition. By May, Bierstadt's public triumph had catapulted him to the rank of full academician at the National Academy of Design, positioning him at the center of the field of visual culture in New York.

Church needed a dramatic image to counter Bierstadt's sudden success, and to protect his market he hastened the completion of his major picture of 1860, *Twilight in the Wilderness* (fig. 113). Although many spectators thought the brilliant sunset of the picture was inspired by Maine, it was clear to most that the invented composition compelled them to gaze westward with the setting sun. Church's powerful image, developed for over a decade since his early visits to Maine's Mount Desert, produced a grand visual metaphor. Only a handful of studio intimates had seen *Sunset* (see fig. 48). His subject was nothing less than the continent of North America itself—stretching from what one critic called the "pillars of fire gleaming below the surface of the waters" in the Northeastern foreground to a blazing western horizon. Church in effect answered Bierstadt's youthful picture of buffalo grazing at the base of the Rocky Mountains with an image of national promise and despair. Representing the sun setting on an uninhabited American wilderness, Church invited spectators to believe they saw this solemn scene for the first time in history. The repose of the picture in the foreground and its contrasting lurid sky, the "fiery ordinance of the firmament," betrayed forebodings of National dis-Union that Northerners dreaded through the turbulent summer of 1860. The painting was wildly popular with New Yorkers, and thousands paid admission to see it at Goupil's Gallery. Its brilliant color was inspired by J. M. W. Turner, and its apocalyptic sky personified Ruskin's call for sunset pictures to be like "armies of angels waving their wings" complete with a "Father of Lights" hovering in the crimson curtain of the sky. With its solemn foreground and its celestial agitation in the sky, *Twilight in the Wilderness* became the seminal picture for the 1860s because it so powerfully articulated conflicting emotions of hope and fear for a nation on the brink.[59] It was the first great Civil War picture, lamenting the impending suspension of national expansion to the West that Church's new rival Bierstadt celebrated.

Newspaper Wars

Throughout the 1860s the rivalry between Bierstadt and Church grew so intense that at times they openly displayed their hostility in public. Manipulation of the "penny press" was raised to new levels by these self-styled "monarchs of landscape painting." Next to the Civil War, one journalist wrote "the fiercest combat of modern times is the controversy now raging among the art-critics of New York. . . . Just now it is the fashion, on the one hand, to extol Mr. Bierstadt as one of the best of masters: and, on the other hand, to defame him as one of the worst of pretenders." Each artist had his advocates for whom he would host private press previews in his studio. Church's early champion George William Curtis at the *New York Tribune* was particularly effective in promoting the youthful painter. Clarence Cook, who became art critic for Horace Greeley's *Tribune* was a major early detractor. He despised the German immigrant Bierstadt who painted in the imported "foreign" style of the Dusseldorf

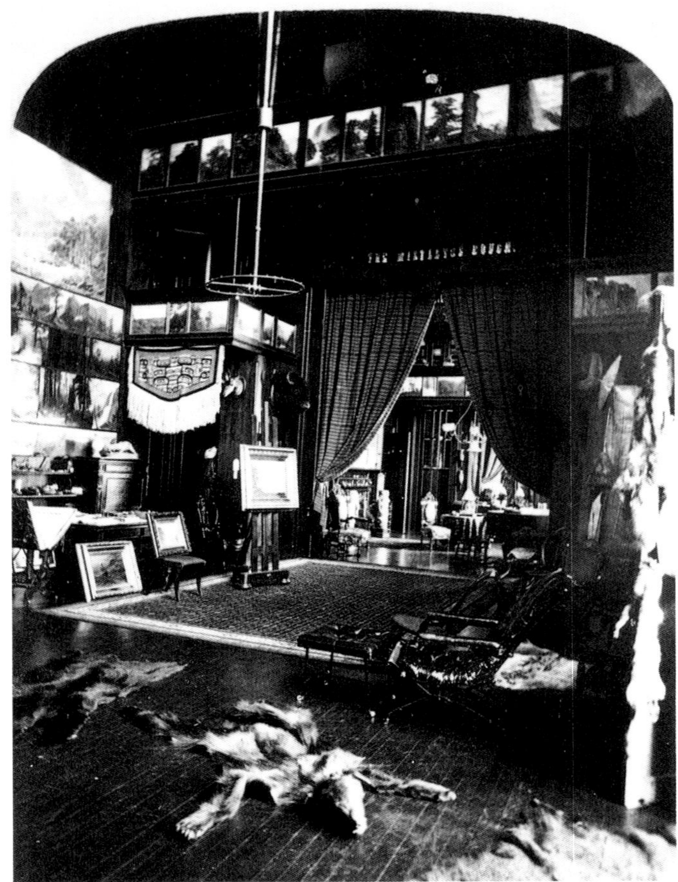

FIG. 114 Charles Bierstadt, *Bierstadt's Studio at Malkasten*. Stereograph Courtesy of The Brooklyn Museum Library Collection, Gift of Joyce Randall Edward, 1996.

Academy, and Cook never missed an opportunity to criticize him savagely. Cook particularly objected to Bierstadt's showmanship, complaining that the *Rocky Mountains* were "at present going through the ceremonies of exhibition and puffery preparation to being engraved. . . . [The] upholsterer has done his work, the tin lorgnettes and the magnifying glasses have been duly provided, the puff-disinterested has been written."[60]

Despite severe criticism from Church's supporters, Bierstadt's advantage in his competition with Church was spurred on by nationalistic enthusiasm for American subjects. While Church ventured farther away geographically than Bierstadt, and showed more interest in contemporary scientific and cultural discourses, Bierstadt reigned through the boom years of the 1860s as the monarch of the western landscape. A reviewer in *Harper's Weekly* captured distinctions between Church's and Bierstadt's subjects and personal styles while reviewing *The Rocky Mountains, Lander's Peak*, noting that Bierstadt's picture was "historic landscape" because of the Indians who were "doomed" to pass away before the coming of civilization. "Unlike Mr. Church's pictures of equatorial mountain scenery of [South] America which . . . forbid hope and leave an impression of profound sadness and desolation, this work of Bierstadt's inspires the temperate cheerfulness and promise of the [West] and the

imagination contemplates it as the possible seat of supreme civilization."[61]

The enterprising zeal of the artist-explorers worried elite art critics like James Jackson Jarves, who complained in 1864 that "the speculating blood infuses itself into art. Within proper limits, the zest of gain is healthful; but if pushed to excess, it will reduce art to the level of trade." "The prominent characteristics of the American landscape school are its realism, vigor, enterprise, and freshness," Jackson continued. But he feared the contaminating influence of sharp business practices: "If it be deceptive, it is so only as trade is, from ambition of success and fervor of competition. Partaking of the enterprise of commerce, it sends its sons to Brazil, to the Amazon, to the Andes, beyond the Rocky Mountains; it orders them in pursuit of icebergs off frozen Labrador; it pauses at no difficulties, distance, expense, or hardship in its search for the new and striking."[62]

Show Studios

In their competition for position and patrons, Bierstadt and Church both built grand villa/studios on the Hudson River. Luxurious theaters of self-fashioning, these elaborate architectural platforms provided illusions of prestige far removed from the harsh realities of business. Exploring-artists lived like gentlemen of leisure and wealth at their country villas, displaying trophies taken on behalf of "art" from their travels to distant places. The studio was the ideal place to enact mystifications of art. Patrons marveled at the brilliant technique and truthfulness of the great men, while reporters were invited to see them at work, admiring the taste and style with which they transformed objects on the walls of their studios into paintings of far away places (fig. 114).[63] The "show studio" became a cultural destination for the wealthiest elite, not unlike the geographical destinations created in the artist-explorers' paintings. In the studio, the transaction of the business of art could be better controlled, and pretensions of disinterest in the business of art could be effectively maintained. Entrepreneurs with new fortunes from Civil War profiteering and transcontinental railroads wanted to complete their cultural transactions in an aestheticized environment detached from the hurly-burly realities of Reconstruction era commerce.

Bierstadt built his architectural fantasy, *Hawksrest,* later renamed *Malkasten* (the paint box), in 1865. Overlooking a vast panorama of the Hudson River, a short trip north by railroad from New York, *Malkasten* was designed to display art and trophies from Bierstadt's expeditions (fig. 115). The villa burned in 1882, and Bierstadt later maintained a succession of other impressive studios around New York. It was said that the more precarious his finances became, the grander and more ostentatious these later studios appeared, evidence of Bierstadt's struggle to maintain

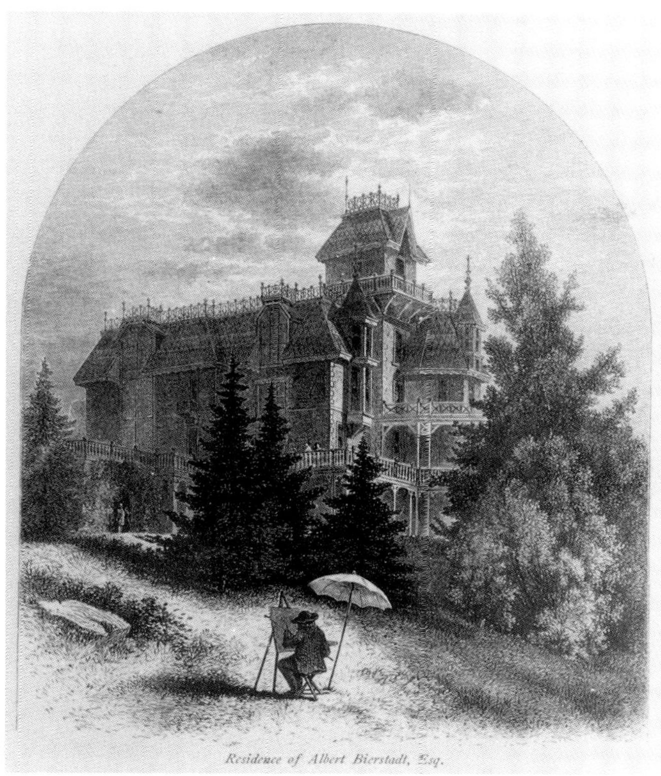

FIG. 115 Martha Lamb, "The Homes of America II," *Art Journal* 2 (1876) "Residence of Albert Bierstadt, Esq.," 45.

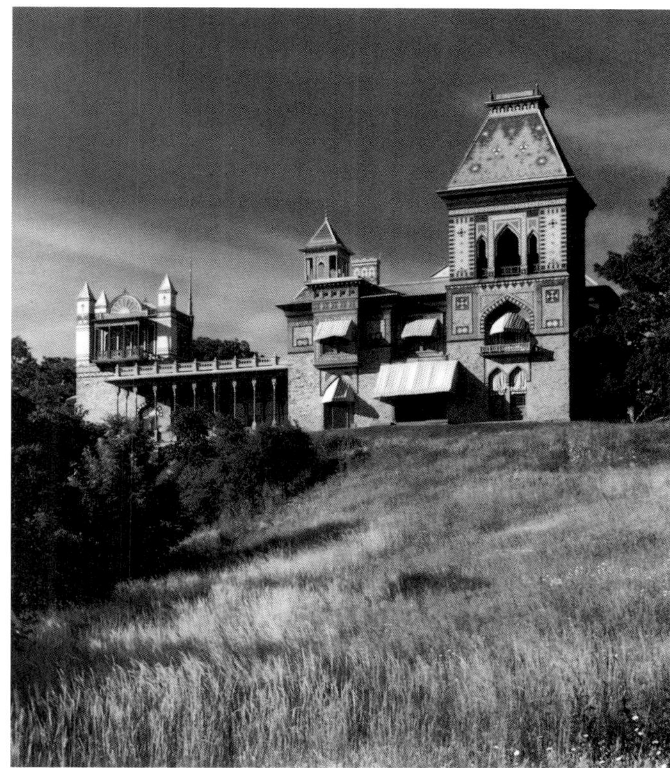

FIG. 116 House of Frederic Edwin Church, *Olana*, Hudson, N.Y. Photograph Courtesy of Olana State Historic Site. © Peter Aaron/Esto.

his position in the New York field of production during the 1870s and 1880s.[64]

Church's studio/villa, *Olana*, a Persian word for "treasure house," built a few years later, overlooked the Hudson River south of Albany, New York (fig. 116).[65] Olana looked across the Hudson to the Catskill Mountains that Cole had made famous. The Catskills were one of the nation's earliest scenic destinations. From Olana's commanding position above the Hudson River, Church could gaze at a panorama of Cole's beloved scenery. At the center of his view was Cole's studio where Church had awakened as an artist. Cole had designed and built the first studio on the Hudson River, and although it was modest, after his death it became a veritable shrine for artists of the Hudson River School. The positioning of Olana overlooking Cole's hallowed studio articulated again Church's claims to the mantle of leadership that Cole had worn, and his own position superior to Bierstadt's Malkasten. Later in his career, when painting became difficult, Olana itself became a symbol of his former preeminence in the field.

At *Malkasten* or *Olana*, or at private receptions in galleries and the Tenth Street Studios, patrons could be made to feel they were privileged "insiders" with a personal relationship to the artist. There, buyers were admitted to the inner sanctuary, the studio—a place seemingly purified of money—where art itself was created. Although visitors today experience only the outward architectural manifestations of the "Castles on the Hudson," and the Tenth Street Studios building was torn down in the 1950s, they were the sites where producers of visual culture directly interacted with representatives of eco-

nomic, political, and institutional power to sell their work. Show studios were molded and shaped by the peculiar and ever-changing conditions governing the consumption and production of culture in a market-driven economy where illusions of pseudo-aristocratic privilege, exclusivity, and the appearance of disinterestedness were essential. The ultimate purpose of the show studio was selling status to patrons by providing elaborate platforms for ritual enactments of high art consumption under the auspices of genteel culture.

Disinterestedness

In the production of personal style a continuing dilemma for artists persisted: the conflict between manipulating aesthetic conventions for personal gain, and the firm proscription that artists must always appear to be disinterested in financial or personal gain, since their work was supposed to concern the ideal, even transcendent, objectives of "Art." Writers reinforced these elite conventions of disinterestedness in the most influential high culture art publications of the period, the *The Crayon* and *The New Path*.[66] Both journals, deeply influenced by English art writer John Ruskin, championed the idea of artists as questing for "higher" quasi-religious purposes. The transatlantic sharing of high art ideas about the role and purpose of art is not surprising considering that the English were also principal investors in expansionistic Antebellum America. They profited enormously from the slave economy in the South, and later financed the transcontinental railroad after Civil War nearly bankrupted the country. Because England was the world's greatest colonial power it was only natural that English ideas about art would shape key aspects of American artistic practice and identity.

The enormous success that Church and Bierstadt also enjoyed in England demonstrated how completely their art conformed to Ruskinian ideas, particularly his new standard of "truth to nature." Ruskin's notions of truth emphasized production of images with a near-scientific objectivity in which a geologist or botanist could recognize the rock or plant types, and at the same time these scientifically accurate representations could remind spectators of moralizing ideas of "nature as God's holy book." Church's originality revealed itself in the way he harnessed these new aesthetic imperatives to a super-realistic, almost photographic-like representation of his subjects accessible to a wide audience.[67]

Ideals of disinterestedness also entered American artistic practice through Thomas Cole. A figure caught between an older European tradition of sustained patronage and the potential fortune of a competitive market economy, the English-born Cole always maintained his sympathy for aristocratic ideas of high art culture, complaining bitterly about his lack of appreciation and patronage in Jacksonian America with its populist embrace of culture for the democratic masses. Because of such conservative ideological attachments, Cole came to believe at the height of his career that he could not succeed as a fine artist in America. The few old aristocrats whose sustaining patronage he hoped to obtain were themselves changing, moving with the times to take advantage of new investment opportunities. Strangely, after his talented student Church left his studio in 1846, Cole became increasingly isolated. His attempts to gain a broad audience with his last allegorical series of paintings were eclipsed by the success of a new genre of moving panoramas specifically designed to attract large audiences, and by his rigid adherence to an obsolete ideal of the artist unconcerned with worldly success.[68] The remarkable potential of his youthful student Church may have also been a contributing factor in his frustration.

Although Cole's financial success in the art market was modest by the later standards of Church and Bierstadt, he was a great exemplar. Considered by many to be the ideal artist, Cole's premature death in 1848 enabled his followers to appropriate him as pseudo-sainted founder of a national school of landscape painting. Elite critics such as William Cullen Bryant eulogized Cole as the American ideal of the "disinterested" artist—the painter-poet-preacher—who loyally labored for society's moral agendas, always working for "truth," and detaching art from "mere" financial concerns.

Thomas Cole's self-fashioned image as a disinterested artist was itself a fiction. In reality, Cole was extraordinarily competitive, and toward the end of his career bitterly jealous of younger artists' success. Cole's public example, and his often-expressed desire for recognition, in turn inspired his ambitious and talented artistic student, Frederic E. Church.

Church was perceived as "fortune's favorite" from the outset. The position he inherited from Cole, or took from Durand, enabled him to capitalize readily on pictorial innovations and historical narratives formulated by Cole, even as he redirected them to serve other more saleable nationalistic interests. Church's images frequently reworked Cole's grand themes of national history, the rise and fall of empires, and he specialized in images that advanced ideas of nature as a transcendent metaphor for "God's holy book." But where Cole had feared the mob, Church relished his celebrity, watching from behind the curtains the crowds who gathered to view his great pictures, and orchestrating the exhibitions and receptions of his great pictures. Like his rival Bierstadt he counted among his patrons leading businessmen such as Cyrus Field, and Church's friend, railroad mogul William H. Osborn.

Social conventions adapted from aristocratic ideas of privilege dictated that an artist present a facade of selflessness. The construction of the ideal artist as a figure free of worldly ambition, laboring for the transcendent rewards of art, not mere entertainers of the people, could not last. By the 1860s Cole's example was largely forgotten, declined by younger artists who decided to engage the art market as they found it. The landscape painter Christopher P. Cranch remarked acidly at the hollowness of notions of disinterestedness. "[The critic] may sneer at your very natural desire to sell your pictures, and preach you a sermon on the duty of despising dirty dollars and living supremely for art. He may tell you that you should be content to feed on air, . . . that, while journalists and critics may count their columns in greenbacks, you must never touch a canvas with an eye to its market value; that the gentlemen of the press may look sharp after their business, but you must 'scorn delights and live laborious days,' and let the heavens drop miraculous manna in your wilderness."[69] Pretenses of aesthetic disinterestedness conflicted sharply with an enterprise- and initiative-driven art market of New York in the 1850s and 1860s. The ever-anxious Jervis McEntee confided to his diary in 1876, "There is great danger that a man in need of money will be induced to work for popular favor and so prevent him from following out his own ideas. An artist above all men should be free from money troubles and I think constantly of how I can order my life so as to be independent in this respect."[70]

VISUAL CONVENTIONS

The images of Bierstadt, Church, and Moran achieved popular success and their great pictures commanded huge prices not because of disinterestedness by their makers, but largely because they so successfully manipulated visual, aesthetic, and pictorial conventions in pursuit of producing personal style and sales. A considerable part of Church, Bierstadt, and Moran's success resulted from their willingness to find new

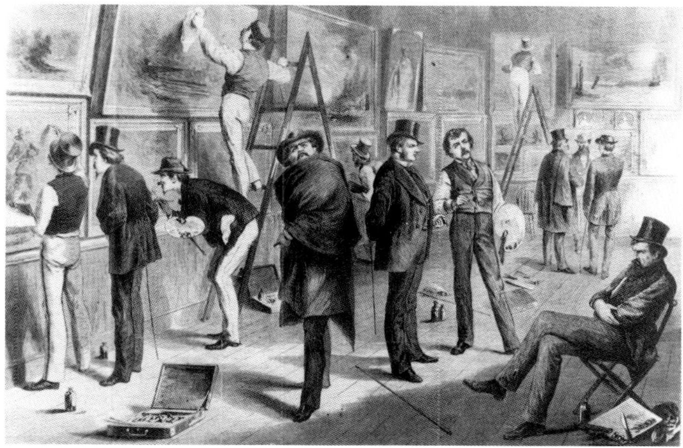

FIG. 117 "Varnishing Day at the National Academy of Design," *Harper's Weekly* (7 May 1870): 292.

ways to use traditional visual conventions to serve requirements of imagination and originality. Their imagery made vast continents to be conquered appear inviting and beautiful. It proclaimed an ideological empire of the eye that was no less persuasive than the transcontinental nation-state spoken and written of by politicians, businessmen, and settlers. Yet how exactly was this ocular empire of representations produced?

The pictorial conventions and visual protocols Hudson River School artists manipulated in their images, the way they organized the space of their pictures through aerial perspective, framing devices, positioning and scale of figures, and personal touch, had evolved over decades of artistic practice. Some of these conventions, like "varnishing day" at the Academy (fig. 117) were largely social or ceremonial, the final additions of an artist's personal touch. Despite exaggerated claims to being entirely original, uniquely American, the core visual conventions practiced by the Hudson River School explorers were developed in European centers of culture and commerce and shared with them. Powerful bonds of language, culture, commerce, and communication linked New York and London. Ruskin promoted the search for originality, imagination, and "truth," on both sides of the Atlantic, and he repeatedly urged artists to develop personal style in pursuit of such objectives.

The Artist's Touch

An important component of personal style in painting was established by stylistic conventions, particularly an artist's "touch," and in more complex ways by the themes and places selected for narrative, and the scale on which they were executed. Art critics of the period discussed individual manner in painting, at length, and individual manner remains one of the determining factors of value for the art market today. In this regard the Hudson River School artists not only claimed geographical turf, but personal style became a major product itself. To a considerable extent an artist defined his personal style as he carved out his position in the field. From that confluence, a handful of superstars emerged, rivals for the best positions. Success meant access to the wealthiest patrons, a place in the echelons of the National Academy, or a presti-

gious studio on Tenth Street, and exhibitions at commercial galleries with the most advanced marketing techniques.

Results of this competition and individual transformations of various components of the reigning aesthetic conventions can be seen in comparing Gifford's works, for example, with their characteristic roseate skies, to Heade's lugubrious sunsets, or through the luminous repose of Kensett that differs so strikingly from McEntee's melancholy scenes. The distinctions between the grand manners of Church and Bierstadt was a point of considerable contention among critics. Moran, on the other hand, was praised and his work long continued to sell because of his thoroughly English style, as befitted "the self-styled American Turner." The possibilities of claiming new new geographical turf narrowed radically as the supply of "unknown" locales diminished following the Centennial. This further increased pressure on the production of personal style. After the Civil War, what at first had only been nuances of individual style or color became increasingly exaggerated. Poetic aestheticism, first evident in the work of Jervis McEntee and George Inness for example, later appeared more dramatically in the figures of James M. Whistler and William Merritt Chase. With this new aestheticism the twentieth-century American artist came into being. For younger, aspiring artists who entered the field after the Centennial, the development of a distinct personal style of painting became almost the only way of claiming a position.

Producing a personal style required the ability to manipulate conventional repertoires of landscape forms whose symbolic and associative equivalencies were codified in English and American art theory and practice. These conventions were grounded in eighteenth-century English aesthetic theories of the Picturesque, the Beautiful, and the Sublime.[71] Particular, often local criteria determined which mountains were considered sublime, which rivers and lakes were deemed beautiful, and which types of trees, rocks, and bushes in the foreground had qualities of the picturesque. According to the constructs of aesthetic theory, mountains, lakes, waterfalls, forests, and rivers were acceptable subjects, but swamps or arid deserts did not fit customary aesthetic ideals.[72] A variety of "views," topographic, documentary, picturesque, pastoral, and eventually sublime were produced by artist-explorers, according to the particular social and cultural function of an image.

Commanding Conventions

Nineteenth-century American audiences looked at landscape representations with complex geographical, political, cultural, and aesthetic expectations. The production of visual meaning was largely accomplished by the manipulation of imported aesthetic conventions, many refined by Cole, and adapted by Church and others. Layers of associations—nostalgic, scenic, nationalistic, or, later, preservationist—engaged spectators either when reading pictures constructed according to the principals of aesthetic theory, or when viewing Yosemite Valley from Inspiration Point.[73] Manipulating these visual and pictorial conventions in an original, imaginative, and convincingly truthful way assured success.

One of the most important issues was the construction of two-dimensional illusions of vast space. The most typical compositional variations situated spectators as if they were looking down from an elevated position. The effect of gazing on a landscape, or a representation of one, from a "wide and commanding prospect" was that of vicarious visual mastery—an effect similar to the emotions experienced in popular entertainments like panoramas and dioramas. A spectator viewing Bierstadt's *Rocky Mountains* was said to have mistaken it for a panorama, "and after waiting awhile asked when *the thing was going to move.*"[74] Artists recirculated panoramic construction of visual space in landscape painting countless times, until it became virtually invisible, a completely naturalized cultural assumption about how the audience expected to see a landscape. With "magisterial gazes" nineteenth-century Americans looked at these panoramic representations of landscapes and dreamed, as Durand recommended, without "care or anxiety" in the comfort of their "favorite easy chair" of national mastery of a continent.[75] Later, at national parks, viewpoints were institutionalized as "outlooks." Ideological constructions of power, gender, and national appropriation of territory were signified at such scenic prospects. Today, a legacy of these ideas persists: principal requirements of valuable real estate include its location; a key aspect must be an impressive view.

In order to make this feeling of visual power more compelling, artists created images of very large size. Church's *Heart of the Andes*, Bierstadt's *Rocky Mountains*, and Moran's large-scale triptych of western wonders, represent the largest landscape productions of the period. Their dramatic size and panoramic, even cinematic effects appealed to crowds of spectators. Bierstadt in particular produced numerous large-scale pictures, and his spacious studio at Malkasten featured great opening doors that allowed large canvases to be rolled outside for completion, and to be easily shown to visiting patrons. Reviewing the Fine Art section at the Centennial Exhibition, Edward Strahan designated the work of Church and Bierstadt as the "panoramic" school of landscape where "the public saw with amazement vast scenes on enormous canvases, that seemed to compete in dimensions with the original. . . . [the viewer] could travel on the magical broomstick of one of [Bierstadt's] colossal brushes into the heart of the Great West."[76] The effect of these very large images painted in brilliant color and exhibited in a theatrical-like setting must have been overpowering in an age before widespread mechanical reproduction made images plentiful and cheap. In great pictures, the nation's grand prospects, captured by its larger-than-life exploring-artists, could be admired in a scale befitting national ideals of continental grandeur and the inspired national mission. In a significant way the cultural work of the great picture was eventually replaced by moving pictures, or, today, perhaps, by the total visual immersion of IMAX cinemas.

Figures and the Gaze

The placement of figures in these large landscapes became particularly important. Figures served a variety of purposes besides their long established function of setting visual scale. Once dismissively termed "staffage," figures provided a position within the image where spectators could enter the pictorial space. Through gesture, costuming, placement, and size, the introduction of figures enabled spectators to vicariously "share" the prospect visually and conceptually. They became an essential part of the process of accumulating associations. In this role, figures often served to direct the spectators' gaze.[77]

Moran's *Grand Canyon of the Yellowstone* shows these conventions at work (see fig. 106). The spectator's eye moves from the foreground ledge inward toward the tiny figures of an explorer and an Indian guide. Yet there was no such Indian guide actually present, and as a publicity stunt Moran asked Hayden to sit for his portrait to insure the "accuracy" of the picture. With their backs to the viewer, the position of the figures on the central foreground promontory facilitated entrance into the visual space of the picture, allowing the spectator to vicariously look over their shoulders, sharing the sight of fantastic rock formations in the valley of the Yellowstone Falls. A similar type of visual control is practiced in Sanford Gifford's and Jervis McEntee's paintings of themselves sketching at Mount Desert from the top of Cadillac Mountain (see fig. 67 and fig. 69). They present themselves not as Indians or explorers, but as artists, spontaneously caught in the act of making oil sketches, in which the spectator is invited to share.

Figures also placed a scene in its historical context. Spectators infrequently gazed on the landscape as if it were being seen in the present moment. More often figures served visually to cue an earlier time, perhaps the storied past of Indian legends. The diminution or even absence of figures signified untouched wilderness before the arrival of explorers or settlers. High art representations of destination scenery required the suppression or elimination of troubling evidences of modernity and generally a reduction or even complete elimination of human presence. Paintings of Niagara Falls were particularly susceptible to this sort of manipulation, and the over-built infrastructure of tourism was seldom glimpsed in paintings of the scene.[78] Bierstadt, Church, and Moran painted the West, or the Maine coast, as if it were an unspoiled wilderness, giving the appearance of places long before pioneer settlements or railroad tourism became visible. A lone American Indian figure often symbolized the fast-

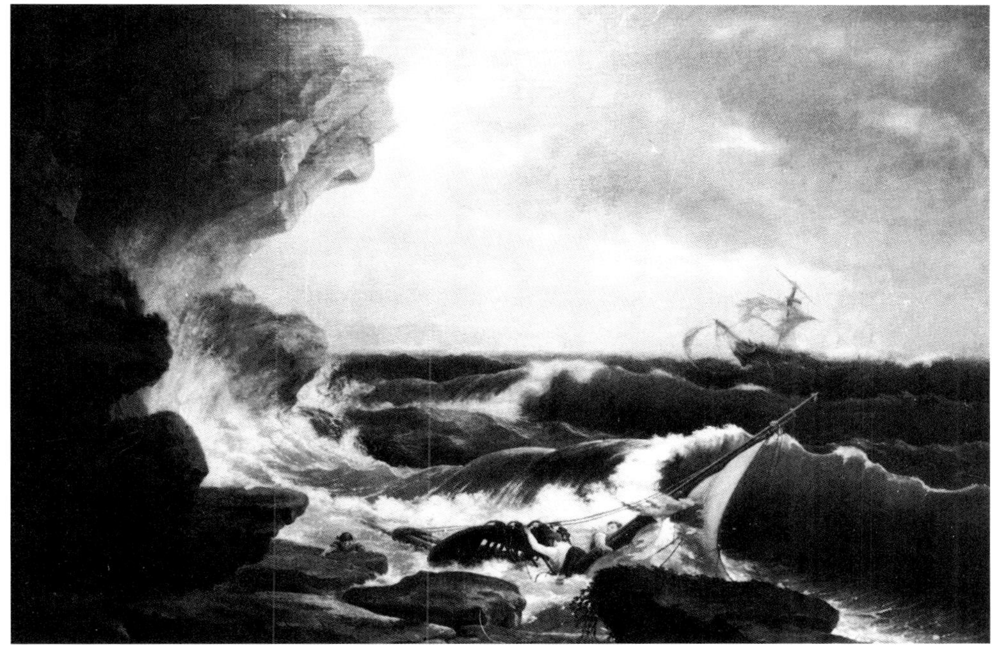

vanishing American past, the "Old America."[79] He represented history that was "destined" to pass away. Native Americans abounded in representations of western landscapes by Hudson River School artists, and their presence lingered well into the twentieth century, when many ways were found to fetishize them. Moran, Hill, and others continued to place Indians in their landscapes. They occupied positions in the field that required production of formula pictures to assuage collectors' nostalgia for the historic "Old West."

Conventions of the Foreground

Hudson River School painters diligently manipulated the foregrounds of their landscape paintings, adhering to Ruskinian notions of "truth to nature," which encouraged the acceptance of an image's visual authenticity by the accumulation and massing of foreground detail. Church's *Heart of the Andes* or Bierstadt's *Rocky Mountains* are classic examples of this visual tactic. James Jackson Jarves noted that Church and Bierstadt "often depart from the literal features of the view. With singular inconsistency of mind they idealize in composition and materialize in execution, so that though the details of the scenery are substantially correct, the scene as a whole is false."[80]

Through repetition of detail, objects could appear to multiply endlessly, thereby expanding the sense of specificity and immediacy of the foreground into the distance. The handling of detail provoked a critic to say that Church painted as Charles Dickens wrote, *"by the inch."* Coupled with the mechanistic, almost scientific sense of optical scrutiny of objects, this precision led hostile critics, like Jarves, to complain of a cold and unpoetic quality in Bierstadt and Church. The new medium of photography assisted in producing startling visual effects of detailed realism and became the standard against which foreground representations were measured during the 1850s and 1860s. Both Bierstadt and Moran collaborated with

photographers on their expeditions, and all the explorers used photographs in their studios.[81] Although the foreground was often the most real looking part of a painting because of the accumulation of detail, it could also be the most contrived part of a picture. Aesthetic conventions allowed artists great flexibility in manipulating foreground elements as long as the result seemed to meet standards of plausibility.

Emblematic Personification

The convention of seeing faces and figures in the environment that Winthrop and Church shared on their expedition to Mount Katahdin, and that Church painted in numerous representations, was an adaptable device for the production of meaning. It was employed by many artists in the New York field who fell under the influence of Cole or Church. Personification was frequently used to support or emphasize narrative, ranging from simple representations of desirable scenery to the complex and subtly inflected ideological imagery of Church, Bierstadt, Gifford, and others. The convention of emblematic personification did not originate with the Hudson River School painters, but had antecedents deep within European traditions. Cole was a major force in its insertion in American landscape painting. One common source from which the convention derived was found in the immensely popular genre of Protestant emblem books with their many small prints. An early and incontrovertible example of a one-to-one link between an emblem book prototype and a painting is found in Thomas Birch's marine painting *The Rescue* (fig. 118). In Birch's picture, a prominent rocky cliff looms impassively above the shipwrecked sailors at the bottom right. Etched into the rock is a craggy face that bears a grim expression. Church's drawing with the word "face" written on a similar profiled configuration comes to mind, as do the solemn visages of his early works like *Otter Creek,* or his subtle anti-war personifications *in Coast Scene, Mount*

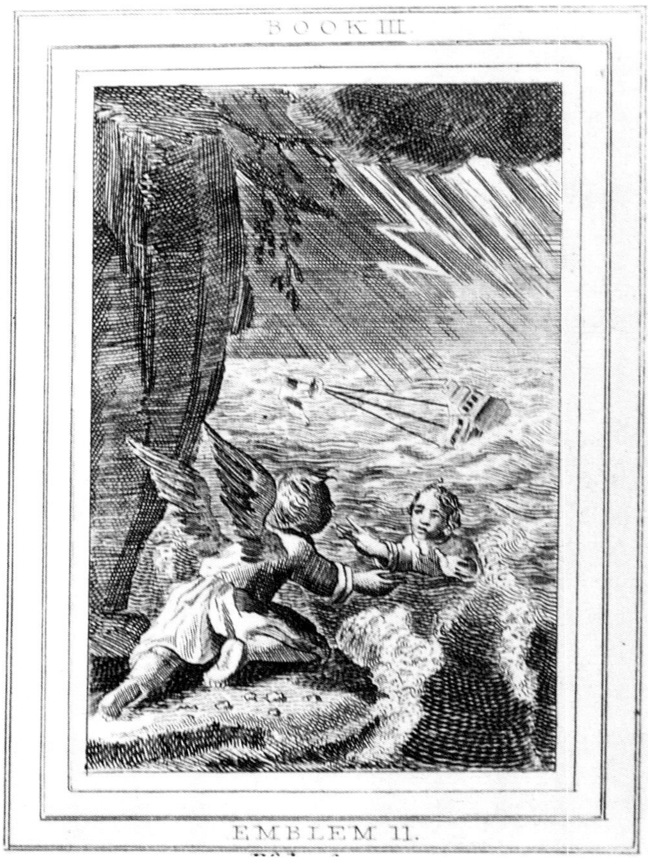

FIG. 119 Francis Quarles, *Emblems: Divine and Moral,* 44 editions, 1639–1854, "Emblem II."

Desert (see fig. 32, fig. 33 and fig. 52) where the enduring presence and gaze of New England rocks became metaphors for national hope. In Birch's painting, the image is directly translated from the small printed image to the large canvas, while in Cole's and Church's pictures it was often freely manipulated to serve a variety of expressive and iconographic functions in the production of meaning and personal style. The effect of such visages in rocks was not taken from nature, as evidenced by *The Rescue's* striking resemblance to a printed emblem that appeared in one of the many editions of the book: *Emblems: Divine and Moral* by Francis Quarles (1639–1854), (fig. 119). In the emblem source for Birch's painting the profiled face in the rock, which gazes toward the sinking ship on the horizon, reveals itself on closer observation to be complete with forehead, nose, eye sockets, mouth, and chin, not unlike the profiled face in the cliff of Cole's *View Across Frenchman's Bay* (see fig. 23).[82]

The visual rhetoric of emblematic personification was a passing moment in the history of American painting—an example, like the enormously popular panoramas of Bunyon's *Pilgrim's Progress,* of a momentary conjunction of the interests of high-art culture and popular traditions of emblem books. Although this sometimes overly didactic convention persisted in the Hudson River School from Cole's early work through the great pictures of Church and others of the Tenth Street Studios Building, it began to wane after the Civil War as more intimate and poetic landscapes became

fashionable, and new issues of claiming positions in the market emerged. Jervis McEntee, a leader in this new style, noted that personification was transformed from the over-determined historical and nationalistic imagery of Cole, Church, and Bierstadt to more intimate emotional styles. Suggesting this new direction, McEntee stated, "I look upon a landscape as I look upon a human being—its thoughts, its feelings, its moods, are what interest me; and to these I try to give expression. What it says, and thinks, and experiences, this is the matter that concerns the landscape painter."[83]

The Anonymous Hand of the Producer

A final example of the subtle way that Hudson River School artists produced personal style was a flat, often thinly painted brushstroke. When brush work is almost invisible, the presence of the artist recedes for a moment. Such depersonalized techniques promoted illusions of scientific accuracy and disinterestedness. For a time in the 1960s and 1970s, formalist art historians isolated the self-effacing brush work of the Hudson River School artists as one of its defining characteristics. Evidence of claims that this convention of style represented spiritual transcendence was hailed in Emersonian notions of the "transparent eyeball." "Luminism," a word coined in the mid-twentieth century to categorize the many paintings of the school that shared this convention, became a useful term used to market them to the public as an established national movement in art.

CONCLUSION

The production of visual art by artist-explorers intersected at every point with economic, political, and institutional fields of power. The works of art they produced functioned in concert with publishers, travel agents, steamship and railroad companies, travel guide writers, hotel operators, lobbyists, politicians, art dealers, patrons, and critics, and they appealed in an unprecedented way to a new urban audience with wealth and leisure. Such paintings encouraged elaborate scenic pilgrimages to Mount Desert, to Yosemite, to Yellowstone, or to the Grand Canyon. The invention of national parks resulted in a very significant way from this cultural work. The leading artists worked to position themselves as "great men" producing "great pictures" for a "great nation," and it was this construction that entered the early history of American art by Tuckerman. He described Church and Bierstadt as modern culminations of a national school of landscape painters that began with Cole. These early historical narratives assumed that the role of the artist was one of disinterest in commerce, repeating and promoting the idea that what they produced was Art—not a market and a public for art.

The struggle for position, prestige, and patrons, sometimes thought of as unique to the contemporary art market

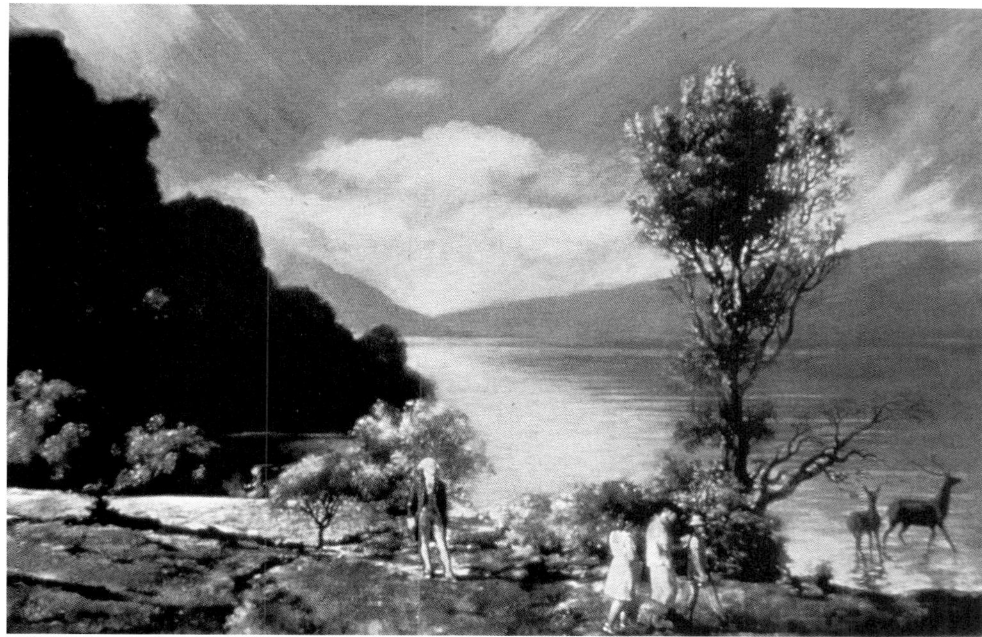

of today, were refined and perfected in New York by Church and Bierstadt, among others, during the 1850s and 1860s. What was new about the artists who comprised what might be called the "Hudson River Company of Artistic Marketing and Tourism Promotion" was their unprecedented concentration in pursuit of personal specialization and originality. Individual entrepreneurship and a new necessity of promoting popular interest in order to maximize profits from sales of paintings, reproductions, and fees from touring exhibitions, dominated the emerging field of visual culture. These profits were the economic capital they reaped from their labors. The cultural capital they harvested included social status, prestige, and life-styles of refinement and leisure.

After the Centennial, the terms of engagement for artists began to shift more rapidly in New York. The production of landscapes for an urban audience in the market economy became problematic.[84] By the end of the century social and economic changes that began in the 1850s resulted in the formation of the modern capitalist nation-state. The idea of the disinterested artist destabilized as it was further contested and reshaped by competitive forces in the market field in the 1890s. Many of the famed artist-explorers found their work marginalized by the 1880s. Their prior personal investment in established positions within the field of production prevented them from further participating in the invention of the modern artist during the Gilded Age.[85] For producers of visual culture, the change might be summarized by remembering that by 1900, Church, Bierstadt, and Moran had been replaced by figures such as William Meritt Chase, George Inness, Winslow Homer, and the American Impressionists as representatives of the epitome of "modern art."

Demystifying the construction of visual artifacts that had the power to motivate major social changes requires a recognition that art-making itself is embedded in political, economic, and institutional power. The formal and thematic conventions that held together these systems of visual cultural production developed over long periods and were sustained by their repeated manipulation. The conventions necessary for the production of meaning in a landscape painting ranged from the almost inchoate painted mark of the artist's brush, to more complex signs, markers, and symbols that supported an elaborate nationalistic iconology. Art makers infused techniques, forms, and aesthetic conventions with iconological and narrative significance, always seeking new ways to attract elite buyers by exhibiting the most precious and expensive of all commodities—imagination and originality.

Teasing out the legacy and the complex play of landscape conventions and societal memory has been an objective of the contemporary conceptual artists Komar and Melamid. They produce landscapes by using scientific polling and statistical sampling techniques. The result demonstrates what the most popular painting in America might look like today. Not surprisingly this painting has an uncanny resemblance to the works of Hudson River School artist-explorers such as Cole, Church, Bierstadt and, Moran (fig. 120).[86] Komar and Melamid critique, from a post-modern perspective, issues that first surfaced with the invention of the Hudson River School: the uneasy relationship between the production of fine art in a democratic, highly commercialized society, and high art conventions, elitism, and art's pretense of disinterestedness. Their satirical work enables us to grasp how deeply the American imagination remains imprinted with the cultural work of its nineteenth-century artist-explorers, and how unrelenting were the market conditions that emerged with them to define a modern field of visual arts production in mid-nineteenth-century New York.

J. Gray Sweeney
Arizona State University

NOTES

1. The first study of the subject was William H. Truettner and Robin Bolton Smith, *National Parks and the American Landscape* (Washington, D.C.: Smithsonian Institution Press for National Museum of American Art, 1972). See J. Gray Sweeney, "Drawing Borders: Art and Cultural Politics of the U. S.-Mexico Boundary Survey 1850–1853, in *Drawing the Borderline: Artist-Explorers of the U. S.-Mexico Boundary Survey* (Albuquerque, N.M.: The Albuquerque Museum/University of New Mexico Press, 1996), 23–75; and Sweeney, "Artist-Explorers and the American West, 1860–1880" (Ph.D. diss., Indiana University, 1975). See also William H. Truettner, ed., *The West as America: Reinterpreting Images of the Frontier, 1820–1920* (Washington, D.C.: Smithsonian Institution Press, 1991); Jules David Prown, ed., *Discovered Lands; Invented Pasts: Transforming Visions of the American West* (New Haven: Yale University Press, 1992).

2. See John F. Sears, *Sacred Places: American Tourist Attractions in the Nineteenth Century* (New York: Oxford University Press, 1989); Dean MacCannell, *The Tourist: A New Theory of the Leisure Class* (New York: Schocken Books, 1976); Peter J. Schmitt, *Back to Nature: The Arcadian Myth in Urban America* (New York: Oxford University Press, 1969); and Kenneth Myers, *The Catskills: Painters, Writers, and Tourists in the Mountains, 1820–1895* (Yonkers, N.Y.: Hudson River Museum of Westchester, 1987).

3. See Nancy K. Anderson and Linda S. Ferber, *Albert Bierstadt: Art and Enterprise* (New York: Brooklyn Museum, 1991); and Nancy K. Anderson, *Thomas Moran* (Washington, D.C.: National Gallery of Art, 1997). For the idea of Moran's triptych see Joni Louise Kinsey, *Thomas Moran and the Surveying of the American West* (Washington, D.C.: Smithsonian Institution Press, 1992).

4. Barbara Novak, *American Painting of the Nineteenth Century: Realism, Idealism, and the American Experience* (New York: Praeger, 1969), 94.

5. See Pierre Bourdieu, *The Field of Cultural Production: Essays on Art and Literature* (New York: Columbia University Press, 1993); and Derek Robbins, *The Work of Pierre Bourdieu: Recognizing Society* (Buckingham, U.K.: Open University Press, 1991).

6. See Jack Greene, *The Intellectual Construction of America: Exceptionalism and Identity from 1492–1800* (Chapel Hill University of North Carolina Press, 1993); Stephen Jay Greenblatt, *Marvelous Possessions: The Wonder of the New World* (Chicago: University of Chicago Press, 1992); David E. Stannard, *American Holocaust: The Conquest of the New World* (New York: Oxford University Press, 1993); Richard C. Trexler, *Sex and Conquest: Gendered Violence, Political Order, and the European Conquest of the Americas* (Ithaca: Cornell University Press, 1995); Hugh Honour, *The New Golden Land: European Images of America from the Discoveries to the Present Time* (New York: Pantheon, 1975); Susan Danforth, *Encountering the New World, 1493 to 1800* (Providence, R.I.: John Carter Brown Library, 1991); and Rachel Doggett, ed., *New World of Wonders: European Images of the Americas, 1492–1700* (Washington, D.C.: Folger Shakespeare Library, 1992).

7. See Bernard Smith, *European Vision and the South Pacific, 1768–1850: A Study in the History of Art and Ideas* (Oxford, U.K.: Oxford University Press, 1960); Barbara Maria Stafford, *Voyage into Substance: Art, Science, Nature and the Illustrated Travel Account, 1760–1840* (Cambridge, Mass.: MIT Press, 1984); and Karol A. Lawson, "A New World of Gladness and Exertion: Images of the North American Landscape in Maps, Portraits, and Serial Prints before 1820" (Ph.D. diss., Univ. of Virginia, 1988).

8. See Amy R. W. Meyers, "Imposing Order on the Wilderness: Natural History Illustrations and Landscape Portrayal" in Edward J. Nygren, *Views and Visions: American Landscape Before 1830* (Washington, D. C.: Corcoran Gallery of Art, 1986.)

9. Henry T. Tuckerman, *Book of the Artists: American Artist Life Comprising Biographical and Critical Sketches of American Artists, First Published 1867* (reprint, New York: James F. Carr, 1967), 424.

10. Angela Miller, *The Empire of the Eye: Landscape Representation and American Culture Politics, 1825–1875* (Ithaca, N.Y.: Cornell University Press, 1993). For the ideological critique see Anders Stephanson, *Manifest Destiny: American Expansionism and the Empire of Right,* (New York: Hill and Wang, 1995); Reginald Horsman, *Race and Manifest Destiny: The Origins of American Racial Anglo-Saxonism* (Cambridge, Mass.: Harvard University Press, 1981); Frederick Merk, *Manifest Destiny and Mission in American History* (New York: Vintage Books, 1963); and Henry Nash Smith, *Virgin Land: The American West as Symbol and Myth* (Cambridge, Mass.: Harvard University Press, 1971).

11. See William H. Goetzmann, *Exploration and Empire: The Explorer and the Scientist in the Winning of the American West* (New York: W. W. Norton, 1978); and Stephen E. Ambrose, *Undaunted Courage: Meriwether Lewis, Thomas Jefferson, and the Opening of the American West* (New York: Simon & Schuster, 1996).

12. Kenneth Haltman, "The Poetics of Geologic Reverie: Figures of Source and Origin in Samuel Seymour's Landscapes of the Rocky Mountains," *Huntington Library Quarterly* 59, 2 & 3 (1997): 303–47. See also Kenneth Haltman, "Titian Ramsey Peale's Specimen Portraiture; or, Natural History as Family History," in Lillian B. Miller, ed., *The Peale Family: Creation of a Legacy, 1770–1870* (Washington and New York: Abbeville Press/National Portrait Gallery, 1996), 186–201; Patricia Trenton and Peter H. Hassrick, *The Rocky Mountains: A Vision for Artists in the Nineteenth Century* (Norman: University of Oklahoma Press, 1983); and Roger L. Nichols and Patrick L. Halley, *Stephen Long and American Frontier Exploration* (Newark: University of Delaware Press, 1980).

13. See Brian W. Dippie, *Catlin and His Contemporaries: The Politics of Patronage* (Lincoln: University of Nebraska Press, 1990); and William H. Truettner, *The Natural Man Observed: A Study of Catlin's Indian Gallery* (Washington, D.C.: Smithsonian Institution Press, 1979).

14. George Catlin, *Letters and Notes on the Manners, Customs, and Conditions of the North American Indians,* first published 1841, (New York: Dover Publications, 1973), vol. I, 260–2.

15. See David C. Hunt and Marsha V. Gallagher, *Karl Bodmer's America* (Omaha: Joslyn Art Museum, and Lincoln: University of Nebraska Press, 1984); and Ron Tyler, ed., *Alfred Jacob Miller: Artist on the Oregon Trail* (Fort Worth: Amon Carter Museum, 1982).

16. See Ron Tyler, *Prints of the West* (Golden, Colo.: Fulcrum Press, 1994).

17. Julie Schimmel, "John M. Stanley," in *Artists of Michigan from the Nineteenth Century* (Muskegon: Muskegon Museum of Art, 1987), 39–55; and Dippie, "Far Superior to Catlin's: Stanley and His Indian Gallery," in *Catlin and His Contemporaries,* 265–317; see also Ben W. Huseman, *Wild River, Timeless Canyons: Balduin Möllhausen's Watercolors of the Colorado* (Fort Worth: Amon Carter Museum, 1995); and J. Russell Harper, *Paul Kane's Frontier* (Austin, University of Texas Press, 1971).

18. *The Crayon* (March 1860): 83.

19. Tuckerman, *Book of the Artists,* 371.

20. David C. Huntington, *The Landscapes of Frederic Edwin Church: Vision of an American Era* (New York: Braziller, 1966), 1–5.

21. Thomas Starr King, *A Vacation Among the Sierras: Yosemite in 1860* (San Francisco, 1860), 20; see also Rebecca Solnit, *Savage Dreams: A Journey into the Hidden Wars of the American West* (San Francisco: Sierra Club Books, 1994); and William Cronon, *Changes in the Land: Indians, Colonists, and the Ecology of New England* (New York: Hill and Wang, 1983).

22. See David Robertson, *West of Eden: A History of the Art and Litera-*

ture of Yosemite (Yosemite: Yosemite Natural History Association and Wilderness Press, 1984); for California in general see David Wyatt, *The Fall into Eden: Landscape and Imagination in California* (New York: Cambridge University Press, 1986); and Anne Farrar Hyde, *An American Vision: Far Western Landscape and National Culture, 1820–1920* (New York: New York University Press, 1990).

23. Frederick L. Olmsted, "The Yosemite Valley and the Mariposa Big Trees, A Preliminary Report," *Landscape Architecture* 43 (1952): 16.

24. "Bierstadt's Picture of the Rocky Mountains," *The Round Table* (27 Feb. 1864): 169; see also *The New York Times* (14 May 1868).

25. See Katherine Emma Manthorne, *Tropical Renaissance: North American Artists Exploring Latin America, 1839–1879* (Washington, D.C.: Smithsonian Institution Press, 1989); Manthorne, *The Landscapes of Louis Rémy Mignot: A Southern Painter Abroad* (Washington, D.C.: Smithsonian Institution Press, 1996); and Lewis A. Shepard, *American Painters of the Arctic* (Amherst, Mass.: Mead Art Gallery, 1975).

26. See Janice T. Driesbach, *Drawn from Nature: The Oil Sketches of Thomas Hill* (Yosemite National Park Association in association with the Crocker Art Museum, Sacramento, Calif., 1997). Carleton Watkins's photographs of Yosemite served a very similar function, although they were addressed to a different segment of the market.

27. Ferdinand V. Hayden, "The Wonders of the West, II: More About the Yellowstone," *Scribner's* 3 (1872): 396.

28. William H. Jackson, "Famous American Mountain Paintings, I: With Moran in the Yellowstone," *Appalachia* 21 (1936): 157.

29. See Joni Louise Kinsey, "Moran and the Art of Publishing," in Anderson, *Thomas Moran*, 1997, 300–321; Sandra D'Emilio and Suzan Campbell, *Visions and Visionaries: The Art and Artists of the Santa Fe Railway* (Salt Lake City, Utah: Peregrine Smith Books, 1991); and T. C. McLuhan, *Dream Tracks: The Railroad and The American Indian, 1890–1930* (New York: Abrams, 1985).

30. Alan Wallach, "Thomas Cole and the Course of American Empire," in William H. Truettner and Alan Wallach, eds., *Thomas Cole: Landscape into History* (New Haven: Yale University Press, and Washington, D.C.: National Museum of American Art, 1994), 22–111.

31. See Sue Rainey, *Creating Picturesque America: A Monument to the National and Cultural Landscape* (Nashville, Tenn.: Vanderbilt University Press, 1994).

32. Tuckerman, 21.

33. Ibid., 31.

34. Ibid., 23.

35. Ibid., 27.

36. See J. Gray Sweeney, *The Columbus of the Woods: Daniel Boone and The Typology of Manifest Destiny* (St. Louis: Washington University Gallery of Art, 1992); and Angela Miller, "The Mechanisms of the Market and the Invention of Western Regionalism: The Example of George Caleb Bingham," in David C. Miller, ed., *American Iconology: New Approaches to Nineteenth Century Art and Literature* (New Haven: Yale University Press, 1993), 112–34.

37. Tuckerman, 30.

38. The term "great picture" originated in descriptive literature from the period; creating "great pictures" originated in England and France in academic exhibitions after about 1800. The phrase describes images specifically designed to be displayed as public spectacle, and as part of a larger promotional arrangement. The term has recently been revived by art historians to describe this marketing practice, and Gerald L. Carr has documented the practice, and its importance for Church. Its importance for Bierstadt and others of the Tenth Street Studios is admirably discussed by Linda Ferber in "Albert Bierstadt: A History of Reputation," in Anderson and Ferber, *Albert Bierstadt: Art and Enterprise*, 24-25, n. 14.

39. Tuckerman, 383.

40. See Alan Wallach, "Long-Term Visions, Short-Term Failures: Art Institutions in the United States, 1800–1860," in *Exhibiting Contradictions: Essays on the Art Museum in the United States* (Amherst: University of Massachusetts Press, 1998).

41. See Annette Blaugrund, *The Tenth Street Studio Building: Artist-Entrepreneurs from the Hudson River School to the American Impressionists* (Southampton, N. Y.: Parrish Art Museum, 1997). For another perspective on the year 1857, see Kenneth M. Stampp, *America in 1857: A Nation on the Brink* (New York: Oxford University Press, 1990.)

42. Tuckerman, 20.

43. Ibid., 22.

44. J. Gray Sweeney, *McEntee and Company* (New York: Beacon Hill Fine Arts, 1997), 12.

45. Tuckerman, 30.

46. Asher B. Durand, "Letters on Landscape Painting, 1," *The Crayon* 1 (3 January 1855): 1; and Durand, "Letters on Landscape Painting, IV," *The Crayon* 1 (14 February 1855): 97.

47. Durand, "Letters," (14 February 1855): 98.

48. See Joseph D. Ketner, *The Emergence of the African-American Artist: Robert S. Duncanson, 1821–1872* (Columbia: University of Missouri Press, 1993).

49. J. Gray Sweeney, "Endued with Rare Genius: Frederic Edwin Church's *To the Memory of Cole*," *Smithsonian Studies in American Art* (Winter 1988): 45–71.

50. Sweeney, "Endued with Rare Genius," 68, n. 21.

51. See John Durand, *The Life and Times of A. B. Durand* (New York: Kennedy Graphics, 1970).

52. See John Davis, *The Landscape of Belief: Encountering the Holy Land in Nineteenth-Century American Art and Culture* (Princeton, N.J.: Princeton University Press, 1998).

53. Kevin J. Avery, *Church's Great Picture: The Heart of the Andes* (New York: Metropolitan Museum of Art, 1993), 38.

54. *New York Herald*, 24 April 1860, cited in Anderson and Ferber, *Albert Bierstadt*, 146.

55. *New York Leader,* 2 April 1863, cited in Anderson and Ferber, *Albert Bierstadt,* 78.

56. "The New Pictures," *Harper's Weekly* (26 March 1864): 194–5; and *New York Leader,* 2 April, 1864, cited in Anderson and Ferber, *Albert Bierstadt*, 75, 78.

57. "Art Gallery of the Sanitary Fair," *New York Times,* 11 April 1864; see Kevin Avery, *Church's Great Picture: The Heart of the Andes* (New York: The Metropolitan Museum of Art, 1993).

58. Z., "Correspondence of the Transcript, New York, April 2, 1860," *Boston Evening Transcript,* 7 April 1860, 6.

59. J. Gray Sweeney, "The Nude of Landscape Painting: Emblematic Personification in the Art of the Hudson River School," *Smithsonian Studies in American Art* (Fall 1989): 57–58; and Franklin Kelly, *Frederic Edwin Church and the National Landscape* (Washington, D.C: Smithsonian Institution Press, 1988).

60. Clarence Cook, "Bierstadt's 'Rocky Mountains'," *New Path* 1 (April 1864): 160–1.

61. "The New Pictures," *Harper's Weekly* 8 (26 March 1864): 194–5.

62. James Jackson Jarves, *The Art Idea: Sculpture, Painting, and Architecture in America* (New York: Hurd and Houghton, 1864, reprint Cambridge, Mass.: Harvard University Press, 1960), 195.

63. See Sandra S. Phillips, et al., eds., *Charmed Places: Hudson River Artists and Their Houses, Studios, and Vistas* (New York: Harry

Abrams, 1988); and Gerald L. Carr, *Olana Landscapes: The World of Frederic E. Church* (New York: Rizzoli, 1989).

64. Ferber, "Albert Bierstadt: The History of a Reputation," in *Albert Bierstadt: Art and Enterprise, 34–39.*

65. See Carr, *Olana Landscapes* (New York: Rizzoli, 1989), 2.

66. Linda S. Ferber and William H. Gerdts, *The New Path: Ruskin and the American Pre-Raphaelites* (Brooklyn: The Brooklyn Museum, 1985).

67. See Nygren, *Views and Visions.*

68. See Kevin Avery, "Movies for Manifest Destiny: The Moving Panorama Phenomenon in America," in *The Grand Moving Panorama of Pilgrim's Progress* (Montclair, N.J.: Montclair Art Museum, 1999).

69. Christopher P. Cranch, "Art Criticism Reviewed," *Galaxy* 4 (May 1867): 80.

70. Jervis McEntee, diary entry, Wed., 30 September 1876, cited in Sweeney, *McEntee,* 38.

71. See Terry Eagleton, *The Ideology of the Aesthetic* (Oxford: Basil Blackwell, 1990); see also Raymond Williams, *Culture and Society, 1780–1950* (New York: Columbia University Press, 1958); Walter J. Hipple, *The Beautiful, the Sublime, & the Picturesque in Eighteenth-Century British Aesthetic Theory* (Carbondale: Southern Illinois University Press, 1957); and Joseph D. Ketner, ed., *The Beautiful, The Sublime, and The Picturesque: British Influence on American Landscape Painting* (St. Louis: Washington University Gallery of Art, 1984).

72. See David C. Miller, *Dark Eden: The Swamp in Nineteenth-Century American Culture* (New York: Cambridge University Press, 1989).

73. Bruce Robertson, "The Picturesque Traveler in America," in Nygren, *Views and Visions,* 187–210.

74. Jarves, *The Art Idea,* 204.

75. See Albert Boime, *The Magisterial Gaze: Manifest Destiny and the American Landscape Painting, c. 1830–1865* (Washington, D.C.: Smithsonian Institution Press, 1991).

76. Edward Strahan, *The Masterpieces of the International Exhibition 1876: The Art Gallery* (Philadelphia: Gebbie & Barrie, 1876), 39–42.

77. See John Barrell, *The Dark Side of the Landscape: The Rural Poor in English Painting, 1730–1840* (New York: Cambridge University Press, 1980); Ann Bermingham, *Landscape and Ideology: The English Rustic Tradition, 1740–1860* (Berkeley: University of California Press, 1986); W. J. T. Mitchell, ed., *Landscape and Power* (Chicago: University of Chicago Press, 1994); and more recent is Michael Rosenthal, Christiana Payne, and Scott Wilcox, eds., *Prospects for the Nation: Recent Essays in British Landscape, 1750–1880* (New Haven: Yale University Press, 1997).

78. See Jeremy Adamson, *Niagara: Two Centuries of Changing Attitudes, 1697–1901* (Washington, D.C.: Corcoran Gallery of Art, 1985); and Elizabeth R. McKinsey, *Niagara Falls: Icon of the American Sublime* (New York: Cambridge University Press, 1985).

79. See Alexander Nemerov, *Frederic Remington & Turn of the Century America* (New Haven: Yale University Press, 1995).

80. Jarves, *The Art Idea,* 191.

81. See Peter B. Hales, *William Henry Jackson and the Transformation of the American Landscape* (Philadelphia: Temple University Press, 1988); Weston J. Naef and James N. Wood, *Era of Exploration: The Rise of Landscape Photography in the American West, 1860–1885* (New York: New York Graphic Society for Albright-Knox Art Gallery, 1975).

82. Alan Wallach, "The Voyage of Life as Popular Art," *Art Bulletin* 59 (June 1977): 234–41. Cole's awareness of emblems and their importance in his art has long been recognized.

83. G. W. Sheldon, *American Painters* (New York: D. Appleton, 1879), 52.

84. See Christine Stansell and Sean Wilentz, "Cole's America," in Truettner and Wallach, *Thomas Cole;* Neil Harris, *The Artist in American Society: The Formative Years, 1790–1860* (New York: George Braziller, 1966); and Lillian B. Miller, *Patrons and Patriotism: The Encouragement of the Fine Arts in the United States, 1790–1860* (Chicago: University of Chicago Press, 1966).

85. See Sarah Burns, *Inventing the Modern Artist: Art and Culture in Gilded Age America* (New Haven: Yale University Press, 1996).

86. See JoAnn Wypijewski, ed., *Painting by Numbers: Komar and Melamid's Scientific Guide to Art* (New York: Farrar Straus & Giroux, 1997).

SELECT BIBLIOGRAPHY

Adamson, Jeremy. "Frederic Church's Niagara: The Sublime as Transcendence." Ph.D. diss., University of Michigan, 1981.

———. *Niagara: Two Centuries of Changing Attitudes, 1697–1901.* Washington, D.C.: The Corcoran Gallery of Art, 1985.

Adelson, Fred B. "Alvan Fisher (1792-1863): Pioneer in American Landscape Painting." Ph.D. diss., Columbia University, 1982.

———. "Alvan Fisher in Maine: His Early Coastal Scenes." *The American Art Journal* 18, no. 3 (1986): 63–73.

"Affairs of the Association." *Bulletin of the American Art-Union* (December 1851): 153.

Agamont House Register, 1855. Bar Harbor Historical Society.

Agassiz, Louis. *Geographical Sketches.* Boston: Houghton, Mifflin and Co., 1896.

Albany Institute of History and Art. *The Works of Thomas Cole: 1801–1848.* Albany, N.Y.

Albright, Horace M. *The Birth of the National Park Service.* Salt Lake City: Howe Brothers, 1985.

Allin, Craig W. *The Politics of Wilderness Preservation.* Westport, Conn.: Greenwood Press, 1982.

Ambrose, Stephen E. *Undaunted Courage: Meriwether Lewis, Thomas Jefferson, and the Opening of the American West.* New York: Simon & Schuster, 1996.

"American Genius as Expressed in Art." *The Round Table* (26 December 1863): 21–22.

"The American White Head or Bald Eagle." *The Crayon* 2 (July 1855): 25.

Amory, Cleveland. *The Last Resorts.* New York: Harper and Brothers, 1952.

Amory, Dita, and Marilyn Symmes. *Nature Observed, Nature Interpreted: Nineteenth-Century American Landscape Drawings and Watercolors from the National Academy of Design and Cooper-Hewitt, National Design Museum, Smithsonian Institution.* New York: National Academy of Design, with Cooper-Hewitt, National Design Museum, Smithsonian Institution, 1995.

Anderson, Nancy K., and Linda S. Ferber. *Albert Bierstadt: Art and Enterprise.* New York: Brooklyn Museum, 1991.

———. *Thomas Moran.* Washington, D.C.: National Gallery of Art, 1997.

"Art and Artists." *The Home Journal* (8 February 1851): 3.

"Art and Artists." *The Home Journal* (15 February 1851): 3.

"Art and Artists." *The Home Journal* (22 March 1851): 3.

"Art and Artists." *The Home Journal* (12 April 1851): 3.

"Art and Artists." *The Home Journal* (10 May 1851): 3.

"Art and Artists." *The Home Journal* (21 June 1851): 3.

"Art and Artists." *The Home Journal* (9 August 1851): 3.

"Art and Artists in New York." *Boston Evening Transcript,* 17 November 1864.

"Art and the Century Club." *The Round Table* 1, no. 9 (13 February 1864): 139.

"Art Gossip." *Cosmopolitan Art Journal* 4, no. 3 (September 1860): 126.

Avery, Kevin J. *Church's Great Picture:* The Heart of the Andes. New York: The Metropolitan Museum of Art, 1993.

———. *The Grand Moving Panorama of Pilgrim's Progress.* Montclair, N.J.: Montclair Art Museum, 1999.

Axtell, James. *The Invasion Within: The Contest of Cultures in Colonial North America.* New York: Oxford University Press, 1985.

Baigell, Matthew. *Thomas Cole.* New York: Watson Guptill Publications, 1981.

Baird, Jenny Caroline. "A Catalogue of the Early Landscapes of Frederic Church, 1844–1853." Thesis, Rice University, 1986.

Bar Harbor Blue Book and Mount Desert Guide with Maps and Tables. Boston: Albert W. Bee, 1881.

"Bar Harbor Express." *Yankee* 31 (August 1967): 139.

Barrell, John. *The Dark Side of the Landscape: The Rural Poor in English Painting, 1730–1840.* New York: Cambridge University Press, 1980.

———. *The Idea of Landscape and the Sense of Place, 1730–1840.* Cambridge: Cambridge University Press, 1972.

Barth, Gunther. *Fleeting Moments: Nature and Culture in American History.* New York: Oxford University Press, 1990.

Bartlett, Irving H. *The American Mind in the Mid-Nineteenth Century.* 2d ed. Arlington Heights, Ill.: Harlan Davidson, Inc., 1982.

Bauer, Juliette. "Humboldt." *New-York Daily Times,* 5 May 1853.

Bayley, W. P. "Mr. Church's Picture of The Icebergs." *Art Journal* (London) 15 (1 September 1863): 187–8.

———. "Mr. Church's Pictures: Cotopaxi, Chimborazo, and the Aurora Borealis." *Art Journal* (London) 27 (September 1865): 265–8.

Bedell, Rebecca Bailey. "The Anatomy of Nature: Geology and American Landscape Painting, 1825–1875." Ph.D. diss., Yale University, 1989.

———. "Haseltine, Agassiz, and the Rocks at Nahant." *Nineteenth Century* 14, no. 1 (1994): 3–9.

———. "Thomas Cole and Fashionable Science. Art and Science in America: Issues in Representation." *Huntington Library Quarterly* 59, nos. 2, 3 (1998): 349–78.

Beebe, William, ed. *The Book of Naturalists: An Anthology of the Best Natural History.* New York: Alfred A. Knopf, Inc., 1944; reprint, Princeton: Princeton University Press, 1988.

Beecher, Henry Ward. "Nature as Minister of Happiness." Chap. in *Star Papers; or, Experiences of Art and Nature.* New York: J.C. Derby, 1855.

Belasco, Warren J. *Americans on the Road: From Autocamp to Motel, 1910–1945.* Cambridge: MIT Press, 1979.

Bercovitch, Sacvan. *The American Jeremiad.* Madison: University of Wisconsin Press, 1978.

———. *The Puritan Origins of the American Self.* New Haven: Yale University Press, 1975.

Bermingham, Ann. *Landscape and Ideology: The English Rustic Tradition, 1740–1860.* Berkeley: University of California Press, 1987.

Blaugrund, Annette. "The Evolution of American Artists' Studios, 1740–1860." *Antiques* 141, no. 1 (January 1992): 214–25.

———. "The Tenth Street Studios Building." Ph.D. diss., Columbia University, 1987.

———. *The Tenth Street Studios Building: Artist-Entrepreneurs from the Hudson River School to the American Impressionists.* Southampton, N.Y.: The Parrish Art Museum, 1997.

Boime, Albert. *The Magisterial Gaze.* Washington, D.C.: Smithsonian Institution Press, 1991.

Bonomi, Patricia U. *Under the Cope of Heaven: Religion, Society, and Politics in Colonial America.* New York: Oxford University Press, 1986.

Bourdieu, Pierre. *The Field of Cultural Production: Essays on Art and Literature.* New York: Columbia University Press, 1993.

Bredeson, Robert C. "Landscape Description in Nineteenth-Century American Travel Literature." *American Quarterly* 20, no. 1 (Spring 1968): 86–94.

Brown, Dona. *Inventing New England: Regional Tourism in the Nineteenth Century.* Washington, D. C.: Smithsonian Institution Press, 1995.

Brown, Lenard E. *Acadia National Park Maine.* Washington, D.C.: Office of History and Historic Architecture, Eastern Service Center, 1971.

Brumm, Ursula. *American Thought and Religious Typology.* New Brunswick, N.J.: Rutgers University Press, 1970.

Bryant, William Cullen, ed. *Picturesque America: or the Land We Live In.* New York: D. Appleton and Company, 1872.

Bryant, William M. *Philosophy of Landscape Painting.* St. Louis: St. Louis News Co., 1882.

———. "Review of the Loan Exhibition at Crow Museum." *The Western,* 1881.

Buell, Lawrence. *The Environmental Imagination: Thoreau, Nature Writing, and the Formation of American Culture.* Cambridge: The Belknap Press of Harvard University Press, 1995.

Buettell, Roger B. "The Bar Harbor Express." *Yankee* 31 (August, 1867): 138–47.

Bunske, Edmunds V. "Humboldt and an Aesthetic Tradition in Geography." *The Geographical Review* 71, no. 2 (April 1981): 127–46.

Burdick, Neal Stephens. "The Evolution of the Environmental Consciousness in Nineteenth-Century America: An Interdisciplinary Study." Ph.D. diss., Case Western Reserve University, 1981.

Burke, Doreen Bolger. "Frederic Edwin Church and The Banner of Dawn." *American Art Journal* 17, no. 3 (Summer 1985): 2–17.

Burns, Sarah. *Inventing the Modern Artist: Art and Culture in Gilded Age America.* New Haven: Yale University Press, 1996.

Butcher, Devereux. *Exploring our National Parks and Monuments.* New York: Oxford University Press, 1947.

Butler, Jon. *Awash in a Sea of Faith: Christianizing the American People.* Cambridge: Oxford University Press, 1990.

Butler, Joyce. *Wildfire Loose: The Week Maine Burned.* 2d ed. Camden, Maine: Down East Books, 1979.

Callow, James T. *Kindred Spirits: Knickerbocker Writers and American Artists, 1807–1855.* Chapel Hill: University of North Carolina Press, 1967.

Campbell, Katherine H., Donald D. Keyes, Robert L. McGrath, and R. Stuart Wallace. *The White Mountains: Place and Perceptions.* Hanover, N.H.: University Press of New England, 1980.

"Camps and Tramps about Ktaadn." *Scribner's Monthly* 16 (May 1878): 33–47.

Cantor, Jay E. "The New England Landscape of Change." *Art in America* 64, no. 1 (January-February 1976): 51–54.

Canup, John. *Out of the Wilderness: The Emergence of an American Identity in Colonial New England.* Middletown, Conn.: Wesleyan University Press, 1990.

Cape Ann Historical Society. *Paintings and Drawings by Fitz Hugh Lane.* Gloucester, Mass.: Cape Ann Historical Association, 1974.

Carpenter, Frederic I. "'The American Myth': Paradise (To Be) Regained." *Publications of the Modern Language Association of America* 74, no. 5 (December 1959): 599–606.

Carpenter, Geoffrey Paul. "Deforestation in Nineteenth-Century Maine: The Record of Henry David Thoreau." *Maine History* 38, no. 1 (Summer 1998): 2–35.

Carr, Gerald L. *Frederic Edwin Church: Catalogue Raisonné of Works of Art at Olana State Historic Site.* 2 vols. New York: Cambridge University Press, 1994.

———. *Frederic Edwin Church: The Icebergs.* Dallas: Dallas Museum of Fine Arts, 1980.

———. "Master and Pupil: Drawings by Thomas Cole and Frederic Church." *Bulletin of the Detroit Institute of the Arts* 66 (1990): 46–60.

———. *Olana Landscapes: The World of Frederic E. Church.* New York: Rizzoli, 1989.

———. "Out on 'Rocks' and 'Peaks' all Day: Frederic Church and Mount Desert Island." Unpublished lecture, Bar Harbor Historical Society, July 1997, 10.

Carroll, Peter N. *Puritanism and the Wilderness: The Intellectual Significance of the New England Frontier 1629–1700.* New York: Columbia University Press, 1969.

Carter, Robert. *A Summer Cruise on the Coast of New England.* 1864. Reprint, Boston: Cupples and Hurd Publishers, 1888.

Cash, Sarah. *Ominous Hush: The Thunderstorm Paintings of Martin Johnson Heade.* Fort Worth, Tex.: Amon Carter Museum, 1994.

Catlin, George. *Letters and Notes on the Manners, Customs, and Conditions of the North American Indians.* First published 1841. New York: Dover Publications, 1973.

Century Association. *Gifford Memorial Meeting of the Century, Friday Evening, November 19th, 1880.* New York: The Century Association, 1880.

Chickering Hall. *The Sanford R. Gifford Collection: A Catalogue of Valuable Oil Paintings, Works of the Famous Artist, Sanford R. Gifford, N.A., Deceased, to Be Sold without Reserve.* Part I, 11 and 12 April; Part II, 28 and 29 April. New York: Thomas E. Kirby and Co., 1881.

Chmaj, Betty E. "The Journey and the Mirror: Emerson and the American Arts." *Prospects* 10 (1987): 353–408.

"Chronicle of Facts and Opinions: American Art and Artists." *Bulletin of the American Art-Union* 89 (August 1850): 81.

Church, Frederic E. "Mountain Views and Coast Scenery, by a Landscape Painter." *Bulletin of the American Art-Union* (November 1850): 129–31.

Church, Frederic Edwin, to William H. Osborn, 7 July 1864, Church Papers, Olana State Historic Site, Hudson, New York.

Cikovsky, Nicolai, Jr. "'The Ravages of the Axe': The Meaning of the Tree Stump in Nineteenth-Century American Art." *The Art Bulletin* 61, no. 4 (December 1979): 611–26.

———. *Sanford Robinson Gifford 1823–1880.* Austin: University of Texas Art Museum, 1970.

Clark, Lewis Gaylord, ed. *The Literary Remains of the Late Willis Gaylord Clark.* New York: Burgess, Stringer, & Co., 1847.

Clark, Willis Gaylord. "Ollapodiana. Number Twenty." *The Knickerbocker* 10 (August 1837): 171–2.

Cole, Nan. "Personal Glimpses of Bar Harbor's Lush Era." *Down East* 15 (July 1969): 22–47, 81–83, 87–89.

Cole, Thomas. *The Collected Essays and Prose Sketches.* Marshall B. Tymn, ed. St. Paul, Minn.: John Colet Press, 1980.

———. *Thomas Cole's Poetry.* Marshall B. Tymn, ed. York: Penn.: Liberty Cap Books, 1972.

———. "Essay on American Scenery." *The American Monthly Magazine* 7 (January 1836): 1–12.

———. Mount Desert, to Maria Cole, Catskill, 22 August 1844, Thomas Cole Papers, McKinney Library, Albany Institute of History & Art.

———. Mount Desert, to Maria Cole, Catskill, 30 August 1844. Thomas Cole Papers, McKinney Library, Albany Institute of History & Art.

Collier, Sargent F. *Mount Desert Island and Acadia National Park: An Informal History.* Revised and edited by G. W. Helfrich. Camden, Maine: Down East Books, 1978.

Conforti, Joseph A. *Jonathan Edwards, Religious Tradition, and American Culture.* Chapel Hill: The University of North Carolina Press, 1995.

Conser, Walter H., Jr. *God and the Natural World: Religion and Science in Antebellum America.* Columbia: University of South Carolina Press, 1993.

Cook, Clarence. "Bierstadt's 'Rocky Mountains'," *New Path* 1 (April 1864): 160–1.

———. "Letters on Art - No. IV." *The Independent* (New York), 7 September 1854.

Cooper, J. Fenimore. *A Landscape Book, by American Artists and American Authors.* New York: G.P. Putnam & Son, 1868.

Cowdrey, Mary Bartlett. *National Academy of Design Exhibition Record, 1826–1860.* 2 vols. New York: New-York Historical Society, 1943.

Cowdrey, Mary Bartlett, Theodore Sizer, et al. *American Academy of Fine Arts and American Art-Union Exhibition Record, 1816–1852.* 2 vols. New York: New-York Historical Society, 1953.

Cranch, Christopher P. "Art Criticism Reviewed." *Galaxy* 4 (May 1867): 80.

Crawford, F. Marion. *American Summer Resorts: Bar Harbor.* New York: Charles Scribner's Sons, 1896.

Cressy, David. "The Vast and Furious Ocean: The Passage to Puritan New England." *New England Quarterly* 54, no. 4 (1984): 511–32.

Croce, Paul Jerome. *Science and Religion in the Era of William James.* Vol. 1, "Eclipse of Certainty, 1820–1880." Chapel Hill: The University of North Carolina Press, 1995.

Cronon, William. *Changes in the Land: Indians, Colonists, and the Ecology of New England.* New York: Hill and Wang, 1983.

Cronon, William, ed. *Uncommon Ground: Rethinking the Human Place in Nature.* New York: W. W. Norton, 1995.

Cropsey, Jasper F. "Up Among the Clouds." *The Crayon* 2 (8 August 1855): 79–80.

Curry, Larry. "Some Reflections on the State of Science in America During the Nineteenth Century." *Proceedings of the National Academy of Sciences* 45 (1959): 666–77.

Curti, Merle. *Human Nature in American Thought.* Madison: University of Wisconsin Press, 1980.

Curtis, George William. "The Fine Arts: Exhibition of the National Academy, III." *New-York Daily Tribune,* 10 May 1851.

———. "The Fine Arts: Exhibition of the National Academy, IV." *New-York Daily Tribune,* 8 May 1852.

Czestochowdki, Joseph S. *The American Landscape Tradition.* New York: E. P. Dutton, Inc., 1982.

Dalton, John Vasmar. "Ministers, Metaphors, and the New England Wilderness, 1650–1700." Ph.D. diss., University of New Hampshire, 1981.

Danforth, Susan. *Encountering the New World, 1493 to 1800.* Providence, R.I.: John Carter Brown Library, 1991.

Daniels, Stephen. *Fields of Vision: Landscape Imagery and National Identity in England and the United States.* Princeton: Princeton University Press, 1993.

Davis, John. "Frederic Church's Sacred Geography." *Smithsonian Studies in American Art* 1 (Spring 1987): 78–96.

———. *The Landscape of Belief: Encountering the Holy Land in Nineteenth-Century American Art and Culture.* Princeton, N.J.: Princeton University Press, 1998.

DeCosta, B. F. *Rambles in Mount Desert.* New York: Randolph & Co., 1871.

Dee, Elaine Evans. *Frederic E. Church: Under Changing Skies. Oil Sketches and Drawings from the Collection of the Cooper-Hewitt, National Museum of Design, Smithsonian Institution.* Philadelphia: Arthur Ross Gallery at the University of Pennsylvania, 1992.

———. *Nineteenth-Century American Landscape Drawings in the Collection of the Cooper-Hewitt Museum.* Washington, D.C.: Smithsonian Institution Press, 1982.

———. *To Embrace the Universe: The Drawings of Frederic Edwin Church.* Yonkers: The Hudson River Museum, 1984.

D'Emilio, Sandra, and Suzan Campbell. *Visions and Visionaries: The Art and Artists of the Santa Fe Railway.* Salt Lake City: Peregrine Smith Books, 1991.

Dippie, Brian W. *Catlin and His Contemporaries: The Politics of Patronage.* Lincoln: University of Nebraska Press, 1990.

Docherty, Linda Jones. "A Search for Identity: American Art Criticism and the Concept of the 'Native School,' 1876–1893." Ph.D. diss., University of North Carolina, Chapel Hill, 1985.

Dodge, E. H. *Dodge's Guide Book and Map to and over Mount Desert Island.* Portland: Loring, Short & Harmon, 1872.

Doggett, Rachel, ed. *New World of Wonders: European Images of the Americas, 1492–1700.* Washington, D.C.: Folger Shakespeare Library, 1992.

"Domestic Art Gossip." *The Crayon* 7 (December 1860): 353.

Doolittle, Duane, ed. *Only in Maine: Selections from "Down East Magazine."* Barre, Mass.: Barre Publishers, 1969.

Dorr, George B. *Acadia National Park: Its Origins and Background.* Bangor, Maine: Burr Printing Co., 1942.

———. *Acadia National Park: Its Growth and Development.* Bangor, Maine: Burr Printing Co., 1948.

———. *The Story of Acadia National Park.* Bar Harbor, Maine: Acadia Publishing Co., 1985.

Dorr, George B., Ernest Howe Forbush, and M. L. Fernald. "The Unique Island of Mount Desert." *National Geographic Magazine* 26 (July 1914): 75–89.

Drake, Samuel Adams. *Nooks and Corners of the New England Coast.* New York: Harper & Brothers, 1875.

Driesbach, Janice T. *Drawn from Nature: The Oil Sketches of Thomas Hill.* Yosemite National Park Association / Crocker Art Museum, Sacramento, Calif., 1997.

Durand, Asher B. "Letters on Landscape Painting." *The Crayon* 1 (3 January 1855).

———. "Letters on Landscape Painting." *The Crayon* 1 (14 February 1855).

Durand, John. *The Life and Times of A. B. Durand.* New York: Kennedy Graphics, 1970.

Dutton, Henry W. "Personal." *Boston Evening Transcript,* 6 March 1880.

Eager, Gerald. "The Iconography of the Boat in 19th Century American Painting." *Art Journal* 35, no. 3 (Spring 1976): 224–30.

Eagleton, Terry. *The Ideology of the Aesthetic.* Oxford: Basil Blackwell, 1990.

Eitner, Lorenz. "The Window and the Storm-Tossed Boat: An Essay in the Iconography of Romanticism." *The Art Bulletin* 37, no. 4 (December 1955): 281–90.

Ekirch, Arthur A., Jr. *Man and Nature in America.* New York: Columbia University Press, 1963.

Eliot, Charles W. "The Need of Conserving the Beauty and Freedom of Nature in Modern Life." *National Geographic Magazine* 26 (July 1914): 67–73.

———. *The Right Development of Mount Desert.* Privately printed, 1904.

———. "The Forgotten Millions." *Century Magazine* 40 (August 1890): 556–64.

Evernden, Neil. "The Ambiguous Landscape." *The Geographical Review* 71, no. 2 (April 1981): 147–57.

Everson Museum of Art. *American Ship Portraits and Marine Painting.* Syracuse, N.Y.: Everson Museum of Art, 1970.

"Exhibition of the National Academy." *The Knickerbocker* 39 (June 1852): 567.

Exhibition of the Paintings of the Late Thomas Cole, at the Gallery of the American Art-Union. No. 497 Broadway. New York: Snowden & Prall, 1848.

Felker, Tracie. "Charles Codman: Early Nineteenth-Century Artisan and Artist." *American Art Journal* 22, no. 2 (1990): 60–86.

Ferber, Linda S., and William H. Gerdts. *The New Path: Ruskin and the American Pre-Raphaelites.* Brooklyn: The Brooklyn Museum, 1985.

"The Fine Arts: Exhibition at the National Academy." *The Literary World* (15 May 1847): 348.

"The Fine Arts: Exhibition at the National Academy." *The Literary World* (19 April 1851): 320.

"The Fine Arts." *International Monthly Magazine* 3 (June 1851): 327.

"Fine Arts." *The Nation* (2 June 1870): 357.

"The Fine Arts: National Academy of Design." *The Knickerbocker* 16 (July 1940): 81.

"Fine Arts, The National Academy of Design - No. III." *The Albion* (27 April 1850): 201.

"Fine Arts, The National Academy of Design - No. III." *The Albion* (8 May 1852): 225.

"Fine Arts, The National Academy of Design - No. IV." *The Albion* (10 May 1862): 225.

"Fine Arts: The National Academy of Design - No. IV." *The Albion* (3 June 1865): 261.

"Fine Arts." *Putnam's Monthly* 1, no. 6 (June 1853): 700–3.

Flexner, James Thomas. *Nineteenth Century American Painting.* New York: G.P. Putnam's Sons, 1970.

———. *That Wilder Image.* Boston: Little, Brown, & Co., 1962.

Foner, Eric. *Politics and Ideology in the Age of the Civil War.* New York: Oxford University Press, 1980.

Foster, Edward Halsey. *The Civilized Wilderness: Backgrounds to American Romantic Literature, 1817–1860.* New York: The Free Press, 1975.

"Fourth Artist's Reception." *New York Daily Tribune,* 26 March 1864.

Frome, Michael. *Battle for the Wilderness.* New York: Praeger Publishers, 1974.

Gardner, Albert Ten Eyck. "Scientific Sources of the Full-Length Landscape: 1850." *The Metropolitan Museum of Art Bulletin* 4, no. 2 (October 1945): 59–65.

Gaunt, William. *Marine Painting: An Historical Survey.* New York: Viking Press, 1975.

Gerdts, William H. "American Landscape Painting: Critical Judgments, 1730–1845," *The American Art Journal* 17, no. 1 (Winter 1985): 56.

———, Curator, The Newark Museum, to the Director, The Newark Museum, 28 March (probably 1960s).

———. "'The Sea is His Home': Clarence Cook Visits Fitz Hugh Lane." *The American Art Journal* 17, no. 3 (Summer 1985): 44–49.

Gill, Sam. *Mother Earth.* Chicago: University of Chicago Press, 1987.

Gilpin, William. *Mission of the North American People: Geographical, Social, and Political.* Philadelphia: J. B. Lippincott & Co., 1873.

Godkin, Edwin Lawrence. *Reflections and Comments: 1865–1895.* New York: Charles Scribner's Sons, 1896.

Goedde, Lawrence Otto. *Tempest and Shipwreck in Dutch and Flemish Art.* University Park: Pennsylvania State University Press, 1989.

Goetzmann, William H. *Exploration and Empire: The Explorer and the Scientist in the Winning of the American West.* New York: W. W. Norton, 1978.

Gombrich, E. H. *Art and Illusion.* 2d ed. New York: Pantheon Books, 1972.

Goodrich, A. T. *The North American Tourist.* New York: A. T. Goodrich, 1839.

Goodyear, Frank H., Jr. *Thomas Doughty 1793–1856: An American Pioneer in Landscape Painting.* Philadelphia: Pennsylvania Academy of the Fine Arts, 1973.

"Going to Mount Katahdin." *Putman's Monthly* 8, no. 45 (September 1856): 242–56.

Greenblatt, Stephen Jay. *Marvelous Possessions: The Wonder of the New World.* Chicago: University of Chicago Press, 1992.

Greene, Mott. *Geology in the Nineteenth Century: Changing Views of a Changing Land.* Ithaca: Cornell University Press, 1982.

Grossinger, Richard. *Book of the Cranberry Islands.* Los Angeles: Black Sparrow Press, 1974.

Hale, Richard Walden, Jr. *The Story of Bar Harbor.* New York: Ives Washburn, Inc., 1949.

Hales, Peter B. *William Henry Jackson and the Transformation of the American Landscape.* Philadelphia: Temple University Press, 1988.

Haltman, Kenneth. "The Poetics of Geologic Reverie: Figures of Source and Origin in Samuel Seymour's Landscapes of the Rocky Mountains." *Huntington Library Quarterly* 59, 2 & 3 (1997): 303–47.

Hammel, Margaret F. "Bar Harbor's Great Cottages." *Down East* 19 (June 1973): 58–63.

Harland, John H. *Seamanship in the Age of Sail.* London: Conway Maritime Press, 1984.

Harper, J. Russell. *Paul Kane's Frontier.* Austin: University of Texas Press, 1971.

Harris, David V., and Eugene P. Kiver. *The Geologic Story of the National Parks and Monuments.* New York: John Wiley and Sons, 1985.

Harris, Neil. *The Artist in American Society: The Formative Years 1790–1860.* New York: George Braziller, 1966.

Harrison, Mrs. Burton. *Golden-Rod: An Idyll of Mount Desert.* New York: Harper & Brothers, 1880.

———. *Bar Harbor Days.* New York: Harper & Brothers, 1887.

———. *A Virginia Cousin & Bar Harbor Tales.* Boston: Lamson & Wolffe, 1895.

Harvey, Eleanor Jones. *The Painted Sketch: American Impressions from Nature, 1830–1880.* Dallas, Tex.: Dallas Museum of Art, 1998.

Hawes, Louis. "A Sketchbook by Thomas Cole." *Record of the Art Museum, Princeton University* 15, no. 1 (1956): 2–23.

———. *Presences of Nature: British Landscape 1780–1830.* New Haven: Yale Center for British Art, 1982.

Hayden, Ferdinand V. "The Wonders of the West, II: More About the Yellowstone," *Scribner's* 3 (1872): 396.

Hayes Augustus Allen. *The Jesuit's Ring: A Romance of Mount Desert.* New York: Charles Scribner's Sons, 1887.

H.B.H. "A Visit to the Studios of Some American Painters." *The Art Journal* 48 (December 1865): 362–3.

Helfrich, G. W., and Gladys O'Neil. *Lost Bar Harbor.* Camden, Maine: Down East Books, 1982.

Hepburn, Andrew. *Great Resorts of North America.* Garden City, N.Y.: Doubleday, 1965.

Hipple, Walter J. *The Beautiful, the Sublime, & the Picturesque in Eighteenth-Century British Aesthetic Theory.* Carbondale: Southern Illinois University Press, 1957.

Hobsbawm, Eric. *On History.* New York: The New Press, 1997.

Hobsbawm, Eric, and Terence Ranger. *The Invention of Tradition.* New York: Cambridge University, 1983.

Hodgson, Alice Doan. "Henry Cheever Pratt (1803–1880)." *The Magazine Antiques* 102, no. 5 (November 1972): 842–7.

Holliday, Joseph E. "Collector's Choice of the Gilded Age." *The Cincinnati Historical Society Bulletin* 28, no. 4 (Winter 1970): 294–315.

Holmes, Rev. William, and John W. Barber. *Religious Emblems: Being a Series of Emblematic Engravings, with Written Explanations, Miscellaneous Observations, and Religious Reflections, Designed to Illustrate Divine Truth, in Accordance with the Cardinal Principles of Christianity.* Cincinnati, Ohio: John H. Johnson, 1851.

Homer, William I. "Thomas Cole and Field's 'Chromatography'." *Record of the Art Museum, Princeton University* 19 (1960): 26–30.

Honour, Hugh. *The New Golden Land: European Images of America from the Discoveries to the Present Time.* New York: Pantheon, 1975.

Horsman, Reginald. *Race and Manifest Destiny: The Origins of American Racial Anglo-Saxonism.* Cambridge: Harvard University Press, 1981.

Horwitz, Howard. *By the Laws of Nature: Form and Value in Nineteenth-Century America.* New York: Oxford University Press, 1991.

Howat, John K., et al. *American Paradise: The World of the Hudson River School.* New York: The Metropolitan Museum of Art, 1987.

Howe, Susan. *The Birth-Mark: Unsettling the Wilderness in American Literary History.* Hanover, N.H.: Wesleyan University Press, 1993.

Hudson, W. P. "Archibald Allison and William Cullen Bryant." *American Literature* 12, no. 1 (March 1940): 59–68.

Humboldt, Alexander von. *Cosmos: A Sketch of the Physical Discription of the Universe.* 2 vols. New York: Harper and Brothers, 1858; reprint, Baltimore: The John Hopkins University Press, 1997.

Hunt, David C., and Marsha V. Gallagher. *Karl Bodmer's America.* Omaha: Joslyn Art Museum, and Lincoln: University of Nebraska Press, 1984.

Huntington, David C. *Art and the Excited Spirit.* Ann Arbor: University of Michigan Museum of Art, 1972.

———. "Frederic Edwin Church, 1926–1900: Painter of the Adamic New World Myth." Ph.D. diss., Yale University, 1960.

———. *Frederic Edwin Church.* Washington, D.C.: National Collection of Fine Arts, 1966.

———. "Frederic Church's *Niagara*: Nature and the Nation's Type." *Texas Studies in Literature and Language* 25, no. 1 (Spring 1983): 100–38.

———. *The Landscapes of Frederic Edwin Church: Vision of an American Era.* New York: George Braziller, 1966.

Huseman, Ben W. *Wild River, Timeless Canyons: Balduin Möllhausen's Watercolors of the Colorado.* Fort Worth: Amon Carter Museum, 1995.

Huth, Hans. *Nature and the American: Three Centuries of Changing Attitudes.* Berkeley: University of California Press, 1957; Lincoln: University of Nebraska Press, 1990.

Hyde, Anne Farrar. *An American Vision: Far Western Landscape and National Culture, 1820–1920.* New York: New York University Press, 1990.

"The Idea of a Picture." *The Crayon* 5 (February 1858): 63–66.

The Independent 15 (18 June 1863): 6.

Jackson, John Brinckerhoff. *The Necessity for Ruins.* Amherst: University of Massachusetts Press, 1980.

Jackson, William H. "Famous American Mountain Paintings, I: With Moran in the Yellowstone." *Appalachia* 21 (1936): 157.

James, Harlean. *Romance of the National Parks.* New York: Arno Press, 1972.

Jarves, James Jackson. *The Art Idea: Sculpture, Painting, and Architecture in America.* New York: Hurd and Houghton, 1864; reprint Cambridge: Harvard University Press, 1960.

Johnson, Owen. "The Building of Arts at Bar Harbor." *The Century Magazine* 76 (August 1908): 676–8.

Kandorian, Nancy A. *"Supreme and Distinctive" on the East Coast; The Mapping of Acadia National Park.* Jenny Marie Johnson, ed. *Exploration and Mapping of the National Parks.* Occasional paper No. IV. By Map and Geographical Round Table of the American Library Association. Winetka, Ill.: Speculum Orbis Press, 1994.

Kasson, Joy S. *Artistic Voyagers: Europe and the American Imagination in the Works of Irving, Allston, Cole, Cooper, and Hawthorne.* Westport, Conn.: Greenwood Press, 1982.

Kazin, Alfred. *A Writer's America: Landscape in Literature.* New York: Alfred A. Knopf, 1988.

Kelly, Franklin. *Frederic Edwin Church and the National Landscape.* Washington, D.C.: Smithsonian Institution Press, 1988.

———. *The North American Landscapes of Frederic Edwin Church.* Washington, D. C.: Smithsonian Institution Press, 1988.

Kelly, Franklin, and Gerald L. Carr. *The Early Landscapes of Frederic Edwin Church, 1845–1854.* Fort Worth: Amon Carter Museum, 1987.

Kelly, Franklin, Stephen Jay Gould, James Anthony Ryan, and Debora Rindge. *Frederic Edwin Church.* Washington, D.C.: National Gallery of Art and Smithsonian Institution Press, 1989.

Ketner, Joseph D. *The Emergence of the African-American Artist: Robert S. Duncanson, 1821–1872.* Columbia: University of Missouri Press, 1993.

Ketner, Joseph D., II, and Michael J. Tammenga. *The Beautiful, The Sublime, and The Picturesque: British Influences on American Landscape Painting.* St. Louis: Washington University Gallery of Art, 1984.

King, Thomas Starr. *A Vacation Among the Sierras: Yosemite in 1860.* San Francisco: 1860.

Kinsey, Joni Louise. *Thomas Moran and the Surveying of the American West.* Washington, D.C.: Smithsonian Institution Press, 1992.

Knight, Janice. *Orthodoxies in Massachusetts: Rereading American Puritanism.* Cambridge: Harvard University Press, 1994.

Kohl, Lawrence Frederick. *The Politics of Individualism: Parties and the American Character in the Jacksonian Era.* New York: Oxford University Press, 1989.

Kolodny, Annette. *The Land Before Her: Fantasy and Experience of the American Frontier, 1630–1860.* Chapel Hill: University of North Carolina Press, 1984.

———. *The Lay of the Land: Metaphor as Experience and History in American Life and Letters.* Chapel Hill: University of North Carolina Press, 1975.

Krasner, James. *The Entangled Eye: Visual Perception and the Representation of Nature in Post-Darwinian Narrative.* New York: Oxford University Press, 1992.

Lapham, W. B. *Bar Harbor and Mount Desert Island*. New York: Liberty Printing, 1886.

Lawson, Karol A. "A New World of Gladness and Exertion: Images of the North American Landscape in Maps, Portraits, and Serial Prints before 1820." Ph.D. diss., University of Virginia, 1988.

Leffingwell, Alsop. *The Mystery of Bar Harbor: A Melo-Dramatic Romance of France and Mt. Desert*. New York: G.W. Dillingham, 1887.

Lemelin, Robert. *Pathway to the National Character, 1830–1861*. Port Washington, N.Y.: Kennikat Press, 1974.

Levitine, George. "Vernet Tied to a Mast in a Storm: The Evolution of an Episode of Art Historical Romantic Folklore." *The Art Bulletin* 49, no. 2 (June 1967): 92–100.

Lewis, Charles. *Mount Desert and Eastern Shore Land Company: Description of Mount Desert Island*. Boston: Privately printed, 1889.

Lewis, Richard Warrington Baldwin. *The American Adam: Innocence, Tragedy, and Tradition in the Nineteenth Century*. Chicago: University of Chicago Press, 1955.

Liancourt, Duke De La Rochefoucault. *Travels Through the United States of America, The Country of the Iroquois, and Upper Canada in the Years 1795, 1796, and 1797; with an Authentic Account of Lower Canada*. London: 1799.

Lindquist-Cock, Elizabeth. "Frederic Church's Stereographic Vision." *Art in America* 61, no. 5 (September-October 1973): 70–75.

———. *The Influence of Photography on American Landscape Painting 1839–1880*. New York: Garland Publishing, Inc., 1977.

Lowance, Mason I., Jr. *The Language of Canaan: Metaphor and Symbol in New England from the Puritans to the Transcendentalists*. Cambridge: Harvard University Press, 1980.

Lowenthal, David. *The Path is a Foreign Country*. New York: Cambridge University Press, 1985.

Lowenthal, David, ed. *Geographies of the Mind: Essays in Historical Geosophy*. New York: Oxford University Press, 1976.

Lurie, Edward. *Nature and the American Mind: Louis Agassiz and the Culture of Science*. New York: Science History Publications, 1974.

Lutz, Tom. *American Nervousness 1903: An Anecdotal History*. Ithaca: Cornell University Press, 1991.

MacCannell, Dean. *The Tourist: A New Theory of the Leisure Class*. New York: Schocken Books, 1976.

Magoon, E. L. *The Home Book of the Picturesque: or American Scenery, Art, and Literature*. New York: G.P. Putnam, 1852; facsimile edition, Gainesville, Fla.: Scholars' Facsimiles and Reprints, 1967.

Manthorne, Katherine E. *American Painters of the Arctic*. Amherst, Mass.: Mead Art Gallery, 1975.

———. *Creation and Renewal: Views of Cotopaxi by Frederic Edwin Church*. Washington, D.C.: Smithsonian Institution Press, for the National Museum of American Art, 1985.

———. *The Landscapes of Louis Rémy Mignot: A Southern Painter Abroad*. Washington, D.C.: Smithsonian Institution Press, 1996.

———. *Tropical Renaissance: North American Artists Exploring Latin America, 1839–1879*. Washington, D.C.: Smithsonian Institution Press, 1989.

Marlor, Clark S. *A History of the Brooklyn Art Association with an Index of Exhibitions*. New York: James F. Carr, 1970.

Marsh, George P. *Man and Nature*. Edited by David Lowenthal. 1864; reprint, Cambridge: Belknap Press, Harvard University Press, 1965.

Martin, Clara Barnes. *Mount Desert on the Coast of Maine: "Infinite Riches in a Little Room."* Privately Printed, 1867; 4th ed., Portland, Maine: Loring, Short, and Harmon, 1877.

Marx, Leo. *The Machine in the Garden: Technology and the Pastoral Ideal in America*. New York: Oxford University Press, 1964.

———. *The Pilot and the Passenger*. New York: Oxford University Press, 1988.

Maurault, J. A. *Histoire des Abenakis, Depuis 1605 Jusqu'a Nos Jours*. Quebec: Sorel, 1866; Facsimile reprint, New York: Johnson Reprint Corp., 1969.

Mazlish, Anne, ed. *The Tracy Logbook: 1855, A Month in Summer*. Bar Harbor: Acadia Publishing Co., and Mount Desert Island Historical Society, 1997.

McClelland, Linda Flint. *Building the National Parks: Historic Landscape Design and Construction*. Baltimore: The John Hopkins University Press, 1998.

McCosh, Rev. James. *Typical Forms and Special Ends in Creation*. New York: Robert Carter and Brothers, 1872.

McCoy, Garnett. *Archives of American Art: A Directory of Resources*. New York: Bowker, 1972.

———. "Visits, Parties, and Cats in the Hall: The Tenth Street Studios Building and Its Inmates in the Nineteenth Century." *Archives of American Art Journal* 6, no. 1 (January 1966): 1–8.

McCoy, Garnett, ed. "Jervis McEntee's Diary." *Archives of American Art Journal* 8, nos. 3–4 (July-October 1968).

McGrath, Robert L., and Barbara J. MacAdam. *"A Sweet Foretaste of Heaven": Artists in the White Mountains, 1830–1930*. Hanover, N.H.: University Press of New England, 1988.

McKinsey, Elizabeth. *Niagara Falls: Icon of the American Sublime*. Cambridge: Cambridge University Press, 1985.

McLoughlin, William G. *The Meaning of Henry Ward Beecher: An Essay on the Shifting Values of Mid-Victorian America, 1840–1870*. New York: Alfred A. Knopf, 1970.

McLuhan, T. C. *Dream Tracks: The Railroad and The American Indian, 1890–1930*. New York: Abrams, 1985.

McNulty, J. Bard, ed. *The Correspondence of Thomas Cole and Daniel Wadsworth*. Hartford: The Connecticut Historical Society, 1983.

McShine, Kynaston, ed. *The Natural Paradise: Painting in America 1800–1950*. New York: The Museum of Modern Art, 1961.

Melbo, Irving Robert. *Our Country's National Parks*. New York: Bobbs-Merrill, 1973.

Mellon, Gertrude A., ed. *Maine and Its Role in American Art*. New York: Viking Press, 1963.

Merchant, Carolyn. *The Death of Nature: Women, Ecology, and the Scientific Revolution*. San Francisco: Harper and Row, 1981.

———. *Ecological Revolutions: Nature, Gender, and Science in New England*. Chapel Hill: University of North Carolina Press, 1989.

Merk, Frederick. *Manifest Destiny and Mission in American History*. New York: Vintage Books, 1963.

Merritt, Howard S. *Thomas Cole*. Rochester, N.Y.: Memorial Art Gallery of the University of Rochester, 1969.

———. *To Walk with Nature: The Drawings of Thomas Cole*. Yonkers, N.Y.: The Hudson River Museum, 1981.

Meservey, Anne Farmer. "The Role of Art in American Life: Critics' Views on Native Art and Literature, 1830–1865." *American Art Journal* 10, no. 1 (May 1978): 72–89.

The Metropolitan Museum of Art. *A Memorial Catalogue of the Paintings of Sanford Robinson Gifford, N.A.* New York: The Metropolitan Museum of Art, 1881. Reprint. New York: Olana Gallery, 1974.

Miller, Angela. *Empire of the Eye: Landscape Representation and American Cultural Politics, 1825–1875*. Ithaca: Cornell University Press, 1993.

Miller, David C. *Dark Eden: The Swamp in Nineteenth-Century American Culture*. New York: Cambridge University Press, 1989.

Miller, David, ed. *American Iconology: New Approaches to Nineteenth-Century Art and Literature*. New Haven: Yale University Press, 1993.

Miller, Lillian B. "Patronage, Patriotism and Taste in Mid-19th Century America." *Magazine of Art* 45 no. 7 (November 1952): 322–8.

———. *Patrons and Patriotism: The Encouragement of the Fine Arts in the United States 1790–1860.* Chicago: University of Chicago Press, 1966.

Miller, Lillian B., ed. *The Peale Family: Creation of a Legacy, 1770–1870.* Washington and New York: Abbeville Press/National Portrait Gallery, 1996.

Miller, Perry. *Errand into the Wilderness.* 1956. 2d ed. Cambridge: Belknap Press of Harvard University Press, 1984.

———. *The Life of the Mind in America: From the Revolution to the Civil War.* New York: Harcourt Brace Jovanovich, Publishers, 1965.

———. *Nature's Nation.* Cambridge: Belknap Press of Harvard University Press, 1967.

Miller, Ralph N. "American Nationalism as a Theory of Nature." *William and Mary Quarterly* 12 (January 1955): 74–95.

Mitchell, W. J. T., ed. *Landscape and Power.* Chicago: University of Chicago Press, 1994.

Moore, James Collins. "The Storm and the Harvest: The Image of Nature in Mid-Nineteenth Century American Landscape Painting." Ph.D. diss., Indiana University, Bloomington, 1974.

Morison, Samuel Eliot. *The Story of Mount Desert Island, Maine.* Boston: Little, Brown & Co., 1960.

Morrison, Kenneth M. *The Embattled Northeast: The Elusive Ideal of Alliance in Abenaki-Euramerican Relations.* Berkeley: University of California Press, 1984.

"Mount Desert." *Harper's New Monthly Magazine* 45, no. 267 (August 1872): 321–41.

"Mr. Church's Pictures." *The Art Journal* (December 1865): 688.

Mugerauer, Robert. *Interpreting Environments: Tradition, Deconstruction, Hermeneutics.* Austin: University of Texas Press, 1996.

Muir, John. *Our National Parks.* Cambridge: The Riverside Press, 1901.

Mulvey, Christopher. *Anglo-American Landscapes: A Study of 19th Century Anglo-American Travel Literature.* New York: Cambridge University Press, 1983.

Murphy, Francis. *The Book of Nature: American Painters and the Natural Sublime.* New York: The Hudson River Museum at Yonkers, 1983.

Myers, Kenneth. *The Catskills: Painters, Writers, and Tourists in the Mountains 1820–1895.* Yonkers, N.Y.: Hudson River Museum of Westchester, 1987.

Naef, Weston J., and James N. Wood. *Era of Exploration: The Rise of Landscape Photography in the American West, 1860–1885.* New York: New York Graphic Society for Albright-Knox Art Gallery, 1975.

Nash, Roderick F. "The American Invention of National Parks." *American Quarterly* 22, no. 3 (Fall 1970): 726–35.

———. *The Rights of Nature: A History of Environmental Ethics.* Madison: University of Wisconsin Press, 1989.

———. *Wilderness and the American Mind.* 3rd ed. New Haven: Yale University Press, 1982.

"The National Academy of Design." *The Evening Post,* 13 May 1863.

"National Academy of Design." *The New York Daily Tribune,* 24 April 1845.

"National Academy of Design." *The New York Daily Tribune,* 26 April 1845.

"National Academy of Design." *The New York Evening Post,* 31 May 1865.

"The National Academy of Design." *New York Herald,* 28 April 1845.

"The National Academy of Design." *The New York Times,* 24 June 1863.

Naylor, Maria. *The National Academy of Design Exhibition Record, 1861–1900.* 2 vols. New York: Kennedy Galleries, 1973.

Nemerov, Alexander. *Frederic Remington & Turn of the Century America.* New Haven: Yale University Press, 1995.

"The New Pictures." *Harper's Weekly* 8 (26 March 1864): 194–5.

Newhall, Nancy. *A Contribution to the Heritage of Every American: The Conservation Activities of John D. Rockefeller, Jr.* New York: Alfred A. Knopf, 1957.

Newirth, Steven P. "The Images of Place: Puritans, Indians, and the Religious Significance of the New England Frontier." *The American Art Journal* 18, no. 2 (1986): 42–53.

Nichols, Roger L., and Patrick L. Halley. *Stephen Long and American Frontier Exploration.* Newark: University of Delaware Press, 1980.

Nicolson, Marjorie Hope. *Mountain Gloom and Mountain Glory: The Development of the Aesthetics of the Infinite.* New York: W. W. Norton & Company, Inc., and Cornell University, 1963.

Noble, Louis Legrand. *After Icebergs with a Painter: A Summer Voyage to Labrador and Around Newfoundland.* New York: D. Appleton and Company, 1861. Reprint. New York: Olana Gallery, 1979.

———. *Church's Painting,* The Heart of the Andes. New York: D. Appleton and Company, 1859.

———. *The Course of Empire, Voyage of Life, and Other Pictures of Thomas Cole, N.A., with Selections from His Letters and Miscellaneous Writings: Illustrative of His Life, Character, and Genius.* New York: Cornish Lambert & Company, 1853.

———. *The Life and Works of Thomas Cole.* Elliot S. Vessel, ed. 1853; reprint, Cambridge: Belknap Press of Harvard University Press, 1964.

Novak, Barbara. *American Painting of the Nineteenth Century: Realism, Idealism, and the American Experience.* New York: Harper & Row Publishers, 1979.

———. "The Double-Edged Axe." *Art in America* 64, no. 1 (January-February 1976): 44–50.

———. *Landscape Paintings from the National Academy of Design.* New York: Harper & Row Publishers, 1980.

———. *Nature and Culture: American Landscape Painting, 1825–1875.* New York: Oxford University Press, 1980.

Novak, Barbara, and Annette Blaugrund, eds. *Next to Nature: Landscape Paintings from the National Academy of Design.* New York: Harper & Row Publishers, for the National Academy of Design, 1980.

Novak, Barbara, David Warren, and Simon de Pury. *The Thyssen-Bornemisza Collection, Nineteenth-Century American Painting.* New York: Vendome Press, 1986.

Nygren, Edward J. *Views and Visions: American Landscape before 1830.* Washington, D.C.: The Corcoran Gallery of Art, 1986.

Nyiri, Alan. *Acadia National Park: Maine's Intimate Parkland.* Camden, Maine: Down East Books, 1986.

Oelschlaeger, Max. *The Idea of Wilderness: From Prehistory to the Age of Ecology.* New Haven: Yale University Press, 1991.

Olmsted, Frederick L. "The Yosemite Valley and the Mariposa Big Trees, A Preliminary Report." *Landscape Architecture* 43 (1952): 16.

"Painting." *The Anglo American* (26 April 1845).

Parker, Charles Franklin. *Come Unto Me: Pictorials from the National Parks of the United States.* New York: Rinehart & Co., 1949.

Parkes, Henry Bamford. *The American Experience: An Interpretation of the History and Civilization of the American People.* New York: Vintage Books, 1959.

Parkman, Francis. *France and England in North America.* 9 vols. American Classic Series. New York: Frederick Unger Publishers, 1965.

Parrington, Vernon Louis. *Main Currents in American Thought.* New York: Harcourt, Brace and Company, 1930.

Parry, Ellwood C. *The Art of Thomas Cole: Ambition and Imagination.* Newark: University of Delaware Press, 1988.

Pearl, Rev. Cyril. "Maine, As a Field for Moral and Religious Enterprise." *The American Quarterly Register* 10 (1837): 185–92.

Perkins, Robert F., Jr., and William J. Gavin III. *The Boston Athenaeum Art Exhibition Index, 1827–1874.* Boston: Library of the Boston Athenaeum, 1980.

Perrin, Noel. "Forever Virgin: The American View of America." *Antaeus* no. 57 (Autumn 1986): 13–22.

"Personal." *Boston Evening Transcript*, 6 March 1880.

Philbrick, Thomas. *James Fenimore Cooper and the Development of American Sea Fiction.* Cambridge: Harvard University Press, 1961.

Phillips, Sandra S., et al., eds. *Charmed Places: Hudson River Artists and Their Houses, Studios, and Vistas.* New York: Harry Abrams, 1988.

Pinto, Holly Joan. *William Cullen Bryant and the Hudson River School of Painting.* Roslyn, N.Y.: Nassau County Museum of Fine Art, 1981.

Plowden, Helen Haseltine. *William Stanley Haseltine: Sea and Landscape Painter.* London: Frederick Muller, 1947.

Prown, Jules David, ed., *Discovered Lands: Invented Pasts: Transforming Visions of the American West.* New Haven: Yale University Press, 1992.

Rainey, Sue. *Creating Picturesque America: Monument to the Natural and Cultural Landscape.* Nashville, Tenn.: Vanderbilt University Press, 1994.

Richards, T. Addison, ed. *Appleton's Illustrated Hand-book of American Travel.* New York: D. Appleton & Co., 1857.

Riley, Phil M. "Adapting the Italian Villa to the Maine Coast." *Country Life in America* 24, no. 4 (August 1913): 27–31.

Rivard, Nancy J. "Notes on the Collection: *Cotopaxi*." *Bulletin of the Detroit Institute of the Arts* 56, no. 1 (1977): 193–6.

Robbins, Derek. *The Work of Pierre Bourdieu: Recognizing Society.* Buckingham, U.K.: Open University Press, 1991.

Roberts, Ann Rockefeller. *Mr. Rockefeller's Roads.* Camden, Maine: Down East Books, 1990.

Robertson, David. *West of Eden: A History of the Art and Literature of Yosemite.* Yosemite Natural History Association and Wilderness Press, 1984.

Robinson, Christine, et al. *Thomas Cole: Drawn to Nature.* Albany, N.Y.: Albany Institute of History and Art, 1993.

Ronnberg, Eric A. R., Jr. "A Few Words About this Picture." *Invention and Technology* 4, no. 2 (Fall 1988): 15–20.

———. "Fitz Hugh Lane: A Storm, Breaking Away, Vessel Slipping her Cable, 1858." Chapter in *Twelve American Masterpieces.* New York: Spanierman Gallery, 1998.

Rosen, Charles, and Henry Zerner. *Romanticism and Realism: The Mythology of Nineteenth-Century Art.* New York: W. W. Norton & Company, 1984.

Rosenthal, Michael, Christiana Payne, and Scott Wilcox, eds. *Prospects for the Nation: Recent Essays in British Landscape: 1750–1880.* New Haven: Yale University Press, 1997.

Roth, Robert. *Acadia: The Story Behind the Scenery.* Las Vegas, Nev.: KC Publications, 1979.

Rowe, William Hutchinson. *The Maritime History of Maine: Three Centuries of Shipbuilding & Seafaring.* New York: W. W. Norton & Co., 1948.

Runte, Alfred. *National Parks: The American Experience.* 2d ed. rev. Lincoln: University of Nebraska Press, 1989.

Rutledge, Anna Wells. *Cumulative Record of Exhibition Catalogues: The Pennsylvania Academy of the Fine Arts.* Philadelphia: The American Philosophical Society, 1955.

Scharf, Frederic Alan. "Fitz Hugh Lane: Visits to the Maine Coast, 1848–1855." *Essex Institute Historical Collections* 98 (April 1962): 112.

Schauffler, Robert Haven. "Unique Mount Desert." *The Century Magazine* 82, no. 4 (August 1911): 477–90.

Schimmel, Julie. *Artists of Michigan from the Nineteenth Century.* Muskegon: Muskegon Museum of Art, 1987.

Schivelbusch, Wolfgang. *The Railway Journey: Trains and Travel in the 19th Century.* New York: Urizen Books, 1979.

Schmitt, Peter J. *Back to Nature: The Arcadian Myth in Urban America.* New York: Oxford University Press, 1969.

Schulman, Lydia Dittler. *Paradise Lost and the Rise of the American Republic.* Boston: Northeastern University Press, 1992.

Schweizer, Paul D., ed. *The Voyage of Life by Thomas Cole: Paintings, Drawings, and Prints.* Utica, N.Y.: Munson-Williams-Proctor Institute, 1985.

Sears, John F. *Sacred Places: American Tourist Attractions in the Nineteenth Century.* New York: Oxford University Press. 1989.

Seligmann, Herbert J. "Bar Harbor: From Eden to Tourism." *Down East* 4 (August 1957): 24–29, 45–46.

Sellers, Charles. *The Market Revolution: Jacksonian America, 1815-1846.* New York: Oxford University, 1991.

Sharf, Frederic Alan. "Fitz Hugh Lane: Visits to the Maine Coast, 1848–1855." *Essex Institute Historical Collections* 98 (April 1962): 111–20.

Shepard, Paul, Jr. "Paintings of the New England Landscape: A Scientist Looks at Their Geomorphology." *College Art Journal* 17 (Fall 1957): 30–42.

Short, Vincent, and Edwin Sears. *Sail and Steam: Along the Maine Coast.* Portland, Maine: Bond Wheelwright Co., 1955.

Simon, Janice. "The Crayon, 1855–1861: The Voice of Nature in Criticism, Poetry, and the Fine Arts." Ph.D. diss., University of Michigan, 1990.

Simpson, Marc, Andrea Henderson, and Sally Mills. *Expressions of Place: The Art of William Stanley Haseltine.* San Francisco: The Fine Arts Museums of San Francisco, 1992.

Skalet, Linda Henfield. "The Market for American Painting in New York, 1870–1915." Ph.D. diss., The Johns Hopkins University, 1980.

"Sketchings: Domestic Art Gossip." *The Crayon* (November 1859): 349.

"Sketchings: The National Academy of Design." *The Crayon* 1 (3 January 1855): 12.

Smith, Bernard. *European Vision and the South Pacific, 1768–1850: A Study in the History of Art and Ideas.* Oxford, U.K.: Oxford University Press, 1960.

Smith, Henry Nash. *Virgin Land: The American West as Symbol and Myth.* New York: Vintage Books, 1950.

Solnit, Rebecca. *Savage Dreams: A Journey into the Hidden Wars of the American West.* San Francisco: Sierra Club Books, 1994.

Spafford, Horatio Gates. *Gazetteer of the State of New-York.* Albany, N.Y.: H. C. Southwick, 1813.

"A Special Issue: The Drawings of Thomas Cole." *Bulletin of the Detroit Institute of the Arts* 66, no. 1 (1990): 4–60.

Sperling, Lynda Joy. "Northern European Links to Nineteenth-Century American Landscape Painting: The Study of American Artists in Dusseldorf." Ph.D. diss., University of California, Santa Barbara, 1985.

Splbester, W. "Sunsets." *The Crayon* 2 (26 September 1855): 191–2.

Stafford, Barbara Maria. *Voyage into Substance: Art, Science, Nature and the Illustrated Travel Account, 1760–1840.* Cambridge: MIT Press, 1984.

Stampp, Kenneth M. *America in 1857: A Nation on the Brink.* New York: Oxford University Press, 1990.

Stannard, David E. *American Holocaust: The Conquest of the New World.* New York: Oxford University Press, 1993.

Steadman, Edmund C., and George M. Gould. *Life and Letters of Edmund Clarence Steadman.* New York: Moffat and Yard, 1910.

Stebbins, Theodore E., Jr. *Close Observation: Selected Oil Sketches by Frederic E. Church.* Washington: Smithsonian Institution Press, 1978.

Stein, Roger B. *John Ruskin and Aesthetic Thought in America, 1840–1900.* Cambridge: Harvard University Press, 1967.

———. *Seascape and the American Imagination.* New York: Whitney Museum of American Art, 1975.

Stephanson, Anders. *Manifest Destiny: American Expansionism and the Empire of Right.* New York: Hill and Wang, 1995.

Stevens, Joseph L., Jr., Boston, to Mr. Mansfield, Gloucester, 17 October 1903, Cape Ann Historical Society.

———. *Gloucester Daily Telegraph,* 17 September 1850.

Stilgoe, John R. "A New England Coastal Wilderness." *The Geographical Review* 71, no. 1 (January 1981): 33–50.

———. "Fair Fields and Blasted Rock: American Land Classification Systems and Landscape Aesthetics." *American Studies* 22 (Spring 1981): 21–33.

Strahan, Edward. *The Masterpieces of the International Exhibition 1876: The Art Gallery.* Philadelphia: Gebbie & Barrie, 1876.

Street, George E. *Mount Desert, a History.* Edited by Samuel A. Eliot. 2d rev. ed. New York: Houghton Mifflin Co., 1926.

Sweeney, J. Gray. "The Artist-Explorers of the American West, 1860–1880." Ph.D. diss., Indiana University, 1975.

———. *The Columbus of the Woods: Daniel Boone and The Typology of Manifest Destiny.* St. Louis: Washington University Gallery of Art, 1992.

———. *Drawing the Borderline: Artist-Explorers of the U. S.-Mexico Boundary Survey.* Albuquerque, N.M.: The Albuquerque Museum/University of New Mexico Press, 1996.

———. "'Endued With Rare Genius': Frederic Edwin Church's To the Memory of Cole." *Smithsonian Studies in American Art* 2, no. 1 (Winter 1988): 45–71.

———. "Inventing Luminism." (Unpublished manuscript in preparation).

———. *McEntee and Company.* New York: Beacon Hill Fine Arts, 1997.

———. "The Nude of Landscape Painting: Emblematic Personifications in the Art of the Hudson River School." *Smithsonian Studies in American Art* 3, no. 4 (Fall 1989): 42–65.

———. Review of *Frederic Edwin Church and the National Landscape,* by Franklin Kelly; and *Frederic Edwin Church,* by Franklin Kelly & Others. In *Archives of American Art Journal* 28, no. 4 (1988): 25–29.

———. *Themes in American Painting.* Grand Rapids: The Grand Rapids Art Museum, 1977.

———. "A 'Very Peculiar' Picture: Martin J. Heade's Thunderstorm over Narragansett Bay." *Archives of American Art Journal* 28, no. 4 (1988): 2–14.

Sweetser, Moses Foster. *Summer Days Down East.* Portland, Maine: Chisholm Brothers, 1883.

Swift, H. W., and D. Bush. *Mount Desert in 1873. Portrayed in Crayon and Quill.* Boston: J. R. Osgood, 1874.

Swift, Jeremy. *The Other Eden: A New Approach to Man, Nature and Society.* London: J. M. Dent & Sons Limited, 1974.

Takaki, Ronald. *A Different Mirror: A History of Multicultural America.* Boston: Little, Brown & Co., 1993.

Taylor, Joshua, ed. *Nineteenth-Century Theories of Art.* Berkeley: University of California Press, 1987.

Taylor, William Leonhard. *A Productive Monopoly: The Effect of Railroad Control on New England Coastal Steamship Lines, 1870–1916.* Providence: Brown University Press, 1978.

"Theodore Winthrop." *Atlantic Monthly* 8, no. 46 (August 1861): 242–51.

Thomas, George M. *Revivalism and Cultural Change: Christianity, Nation Building, and the Market in Nineteenth-Century United States.* Chicago: University of Chicago Press, 1989.

Thoreau, Henry David. *Cape Cod.* 1865; reprint, New York: Thomas Crowell, 1966.

———. *The Maine Woods.* Edited by Joseph J. Moldenhauer. Princeton: Princeton University Press, 1972.

Thwaites, Reuben Gold. *France in America, 1497-1763.* 1905; reprint, New York: Haskell House Publishers, 1969.

Tilden, Freeman. *The National Parks.* 3rd rev. ed. New York: Alfred A. Knopf, 1986.

Tocqueville, Alexis de. *Democracy in America.* Translated by Henry Reeve. New York: Oxford University Press, 1947.

———. *Journey To America.* Translated by George Lawrence. Edited by J. P. Mayer. New Haven: Yale University Press, 1959.

Tracy, Charles. "Log of a Voyage from New York to Mount Desert and Return, July–September 1855." Typescript copy at Bar Harbor Historical Society, Jesup Memorial Library, Bar Harbor, John Pierpont Morgan Library, New York.

Trenton, Patricia, and Peter H. Hassrick. *The Rocky Mountains: A Vision for Artists in the Nineteenth Century.* Norman: University of Oklahoma Press, 1983.

Trexler, Richard C. *Sex and Conquest: Gendered Violence, Political Order, and the European Conquest of the Americas.* Ithaca: Cornell University Press, 1995.

Troyen, Carol. "Retreat to Arcadia: American Landscape and the American Art-Union." *The American Art Journal* 22, no. 1 (1991): 20–37.

Truettner, William H. "The Art of History: American Exploration and Discovery Scenes, 1840–1860." *American Art Journal* (Winter 1982): 4–31.

———. "The Genesis of Frederic Edwin Church's *Aurora Borealis*." *Art Quarterly* 31, no. 3 (Autumn 1968): 267–83.

———. *The Natural Man Observed: A Study of Catlin's Indian Gallery.* Washington, D.C.: Smithsonian Institution Press, 1979.

Truettner, William H., ed. *The West as America: Reinterpreting Images of the Frontier, 1820–1920.* Washington, D.C.: Smithsonian Institution Press, 1991.

Truettner, William H., and Robin Bolton-Smith. *National Parks and the American Landscape.* Washington, D.C.: Smithsonian Institution Press, 1972.

Truettner, William H., and Alan Wallach, eds. *Thomas Cole: Landscape into History.* New Haven: Yale University Press, for the National Museum of American Art, 1993.

Tuckerman, Henry T. *America and Her Commentators.* 1864; reprint, New York: Antiquarian Press, 1961.

———. *Book of the Artists: American Artist Life, Comprising Biographical and Critical Sketches of American Artists: Preceded by an Historical Account of the rise and Progress of Art in America.* New York: G.P. Putman & Sons, 1867.

———. *The Optimist.* New York: G.P. Putman & Son, 1850.

Tunnard, Christopher. *A World with a View: An Inquiry into the Nature of Scenic Value.* New Haven: Yale University Press, 1978.

"Twentieth Annual Exhibition of the Academy of National Design [sic]." *The Broadway Journal* (3 May 1845): 275–6.

"Twenty-Sixth Exhibition of the National Academy of Design." *Bulletin of the American Art-Union* 4 (1 May 1851): 23.

"Twilight in the Wilderness." *New York World,* 20 June 1860.

Tyler, Ron. *Prints of the West.* Golden, Colo.: Fulcrum Press, 1994.

Tyler, Ron, ed. *Alfred Jacob Miller: Artist on the Oregon Trail.* Fort Worth: Amon Carter Museum, 1982.

U.S. Department of the Interior. *Glimpses of our National Monuments.* Washington, D.C.: Government Printing Office, 1926.

Van Den Abbeele, Georges. "Sightseers: The Tourist as Theorist." *Diacritics* 10, no. 4 (Winter 1980): 2–14.

Vanneman, Reeve, and Lynn Weber Cannon. *The American Perception of Class.* Philadelphia: Temple University Press, 1987.

Vaughan, Alden T. *New England Frontier Puritans and Indians, 1620–1675.* Boston: Little, Brown & Co., 1965.

Wadsworth Atheneum. *Thomas Cole 1801–1848: One Hundred Years Later.* Hartford, Conn.: Wadsworth Atheneum, 1949.

Wagner, Virginia L. "Geological Time in Nineteenth-Century Landscapes." *Winterthur Portfolio* 24, no. 2-3 (1989): 153–63.

———. "John Ruskin and Artistical Geology in America." *Winterthur Portfolio* 23, no. 2-3 (1988): 151–67.

Wallach, Alan. *Exhibiting Contradictions: Essays on the Art Museum in the United States.* Amherst: University of Massachusetts Press, 1998.

———. "Making a Picture of the View from Mount Holyoke." *Bulletin of the Detroit Institute of the Arts* 66, no. 1 (1990): 35–45.

———. "Thomas Cole and the Aristocracy." *Arts Magazine* 56, no. 3 (November 1981): 84–106.

W. B. "The Late F. H. Lane, Marine Artist." *Daily Evening Transcript,* 19 August 1865.

Weinberg, Albert K. *Manifest Destiny: A Study of Nationalist Expansionism in American History.* Baltimore: Johns Hopkins University Press, 1935.

Weiskel, Thomas. *The Romantic Sublime: Studies in the Structure and Psychology of Transcendence.* Baltimore: Johns Hopkins University Press, 1976.

Weiss, Ila. *Poetic Landscape: The Art and Experience of Sanford R. Gifford.* Newark: University of Delaware Press, 1987.

———. *Sanford Robinson Gifford, 1823–1880.* New York: Garland Publishing, Inc., 1977.

Wescott, Richard R. "Early Conservation Programs and the Development of the Vacation Industry in Maine 1865–1900." *Maine Historical Society Quarterly* 27, no. 1 (Summer 1987): 2–13.

Williams, Raymond. *Culture and Society, 1780–1950.* New York: Columbia University Press, 1958.

Willis, Nathaniel Parker. *American Scenery.* 2 vols. London: George Virtue, 1840.

Wilmerding, John. *American Views: Essays on American Art.* Princeton: Princeton University Press, 1991.

———. *American Marine Painting.* Richmond: Virginia Museum of Fine Arts, 1976; Newport News, Va.: The Mariners' Museum, 1976.

———. *American Marine Painting.* 2d ed. New York: Harry N. Abrams, Inc., 1987.

———. *The Artist's Mount Desert: American Painters on the Maine Coast.* Princeton: Princeton University Press, 1984.

———. *Fitz Hugh Lane 1804–1865: American Marine Painter.* Salem, Mass.: Essex Institute, 1964; reprint, Gloucester, Mass.: Peter Smith, 1967.

———. *Fitz Hugh Lane.* New York: Praeger Publishers, 1971.

———. *Paintings by Fitz Hugh Lane.* Washington, D.C.: National Gallery of Art, 1988.

———. "Thomas Cole in Maine." *Record of the Art Museum, Princeton University* 49, no. 1 (1990): 2–23.

———. "William Stanley Haseltine's Drawings of Maine." *Master Drawings* 31 (Spring 1993): 3–20.

Wilmerding, John, et al. *American Light: The Luminist Movement 1850–1875.* Princeton: Princeton University Press, 1989.

Wilmerding, John, Earl A. Powell, and Linda Ayres. *An American Perspective: Nineteenth Century Art from the Collection of Jo Ann and Julian Ganz, Jr.* Washington, D.C.: National Gallery of Art, 1981.

Wilson, Christopher Kent. "The Landscape of Democracy." *American Art Journal* 18, no. 3 (1986): 20–39.

Winship, George Parker. *Sailors Narratives of Voyages Along the New England Coast, 1524–1624.* New York: Burt Franklin, 1905.

Winsor, Luther S. *Acadia National Park: A Study of Conservation Objectives Relating to its Establishment and Boundary Adjustments.* Washington, D.C.: U.S. Department of the Interior, 1955.

Winthrop, John. *Winthrop's Journal: History of New England.* Edited by James Kendall Hosmer. New York: Charles Scribner's Sons, 1908.

———. *Winthrop Papers. Vol. 2, 1623–1630.* Massachusetts Historical Society, 1931.

Winthrop, Theodore. *Life in the Open Air, and Other Papers.* Boston: Ticknor and Fields, 1863.

Wolf, Bryan Jay. *Romantic Re-Vision: Culture and Consciousness in Nineteenth-Century American Painting and Literature.* Chicago: University of Chicago Press, 1982.

Wood, Richard George. "A Bibliography of Travel in Maine, 1783–1861." *New England Quarterly* 6 (June 1933): 426–39.

Wyatt, David. *The Fall into Eden: Landscape and Imagination in California.* New York: Cambridge University Press, 1986.

Wypijewski, JoAnn, ed. *Painting by Numbers: Komar and Melamid's Scientific Guide to Art.* New York: Farrar Straus & Giroux, 1997.

Yard, Robert Sterling. *The Book of the National Parks.* New York: Charles Scribner's Sons, 1919.

———. *The National Parks Portfolio.* Washington, D.C.: U.S. Government Printing Office, 1928.

Yarnall, James L., and William H. Gerdts. *The National Museum of American Art's Index to American Art Exhibition Catalogues from the Beginning through the 1876 Centennial Year.* Boston: G. K. Hall, 1986.

Z. "Correspondence of the Transcript, New York, April 2, 1860," *Boston Evening Transcript,* 7 April 1860.

Paintings of Mount Desert, Exhibited from 1836–1894

AAU

American Art Union

BA

Robert F. Perkins, Jr., and Willliam J. Gavin III, *The Boston Athenaeum Art Exhibition Index, 1827-1874*, Boston: Library of the Boston Athenaeum, 1980.

NAD

Mary Barttlett Cowdrey, *American Academy of Fine Arts and American Art Union Exhibition Record, 1816-1852*, Vol. 77: Collections of the New York Historical Society, New York: New-York Historical Society, 1953: National Academy of Design Exhibition Record, 1826-1860, Vol. 74: Collections of the New-York Historical Society, New York: New-York Historical Society. 1943; and Maria Taylor, *The National Academy of Design Exhibition Record, 1861-1900*, New York: Kennedy Galleries, 1973.

NMAA-Index

James L. Yarnell and William H. Gerdts, *The National Museum of American Art's Index to American Art Exhibition Catologues: From the Beginning through the 1876 Centennial Year*, Boston: G.K. Hall and Co., 1986.

PA

Ann Wells Rutledge, *Cumulative Record of Exhibition Catologues: The Pennsylvania Academy of Fine Arts*, Philadelphia: The American Philosophical Society, 1955.

Note

The NMAA Index by Yarnall is not a definitive source. It is incomplete and many pictures are listed without dates or exhibition place. Moreover, paintings may have been exhibited under alternate title.

Armstrong, David Maitland (1836–1918)

Bar Harbor, Mt. Desert, NMAA-Index, Exhibited November 4, 1876 at Century Association, New York, no. 7.

View at Mount Desert, NMAA-Index, Exhibited December 1876 at Century Association, New York, no. 23.

Bonfield, George R. (1805–1898)

Somes' Sound, Mount Desert Island, 1851, PA, Exhibited 1851 Pennsylvania Academy, no. 115.

Scene in Mt. Desert, Maine, 1852, PA, Exhibited 1852 Pennsylvania Academy, no. 100.

Mount Desert, 1854, PA, Exhibited 1854 Pennsylvania Academy, no. 109.

Bricher, Alfred Thompson (1837–1908)

Mount Desert, Maine, BA, Exhibited 1864, no. 176, and NMAA-Index, Sailors' Fair, Boston, 1864, no. 176.

Sunset and Moonrise on Ironbound Island, Mt. Desert, Maine, NAD, Exhibited Summer 1871 at National Academy, no. 139, owner—William Schaus.

On Iron Bound Island, Mt. Desert, Maine, NMAA-Index, Exhibited 1875, Chicago Interstate Industrial Exposition, no. 150.

Under Schooner Head, Mt. Desert Island, 1894, NAD, Exhibited 1894 at National Academy, no. 287.

Brown, Harrison Bird (1831–1915)

Storm Off Mount Desert, NMAA-Index, Exhibited 4 October 1859 at Maine Mechanical Association, Portland, Maine, no. 29.

Frenchman's Bay, Mount Desert, 1859, NAD, Exhibited 1859 at National Academy, no. 680.

Frenchman's Bay, 1863, BA, Exhibited 1863 at Boston Athenaeum, no. 253.

Mount Desert, NMAA-Index, Exhibited 1871 at Utica Art Association, New York, no. 74, sold for $225.

Church, Frederic E. (1826–1900)

An Old Boat, 1850, (Thyssen-Bornemisza Collection, London), NAD, Exhibited 1851 at National Academy, no. 166.

Otter Creek, Mount Desert, c.1850–51, (Museum of Fine Arts, Boston, #1982.419), PA, Exhibited 1851 at Pennsylvania Academy, no. 37, and NMAA-Index, Exhibited c.1863 at Weehawken Gallery, New Jersey, no. 25.

Twilight, a Scene at Mount Desert Islands, 1851, PA, Exhibited 1851 at Pennsylvania Academy, no. 171.

Beacon, off Mount Desert Island, 1851, (Private Collection), NAD, Exhibited 1851 at National Academy, no. 371, and AAU, Exhibited 1851 at American Art-Union, no. 226, and NMAA-Index, Exhibited December 15–17, 1852 at American Art-Union, no. 350, to be auctioned, owner—American Art-Union.

Lake Scene in Mount Desert, 1851, NAD, Exhibited 1851 at National Academy, no. 383.

Fog Off Mount Desert Island, Maine, 1850, (Private Collection), AAU, Exhibited 1852 at American Art-Union, no. 135, NMAA-Index, Exhibited December 15–17, 1852 at American Art-Union, no. 119, to be auctioned, owner-American Art-Union.

The Wreck, 1852, (The Parthenon, Nashville, Tennessee, #29.2.14), NAD, Exhibited 1852 at National Academy, no. 145.

Mount Desert Scenery, NMAA-Index, Exhibited 1859 at Young Men's Association, New York, no. 36, owner—A. R. Smith.

Coast Scene, Mount Desert, 1863, (Wadsworth Atheneum, Hartford, #1948.178), NAD, Exhibited 1863 at National Academy, no. 74, and Exhibited 1864 at Albany Sanitary Fair, Albany, New York, no. 10.

Twilight (Mount Desert Island), 1865, (Washington University, St. Louis, Missouri, #1923.2175), NAD, Exhibited 1865 at National Academy, no. 31.

Landscape, Mount Desert Island, NMAA-Index, Exhibited 1867 at Derby Gallery, New York, no. 24, for sale, owner—Derby's New Art Rooms.

Cole, Thomas (1801–1848)

Frenchman's Bay, Mount Desert Island, Maine, c. 1845, (Albany Institute of History and Art, New York, #1964.69).

View Across Frenchman's Bay, From Mount Desert Island, Maine, After a Squall, 1845, (Cincinnati Art Museum, #1925.569), NAD, Exhibited 1845 at National Academy, no. 88, sold to William W. Scarborough.

Desert House on Mount Desert Island, c. 1845, (Fogg Art Museum, Harvard University, #1956.222), AAU, Exhibited 1845 at the American Art-Union, no. 82, sold to Nathaniel Silsbee, Salem, Massachusetts.

Mount Desert, NMAA-Index, Exhibited 1875 at Cincinnati Industrial Exposition, no. 125, owner—W. W. Scarborough. This picture is probably *View Across Frenchman's Bay.*

DeHass, W. F. (1830–1873)

Mount Desert, NMAA-Index, Exhibited 1876 Chicago Interstate Industrial Exposition, no. 392, owner J. G. Shortall.

Showery Day off Mt. Desert, Maine, NMAA-Index, Exhibited 1876 Chicago Industrial Exposition, no. 97.

Dix, C. T. (1838–1873)

Mount Desert, NMAA-Index, Exhibited 1860 at Washington Art Association, no. 22.

Doughty, Thomas (1793–1856)

Desert Rock Lighthouse, Maine, 1836, (Collection of Mrs. Gustav D. Klimann), BA, Exhibited 1836 at Boston Athenaeum, no. 46.

View of Mount Desert, Maine, 1848, NMAA-Index, Exhibited 1848 at Albany Gallery of Fine Arts, Albany, New York, no. 122.

Falconer, J. M. (1820–1903)

Bridge at Mt. Desert, Maine, NMAA-Index. Exhibited January 28, 1872 at American Society of Painters in Water Colors, New York, no. 472.

Ferguson, Henry A. (1842–1911)

Mt. Desert, from Green Mountain, 1868, Ex. PA no. 118.

Mt. Desert, Coast of Maine, NMAA-Index, Exhibited 1868 at Utica Art Association, Utica, New York, no. 138.

Fisher, Alvan (1792–1863)

View of Mt. Desert From Cranberry Island, NMAA-Index, Exhibited in 1850 and 1851 at New England Art Union, Boston, Massachusetts.

Island of Mount Desert, Maine, 1856, BA, Exhibited in 1856 at Boston Athenaeum, no. 239.

Frost, Francis Shedd (1821–1910)

Mount Desert, Maine, 1856, BA, Exhibited 1856 at Boston Athenaeum, no. 106.

Mount Desert, NMAA-Index, Exhibited 1866 by Opera House Art Assoc., Chicago, to be distributed.

Landscape, Mount Desert, 1856, BA, Exhibited 1856 at Boston Athenaeum, no. 350.

Frenchman's Bay, Mt. Desert, 1857, BA, Exhibited at Boston Athenaeum, no. 293.0

Gay, Winckworth Allan (1821–1910)

Mount Desert, Maine, 1863, BA, Exhibited 1863 at Boston Athenaeum, no. 246.

Southwest Harbor Mount Desert, Maine, NMAA-Index, Exhibited 1874 at Cincinnati Industrial Exposition, no. 8.

Gerry, Samuel Lancaster (1813–1891)

Wood Study at Mount Desert, Maine, 1859, NAD, Exhibited 1859 at National Academy, no. 575.

Gifford, Sanford Robinson (1823–1880)

Lake on Mt. Desert, 1865, BA, Exhibited 1865 at Boston Athenaeum, no. 265.

From the Green Mountains-Mount Desert (Artist Sketching at Mount Desert, Maine), 1865, (Collection Jo Ann and Julian Ganz Jr.), BA, Exhibited 1865 at Boston Athenaeum, no. 245, and NMAA-Index, Exhibited 1865 at Artists' Fund Society, New York, no. 50.

Gignoux, Regis Francois (1814–1882)

Mount Desert, Maine, NMAA-Index, Exhibited 1863 and 1864 at Buffalo Fine Arts Academy, Buffalo, New York, no. 7.

Mount Desert, Maine, NMAA-Index, Exhibited every year from 1865 to 1876 at Buffalo Fine Arts Academy, Buffalo, New York, no. 3.

Griggs, Samuel W. (1827–1898)

Foggy Morning off Mt. Desert, 1860, BA, Exhibited 1860 at Boston Athenaeum, no. 211.

Coast Scene, Mt. Desert, 1860, BA, Exhibited 1860 at Boston Athenaeum, no. 205.

Haight, H. J.

Eagle Lake, Mt. Desert, NMAA-Index, Exhibited Summer 1870 at National Academy, no. 278.

Hart, William (1823–1894)

Mount Desert, NMAA-Index, Exhibited c. 1845 at Cleaveland and Osgood Gallery, no. 62.

Close of Day on Mount Desert, 1857, NAD, Exhibited 1857 at National Academy, no. 85.

View of Mount Desert, Maine, NMAA-Index, Exhibited 1857 at Washington Art Association, Washington, D.C., no. 55.

Coast Scene, Mount Desert, NMAA-Index, Exhibited 1860 at Young Men's Association, Troy, New York, no. 6.

Mount Desert, NMAA-Index, Exhibited February 15, 1864 at Yonkers Fair, New York, no. 89.

Coast of Mt. Desert, NMAA-Index, Exhibited April 1864 at Maryland State Fair, Baltimore, no. 44.

Mount Desert, NMAA-Index, Exhibited February 27, 1865 at Montreal Art Association, Montreal, Canada, no. 126.

Near Mount Desert, NMAA-Index, Exhibited November-December 1872 at St. Louis Mercantile Library, no. 126.

Haseltine, William Stanley (1835–1900)

Mount Desert, 1860, PA, Exhibited 1860 at Pennsylvania Academy, no. 87.

Near Mount Desert, NMAA-Index, Exhibited 1857 at United States Christian Commission, Philadelphia, no. 131.

Schooner Head, Mount Desert, Maine, NMAA-Index, Exhibited 1862 at Artists' Fund Society, New York, no. 68.

Near Mount Desert Island, NMAA-Index, Exhibited 1869 at Claghorn Collection, Philadelphia, no. 19.

Heine, Wilhelm (William) (1827–1885)

Southwest Harbour, Mount Desert, Maine, 1858, NAD, Exhibited 1858 at National Academy, no. 491.

Hill, J. W.

Rocks at Mt. Desert, NMAA-Index, Exhibited 1866 at Artists' Fund Society, no. 67.

Hillyer, H. L.

Eagle Lake, Mount Desert Island, NMAA-Index, Exhibited December 21, 1863 at Artists' Fund Society, New York, no. 132.

Somer [sic] Sound, Mt. Desert, NMAA-Index, Exhibited December 21, 1863 at Artists' Fund Society, New York, no. 68.

Refuge Bay on Somes Sound, NMAA-Index, Exhibited 1865 at Artists' Fund Society, New York, no. 53.

Holmes, P. H.

Off Mount Desert, NMAA-Index, Exhibited c. 1845 at Holmes' Art Sale, Portland, Maine, no. 25.

Mount Desert, NMAA-Index, Exhibited c. 1845 at Holmes' Art Sale, Portland, Maine, no. 23.

View at Mount Desert, NMAA-Index, Exhibited c. 1845 at Holmes' Art Sale, Portland, Maine, no. 29.

Hubbard, Richard William (1816–1888)

View of Sandy Beach, Mount Desert, 1851, NAD, Exhibited 1851 at National Academy, no. 387.

Huntington, Daniel (1816–1906)

Coast of Mount Desert, Maine, NMAA-Index, Exhibited 1862 at Artists' Fund Society, New York, no. 231.

Lagerfeldt, T. O.

Great Head, Mt. Desert, NMAA-Index, Exhibited January 12–February 2, 1976 at Boston Art Club, Boston, Massachusetts, no. 23.

The Bar, Bar Harbor, Mount Desert, NMAA-Index, Exhibited 1876 at Boston Art Club, Boston, Massachusetts, no. 25.

Thunder Hole, Mt. Desert, NMAA-Index, Exhibited January 12–February 2, 1876 at Boston Art Club, no. 30.

Lane, Fitz Hugh (1804–1865)

Mt. Desert Light House, 1855, BA, Exhibited 1855 at Boston Athenaeum, no. 218.

Linsley, Wilford

At Bar Harbor, Mount Desert, NMAA-Index, Exhibited 1873 at American Society of Painters in Water Colors, New York, no. 50.

Balance Rock, Mt. Desert, NMAA-Index, Exhibited 1875 at Chicago Interstate Industrial Exposition, no. 835.

Livingston, Montgomery (1816–1916)

Mount Desert, Maine, 1852, NAD, Exhibited 1852 at National Academy, no. 85.

Mount Desert, Maine, 1852, NAD, Exhibited 1852 at National Academy, no. 396.

Nichols, George Ward

Porcupine Islands, The Wind and Storm Just Gathering, Mt. Desert, Maine, NMAA-Index, Exhibited 1868–1869 at Cincinnati Academy, Cincinnati, Ohio, no. 24.

The Sands at Evening, Mt. Desert, Maine, NMAA-Index, Exhibited 1868–1869 at Cincinnati Academy, Cincinnati, Ohio, no. 28.

Parsons, Charles (1821–1910)

Coast of Mt. Desert, Maine, NMAA-Index, Exhibited 1863 at Derby Gallery, New York, no. 49.

Frenchman's Bay, Mt. Desert, Maine, NMAA-Index, Exhibited 1864 at Artists Fund Society, New York, no. 28.

Entrance to Somes' Sound, Mt. Desert, NMAA-Index, Exhibited 1863 at Derby Gallery, New York, no. 1.

Pratt, Henry Cheever (1803–1880)

View of Sand Beach, Mt. Desert, Maine Taken From Nature, in 1844, 1845, BA, Exhibited 1845 at Boston Athenaeum, no. 70.

View of "Dog Mountain" and "Somes' Sound," and Near South-West Harbor, Mount Desert Island, Maine, NMAA-Index, Exhibited 1872 at Studio Building, Boston, Massachusetts, no. 3.

Rawstorne, Edward

Study of Rocks: Mount Desert, 1860, NAD, Exhibited 1860 at National Academy, no. 516; and BA, Exhibited 1860 at Boston Athenaeum, no. 96 1/2; and NAD, Exhibited 1861 at National Academy, no. 211.

View Near South-West Harbor, Mt. Desert, 1861, NAD, Exhibited 1861 at National Academy, no. 396.

Richards, William Trost (1833–1905)

Mount Desert, NMAA-Index, Exhibited September 3, 1867 at Rhode Island Society for Domestic Industry, Providence, Rhode Island, no. 151.

Mount Desert Island, NMAA-Index, Exhibited February, 1867 at Artists' Fund Society, Philadelphia, no. 36.

Mount Desert Island, 1868, PA, Exhibited 1868 at Pennsylvania Academy, no. 228.

Rood, O. N., Prof. (1811–1902)

Great Head, On Mount Desert Island, Coast of Maine, NMAA-Index, Exhibited 1867–1868 at American Society of Painters in Water Colors, no. 429.

Great Head, Mt. Desert, NMAA-Index, Exhibited Spring 1868 at Artists' Fund Society, Philadelphia, no. 63.

Shattuck, Aaron Draper (1832–1928)

Coast of Mount Desert, 1862, BA, Exhibited 1862 at Boston Athenaeum, no. 273.

Morning at Mount Desert, 1864, NAD, Exhibited 1864 at National Academy, no. 220.

Marine of Mt. Desert, NMAA-Index, Exhibited June 1865 at Northwestern Fair, Chicago, no. 80.

Moonlight at Mount Desert, NMAA-Index, Exhibited 1875 at Chicago International Industrial Exposition, no. 46.

Warren, A. W. (1823–1873)

Easterly Gale off Mt. Desert, NMAA-Index, Exhibited 1862 at Artists' Fund Society, New York, no. 151.

Bar Island, Maine, NMAA-Index, Exhibited 1866 at Utica Art Association, Utica, New York.

Williams, Isaac L. (1817–1895)

Mt. Desert-Evening, 1852, PA, Exhibited 1852 at Pennsylvania Academy, no. 52.

Mount Desert, NMAA-Index, Exhibited January 1851–May 1851 at Philadelphia, no. 70.

Mount Desert, NMAA-Index, Exhibited September 1851–January 1852 at Philadelphia Art-Union, no. 111.